THE
AHOMS

THE
AHOMS

A

REIMAGINED

HISTORY

ARUP KUMAR DUTTA

HarperCollins *Publishers* India

First published in India by HarperCollins *Publishers* 2022

HarperCollins *Publishers* India, Cyber City, Building 10-A, Gurugram,
Haryana – 122002, India
www.harpercollins.co.in

4 6 8 10 9 7 5 3

P-ISBN: 978-93-5629-414-1
E-ISBN: 978-93-5629-415-8

Typeset in 11.5/15.5 Goudy Old Style at
Manipal Technologies Limited, Manipal

*

HarperCollins *Publishers*, Macken House, 39/40 Mayor Street Upper,
Dublin 1, D01 C9W8, Ireland

For Arnab and Susmita

Contents

Introduction

IT WAS AN AMAZINGLY FERTILE VALLEY, FLANKED BY MOUNTAIN ranges on the north, east and south. A mammoth river, fed by innumerable tributaries, meandered through it. This emerald vale enjoyed a central geo-ethnologic position vis-à-vis China, Myanmar (Burma), Southeast Asia, Tibet, Bhutan and the Indian subcontinent. Little wonder that the land across which the mighty river Brahmaputra flowed had, through millennia, attracted migrant settlers from every direction.

They—the Australoid, Dravidians, Caucasoid and Mongoloid—arrived in different phases of time. The Mongoloids who had their origins in west China came in sporadic waves to become the dominant grouping, imparting to Northeast India its distinct ethnic identity. New arrivals clashed with and occasionally drove out old settlers from more salubrious spots on the riverbanks, forcing them to shift to the mountains. The constant but periodic inflow initiated a process of conflicts and dispersals till the settlers colonized the valleys and mountains in a mind-boggling number of communities contained within small kingdoms or principalities, each possessing a distinct language and culture of its own, yet simultaneously sharing certain common affinities, having come from similar origins and evolving within a common environment.

For instance, in Nagaland we have no less than seventeen Naga tribes: Angami, Ao, Chakhesang, Chang, Dimasa Kachari, Khiamniungan, Konyak, Kuki, Lotha, Phom, Pochury, Rengma, Sangtam, Sumi, Tikhir, Yimkhiung, Zeliang; Mizoram is peopled by Lushais and Kukis; Meghalaya by Garos, Jaiantias and Khasis. Most variegated is the ethnic composition of Arunachal Pradesh, which has over twenty-six tribes such as Monpa, Miji, Sulung, Nishi, Aka, Tagin, Gallong, Apatani, Sherdukpen, Khowa, Adi, Dafla, Padam, Minyong, Bokar, Bori, Digaru, Mishmi, Khampti, Singpho, Tangsa, Nocte, Wanchoo, etc., and over 100 sub-tribes. In the Brahmaputra Valley itself we have the great Bodo ethno-linguistic group, comprising numerous tribes such as Kachari, Lalung, Dimasa, Rabha, Chutiya, Moran, Tippera, Hajong, etc. Add to these the dozens of non-Bodo tribes inhabiting the rest of Assam, such as the Mishings, Karbis, etc., as well as the tribes of Manipur and Tripura, and the ethnologic mosaic that is Northeast India is unparalleled in any other region of the world of a similar limited size.

From time to time, throughout history, an ambitious chieftain would wage war against the neighbouring principalities and subjugate them, and build up empires of magnitude, whose existence is testified to by indirect sources such as allusions in the Indian epics and the Puranas. But these lasted for too brief a period to act as an authentic coalescing force amongst the inhabitants of the valley and mountains, and the pattern of synthesis and fragmentation continued.

Then, in 1228 CE, an event of great significance occurred, one which changed the destiny of the Brahmaputra Valley and the surrounding mountains. A group of Shan or Tai warriors, led by a brave and far-sighted leader named Sukapha, left its original home in the Shan country, which encompassed Myanmar and the Yunnan Province of China, swept through the Patkai range of mountains into the upper part of the Brahmaputra Valley, and set up the nucleus of what was later to become the powerful Ahom Empire.

Gradually, decade by decade, the Ahom rulers expanded their tiny principality till they held sway over the entire Brahmaputra Valley and the surrounding hills. They brought under their dominion not only rival settlers of the Bodo ethnic groups, such as the Chutiyas and Dimasas, but also the hill people such as the Nagas and Karbis; during the days of their greatest glory almost all the tribes in the region, including the Kacharis, Khasis and Jaintias, owed allegiance to them.

By the time of their arrival, Hinduism had percolated from the Indian subcontinent and was the principal prevalent religion in the Brahmaputra Valley. Also, by then, a common language, which today we term as Assamese, was evolving amongst the disparate tribes in the valley. The Ahoms were non-Hindus—they had a religion of their own, with defined rituals practised by their priests, as well as a language belonging to the Sino-Tibetan Tai group. They were a highly cultured people who had books on history, astrology, religious ethics, mythology; scriptures; political treatises, etc. written in the Tai language. Yet the early Ahom kings gradually gave up exclusive practice of their own language and religion to adopt those of their subjects, because they were aware that this would create between the rulers and the ruled the empathy so essential for the well-being and continuation of their dynasty.

From the time Sukapha entered Assam in 1228 till this region was annexed by the British in 1826, for nearly six centuries his descendants reigned over a greater part of the Brahmaputra Valley. Few dynasties in the world, let alone Asia, have enjoyed such a long period of almost unbroken rule. No doubt, throughout these 600 years the cycle of conflict and synthesis continued, and many of the Ahom kings had to wage war in order to subjugate other ethnic groups, as also to quell uprisings. Yet, simultaneously, by bringing the valley under a single administration and providing a generally enlightened and stable rule, they initialized a process of homogenization.

It was primarily due to the Ahom dynasty that the pre-colonial Assamese nation was born. Its reign witnessed the synthesis of the disparate ethnic entities inhabiting the Brahmaputra Valley and the evolution of a distinct Assamese language, culture and nationalist identity. Greater political and cultural intercourse, intermarriages and other social exchanges between tribes ultimately broke racial and cultural barriers, and imbued a solidarity and nationalistic spirit to the people.

Periodic, unrelenting assaults by Muslim rulers from the west, which had to be repulsed, reinforced this Assamese nationalism, the disparate tribes being also bonded together by the religious and cultural renaissance ushered in by Vaishnava saints such as Mahapurush Sankardev.

However, apart from its longevity and its role in coalescing the diverse peoples of Assam, what marks out the Ahom dynasty was the part it played in shaping the religious and cultural profile of Asia. In comparison to, say, the great Chinese dynasties, the area ruled by the Ahoms, even at the zenith of their power, was relatively small. Yet the Brahmaputra Valley was strategically located, with the river, cutting as it did across the entire valley from east to west, becoming a highway for religious and cultural transference between the two ancient civilizations of India and China, as also between India and Southeast Asia.

The Brahmaputra–Ganges link had, since the primordial past, provided easy access to the valley from the west. At the eastern edge of the Brahmaputra Valley there were quite a few land routes to Myanmar, China and other regions of Southeast Asia, much used by traders, pilgrims and proselytizers. For instance, one land-based extension of the Brahmaputra–Ganges link was the 'Silk Route' to China. From Sadiya at the easternmost extremity of the Brahmaputra Valley, this route traversed the Patkai Mountains to the banks of the Irrawaddy River, from where merchants going to Ava descended the river, while those going to the Yunnan Province of China travelled upstream. Another route from Tonkin to Assam was mentioned by the ninth-century Chinese traveller Kya Tang.

Thus, the Brahmaputra Valley formed a natural corridor across which expansionist Brahmanical Hinduism could travel to Myanmar and Southeast Asian regions as early as the first century CE. It can be surmised that the Hindu King Samuda, who ruled Myanmar in 105 CE, had proceeded there through Assam, as did the Hindu rulers who led the Shan conquest of the mouth of the Mekong in 280 CE. The valley, therefore, played a seminal role in carrying Hinduism and later Buddhism to regions of Southeast Asia. It was also the route through which Indian ideas and literature, including the two epics Ramayana and Mahabharata, travelled to these nations.

In the process, Southeast Asia during ancient times was widely Hinduized—aggressive propagation by Hindu proselytizers led to the erection of numerous Hindu kingdoms—the Champa civilization in Vietnam, Funan in Cambodia, the Khmer Empire in Indo-China, the Langasuka, Ganganegara and Old Kedah in the Malayan Peninsula, and the Srivijayan, Singhasari and Majapahit kingdoms of Indonesia, etc. The language and cultures of many countries were influenced by the Indian civilization and Indian epics were adapted to suit local conditions.

No doubt Brahmanical Hinduism was gradually supplanted by Buddhism between the first and fifth centuries CE, and later by Islam in some regions of Southeast Asia in the fifteenth century and Christianity in the early sixteenth, but vestiges of the Hindu civilization remain in the form of magnificent relics, or ingrained in customs and mores. Amongst the Hindu monuments still extant can be mentioned Angkor Wat in Cambodia, the largest Hindu temple complex in the world, and the Prambanan group of temples on the island of Java in Indonesia. Amongst the numerous Southeast Asian adaptations of the epics we have the Ramayanas of Laos and Myanmar; many Hindu gods continue to be worshipped today in Buddhist Myanmar and Thailand; Hindu figures like Garuda have been adopted as icons in Indonesia.

Having themselves converted and become Hindus, the Ahoms and their neighbours in the west, the Koches, while facilitating Hindu expansionism in Southeast Asia, actually prevented Islamic influence from penetrating into Myanmar and beyond to other nations across the land route. Later, when the Koch kingdom became a vassal of the mighty Mughals at Delhi, it was left to the Ahoms to repulse the repeated assaults of the Muslim invaders and retain the sovereignty of the region as well as its broad Hindu character. This came during the fourteenth to sixteenth centuries when Islam was expanding across Asia and north Africa; with the land route to the east blocked, proponents of that religion shared the sea route with traders in order to reach Southeast

Asia, which explains why the Indonesian archipelago was the first region where Islam could get a toehold before spreading in the region.

Though there are records of Muslim traders being present in Indonesian ports in the tenth to twelfth centuries, it was only in the thirteenth century that notable conversion of the indigenous Hindu population took place. Marco Polo, who visited the archipelago towards the end of the thirteenth century, records that two small Muslim principalities existed in Aceh province of Sumatra. The fourteenth century saw the strengthened Muslim principalities engage in wars, with an element of 'jihad', against non-Muslim neighbours, and finally supplant Hinduism and Buddhism in Indonesia. Islamic influence inexorably spread northwards to claim the Malay peninsula and parts of southern Thailand; the creation of the Sultanate of Brunei led to parts of southern Philippines coming under Islamic influence. However, strong Buddhist presence stemmed the spread of Islam further—it might, of course, have been a different matter had expansionist Islam been able to utilize the land route through Myanmar.

It is interesting to note that the Ahoms' expansion of their kingdom coincided with the Islamic expansion in Southeast Asia. Wave after wave of assaults by the Muslim rulers in Delhi to subjugate the Ahoms in order to open a gateway to Myanmar and beyond were repulsed and terminated at the Brahmaputra Valley itself. There can be no doubt that the Ahoms were responsible for stemming the flow of Muslim invasions into Myanmar and beyond with the attendant conquest, colonization and conversion—had they not done so the religio-cultural scenario in this region might have been entirely different from what it is today.[*] This is indubitably the most significant contribution of the Ahoms as far as Asia is concerned and an abiding factor of the legacy they left behind.

The renowned Bengali scholar Suniti Kumar Chatterjee (Padma Vibhushan), amongst others, advocated this postulate:

---

[*] There are a number of references to substantiate this theory. Please refer to Gait, *A History of Assam* (1905) and Acharyya, *The History of Medieval Assam* (1992), for instance.

The most noteworthy military achievement of the Ahoms was their holding the Mohammadan expansion from north India through Bengal .... There were persistent efforts on the part of the Muslim rulers of Bengal (Turkey, Pathan and Indian Muslim) to conquer Assam all through the centuries, and we have very detailed account of the campaigns of the Moghul generals in Assam. But these fights between Ahom ruling houses, between their Ahom and Bodo and Hindu Assamese troops, on the one hand, and the Bengalised Turki and Pathan and North Indian Muslims as well as Rajput and other Hindu troops under the Moguls on the other, show Assam in a particularly favourable light. Assamese kings stopped the Muslim flood from penetrating into Burma and beyond in a wave of aggressive warfare and conquest. Colonisation, proselytization and then conquest of Arab merchants and their religious teachers in Indonesia led to the final Islamisation of Indonesia. The Arabs and later on Indian Muslim merchants from Western India found a direct line of access by sea to Malaya and Indonesia, but a land route for aggressive advance was denied to the Indian Muslims by the Ahoms of Assam. Otherwise, the history of Burma and Indo-China might have been different.

(Chatterji, *The Place of Assam in the History and Civilization of India*, 1970)

With the coming of the Ahoms also began the recorded history of the Brahmaputra Valley. For events prior to their advent, historians have had to rely on myths, legends, ancient religious manuscripts and stone inscriptions to decipher the history of this region. But the Ahoms actually recorded contemporary events in the form of chronicles called buranjis. These were historical manuscripts written upon strips of bark by priests or other court dignitaries, and brought up to date from time to time. Written originally in their native language and later in Assamese, these recorded chronicles provide an authentic account of the history of the valley from the thirteenth century onwards till its annexation by the British in the nineteenth century. In fact, some of the older buranjis record 'events' which actually belong to the mythical realm, such as how the world was created or how the ancestors of the Ahoms descended from Heaven; however, the chronicles from the year 1228 CE, when Sukapha entered the valley, can be trusted as a true account of events.

The Ahom dynasty was one of the greatest political entities in medieval Asia, equal to if not greater than their more well-known counterparts in China or Japan. Their 600 years of rule is replete with fascinating tales of war, bravery, brutality, love, loyalty, treachery and treason. Many volumes would be required to fully mirror these in their totality; only a mere glimpse can be provided here.

In writing this book, the objective of the author has been to broadly familiarize the reader with the fascinating history of the Ahom dynasty. The primary sources of historians tracing this history are the 'buranjis' or chronicles maintained by the Ahoms. However, these buranjis do not provide detailed accounts of events, or of the personae involved, but only record happenings in a concise, matter-of-fact manner. The author has taken these recorded materials and expanded them in an imaginative way.

For instance, the tale of Sudangpha or the Brahmin Prince, is recounted in the buranjis in two brief paragraphs. The author has taken the skeletal facts and expanded them into an entire chapter, adding backdrops, characters, situations, etc. Thus, the village of Kalabari, characters such as Surjya Bipra, Khenkham, Baduli, and incidents such as the sending of a spy to hunt for the younger queen which do not figure in the buranjis have been included. This is true of the entire book, and the reader must bear in mind that though historical accuracy is maintained, much of the book is a creative retelling of the original material.

THE NARRATOR

'Listen to my words,' the Narrator said. 'Then let your imagination fly. Go back to the past so that you can see the events of which I speak unfold.'

In this part of the Upper Brahmaputra Valley, the sun sets earlier than the rest of the country; during winters, the night, with amazing swiftness, rushes breathlessly in. But a huge bonfire had been lit in the community field of this Ahom village. The flames kept the pitch-black darkness away, as also the damp mist which in time would thicken into fog.

The flames lit up the features of those who squatted upon the ground: men and women, boys and girls in their prime, youngsters, their rapt faces upturned towards the Narrator who stood before them, gazes transfixed upon him. Though none too tall, and thin and bony, with wizened features and limbs so withered that the black veins could be seen, he loomed in their minds as a towering figure; one who spoke in the voice of thunder.

The Narrator was of Deodhai lineage—his ancestors since time immemorial had been acting as priests for Ahom monarchs. But the sun had set long ago on the once mighty Ahom Empire; in these modern times, the need for traditional Ahom Deodhai or Bailung priests had grown less and less. In fact, he was the last of his profession; his own children had branched out into different and more lucrative jobs.

Yet he remained the custodian of the Ahom heritage; empowered with an astonishing memory, he could trace the history of his people to their beginnings. Names, events, years—these had been handed down generation after generation through a remarkably resilient oral tradition; he was its last human receptacle. His knowledge, of course, was not merely dependent upon what his elders had told him; a scholar, he had since childhood studied the Ahom buranjis and scriptures—no, not the spurious, translated versions, but the original sanchi-paat chronicles, or manuscripts made of the bark of the sanchi tree, penned both in the Tai language as well as Assamese languages.

This had become almost an annual ritual in this village. Each year, just after the harvest festival was over and while the embers of the bonfires lit during the community feast remained alive, the villagers would gather in the evening after their supper around the rebuilt bonfire to listen to a narration of their glorious past. The old priest in a firm voice would retrace the course of Ahom history from the very inception; someone or the other would tend the bonfire to keep it blazing as the Narrator spoke deep into the night.

'The past I speak of is not a creation of my imagination,' he said. 'Each event, even those from mythical realms, is recorded in the Ahom buranjis—our historical annals or chronicles. "Bu" in our Tai language translates as ignorant, "ran" is to teach and "ji" means a granary. Thus, a buranji is a storehouse which teaches the ignorant. You, my people, are the ignorant ones. Not only have you lost the power and glory you once commanded, you have also lost knowledge of your past. Tonight, I shall remove your ignorance and enlighten you of your history.

'If you wish to know of your history, you will need to be told of specific years and when events took place. But you are ignorant of the Ahom system of counting years! We count the years by a system called Lakli. It is different from the Gregorian calendar of the English, or our Assamese calendar with which you are familiar. For instance, in the English calendar every 100 years constitute a century, from where a new era starts. In our Lakli system, on the other hand, a new era starts every sixty years. I shall not, however, try to teach you our system tonight. So know you this, my people, when I speak of dates and years I speak in the English way.'

The silence was so thick that one could almost touch it. The audience made no sound; the youngsters did not fidget. Only the wood in the bonfire hissed and crackled as red-yellow flames turned them to embers.

'We, the Ahoms,' said the Narrator, 'are Tais. The word Tai means "of celestial origin". We, my people, are a race that descended from Heaven itself. Our kings descended from the thunder-wielding Lord of Heaven, Lengdon; our two principal noble clans, Bargohain and Buragohain, from Khuntun the moon god and Khunban the sun god; our Deodhai and Bailung priests from Loakhri and Pujakoji, the teacher of the gods; and our subjects from the Khun race that once dwelt in Heaven ...'

Mythical Realms

〜

IN THE BEGINNING THERE WAS NOTHING. NOT THE EARTH YOU plough, no trees that give you fruits and shade, no sky or cloud or sun or moon. There was no air, but a vast sheet of water did exist. And, of course, there was Pha, the Supreme One, the fount of everything that has or will come into being. He had form yet no form, shape yet no shape, perpetually in motion like a swarm of bees in a hive. He hung suspended within the all-pervading emptiness, emanating the light of a million suns. Then Pha assumed form and shape and created from his own self a creature called Khuntheukham, huge and monstrous, who floated upon the water facing upwards. A lotus bloomed from Khuntheukham's navel. Next Pha created a crab, a tortoise and a snake with eight hoods that spread in eight directions ... also a huge white elephant with tusks. Then Pha caused two mountains to rise in the north and south, placed two pillars upon them, and linked them with a rope. He created two huge golden spiders that floated about in the emptiness ... from their excrement the earth gradually formed upon the water. The spiders also placed eight pillars upon eight directions. Passing quickly from one to the other like a woman working a loom, they wove a web shaped like a golden throne, which became Heaven.

Then Pha, feeling lonely, created a female version of Himself. In due course of time, She laid four eggs, which hatched into four sons.

The eldest son was named Phasang din Khunnyeu and made King of Earth. Sengchaphaphakam, the second son, was made the overlord of eight lakh serpents and the third son, Shengkhampha, overlord of the myriad kinds of thunder. Pha invested his youngest son, Ngingaokham, with the responsibility of further creations. The eldest son inadvertently disobeyed his father and had to suffer death and become a spirit. His son, who succeeded him as King of Earth, also died and became a ghar deuti or a spirit that looks after the well-being of a household.

Pha looked down from Heaven and saw that due to the lack of wise men, the world was not functioning properly. To overcome this, he created a number of wise men who were given the responsibility of governing various parts of the world. I shall not trace the knotty relationships which further ensued through the course of centuries, but know you this, my people, that ultimately were born Khunlung, which in Tai means the Older Prince, and Khunlai, which means the Younger Prince, who descended from Heaven to become progenitors of the Ahom race.'

Heaven, the celestial realm, was ruled by its supreme deity, Lengdon, which means the "powerful one". Later, when the Brahmins came and our religion became intermixed with Hinduism, Lengdon was also referred to as Indra. He had numerous gods and goddesses to do his bidding, such as the goddess of knowledge, Jasingpha, who is the equivalent of the Hindu goddess Saraswati, as well as Lengsheng, the god of light; Laokhri, god of political wisdom, and so on. The earth was peopled by men and women created by Ngingaokham ... he also created animals and plants. Lengdon sent down gods from the Heaven to rule the men and women in different parts of the earth.

Then disaster struck. For a long period there was no rain; the fierce sun heated up the earth till it dried up and many people and animals perished. Finally, the earth cracked apart and boiling water gushed out and killed every living thing—men and women, all creatures and plants.

Only two beings survived, an old man named Thaolipling and a cow, both having taken refuge in a boat of stone. The seething, rising waters carried the boat to the peak of a tall mountain named Ipa in the remote northeast of the earth. Thaolipling and the cow clung to the mountain peak and survived the cataclysm.

The waters subsided. But the corpses of people and animals began to rot and the stench grew terrible. The foul smell went up and up till it polluted Heaven too, forcing Lengdon to send down fire to burn the corpses. You can imagine the heat, my people, a million times greater than of the bonfire beside which you sit. Thaolipling could not endure the intense heat, so he killed the cow and took shelter inside it. What do you think he found within the cow's stomach? A single seed of a gourd, that's what!

Gradually, the heat subsided. The stench wafted away. The rains came. Thaolipling emerged from within the cow and planted the gourd seed in the earth. It grew up into a gigantic gourd plant that threw out four branches towards the four directions. Fierce cold destroyed the northern branch; the southern branch was withered by fire and the western branch by water. But the eastern branch survived.

It produced a gourd of gargantuan proportions, one which contained within it countless men, women, beasts, birds, fish and plants of every kind. But the rind of that gigantic gourd was hard as iron; as unbreakable as the concrete we use to build tall skyscrapers in our cities nowadays. Thus, those living creatures were trapped; they screamed for help, raising a storm of noise which grew loud enough to reach Heaven and fall on Lengdon's ears. Startled, the powerful one sent a messenger named Panthoi to find out what the uproar was all about. Panthoi descended from Heaven and reached the earth; he listened to the screams and cries for help and understood the cause; returning to Heaven he advised the Almighty to break the gourd open, else everything inside would suffocate to death.

And that, my people, was why Aiphalan, the eldest son of Lengdon, was sent down to the earth to break open the gourd with the aid of lightning. Forthwith Aiphalan left Heaven to carry out his task; but the moment he directed his lightning bolt at the point of the gourd where human beings were cringing, they pleaded that he hit another part, lest the force of the bolt kill them all. They promised, if allowed to come out alive, to people the entire earth and cultivate the land. Moved by their entreaties Aiphalan directed his fearsome missile at the point where the cattle were; but they too pleaded to be spared, as human beings would need them to cultivate the land.

Perplexed, time and again Aiphalan tried to aim at different spots of the gourd, but on each occasion he was stopped by the entreaties of the creatures trapped within. The son of Lengdon did not know what to do, but it was at that point of time that the old man Thaolipling, who was sitting where the flower of the plant had withered away after fruition, offered to sacrifice himself if they worshipped and honoured him for it. With the desperate people promising to do so, Aiphalan finally discharged a lightning bolt at the spot where the old man was seated, killing him, but causing the gourd to split open.

Thus it was, my people, that mankind could thrive and spread. Aiphalan taught them various skills; he taught the wild animals how to take care of themselves, the birds how to make nests. And thus it is, my people, why we Deodhais and Bailungs, priests and astrologers of the Ahoms, worship Thaolipling each year and give a feast in his honour. No doubt Lengdon is our chief god, but that will not prevent us from offering obeisance to the one who gave up his own life so that mankind could live.

We, the Ahoms, have an ancient lineage—we are the descendants of Khunlung and Khunlai sent by Lengdon to rule over a kingdom on the earth. Later, my people, Brahmin proselytizers fabricated another tale in order to influence Ahom monarchs and convert them to Hinduism, but that is not recorded in our early buranjis. Yet know you this, both legends attribute to our race divine ancestry; that is why we address an Ahom monarch as Chaopha or Swargadeo, or God of Heaven. The story of gods coming down from Heaven to rule the earth is present all over the part of Asia where the Shans or Tais prevail, so there must be truth to it!

Lengdon, ruler of Heaven, was concerned that none of his lineage ruled any part of the earth. He was also concerned that, due to the absence of good rulers, anarchy prevailed in many parts of the world. He consulted his council of gods and decided that one of his own must be sent down to earth to stop the anarchy and govern wisely and make mankind understand the difference between good and evil. He requested his son Thenkham to go, but the latter was loath to leave Heaven. Thus, it was finally decided that Lendon's grandsons—Thenkham's sons—Khunlung and Khunlai should go.

Accordingly, Khunlung and Khunlai knelt before Lengdon prior to departure and were given the following counsel: 'Go forth and rule with justice and fairness. I am sending with you God Puphishu, who will rule over the forests. In the month of Dinpet or Ahar, you must sacrifice a buffalo and offer a feast to Puphishu, and he will keep you safe. I am gifting you two pairs of roosters; your priests will be able to foretell the future by killing them, cutting them open and studying the beak, entrails and legs. I am giving you a pair of drums; beat upon them in times of difficulty, and I shall aid you. I am gifting you a pair of hengdang, broadbladed swords to slay your enemies with. But above all, I am gifting our idol Somdeo, kept safely within a casket of gold. Take the greatest care and protect it with your very life—the loss of Somdeo would also spell the end of your rule.'

Fortified by Lengdon's advice and assurance, Khunlung and Khunlai descended the golden stairs of Heaven and reached the earth and set up their kingdom at Mungrimungram, which in Tai means 'an uninhabited, deserted country'. It was actually peopled by Shan tribes, but perhaps it was called thus because there was no king to govern the multitude. However, in their haste to leave Heaven, they had forgotten to bring the gifts bestowed on them by Lengdon. So, a follower named Lango was dispatched back to Heaven to fetch them and was made the king of China as a reward.

Unfortunately, my people, gods behave godlike only in Heaven! On earth even gods develop feet of clay. No doubt Khunlung and Khunlai built a holung or city in Mungrimungram and made it their capital. But Khunlai, who harboured a desire for kingship, through a devious subterfuge usurped the throne. Khunlung was forced to leave and set up another kingdom at Mungkhumungjao—which translated means a country of great extent—though he did succeed in taking the Somdeo with him. The elder brother ruled wisely for forty years in his new kingdom. He made his eldest son the ruler of Mungkang or the 'country of the drum', and gave him the Somdeo to protect. Another son was made the king of Ava in today's Myanmar. Perhaps this is why the Ahoms and the Burmese rulers referred to each other as 'brother kings'. You need to bear in mind that during their 600 years of rule in the Brahmaputra Valley, threat to the Ahom kingdom came only from the west. The sole occasion when assault had been made from the east, the death knell of the Ahom kingdom sounded!

Upon Khunlung's demise, his youngest son, Khunchu, succeeded him. Meanwhile, Khunlai and his son ruled for over a century at Mungrimungram—and then the lineage ended. Once again a prince in the line of Khunlung and Khunchu, whose name was Tyaokhunjan, was sent to fill the vacant throne, thereby undoing the objective of Khunlai's treachery. There are many successions in between and many new kingdoms sprang up, which I will not talk of. Enough that you know, in the final decade of the twelfth century of the English era was born a prince named Sukapha, which translates as 'Tiger from Heaven', who was the founder of the Ahom dynasty and the arbiter of the Brahmaputra Valley's destiny for the next 600 years.

The circumstances of Sukapha's birth and lineage are obscured by the mists of history. There are many versions and it is difficult to say with absolute certainty which is the true one. So I will give you but one version; yet, know you this, it may not be the correct one. Only from 1228 onwards, when Sukapha made his way into the Brahmaputra Valley, can we say with certainty that proper buranjis, which were accurate, were written ...

Tiger from Heaven

⁓

THIS WAS HILLY COUNTRY, WHERE THE MAU TRIBE OF THE SHAN people dwelt. Mung in the Tai language meant 'country', so the vast region stretching from Upper Myanmar to the Yunnan Province of China was called Mungmau by its inhabitants. Those beyond its boundaries knew the region as Pong; they also knew that Mungmau or Pong was not a single state but comprised of a number of principalities ruled by different Shan kings, some not much more than mere chieftains of small communities.

The principality of Maulung, ruled over in the first decade of the thirteenth century CE of the Gregorian calendar by King Pameuplung, was of considerable dimensions, reaching across many river valleys and mountain ranges. The Shan tribe inhabiting Maulung used the valleys for wetland rice cultivation, and also cut terraces upon the hills for other crops. The numerous hamlets in Maulung wherein the inhabitants dwelt were set in disparate clusters linked to each other by passable roads and bridle paths cut through dense jungles filled with wild animals which did not hesitate to attack human intruders. So the villagers, while travelling from one place to another, chose not to travel alone but in well-armed groups.

Life was not easy; the summers were wet and the dampness especially in the valleys could bring about strange fevers and skin ailments. The winters, though brief, could be quite harsh. But the people were a hardy lot, unafraid of toil and brave of heart. Every adult male was deemed to be a warrior who would respond to a call for battle by their king if the kingdom was under attack from outside.

The capital of Maulung where the king lived was, however, not built in a valley but higher up in the mountains, flanked on almost all sides by sheer cliffs and gorges, except for the steep slope which led up to it from the valley below. A river, relatively narrow and dry during winter, but which could swell up to a sizeable proportion during the rainy season, cut through the valley, dividing it into halves. A narrow but well-paved road snaked up this slope; every kilometre or so there were checkpoints manned by armed sentries who searched porters carrying provisions and asked about the identity of anyone going to the place 'where King Pameuplung lives', that being the name of the kingdom's capital, none daring to call it by any other name.

The palace of the king was made of wood, bamboo and cane; of sizeable proportion and having many chambers for different purposes, the style similar to traditional Chinese architecture. The entire compound was surrounded by a tall stockade of tree trunks with spiked tops, lashed firmly together with stout ropes of cane. A heavy gate of wood was the sole point of entry; at various points of the stockade watchtowers had been erected, manned by armed sentries, as was the gate. The palace 'where King Pameuplung lives' was secure and well guarded, indeed.

There were smaller palaces built adjacent to the central palace compound, of similar design but smaller in size—these housed the nobles of the king's court. Separate from them were the dwellings of the common citizens—the professional guards and soldiers, servants who worked in the palaces of the king and the nobles, traders who imported exotic goods from far-off places in China, peasants who cut terraces on the mountain side to raise maize and other crops—many of these were rude bamboo chang-type hutments, set upon stilts and with thatched roofs the eaves of which almost touched the ground, some perched precariously on the sides of steep cliffs. All the buildings, hutments, gates and ramparts of the city, by royal decree, were painted in bright red, green and yellow; on a clear summer day, the capital glinted like a diamond which could be seen from far away. There was also a marketplace which bustled during the daytime with life and activity, but fell silent, like the rest of the capital, with the setting of the sun; the night, everyone knew, belonged to the animals of the wild and spirits of the dead.

The man who trudged up the slope to the place 'where King Pameuplung lives' this winter morning was noticeable because he did not travel with a group but alone. His skin was heavily tanned, showing that he was not a native and had apparently come from other climes. Though he carried a heavy bag on his back containing all his personal belongings, he moved strongly and lithely like a leopard.

Naturally, he was challenged by the guards at the very first checkpost at the bottom of the slope. 'Where do you think you are going?' one of the sentries at the gate asked insolently. The man's face was weather-beaten and tired, his clothes somewhat ragged. Reasons enough for the sentry's insolence!

'To the palace where King Pameuplung lives,' the stranger replied haughtily.

'Perhaps our Lord of Heaven has invited you to dine with him?' mocked the sentry.

'Save your insolence for someone else, you lout!' the stranger said in a strident voice, making the sentry suddenly feel uneasy. 'Obviously, you do not recognize me. I am Chenkhung!'

The name instantly struck a chord in the sentry's memory. Everyone had heard of Chenkhung, a member of the royal household who, a few years back, had been afflicted with wanderlust, and set off alone to find out what lay west beyond Mungmau's borders. Everyone had thought that Chenkhung must have by now made a hearty meal for some jungle predator. Yet here he was, back from the dead, his authoritative voice, the piercing quality of his gaze, the regality of his gestures leaving no doubt about his identity in the sentry's mind. The man fell prostrate on the ground before the stranger. His fellow guards, seeing this, prostrated themselves too.

'Get up, you morons,' said the stranger. 'You're of no use to me down on the ground. Open the gate and let me through. One of you—come along with me so that there will be none of this at the other checkpoints. Let another run forth and alert the palace of my return.'

The guards clambered over each other in their eagerness to obey. One of them offered to relieve the stranger of his bag, but he waved him away, and set off once again on the climb.

In a courtyard of the royal palace, the two princes, Sukapha and Sukhanpha, were practising martial arts under the supervision of a trainer. At one edge of the courtyard, seated upon a cane chair, an aged lady of regal bearing basked in the muted warmth of the winter sun, lovingly watching the youths as they went at each other with bamboo swords.

Sukapha was a prince only in name. The actual crown prince was Sukhanpha, the son of Pameuplung. Sukapha's father's name was Tyaosangnyao. He had once been the king of the principality of Munkgkhumungjao. But, worsted by his enemies, he had been forced to flee with his family and clansmen to Maulung and seek shelter under King Pameuplung. The good king not only assured him safety, but also gave him in marriage his own sister and allowed his brother-in-law to stay on in the palace. In due course of time, Sukapha was born.

Since Pameuplung did not have any issue, it was taken for granted that Prince Sukapha would succeed him after his death. But a few years later, a child was born to Pameuplung—they named him Sukhanpha. Sukapha's ill luck did not end there. Sometime later, his parents too died. It was his maternal grandmother—the lady now basking in the sunshine—who had brought him up. Though orphaned and with his hopes of being the king dashed, Sukapha was not disheartened. He loved Sukhanpha very much and wished him well, but he was determined to leave Maulung one day and seek out a kingdom of his own.

A gong suddenly sounded, its loud, discordant clang echoing against the walls of the courtyard. Sukapha and Sukhanpha immediately stopped their practice and knelt upon the paved floor with bowed heads, as did the trainer and other attendants. Only the lady on the chair did not move.

This particular gong was always struck when His Majesty the king was approaching a place, so as to alert others of his imminent arrival. Sure enough, a few minutes later, King Pameuplung swept into the courtyard along with his retinue, including the spittoon-bearer who carried a small but intricately carved receptacle in which His Highness, fond of chewing betel-nut, could periodically spit into.

King Pameuplung, though short, possessed broad shoulders and was powerfully built. On this occasion, he was accompanied by a stranger with skin almost tanned black by the sun though it was winter, wearing ragged clothes and possessing rugged features. No one recognize him and the king chortled.

'Ha, ha,' he laughed with almost childish delight. 'Seems like a tramp, doesn't he? Sukhanpha, Sukapha, don't you recognize Uncle Chenkhung? He has just returned from his travels.'

The two youths sprang up from their positions and ran to embrace Uncle Chenkhung in bear hugs. The newcomer than approached the old lady and prostrated himself before her. 'Arise, Chenkhung,' she spoke in a voice full of authority. 'It's good to see you safely back.'

That evening, in one of the inner sanctums of the royal palace, Chenkhung dined with the king, the queen mother, the queen, Sukhanpha and Sukapha. Naturally, most of the conversation was carried on by the traveller, the others being eager to learn where he had been and what he had seen.

'I knew what lay towards Maulung's north, east and south—we carry on trade with our neighbours and often visitors arrive from even the remotest regions located in these directions. But I did not know much about what lay to our west, the mystical land which our immediate neighbours call Athan or Weithali and others refer to as Weisali or Tekau. So, this was the direction I followed on my travels. It did not take me long to realize why we were so ignorant of what lies to our west, or why none from this region ever visits our land. It is an uncharted route filled with myriad pitfalls; there are dense jungles one has to hack through, which contain weird creatures; there are rivers and mountains to cross. Most important, the people who inhabit the area that lies across this route are not friendly at all; I had to use all my wiles to avoid them; for, from my observations, I came to know that they were headhunters, if not actual cannibals!'

He talked on and on, the interest in the faces of his audience never waning, of the various travails that he had undergone, the dangers he had confronted. 'My advantage was that I travelled alone,' Chenkhung said. 'It was thus possible for me to slip through settlements undetected. If I had gone with a small group, we would surely have been detected and decimated one day or the other. But I finally traversed the treacherous region and came to a beautiful valley lush with flowering forests and meandering rivers. There was, I remember, a mammoth river which cut across this valley; it is a wonderfully fertile land, very sparsely populated. The people I met there, though they did not speak my language, were friendly enough. I spent a long period there learning their language, customs and mores; then I felt sick for home and made my way back over the same treacherous route—and here I am!'

Everyone in that inner sanctum, even the servants—who listened on the sly and would convey the tale next morning outside the palace so that soon it would be heard by each person in Maulung and perhaps beyond—was fascinated, Sukapha most of all. 'Did you find out what this valley is called?' he asked in undisguised excitement.

'Well, they call it by many names. But then I recalled our own Shan folklore which mentions this valley—I remembered we call it Mungdunsunkham. "Mung" in our language means country, "dun" means full of, "sun" means garden and "kham" gold. Thus, Mungdunsunkham means "the country full of golden gardens"!'

'Uncle,' continued Sukapha in the same breathless tone. 'Can you draw the route to that place on a tree-bark sheet, and mark out special features? Also, in the next few days, I would beg your indulgence by picking your brains for memories of your travels.'

'Of course, I will,' said Chenkhung. 'But why this extraordinary interest, Prince Sukapha? Do you plan to make a trip to Mungdunsunkham in the near future?'

The youthful prince laughed. 'You never know, Uncle. I just might go to the country full of beautiful gardens!'

The very next morning, Sukapha went to his grandmother for advice. He sought her counsel even before discussing with the king the plan that was hatching in his mind, and which had made sleep impossible the previous night—she was his mentor and the first confidante since childhood.

'Grandma,' he said, the gravity upon his face indicating the seriousness of the subject he was about to broach with her. 'You know I love all of you, especially Sukhanpha.'

'Of course, I know that, my dear,' the old lady replied. Her shrewd eyes had seen the restlessness within her grandson in the past few years and her mind had grasped the reality that such a moment would arrive. 'You are a young man of character, incapable of treachery, generous of heart. We all love you dearly, too.'

'But I have been overcome with yearnings for some time now—'

'I have guessed that too, my dear,' the old lady said, interrupting her grandson on seeing how much difficulty he was having in coming straight to the subject. 'The whole of Maulung, nay, the whole of Mungmau, had thought you would inherit the throne after my son. Then Sukhanpha was born and your hopes were dashed. Even then my son might have given you the crown—he well knows you have the qualities of a great king. But the laws governing the great Shan tribe to which we Mau people belong ordains that the son of the king has first claim to the throne.'

'I've no regrets, dear Grandma,' Sukapha assured her.

'You're too generous to harbour regrets or grudge Sukhanpha his privilege. But then, you're deeply unhappy inside, for you have been born to be a leader of man and cherish a hope to build up your own individual kingdom. Chenkhung's return has put a notion into your head, isn't it?'

Sukapha smiled. 'You're like one of those magicians who come to perform in the palace! You read my mind as though it were your own.'

'I've reared you ever since you were born, haven't I? It's not bad to harbour ambition, my dear. That, in fact, is a sign of greatness. But then, two tigers cannot live within the same area of the forest; one never knows when their paths might cross! Also, the air of a royal palace does not suit a young man of your nature ... such air is always befouled by suspicions, innuendoes, occasional betrayals. So, what do you plan to do?'

'Depart with a body of men in search of another place where I can erect my own kingdom.'

'Mungdunsunkham? Chenkhung's description of that valley full of golden gardens has mesmerized you, hasn't it? It is a good idea, though the way to that valley seems treacherous indeed. Discuss it with His Royal Highness. I will help. When do you propose to leave?'

'At once, Grandma, though it would break my heart to go.'

'No, my dear. Winter is almost over; the rains will be coming soon. You need to bide your time till the rains stop, for otherwise it will hinder you at the very outset. Also, I must have the time to organize everything— men, animals and materials you will require on your conquering trek. Make that your rule—travel only during the dry season, and when the rains come, set up camp wherever you are and await their end. Your men can cultivate rice and other crops during that season.'

'It will be a difficult wait, Grandma!'

'Patience is the virtue of the great. You have just crossed twenty-four; your whole life lies before you. A few more months will not make a difference. It will, instead, aid in careful preparation. Now, go, broach this with His Majesty and seek his permission.'

King Pameuplung, aware of the ambition burning within his nephew, readily consented to Sukapha's plan. The first April showers would arrive a few months later and then the next six months would witness incessant rains. So, it would be possible for Sukapha to depart only towards end of September—but the eight months this deferment gave to him were actually helpful, for it would enable him to prepare thoroughly for what indubitably was an once-in-a-lifetime journey.

The king would have preferred to conscript by royal decree the men who would accompany Sukapha on his quest for a kingdom, but the young prince requested that the men should be selected only from amongst those who volunteered on their own. His Majesty had been inwardly sceptical about how many able-bodied men could be mustered in this manner. Imagine his surprise when thousands of his subjects, who met the required conditions of being young and unmarried, made their way to the capital to volunteer for the trip! Suddenly, in his heart of hearts, King Pameuplung was glad that Sukapha would be leaving his kingdom—the enormous response to the call for volunteers was clear indication how popular the prince was with the subjects and how they trusted him.

Veteran soldiers from the royal guards had been entrusted with the task of picking out those who were fit enough to undertake a rigorous journey that would involve not only travel, but numerous skirmishes with dwellers of the regions through which the caravan would pass. Though provisions would be carried, the group would need to live off the land too, thus many of the men must be expert hunters. Most important, since the enormous band of men would encamp every year at salubrious spots the moment the rains began and embark on wet-rice cultivation to augment their supplies, the men, apart from being good warriors, needed to be good cultivators.

Finally, a huge body of young male adults, over 8,000 of them, were picked and housed in a makeshift camp built with bamboo and cane in the valley below Maulung's capital. Sukapha himself selected the officers who would train this army in the art of warfare. The next task was to acquire a band of non-combatant specialists—carpenters, cooks, doctors well-versed in traditional medicines, masons, tailors and the like, as well as native priests and astrologers without whom the project could not take off. It had been Sukhanpha who alerted his brother to one aspect that the latter had overlooked. 'Remember, Uncle Chenkhung said that Mungdunsunkham is filled with rivers and water bodies,' he said. 'We are mostly hill folk unused to travel by rivers and streams. You'll need to train up some of your people in the art of building rafts and navigating over waters if you don't wish to get bogged down in that valley.'

This was wise advice indeed, and King Pameuplung lost no time in sending out emissaries to his Shan allies in the Chinese plains and importing a few experts in rivercraft to give the required training. It reassured Sukapha that Sukhanpha, though far younger than him in age, had sense in him, enough to make him a good monarch. With the passing of the days, despite the spells of heavy rain proving to be an obstacle to the preparations, Sukapha grew more satisfied as he watched his army take shape before his eyes.

At one corner of the enormous compound of the royal palace stood a spacious, well-guarded building, all by itself, not linked like the others by passages and corridors. A person had to traverse a gabled courtyard to reach this gaudily painted outhouse. One morning, as September approached and the time of Sukapha's departure drew near, the queen mother made her way over the courtyard, accompanied by her retinue of maidservants.

The guards bowed low and opened the outer door for her. She gestured to her maids to wait outside and then entered the passage as the door was closed behind her. Inside, there was gloom and hushed silence;

so quiet that she could hear the echo of her own footfall as she moved swiftly down the corridor; it opened into a dimly lit room made dimmer by the swirls of smoke from burning incense sticks. Though the queen mother was a woman who feared nothing and no one, yet the eerie aura the room radiated caused the hair at the nape of her neck to rise.

'I have been expecting you,' a disembodied voice emerged from the gloomy interior.

'In that case, you've already performed the ritual and have the results ready?'

'Certainly, Your Royal Highness. The cock whose throat I slit traces its stock from the roosters brought down from Heaven by Khunlung and Khunlai! Looking at its legs and entrails, as is our custom, I've been able to predict the future.'

'So, what say you?'

'Propitious, Your Royal Highness. Highly propitious! Prince Sukapha will achieve the greatest of success in the enterprise of his choosing. He is destined to be the king of his own empire and head a dynasty which will rule for many centuries.'

The queen mother heaved a sigh of relief. This was the head priest speaking and he foretold of auspicious happenings. Strangely enough, she had never seen the head priest in her life. He never emerged from his sanctum sanctorum, choosing to spend his hours praying and studying within its dusky depths. There were many rituals to be performed almost every month in the royal palace and in those of the nobles', the Deodhai and Bailung priests had to cater to the ritualistic needs of the laity, too. But always acolytes of the head-priest were sent for these tasks; the head priest himself only taught them the lore.

'I am greatly relieved to hear that,' the queen mother said, her belief in the prediction absolute and unshakeable. 'I convey my gratitude to you.'

'However, there is something else I must tell you,' the voice spoke again.

'Yes? Is anything wrong?'

'We must again go back to the days Khunlung and Khunlai. When they departed from Heaven, Lengdon had given them the Somdeo, the idol we Shans worship. Unfortunately, as the greater Shan nations broke up into smaller kingdoms, the Somdeo kept changing hands. This had caused us to worship surrogates, the male idol called Sung, and the female idol called Sang. Prince Sukapha is travelling to new lands to spread the seeds of the Shans. It would behove him to have the original Somdeo in his possession when he does so. The Somdeo would guide him safely on his enterprise.'

'I must confess I have never seen this idol, let alone worshipped it. What does it look like? Is it in the likeness of our supreme deity Lengdon?'

'Nor have I, Your Highness. But I've been told of it by others who have seen and worshipped the Somdeo. It is in the likeness of Lengdon, they tell me, though not in form but in spirit. It is a pearl of wondrous beauty, set within a hollow cylinder and placed upon an oblong metal plaque. There is a hook at the upper end, by means of which the Somdeo can be suspended from the neck of a king at the time of his coronation. It is brought out of its place of storage but very rarely—on special occasions such as a coronation or the birth of an heir. The rest of the time it is kept in a set of seven gold caskets, which fit one within the other.'

A look of grim determination came over the queen mother's face. 'Where is the Somdeo now, do you know?'

'Certainly, Your Highness.' The disembodied voice paused theatrically. 'There is not much that goes on in the Heaven and earth that I do not know of. Little sprites come to me and whisper things in my ears.'

'Come, come, where is it?'

'In the custody of King Nyaishanpha. The Mungkang kingdom he rules lies northeast of Maulung.'

'Of course I know where Mungkang is. Where is it kept in Nyaishanpha's palace?'

'In a separate building just like this one. Well guarded, may I warn you, for a little sprite has just whispered to me the sudden notion that has crept into the mind of Your Highness.'

For the first time since entering the high priest's sanctum the queen mother smiled. 'Yes,' she said. 'I do have a plan, for my darling Sukapha must have his Somdeo.'

Having left the head priest's sanctum, the queen mother headed back to her anteroom in the palace and summoned one of her most trusted officers.

'I have met the head-priest,' she said, coming straight to the point. 'He predicts that Sukapha will meet with success in his quest. But he says it would be better if my grandson carried the Somdeo with him.'

'But the Somdeo is not in Maulung,' the officer pointed out.

'That's correct. It is in the possession of King Nyaishanpha, ruler of Mungkang. It is kept in a separate building in the compound of the royal palace … Heavily guarded, I presume.'

'Ah,' said the officer, by now aware what the old lady was up to. 'Every building, no matter how well guarded, has doors and windows which can be broken into. This is particularly true when the owner doesn't expect any break-in. But getting into the palace would be a problem.'

'I think I know how we can manage that. Sukhanpha is maturing into a handsome youth. We are hunting for a bride for him. Nyaishanpha has a beautiful daughter. We can send an embassy to his court to discuss possibilities of a marriage alliance.'

'Of course, Your Highness! I shall myself head the embassy. I'll also ensure that we have the most notorious thief our dungeons can provide in my entourage.'

'I'll write out an authorization so you can make the necessary arrangements. That way, you will not be held culpable if anything goes wrong and can prove you were working on my instructions. Keep everything away from the king's ears. He is of a cautious kind and might nip our plans in the bud.'

Things proceeded smoothly. Nyaishanpha actually did not have a daughter and had expressed his surprise at how misinformed the queen mother of Maulung was. He would have, of course, been more than happy to have formed a marriage alliance with Maulung, but there was no help for it. However, he proved to be a most gracious host and spent no effort to make his guests comfortable during the two nights they spent at the royal palace.

The mission had been accomplished. Three days before Sukapha's departure the Somdeo was in the safekeeping of the queen mother, with the king of Mungkang none the wiser of this fact.

Finally, the fateful day arrived. Sukapha's army would consist of around 8,000, well-trained foot soldiers, 600 bonded workers to carry provisions and so on, scores of carpenters and other professionals, and Deodhai and Bailung priests who could also double as medicine men. There would not be too many women-folk—Sukapha's three wives and their children, wives of the five nobles accompanying the prince, as well as the scores of handmaidens trained to serve their mistresses. A number of palanquins had been constructed, each to be borne on the shoulders of teams of four men, which would carry the women and children in shifts, so that they could travel in comfort and also not be a burden on the rest of the group. While most of the soldiers were bachelors, a handful amongst them were married, but if any family accompanied the head of the household, it had been made clear that they had to fend for themselves. This was the case with the non-combatant professionals too, most of whom were married and had children.

The nobles accompanying Sukapha were absolutely loyal and trustworthy. The highest-ranked amongst them was Chaophrangmung Thaomungmahgrai. Chaophrangmung translated as 'god of a wide country', which implied that particular noble was second in command next to Sukapha. Another noble, the third-ranked in the hierarchy, was Chalothaoung Taomungkan, his designation translating as 'great old god'. Lower in rank, but immediate commander on the ground at the head of the troops, was Phukanlung Takhunlak; Phukanlung, implying 'man of great origin'. Sukapha, as befitted the supreme commander of the group, would travel at the front along with the Chaophrangmung atop a male tusker named Khamkomung ridden by Phongpim the mahout; only a force of fifty heavily armed men on foot led by Takhunlak would precede Sukapha's elephant. The two other nobles would travel upon a female elephant named Kipkeu, always staying a few metres behind the tusker. Lines of soldiers on either side of the non-combatants, including the porters carrying cooking utensils, provisions, etc., stretching right till the back, would guard the flanks, though the biggest number of soldiers would be deployed at the rear, for a surprise attack from that direction was to be feared the most.

The quantity of provisions that had to be taken along was staggering. The route charted out by Chenkhung did not have many towns or hamlets where food for such a huge contingent could be obtained; in any case the area of that part of the country was the least inhabited of the Shan-occupied lands; King Pameuplung had already alerted the rulers of the realms Sukapha would pass through by sending couriers carrying messages that requested safe passage for the group. The primary objective, of course, was to prevent any misapprehension on the part of these rulers that it was an attacking army. Once the caravan passed the Shan-controlled area, it would be on its own. Even if it were to make longer stays to cultivate rice and other crops, it needed to carry provisions which would last at least for nine months. Cattle, both cows and oxen of the hardy, mountain variety, as also buffaloes and goats, would have to be herded along—not for milk, because the Shans were somewhat averse to it, but primarily for meat; there were expert hunters in Sukapha's band, but they would not be able to garner enough meat for almost 1,000 people!

Even the utensils required for cooking needed logistical planning—300 motongs or bronze pots, each large enough to cook for three adults, had been procured, as well as ladles for stirring and serving, and clay pots for drinking from, though plantain leaves collected from the jungles would serve in lieu of dishes. The motongs and other utensils had been distributed amongst members of the party; an officer had been appointed to keep track of the provisions and utensils; foodgrain and other eatables would be rationed out to groups of three for a week before being replenished. Similarly, petty officers were appointed from amongst the soldiers who would be in charge of twenty warriors each, accountable for any breach of discipline or misdemeanor on the part of the subgroup and would undergo punishment on their behalf. All in all, despite the seeming confusion and bustle amongst the group as it readied to depart, there was an underlying tiered structure which gave it balance and cohesion.

Sukapha, accompanied by his wives and children, arrived in the queen mother's private outer chamber almost immediately after sunrise. His grandmother was surrounded by King Pameuplung, his queen, Sukhanpha and a few senior nobles.

One by one, Sukapha and his family touched the feet of their elders and received blessings. An emissary of the head priest carried a bowl from which he sprinkled water upon the migrants and made his exit from the room. Sukapha hugged Sukhanpha in a fierce, fraternal grip.

The queen mother, with fortitude typical of the woman, kept smiling in spite of the fact that her heart was breaking inside. 'All right,' she finally said with feigned severity, 'that's enough of bidding farewell.' She brought out a wooden case, locked from outside, and handed it to the prince, along with a set of iron keys.

'This is our Somdeo, our very own idol for worship. I have procured it with great stealth, without guilt or regret, because the Somdeo belongs to the entire Shan race, to be used for great occasions. And there will be no greater occasion for our people in times to come than the one commencing today. Guard the Somdeo with your life—the priests who accompany you will advise you on when to bring it out and how to worship it. For the time being, only those present in this room know it is with you. But be sure King Nyaishanpha of Mungkang will discover sooner or later that his precious possession is gone and will put two and two together. So be on the alert for an attack from him. Now go forth, Sukapha, the tiger from heaven, and earn the admiration of the entire world.'

The shepherd boy Khumrung had never beheld such a wondrous sight in his young life, nor perhaps would he ever in the future. Perched upon the craggy hillside, he had a bird's eye view of the valley, which this morning swarmed with people—the lad had never imagined that there could be so many in the kingdom! Kinsfolk of those who were leaving had made a beeline to the riverbank to bid goodbye: fathers and mothers hugged their sons and daughters; families of the professionals embraced their loved ones whom they would never see again. The sounds made by the domestic animals and fowls that would be taken along by the migrants added to the din; the noise wafted up to him like a loud, continuous murmur, drowning out the sound of the river's waters.

Though from that height the people and palanquins looked like toys—even the elephants appeared to be miniatures—yet the grandeur of the spectacle overwhelmed Khumrung. Then, to the sound of bugles and brass instruments, the flags carried by standard-bearers glinting in the sunlight, the procession moved; the cloud of dust it raised surpassed the dimensions of the clouds which cover the mountaintops during the rains. A phalanx of soldiers, led by a man who walked all alone at their head, formed the vanguard; two elephants followed. Even from that height Khumrung could make out the dazzling, silky white of the clothes the prince and his nobles were wearing. Next the palanquins and the servants, the professionals and the bondsmen—the latter laden with utensils and provisions—then, herdsmen like himself, calling out to the animals to keep them from straying and breaking the formation; and finally more soldiers at the very end, hundreds of them, their shields and uniforms reflecting the winter sunshine.

Turning his eyes to the left, Khumrung could see the next hamlet which hugged the riverbank some distance away. Although the slow-moving procession would take a couple of hours to reach that settlement, people were already thronging the main thoroughfare that ran through it, awaiting the arrival of Sukapha and his group, to watch it pass and to wave their goodbyes. This would be the case the next few weeks in every settlement that they crossed; for the news of what the elder prince of Maulung was embarking upon had spread throughout Mungmau and even beyond.

Khumrung continued for quite a while to watch that vast, miniature procession slowly inch forward. Then he smiled, raised his hand and bid Prince Sukapha farewell.

Only the prince and nobles knew of it, but expert trackers had been sent long beforehand to prospect the route lying within Mungmau and select suitable places where nocturnal halts could be made. So, the trek within Shan territory had been planned out prior to their departure. However, once they were out of Mungmau, they would have to adopt a different strategy—send out each night advance reconnaissance scouts to chart out the territory lying immediately ahead, locate possible sources of danger, and also select spots where halts could be made. At the same time, a small band of soldiers would be left some way behind, so they could keep watch in case someone with hostile intentions was pursuing them.

The first evening's halt was at a stretch of land beside the river. Easily assembled tents of animal hide were erected for the prince, the nobles and their families; the others would sleep in the open, warmed by the blaze of scores of bonfires which would be lit as soon as it got dark. Apart from providing warmth, these also served to keep wild denizens of the jungle far away. Pretty soon the motongs were being put to good use and the smell of food cooking filled the night air.

Prince Sukapha, accompanied by his nobles, made a round of the encampment, mixing easily with his soldiers, craftsmen and their families, exchanging pleasantries and asking about their state of health and spirit. This would be a ritual he would undertake each evening, not merely to keep in touch with his men, but also to judge the prevailing mood. That first evening he was pleased to discover that everyone was cheerful and excited; tiredness had not set in even amongst the children and women; there was fireside chat and banter; the reality that almost none of them would ever return had not yet set in.

But a month later, the atmosphere within the group had grown markedly different. In his eagerness he had set a relatively quick pace; though progress was slow and they had crossed but a little distance from the bounds of Maulung, yet there was less merry an atmosphere within the camp at evening; fatigue had already set in amongst the children and womenfolk; some of the men had thoughts in their heads of those they had left behind. Fortunately, this being winter and thus a healthy season, and the Shan being a hardy race, no one was struck by any serious ailment; just a minor fever or two and a couple of cases of snake bites, which the accompanying physicians had no difficulty in curing.

Sukapha made some important decisions. The first was to slacken the pace and give breaks in between each day's travel, never mind that this would slow things down even further. He also decided that, once the rains set in, he might, if need be, spend a couple of years in the spot of their choice, so that his group might have the feel of being within a settled community. Last of all, he revealed the ace up his sleeve—a brainwave of his grandmother—that very evening he had conscripted a band of entertainers, who could juggle, perform acrobatics and clown around; they were required to put on a show a couple of evenings each week, and proved to be great spirit-lifters and an anodyne to homesickness.

Life settled into a somewhat slow-paced routine. No longer the bustle and hurry of the first few weeks, to wake up at break of day and get ready at once for the day's march. If the camp spot was scenic and situated on even ground beside a river, the halt was extended by a few days so that the marchers could rest and enjoy frolicking on the river's waters and bank. Sukapha discovered that this was a far more preferable mode of journey, for it kept up spirits. Occasionally, he would set some of his expert hunters after deer; the venison would be distributed equally amongst the inmates of the camp, and there would be great feasting and merriment on such nights.

In the third month since they had set out, there was a break to the routine. One evening, a group of runners sent by King Pameuplung had stumbled into the camp, bearing grave tidings. Spies deployed by the king had learned that King Nyaishanpha of Mungkang had discovered the Somdeo to be missing; it had not taken him long to infer who had purloined the idol and who carried it now. Even as the messengers were conveying this information to Prince Sukapha, a fast-moving host of soldiers from Mungkang was hot on his trail, and would catch up in the matter of two days or three.

The very next morning, Sukapha led his band away from the valley in which they were camping and moved to higher ground, his soldiers hacking away the vegetation that grew there so as to ready the slopes for encampment. 'Illusion,' he told his nobles, 'lies at the heart of success in warfare. We need to show our adversary that we have ten times more resources in terms of men and weapons than we really have.' As night fell, flares stretching over that entire hillock were lit so as to numerically magnify the presence of men. The bonfires and flares, serving also to keep animal predators away, could be seen for miles around—Sukapha hoped Nyaishanpha's troops would take note of these.

He kept to the hillside for the next few days, asking his followers to camouflage themselves so they could not be spotted during daytime, though the flags they carried fluttered for miles on either side, and flares were kept burning throughout the nights. His warriors were ready and on the alert. Spies had been left behind, concealed on treetops, to learn whatever they could of the adversary's strategy, and then report back to their commander.

Three days of nerve-racking wait, but nothing happened. Nyaishanpha's army did not materialize. Then one by one Sukapha's spies began to return, almost all bearing similar information. Nyaishanpha had dispatched a sizeable force to capture Sukapha and bring back the Somdeo, but he had apparently miscalculated the strength of the prince. The officer who led the forces had been informed that he would have to confront just a few hundred warriors, but an entire hill had been lit up during the night, denoting that his force would be met with thousands of well-trained men. Moreover, the enemy was entrenched on higher ground, which gave it a definite edge in any encounter. The commander and his immediate subordinate had come to the conclusion that it would be suicidal to engage Sukapha and his army. Therefore, they had decided to return to Mungkang.

Great jubilation greeted this news. It fired up the men and women with renewed energy and resolve, putting strength into them to continue determinedly on their historic trek.

Five months had passed, but they were yet to cross the Mungmau boundary, marked by a big river on Chenkhung's sketch. Sukapha had long suspected that they had strayed from the route charted out by his uncle, and now they would have to steer their own course. So far, except for the episode involving the Nara king Nyaishanpha of Mungkang, he had met with no resistance. In fact, the further he got from Maulung the fewer settlements they came across; miles and miles of hills and valleys with not a soul in sight. Sukapha did not even know who this realm belonged to—he may have been tempted to claim it as his own, considering the lack of occupants, had it not been for two reasons. The first was his fascination with the country full of golden gardens; the second was more practical—almost all of his warriors were bachelors, and he had to claim a well-populated realm full of eligible women if they were to marry, procreate and propagate his race.

He also continued to see virtue in patience and slow progress, so that he did not unduly tax his folks. After all, he was in no hurry, for Mungdunsunkham would not disappear if he was late reaching there by a year or two. His primary concern was to keep his own band in health and good spirits; undue haste would not serve that end. It was thus, though the rainy season was still at least a month away, when they came upon a wide stretch of even ground between two tall mountain ranges, with a river flowing through, he decided to set up permanent camp. He might not come across another such suitable spot if he continued; also, his advance scouts had warned him that dense jungles lay further ahead, and it would require a great deal of hard work and time to cut a passage through them.

That spot had other advantages. Bamboo plants grew in profusion and cane strands were abundant in the surrounding jungles; the valley itself was filled with tall thatch-grass, which could be dried and used to thatch roofs. No sooner was the command to raise a permanent camp given, his men and women set about erecting it. Slightly higher ground away from the river was selected to erect chang-type structures of bamboo and cane with thatched roofs; large dormitories for the soldiers, suitable for accommodating at least fifty men each; smaller units for families—the biggest of these, having bamboo eaves intricately wrought with palm fronds and cane, was built for the prince. A royal kitchen was constructed at some distance from the buildings housing the prince, his family and those of the nobles. A covered passageway led to the kitchen so that food could be ferried from the latter even when the heavens were pouring down. Similarly, the kitchen buildings where the soldiers and others could cook their meals were built far away from the main cluster of buildings, linked by a covered passageway; kitchens of thatch and bamboo had an occasional propensity to burn down; hence the precaution of keeping them far away so that the fire might not spread to the settlement.

Stretches around the river, though dry now, were left vacant. Sure enough, when the rains came, the river overflowed its banks and swelled into an inordinate size, though the waters did not reach the structures since they had been constructed on higher ground. As the rains abated and water receded, the land around the river grew rich in deposited silt, so wet rice cultivation, with seeds carried from Maulung, could commence. The harvest was good; there was plenty for immediate consumption as well as storing for the future; other crops could also be grown upon the fertile soil to supplement their meals. The poultry and cattle grew fatter; meat was to be had in plenty both from the domestic beasts as well as through hunting. Such was the idyllic nature of the spot that Sukapha decided to spend two rainy seasons there instead of one, augmenting his food resources. Had he known that it would be the final idyllic moment in their trek, he might have been tempted to linger even longer!

At the commencement of the third year, with the rains showing signs of abating, and the priest giving their blessings to recommencement of the journey, the settlement was dismantled, provisions packed and the band was once more on the move. They immediately discovered that the going was more difficult than experienced so far; his men had worked months hacking a path through the dense verdure lying beyond the valley; but the wet climate and fertile soil encouraged astonishingly rapid plant growth, so that no sooner had a path been hacked than it was obliterated in the span of a month. In fact, the need to reopen the trail had resulted in much of the dry spell being wasted and a late departure of the troupe, which in turn meant they had to find the place for next long-term encampment within a shorter spell.

The two elephants now took the lead, their bulk and weight enabling them to push through remnants of foliage and easing things slightly for the people on foot behind them. It was a hard going; the ground was uneven and protruding tree-stumps and creepers, which acted as foot-traps, made some of the trekkers stumble and fall. They could not complete the jungle crossing during the daylight hours; it would be suicidal to try and camp on the trail itself. So for the first time, they had to undertake night travel. Each soldier was ordered to light a flare and hold it aloft; the two elephants were given freedom to make their own way through the darkness; their mahouts were confident the highly intelligent animals would be able to do so without straying. Fathers picked up their children and carried them on their backs; there could be no breaks in between even for the palanquin-bearers. Only towards daybreak could they cross out of that benighted stretch, which meant a continuous trek for twenty-four hours; but though they reached a clearing, it was small and there was no nearby source of water. Sukapha had to make a quick decision as to whether to stay put at the place for the day or move on; he had not envisaged lack of potable water at any stretch of the journey and thus no provision had been made to carry extra water; despite the fatigue that had gripped his band, he ordered that the group carry on and, only towards the end of the day, when they had reached a more convenient spot with a stream, did he raise his hands to bring the company to a halt and make overnight camp.

The weeks which followed were equally stressful; the strain first began to tell on the health of the young ones and the womenfolk, but soon enough the men began to feel it too. By then, in the estimate of Sukapha, they had crossed the bounds of Mungmau; now for months together there was not the least sign of human settlement; only thick jungles and treacherous hillocks; at the very first place which he deemed to possess the basic features required of a more permanent campsite, Sukapha commanded that once again hutments be built and arrangements made for a longer stay.

His advance scouts brought grave tidings. A couple of days' trek ahead lay a settlement peopled by non-Shan clansmen; they appeared to be fierce and warlike and would not be cowed down easily. Sukapha guessed that these must be the first of the Naga tribes Chenkhung had mentioned; his fatigued band needed time to rest and recuperate. Though the spot was not as convenient as the one before, he decided that at least two rainy seasons would have to be spent there.

The rains here were as heavy as elsewhere in Mungmau, the ground as fertile and crops as rich. However, vigil had to be strengthened during the night; there was a risk that the Nagas nearby had learnt of their presence and might launch a surprise attack. In presciently expecting such a possibility, Sukapha had almost taken on the role of an oracle; none of the Deodhais and Bailungs accompanying him had been able to foretell the consequent happenings. One night, at the start of the second rainy season at that spot, during a spell of heavy rain, a host of Nagas stealthily descended on the encampment. Had his men not been on full alert as they had been ordered, things might have taken a precarious turn—but a timely alarm had been raised and a well-rehearsed drill for just such an eventuality had been set in motion. The Shan fighters accompanying Sukapha were no less fierce than the attackers; the latter were repulsed in a matter of hours; three of Sukapha's men had been killed and a dozen injured, while half-a-dozen enemy corpses lay strewn about here and there in the camp.

These corpses were carried into the jungle to be food for scavengers, while Sukapha's dead warriors were given a ceremonial burial, with the priests saying the final prayers and the mandatory mound being raised over the gravesites. The prince wasted little time. The very next day, he led an army of four hundred hand-picked men who, after two days and nights of almost continuous march, descended upon the sprawling settlement of the Nagas at the break of day. With ruthless thoroughness, the men in that village who could not make good their escape into the jungles were slaughtered; women and children were made captives to be taken back to Sukapha's camp and every hutment razed to the ground and all crops and possessions destroyed. The corpses of Naga warriors were tied to bamboo poles and these were stuck to the ground in grotesque, fearful rows.

'This needs to lie at the core of our strategy,' he told his nobles, explaining his seemingly horrible demonstrative act. 'Only civilized people would respond to pacific words and gestures. These tribes are known for their savagery; we need to strike terror in their hearts if we are to subdue them. But, of course, those who escaped today's onslaught will go to others and inform them of our coming. In the near future, we will need to be ready for more fighting.'

Sukapha was not wrong. The more they advanced, the stronger the resistance grew, and despite his unwillingness, the prince had to use methods of increasing savagery to strike fear into his enemies. No doubt he succeeded in doing so, with the chiefs of many settlements along the way pledging allegiance to him; but it was a time-consuming progress and cost him the lives of at least a hundred of his own warriors. Not that his entourage dwindled in numbers; the Naga women and children were quite content to form a part of the troupe; moreover, many Nagas from the subjugated villages expressed their desire to go with Sukapha, vowing solemn oaths that they would not hesitate to fight their own clansmen. The truth, of course, was that there had been always hostility between these tribes, with even neighbouring villages occasionally fighting against each other.

Thus, it took almost a decade of slow progress for Sukapha to cross tribal inhabited areas such as Phakechering, or 'the land of a thousand old stones', as also a pass across the Daikham mountains to reach the plains from where, at a distance, a range comprising nine mountains could be seen. That mountain range had been very much on Chenkhung's sketch; his uncle had called it Daikaorang. 'Dai' in the Tai language meant mountain, 'kao' was nine and 'rang' meant union—thus, Daikaorang meant the coming together of nine mountains. Sukapha was relieved that he and his uncle were on the same course once again; from what the latter had said, his group would have to cross that mountain range through a pass to get to Mungdunsunkham, a treacherous journey that would involve frequent clashes with resisting Naga tribes. Sukapha pondered deeply over his situation and decided that it would perhaps be better for his people to settle down at that place itself and erect his kingdom.

But first they had to find the best spot; a river which the Nagas with him called Khamnangjam had to be crossed. Here, for the first time, the rivercraft taught to his men by the experts from China came into play. The prince marvelled at the skill with which they cut down suitable trees and lashed them together to make rafts. A majority of the animals with them, including the two elephants, crossed the waters on their own, but some, such as the poultry and goats, had to be ferried across. The rafts served well to transport the children, women and men, as also the provisions, equipment and weapons across, the rowers handling them with great dexterity, showing that they had been trained well.

Then, once again, they were on their trek, moving at the same lethargic pace, with the Nagas living in settlements close by deciding to keep well away from their path. They came across a beautiful lake which was called Nongnyang or 'shaking lake'; just beyond it there was a wide swathe of plains called Khamjang. It had taken them over a decade to reach the spot; many of the women and children had perished from illness; his men were exhausted. Sukapha decided to establish his kingdom at Khamjang, the first mung or state established by the prince.

He ordered a permanent settlement to be built, on a more durable and bigger scale than the temporary settlements they had constructed on the way. He even had a miniature palace built to duplicate that of Maulung. When the Naga tribes around the area realized his intentions, they once again embarked on warfare. However, there was no unity amongst his adversaries; they attacked in small groups from individual settlements rather than in a combined army. Though the Nagas fought fiercely, Sukapha's men could ward them off, slaughter many and take many captives. On the boundaries of his settlement complex at Khamjang, he erected bamboo poles with the corpses of defeated warriors slung from them; he even launched surprise counterattacks on Naga villages, telling his men not to kill but try and capture the village chieftains.

With typical resourcefulness, he learnt the local dialect from his captives, negotiated with the defeated chieftains and obtained their allegiance to him. One by one, the chiefs of the Naga villages of Kharukhu, Pungkang, Tithang, Binglau, Latema, Laungpang, Taru, Luklan and Luka signalled their willingness to submit to Sukapha. They had to ceremonially accept his suzerainty over the area and pay tribute to him. More and more, Sukapha emitted the aura of a king rather than a mere prince. The last to submit were the Taputapa Nagas; officers and men were sent to engage with them and soon they too were brought to their knees.

Finally, Sukapha had his own kingdom, but he was not satisfied. Mungdunsunkham continued to haunt him in his dreams; his children were growing up and would soon realize that their father, far from being the monarch of a country full of golden gardens, was merely the ruler of a tiny principality. Moreover, he and his men would forever be at risk from the Nagas who, though they had been forced into submission, did not conceal their hostility to the intruders. Sukapha spent a year at Khamjang and at the onset of the next dry season, leaving one of his most daring and efficient officers, named Kangkhrum, as governor of Khamjang, began his trek across Daikaorang, the place where nine mountains met.

It was the most horrendous portion of the trek they had encountered so far, despite the presence of Naga guides to show them the way. They went on steep and winding mountain trails, sometimes so narrow that his people had to move in a single file, a state of things which increased their vulnerability to attack from their enemies. However, the strong action against the tribes near Khamjang appeared to have subdued those who dwelt upon the Daikaorang range; for the group was not assailed while on the move. This emboldened Sukapha to continue the momentum of his conquest. Though this slowed their party down even more, he launched attacks on tribal villages that fell on the way— the Nagas of Papuk, Tengkham, Khunkhat, Khuntung, Tangchin and Jakhang villages fell one after the other. Though it was against his nature and notion of fairness, the need of the moment was to impose his will upon these fierce people, so he committed atrocities in the villages he would not otherwise have.

Then, thirteen long years since he had left Maulung, he and his band crossed the Daikaorang ranges across the Panchou Pass, and could gaze fascinated at the valley which stretched at some distance yet before them!

The going was far easier now, being downhill and the area devoid of any settlement that might offer resistance. The vegetation, if anything, was even thicker than what they had encountered previously; it being the beginning of winter, many of the trees were in full bloom; seen from higher up, a burst of colours seemed to wrap the area; this had perhaps induced others to name the valley of the river Ti-Lao, which the locals also called Luit, as the country full of golden gardens. The jungles were filled with colourful orchids; there were wild fruit trees, many of them exotic to the Shan newcomers. The combined hearts of the entire group lifted at the realization that their tortuous journey was on the brink of ending, and a less nomadic and more sedentary way of life was in sight.

How wrong they were! The valley, which had looked so beautiful from the mountain heights, proved to be full of pitfalls. True, the thick and almost impassable jungles thinned out somewhat at the banks of the numerous rivers and streamlets—according to Chenkhung, all these tributaries and sub-tributaries finally fell into the mammoth river Ti-Lao which flowed through the middle of the valley. But despite the rains having ended, the land around the rivers had remained swampy; alligators basked on the sand bars, in the shallows and on the pebbled banks; their jaws could cleave a person in two! There were new and highly poisonous varieties of snakes, the likes of which their party had never encountered before, as well as ants, termites, centipedes and leeches.

'Travel by land seems extremely dangerous,' Sukapha told his nobles. 'We must take a river route the very first chance we get.'

'That's very true, Your Highness,' agreed Chaophrangmung Thaomungmahgrai, the chief amongst the nobles. 'Perhaps that is the reason there are so few human settlements in this area.'

'However, we also need to look at the positive side,' Sukapha said. 'We can lay claim to this territory without much resistance. From now on that will be our strategy. Move from place to place, putting up small settlements to be governed by one of our officials. That way we will be able to lay the ground for creating our very own kingdom and expand it when the opportune moment arrives. On finding the most suitable spot, we shall construct the finest capital this valley has seen.'

'What name will you give your kingdom, Sire?' asked Chalothaoung Taomungkan, the second-ranked amongst the nobles.

'Do you need to ask?' Sukapha replied laughingly. 'We shall call my kingdom what our people have called this valley—Mungdunsunkham—or the country full of golden gardens!'

As news of Sukapha's intentions percolated down to his people, they were slightly disappointed that their trek was not destined to end immediately, though they were careful not to show it. They reached the region called Khamhangpung by the Nagas and the going became extremely tough. Alert warriors were told to be on the lookout for hungry reptiles including the python; many in the group fell ill due to the miasma which seemed continually to arise from the damp and slushy ground, and the priests who doubled as medicine men were kept busy. Finally, they arrived at a place which had a number of streams running through it, so Sukapha named it Namruk, 'nam' meaning water and 'ruk' meaning six, thus a place through which six rivers flowed. One of these was a somewhat larger river which, because of the furious nature of the currents, could not be crossed by raft. So, a bridge of bamboo and cane had to be constructed across it.

The fortnight they spent while the bridge was being built was one of the most dangerous periods of their journey thus far. Sukapha ordered his warriors to clear as much of the jungle near the riverbank as possible so as to try and get away from the miasma; they detected the presence of herds of wild elephants and had to build many bonfires at night to keep them and wild carnivores at bay; one day a huge, outlandish, armour-plated animal with a single horn on its snout barged into the tiny clearing and had to be chased away by the soldiers. A dozen of the group, including children and women, perished through fever and stomach ailment in the days which followed. Sukapha was relieved when the bridge was completed and they could cross over to the other side. Conditions, though slightly better there, were not all that salubrious; so, when they reached a wide and navigable river with some open ground upon its banks, Sukapha ordered a halt for the year and got his men to start constructing sturdy rafts to enable them to travel upstream towards higher grounds where perhaps a capital could be built.

The rainy season started. Never in their lives had the Shans in that little community imagined the heavens could pour down so much water! The river swelled up and broke its banks and swept over the settlement; they had to undertake emergency evacuation, desperately clear jungles on higher ground so as to get away from the dreaded floods; there were more deaths and greater misery. His officers warned the prince that they had heard, for the first time, mutterings amongst the people at the prolonged nature of their quest; Sukapha had to address them and instill his own overriding optimism into their hearts.

After what felt like an eternity the rains tapered off, and the group could move again, this time upstream across the wide river on sturdy rafts pulled from the banks by soldiers using ropes. But it soon grew apparent that the land here was even more unfit for permanent dwelling; when they reached a wider patch of ground Sukapha named it as Munglakkhentheusa. He left his officer Khuntang along with some men to maintain that outpost on his behalf and retraced his route down the river. Travel downstream was relatively quick and easy and before the monsoons could set in, they reached an open, riverine area. This appeared to be a far more suitable place to set up camp; a buffalo was sacrificed to thank the river god for the small token of mercy and the priests performed propitiatory rituals. Sukhapa named the place Tipam: 'ti' meaning place and 'pam' meaning to kill as a sacrifice.

However, his assessment of Tipam as a better place was belied the very next rainy season; the area, being close to the mammoth Ti-Lao, proved to be even more susceptible to flooding. It had been twenty-one years since he had departed from Maulung; the mostly young soldiers had slid into middle age, the children had grown up into men and women; he himself was in his forty-fifth year. Most of his band wanted an end to this nomadic, rootless existence; but this was not yet to be. Not a man to compromise, Sukapha was determined to continue his search till actuality coincided with imagination and he could find the ideal nucleus around which he could build his empire.

In search of ground not subject to inundation, he and his band shifted to Munklang Chekhru; this seemed to be a far more ideal spot; instructions were given for permanent dwelling structures to be constructed; the lowlands were immediately opened up for wetland cultivation. Sukapha was sorely tempted to declare this place his capital; but experience had been a great teacher; he had no idea what awaited him. Sure enough, in the fifth year of their stay, their tiny community was overwhelmed with the worst floods they had encountered so far. Many animals and preciously hoarded food and other materials were washed away; fortunately, not a single life had been lost.

'We've been unable to locate a suitable spot where you can build your capital,' said one of his nobles. 'Why don't we try our luck on the other side of Ti-Lao?'

This seemed to be sound advice; once more Sukapha ordered the construction of large rafts made of tree trunks. The crossing, naturally, had to be made during the dry spell when the water level of that huge river was at its lowest and the currents had lost much of their ferocity. Even then, getting to the other side involved great risk and exertion, but the end result was disheartening. The spot they had landed on the northern bank proved to be even more flood-prone; also, his scouts after surveying the area discovered that the mountains which rose from where the flat land ended were settled upon by many tribes who could use the advantage offered by height to descend and attack their settlement. It had been only the strenuous nature of the crossing which would have to be undertaken again that made Sukapha stay there for three years; but then he finally mustered up his energy and resources and re-crossed over to the southern bank of the Ti-Lao.

Rather than trek across land, they put the rafts to good use by travelling eastward along the southern stream of the Ti-Lao till they reached the mouth of another comparatively large river; moving upstream along this tributary of the Ti-Lao, they came across a sub-tributary; Sukapha had the water of this subtributary weighed and judged that it came from Tipam, so travelling up it would be of no avail. Instead, they continued on their journey upon the same tributary and reached a valley which Sukapha christened as Mungringmunkgchin. Up ahead, he weighed the waters of another sub-tributary of the tributary they were on and found it to be two tolas heavier, so named the place Sangtak, in the Tai language, 'sang' meaning two and 'tak' being tola. Staying two years there and not finding the spot to his liking, he and his group once more moved up the Ti-Lao tributary after Sukapha had appointed an officer named Takhunlak to govern the region.

Throughout their peregrination they had come across small human settlements of local tribes who were relatively docile as compared with the Nagas, and offered no resistance to the newcomers. In fact, some youths of these tribes, perhaps impressed by the size of Sukapha's group and that it consisted mostly of well-armed warriors, had joined them; the prince at once set some of his officers to learn the prevalent language of the region. At last, they discovered that the name of the tributary they were on was the Dikhow and the place they were then at was Ligirigaon; the youths urged him to proceed to a place called Simaluguri, which Sukapha did, and finding it to his liking, set up camp. Thinking that perhaps he had reached the end of his journey after thirty-one long years, something that the priests with him agreed on, Sukapha ordained that cattle be killed for meat and a huge feast be held.

But there was to be no immediate respite from trudging on, despite the restiveness he had sensed amongst his people. A local youth suggested that the land eastward from that place, across a river, which Sukapha, because of the reddish colour of its water, had named the Namdang, 'nam' in Tai meaning water and 'dang' red, was highly suitable for the setting up of a permanent capital. The prince, therefore, sent his scouts along with the youth on a reconnaissance mission. They brought back terrible tidings—the river Namdang had 3,300 places on its banks from which people drew water! It meant that the area was heavily populated and well-governed, so his relatively small troupe was vulnerable. Sukapha at once appreciated the danger and ordered the dismantling of his camp and shifted northward away from the river to re-establish camp at a place he named Timan.

Though the land was not at all suitable, to quell the restiveness amongst his group, Sukapha had a prolonged stay. But there seemed to be no staving off the floods, which finally induced him to move to Timak and build a small township called Mungtiuamao there. Almost thirty-six years had elapsed since they had departed from their native land; in truth, the others had long given up hope that they would ever lead a settled life. But not Sukapha. Though sixty years old and long past his prime, he repeated to himself that patience was the greatest virtue a leader of men could possess, so he continued to pray and hope for a miracle.

Then, just as the spell of rains in the thirty-sixth year of their departure was ending, the miracle occurred. He had been sending scouts everywhere in search of a salubrious place; one of these came back with a report that there was a place with hilly terrain not too far from where they were located now. Sukapha along with his nobles and a small group of his troops went atop Khamkomung and Kipkeu to see the place for themselves. The prince at once loved the area and knew that his quest had ended!

The joy amongst his people was boundless. From their prince's words and demeanour, they had surmised that their nomadic life had come to a conclusion. With renewed enthusiasm they began construction of the capital township, which in course of time would expand into a vibrant city. Patterned on the capital of Maulung, the palaces for the prince and the nobles were made of wood while those of the commoners were of bamboo, cane and thatch. Within the compound of the palace was constructed a separate building to house the Somdeo and an aged Deodhai priest appointed to be the resident of the building. Slowly but surely, Cheraidai was developed into a well-planned city; Chaophrangmung Thaomungmahgrai himself supervised construction; the roads were kept wide and provision was made for a central marketplace and large open spaces where children could play and warriors practise their martial arts.

'What shall we name it?' asked Chalotahoung Taomungkan. 'May I suggest Chetamdoi as its name?' 'Che' meant town, 'tam' short and 'doi' a hill, so Chetamdoi meant a 'town on a low hill'.

'Oh, that's too ordinary,' said sixty-two-year-old Sukapha, displaying the excitement of a child. 'Let's call it Cheraidai—the Shining City on a Hill.'

'That's excellent, Your Highness,' Chalothaoung Taomungkan replied. 'The areas we have occupied so far in Mungdunsunkham and are governed by our officers are but small in extent and not very suitable for settling. The more suitable lands naturally have already been settled upon. We need to annex these and extend our kingdom north and westwards.'

'Certainly. But in due course of time. Let us first settle down and consolidate what we have achieved. We are, bear in mind, few in number. I've already dispatched a small group of soldiers to Maulung to inform Sukhanpha of the success of our mission. If willing, more of our people can come to our dominion to augment our population. They will not be confronted with the travails we had to face; they would be guided by our soldiers, and the Naga tribes on the way have already been subjugated. Yes, we'll conquer more land within this valley, but our strategy with our neighbours must not be the same as the one that we adopted towards the Naga tribes. We need to conquer them without arousing much hostility towards us. That'll be a difficult task.'

'Our scouts have brought back good tidings,' said Chaophrangmung Thaomungmahgrai. 'The tribes dwelling in this region, who call themselves Borahis and Morans, are a civilized people ruled by their kings Thakumtha and Baduacha respectively.'

'That is good news. We must not only subjugate them, but also enfold them into our Shan society through marriage with their women. In fact, our main requirement right now is for our soldiers, who have remained bachelors despite having aged so much, to get married and beget children so that we can lay the ground for a future generation of our people. I too will marry again and, hopefully, beget more sons and daughters to ensure that the royal lineage is carried on in perpetuity. You, of course, know that according to Shan tradition none but one descended from me will be able to sit upon my throne in the future.'

Sukapha set this strategy into motion—the conquest of one principality after another was achieved at no great cost to either side. The prince behaved with great clemency and courtesy towards the vanquished, inviting members of the community to live as equal citizens in Cheraidai or settle in any part of his kingdom; he himself took four Borahi and Moran princesses as his wives; the nobles did likewise, while the unmarried soldiers and others in his group were all too happy to settle down and raise families. He learnt the dialect of those whom he had conquered, and ordained that these along with Tai be used in official communications. He also ensured that some officers of his kingdom, including those serving in the royal palace, be appointed from these tribes.

Such generosity towards the vanquished yielded positive results; within a few years, the distinction between the newly arrived Shans and the indigenous communities in the vicinity of Sukapha's kingdom so blurred that the Borahis and Morans began to consider themselves Shans too. Further west lay the powerful Kachari kingdom but Sukapha decided that he did not have the resources to attack it; with his main purpose of getting his soldiers married off realized he was now content with what he had achieved so far. He was now the monarch of a principality bounded by the Daikaorang in the east, the Dikhow in the west, the river Dihing in the north and hills on which dwelt more Naga tribes to the south. Sukapha was content. He had attained his dream and wanted to spend his last few years in peace.

He declared that, rather than call his two principal advisors Chaophrangmung and Chalotahoung, they would now be designated in the indigenous dialect as Bargohain and Buragohain and would henceforth take part in all decision-making involving the state. They were also publicly invested, in consultation with other nobles, to select the next ruler when a king died. Sukapha also made his Deodhai and Bailung priests record his monumental trek and the establishment of his kingdom in the form of buranjis, and also ordered that from then on, meticulous records must be kept on happenings within the realm.

The prince was endowed with an innate genius for administration; he appreciated that decentralization was the key to effective and ameliorative governance. Not only were governors of distant outposts invested with enormous powers, Sukapha built a tiered structure amongst his own warriors, creating new offices and delegating responsibility to specific individuals even for minor activities such as gathering wood or collecting honey. As for the governors of his outposts, Sukapha understood that delegation of power and responsibility had to be monitored by keeping the lines of communication open even during the rains, and making personal visits as also sending his nobles for periodic inspections of the outposts. Since roads were almost non-existent, and the cost of building and maintaining longer roads difficult, the rivers and streams had to be used as highways.

The slow and unwieldy rafts which his men had been using were inadequate if neighbouring tribes were to be fought and conquered; boats were therefore an urgent necessity. The local people were experts at building boats, both of the simple dugout types carved out from a single tree trunk, as well as bigger and more elaborate barges to carry soldiers and provisions. Sukapha at once set up a unit devoted mainly to the manufacture of boats, even as his warriors began training in rivercraft. The biggest boat built by his boatyard was the royal barge, to be used by the king when on the move over water.

Finally, only two things remained to be done. The new capital had to be consecrated and the sixty-two-year-old prince had to be formally crowned as the king.

Cheraidai wore a festive look. While the palaces and other wooden buildings had been newly painted in bright colours, even the humblest hutment had received a fresh coat of whitewash. Festoons and flags were hung up everywhere; the streets echoed with laughter and the sound of music was everywhere. The citizenry was decked out in its finest. Young children, ceremonially dressed, hopped and skipped upon the streets. Traders in the marketplace were doing brisk business and there was much pushing and jostling. The shrill cries of vendors shouting out their wares added to the din. Eatables were being sold by itinerant hawkers. A delicious aroma wafted up and filled the air.

A huge pavillion of bamboo, cane and thatch had been constructed on open ground for the crowning of Prince Sukapha. Almost everyone was heading for that field to watch the ceremony. A temporary fair had opened up a little distance away from the pavillion; it comprised of stalls selling a variety of items; there was even a stall where a puppet show was being performed. Appropriately enough, the story narrated by the puppet master was about the exploits of Prince Sukapha and his people, how they had trekked from distant Maulung to set up a kingdom in an alien land. A balladeer stood on one side of the path leading to the coronation ground; he had composed a ballad on Sukapha and, thrumming the one-stringed musical instrument which the locals called 'been', was singing it in a loud and melodious voice. There were men huddled in groups making wagers on cockfights, eggfights and many other games; soldiers in uniforms patrolled the streets to ensure that no one went overboard with their celebrations.

A gong sounded from the palace, followed by drumbeats. The people stopped whatever they were doing and hurried to the side of the central road which led to the pavillion or to the field itself. Prince Sukapha, his wives and children, the nobles and their families emerged from the palace gate upon a procession of elephants. On beholding their prince, some of those lining the road fell prostrate on the ground. 'Long live Chaolung Sukapha,' others shouted. As their prince waved to his people, there were continued bursts of cheers. Though bareheaded and, as was his nature, wearing but the simplest of ornaments, yet Sukapha looked every inch a king. He had instructed the Deodhai and Bailung priests that the coronation ceremony must be totally bereft of ostentation and only the essential rituals were to be performed. He himself had that morning gone to the house where the Somdeo was kept and, guided by his head priest, offered prayers to it. The priest had picked up the idol, which had a golden chain attached to its top, and placed it around Sukapha's neck. Throughout the ceremony the prince would carry the Somdeo before putting it back in its sacred niche after the coronation.

The nobles too, in deference to the temperament of their leader, had refrained from ostentatious display in matters of clothing and ornaments. 'I must be the people's king,' he had told them. 'Too gaudy a display would only serve to drive a wedge between the ruler and the ruled.' However, the queens-to-be were under no such restriction and were decked up in the finest silks and most glittering jewellery. The procession was led by a band of drummers and cymbal-players; in unhurried pace, it wended its way to the coronation ground. A wooden dais had been built at the further end of the pavillion; upon it had been placed a large throne of wood padded with tiger skin; a number of wooden chairs, stools, benches and bamboo murrahs had been placed by the side of the dais, and, after alighting from the elephants, the royal party made their way and sat upon them. There were rows of chairs a few feet away from the dais, facing it. Even before the arrival of the royal party, these had been occupied by kings and chieftains owing allegiance to Prince Sukapha; the Naga chiefs, dressed in loincloths with the mandatory broad-bladed knife called dao slung at the waist, their faces and bodies painted and heads adorned with brilliant-hued feathers, looked the most exotic amongst the august audience.

Sukapha alone was drawn aside by the priests towards a solitary mulberry tree around which incense sticks and earthen lamps filled with mustard oil burned. They had already performed rituals to please the gods Kamle, Rangle and Rangmao; the prince was made to kneel and touch his head to the ground to complete the rituals as the priests sprinkled him with holy water and chanted benedictions. Then, one by one, as the priests mentioned the gods by name and muttered incantations, Sukapha made offerings to them upon a silver platter and, when this ritual ended, prostrated himself once more at the foot of the tree.

Nearby was tethered a buffalo, its forehead coloured with vermillion and flower garlands around its neck. The prince strode up to it, picked up the hengdang which was placed on a bamboo tray beside it and, with one mighty swing, severed the head from the animal's body. The crowd raised a cheer; women made ululating sounds as the priests now led the prince into the pavillion and gestured him towards the throne. Sukapha, with measured steps, gravely ascended the stairs to the elevated dais and sat upon the throne. A priest handed over the silk headgear, encrusted with a single beautiful jewel, which formed the crown, to the bargohain; the latter climbed up to the dais and ceremonially placed the crown upon Sukapha's head.

'Long live the king!' he raised his hands and shouted.

'Long live the king!' the crowd roared back. There were more cheers and ululations; those who had not been able to make it to the coronation field took up the refrain and the entire capital shook with the words 'Long live the king!'

One by one the chiefs seated in the front rows came up, bowed to the king seated on his throne, and placed the gifts they had brought for the occasion at his feet. Finally, Sukapha rose and addressed the gathering. The hush that fell over the boisterous and noisy crowd was uncanny. Though his voice did not carry far and those beyond the immediate vicinity could not hear him, even they fell silent.

'Noble chiefs, dangoriyas, my people,' he said. 'I thank you all for being at my side through times of danger and times of safety. It had been my ambition to set up a kingdom at Mungdunsunkham and this has been achieved. It is not my doing—it is only sacrifice and exertion on your part that has made it possible. I have been invested with a great responsibility. Today I pledge that I shall rule my kingdom justly and fairly. If there is injustice against anyone, be sure my ears would be open to the pleas of the victims. I shall meet the people in open court once every week to take up your petitions and listen to your grievances. Do not be afraid to speak out, for fear of authority is an enemy of true justice. May our kingdom become prosperous and our citizens happy. May the blessings of Lengdon and Somdeo be showered upon you all.'

Indeed, Prince Sukapha had become King Sukapha!

The years passed. Those were prosperous times. The Shans discovered that the ground was extremely fertile and crops, if they were protected from pests, were bountiful. Sukapha understood all too well that his was only a tiny principality in the valley through which the Ti-Lao flowed; it and its capital Cheraidai was vulnerable to attack by numerically bigger communities that dwelt beyond the borders of the Borahi and Moran people's lands. Therefore, he continued with his conciliatory tactics, taking extreme care not to provoke or antagonize any group, while ensuring that greater assimilation continued to take place between his own people and other indigenous tribes. He particularly welcomed individuals who could augment his army, as also craftsmen and artisans, often luring them with grants of land and gold. He also ensured that communication with his brethren in Mungmau was maintained in case their help was needed in times of distress, annually sending to them gifts of gold and ivory.

Into his fifteenth year as king, tragedy struck the realm and the kingdom was plunged into gloom. As was the Shan custom, there was no public announcement of the fact—but then, there were so many menials in the royal palace that the secret soon leaked out. King Sukapha, into his seventy-seventh year, was gravely ill. The news itself was not surprising. The brave Tiger from Heaven had led a life full of danger and excitement; he had fulfilled his dream and was tired; now he had to slide into eternal rest and ascend upward towards Heaven. Yet the thought that Sukapha was about to die was heart-wrenching.

The gravity of Sukapha's condition was confirmed by the construction of a mausoleum or maidam where he would be buried. In accordance with the king's wishes, there was nothing ostentatious about the maidam. A huge hollow was dug in the side of a hillock and four chambers were constructed therein, their ceilings and walls buttressed by wooden beams. The central and biggest chamber was furnished with a bed covered by a soft mattress and the softest silk bedsheets the weavers in the kingdom could make. Chairs and tables were placed in the central chamber; the other chambers were left empty.

One night there was an unusual flurry of activity in the palace. The nobles were hurriedly summoned to the bedchamber of the king; he looked a shadow of his former, handsome self. Though the head priest himself was there to minister to him, it was clear that the end was nigh. The entire family was within the large chamber, his queens and children, the eldest son Suteupha amongst them. There were tears in every eye; even those of the aged nobles were moist.

'Ask Suteupha to come near me,' the dying man said in a weak voice.

'Yes, father?'

With hands that shook, the king drew off a ring from his right index finger. It was a large ring made of gold. Embossed upon it was the royal seal, used by the king to mark his authority on any decree he issued. He slid the ring onto his eldest son's finger.

'This is my final decree,' Sukapha said. 'You shall rule my beloved Mungdunsunkham after I am gone. Rule wisely, my son. Be the protector of the realm and its people.'

The frail man on the bed let out a long sigh. King Sukapha was dead.

'The king is dead!' announced the buragohain, his voice drowned out by the wailing of the people in the room. 'Long live the king.'

All at once everyone, even the mother of Suteupha, knelt on the ground. Only Suteupha remained standing. 'Arise you all,' said the new king. 'There is deep grief in each of us, but grieving for our departed father must wait, for much now remains to be done. Bargohain, convey the tidings to the people. Our realm shall be in mourning for a month and there will be no celebrations within this period, no marriage, no feasting.'

Suteupha turned to the head priest. 'Commence the embalming of our dear departed father's body. We will place him in the palace courtyard for a week so that subjects from even far away can pay their last respects to him. Then shall he be carried to the maidam and given a burial befitting a king.'

The grief within the realm was overpowering. Thousands lined up each day to prostrate themselves in front of Sukapha's body and sob out their grief. Finally, his bier was carried by his children to the maidam and his body laid upon the bed of the central chamber. Plates and bowls heaped with food, water and wine were brought and placed upon the tables in the chamber so that his soul remained well nourished as he made his way up the ladder towards Heaven. In accordance with his wishes, no jade, diamonds and rubies were placed inside, but five of his favourite servants and two warrior guards, were chosen to accompany the late king on his final journey. The men, all willing volunteers, bade farewell to their loved ones, and walked unhesitatingly into the vault, immediately after which the maidam was sealed. More piles of earth were placed upon it to raise it even higher; turf was laid at the very top and soon no earthly trace remained of the founder of the kingdom and the Tiger from Heaven.

THE NARRATOR

'That, my people, was the tale of Sukapha, the founder of the Ahom kingdom in the Brahmaputra Valley during the thirteenth century. What an incredible tale, my people! Sukapha, born in Maulung in 1191, set out from his place of birth in 1215, at the age of twenty-four years. You recall that he took the Somdeo ... and king of the Nara tribe, Nyaishanpha of Mungkang, sent a force after him to recover the idol. The place from which Nyaishanpha's men returned in failure was later named Naraulta or the spot from where the Naras returned! It took Sukapha thirteen years to approach the object of his quest, the Brahmaputra Valley, which he reached in 1228. The river they had first bridged was the Sessa; the wide and navigable river they had traversed was the Dihing. Only in 1253, after thirty-eight years of an almost nomadic existence, at the age of sixty-two, could he establish his capital at Cheraidai, where he ruled till his death in 1268 at the age of seventy-seven. What an epic journey, people!

'So, historically speaking, the Ahom kingdom was established in 1253, though Sukapha entered the valley in 1228. Now then, you must be wondering why the Shan people, who came from distant Mungmau, came to be called the Ahoms? There are those who might dispute my explanation, but this is the most logical one. You see, Prince Sukapha and his nobles were the most valiant of men. Moreover, his army consisted of choice warriors of the Shan tribe whose fighting skills were unmatched. The way they destroyed the fiercest opponents to their advance had aroused terror into the most savage of hearts! Their reputation of being 'asama' or peerless had preceded them, and this is what the indigenous communities in the Valley called them when they arrived. The Shans themselves could not pronounce the sound 's', pronouncing it as 'h' instead, which meant that asama became ahoma when uttered through their mouths. Thus, in the course of time Sukapha's people came to be called the Ahoms.

'It is also said that the term for the entire region, Assam, too came about the same way. In ancient days the region was called Pragjyotishpur, and later Kamarupa by the people of the lands to the west. The term Assam may have been the latest derivation from the word asama used by the indigenous tribes to describe the Ahoms. Here again, others differ, but the logic remains. Be sure, the names of places keep changing with changing circumstances. For instance, you will not find the name Daikaorang, the place where nine mountains meet, in a map of today. The name changed, my people, to the Patkai hills. In the buranjis, it is written that much later, one of the Ahom princes, in order to dethrone the then Ahom king, took the help of the Nara ruler of Mungkang by lying to him that the Ahom throne had been usurped by an impostor, and advanced towards Mungdunsunkham with a Nara army. An Ahom force was sent to counter it, but in the nick of time the two commanders, through emissaries, discovered that a lie was the only reason they were about to engage in combat. So, they declared a truce and, in 1401, on the bank of Lake Nongnyang, sacrificed a rooster and took oath that they would always be bound in friendship. This oath-taking ceremony is called Patkai-Chengkeu, so the name of the place changed from Daikaorang to Patkai. There are so many such tales within tales in the buranjis, my people. That is what makes our history so fascinating!

'Suteupha, though of adventurous disposition like his father, had learnt statecraft from him. The hills that surrounded the Brahmaputra Valley were peopled by hostile tribes; his own tiny kingdom was sandwiched between bigger and more powerful kingdoms of the Valley. The ancient Chutiya kingdom covered a large portion of the plains and hills to its east; powerful kingdoms like those of the Kacharis, Barabhuyans and Kamatas lay to the west. Following the policy of Sukapha, the new king focused on strengthening his army, increasing the number of his subjects by inviting migrants, enhancing his naval fleet and ensuring economic prosperity within the kingdom. He did enlarge the extent of his domain a little—for instance, his people encroached upon lowlands belonging to tribes such as the Kacharis, but this was not resisted by the latter because the land was of no use to them since they did not know the technique of wetland rice cultivation. He also extended his domain through diplomacy and intermarriage amongst people rather than through combat. Thus, though he ruled for thirteen years and died in 1281, there was no conflict during the period of his rule.

'His son Subinpha, who ruled for twelve years from 1281 to 1293, followed the same maxim of peaceful coexistence rather than conquest. A firm believer in decentralization of power, he delegated the responsibility of running the upper half of his kingdom to his buragohain and the lower half to his bargohain, urging them to build up a tiered structure wherein each officer understood the nature of his duties as well as the consequences of dereliction.

'But his son Sukhangpha, who ascended the Ahom throne after Subinpha's death, was made of sterner stuff. Relatively young when he became the king in 1293, the small confines of his kingdom stifled him. He was bent on extending it, if not to be ruled directly at least by creating vassals who would pay tribute. Four decades had passed since the founding of Cheraidai as capital of the Mungdunsunkham kingdom; its fame had travelled across the valley and others were already beginning to call it the kingdom of the Ahoms; the number of his people had increased; each young man, no matter whether a farmer or an artisan, had to undergo training in combat so that he could pick up a sword or lance on his king's behalf; the time seemed opportune for expansion. However, Sukhangpha was not so rash as to take on the powerful adversaries closer to his kingdom like the Chutiyas and Kacharis. Instead, he went westwards and attacked the kingdom of the Kamatas.

'It proved to be a fruitless exercise, costly in terms of men and material. Finally, both sides grew weary of the combat which had not resulted in decisive victory for one or the other; the Kamata king Pratapdhwaja sent emissaries desiring a treaty to which Sukhangpha readily agreed. To cement their allegiance to each other, Rajni, daughter of Pratapdhwaja, was given in marriage to the Ahom king. Unfortunately, my people, one cannot foresee the grievous consequences of such routine actions. The marriage of Sukhangpha and Rajni was to prove bad for the kingdom's future.

'Having burned his hands once, the Ahom king made no more forays at expansion, though his was a lengthy tenure of thirty-nine years till his death in 1332. Yet it was in his term that the dark clouds of discord first began to gather on the horizons of this fledgling nation. You see, my people, power has allure that can corrupt most individuals. This is why the corridors of palaces are filled with dark niches of intrigue and conspiracies, and the floors stained with spilt blood. It was ultimately the greed for power and the intrigues to attain it, which brought about the fall of the mighty Ahom Empire ... the first shadows were cast during the reign of King Sukhangpha.

'When Sukhangpha died, he left behind four sons, Sukhrangpha, Sutupha, Tyaokhampthi and Chaopulai. The last of these, Chaopulai, was born of the marriage between the Kamata princess Rajni and Sukhangpha. Shan or Tai laws dictate that the eldest son of the king shall succeed him after his death, and accordingly, Sukhrangpha was crowned king in 1332. But now Chaopulai too staked his claim to the Ahom throne! The nobles had no love lost for Sukhrangpha—the pampered prince proved unfit to rule and was unpopular with his people—but there was no disobeying established law. Sukhrangpha felt the hostility of his nobles towards him and thought it more prudent to placate his half-brother by making him the raja of Saring. But Chaopulai had greater things in mind than mere governorship of a small area and hatched a conspiracy against Sukhrangpha.

'But his ruse was uncovered, forcing Chaopulai to escape to Kamatapur and ask his kinsmen for help in raising him to the Ahom throne. The Kamata king sniffed an opportunity—he was being offered a chance to have indirect influence over the Ahom kingdom! He readily agreed and advanced with his army into Ahom territory as far as Saring. Once again Sukhrangpha, suspicious of the loyalty of his nobles as well as his army commanders, opted for conciliation and offered negotiation. The Kamata king, suddenly aware that he would be facing the mighty Ahom warriors, had also developed cold feet. A friendship treaty was signed, the Kamata army withdrew and Chaopulai had to remain content with being the Saring raja.

'Later it was discovered that the bargohain was the one who had poisoned Chaopulai's mind against Sukhrangpha. But the weak-willed king, rather than taking action against the powerful noble, forgave him and took him back in his favour. Sukhrangpha, despite being unpopular with the people, had a long reign of thirty-two years and died in 1364.

'Over a century had elapsed since the establishment of Cheraidai, which today we call Charaideo, as the capital of the Ahom kingdom. The boundaries of the kingdom, notwithstanding the forays of

Sukhangpha against the Kamatas, had not changed greatly since the days of the founder Sukapha. But the Ahom community thrived and the population increased; there was a general atmosphere of peace conducive to prosperity. Yet, as we saw beginning with Chaopulai, discord was beginning to cast its shadow. This is but natural, my people, with all institutions erected by man. Even amongst such as disciplined race as the Shans there would be black sheep in the flock.

'Also, the growing might of the Ahoms was making the neighbours uneasy. Thus, when Sukhrangpha was succeeded by his brother Sutupha, there were occasional clashes with the Chutiya neighbours to the kingdom's east. However, following Sukapha's example, Sutupha too tried to maintain amicable relations with the Chutiyas and offered the hand of friendship to their king. The latter proved treacherous and, pretending to reciprocate, invited Sutupha to a boat race on the Safrai River and assassinated him in 1376. The Ahom nobles were unable to take any action because the assassination had been made to look like an accident, in which Sutupha was gored to death by a runaway bull; at the same time, they were preoccupied with administering the affairs of the kingdom since there was no suitable candidate who could be elevated to the throne.

'Shan laws permitted this, allowing leeway for the nobles to rule the kingdom while leaving the throne vacant. This being the first occasion for such a state of affairs, the nobles themselves faced difficulties. Thus, after four years without a king, in 1380 they put Tyaokhampthi, the third son of Sukhangpha, upon the Ahom throne. No wonder they had delayed, for Tyaokhampthi was arrogant, ruthless and headstrong. His first action after becoming king was to lead a punitive expedition against the Chutiyas for the murder of Sutupha, thereby laying the groundwork for one of the strangest and most romantic tales in the Ahom buranjis, that of the Brahmin Prince ...'

The Brahmin Prince

~~

KALABARI WAS A LARGE BUT TYPICAL VILLAGE IN THE HABUNG AREA on the north bank of the Ti-Lao, also called Luit or the Brahmaputra River. The great King Sukapha, the founder of the Ahom Empire, had tried to settle in the region between 1240 and 1244 but had to leave because it was prone to floods. But he had brought the native chieftains of the area under his suzerainty, so Kalabari lay within the Ahom kingdom. Since the days of Sukapha, the Ahoms had freely intermixed with the indigenous communities; the population of this village was therefore varied, consisting of both Ahoms and non-Ahoms.

Kalabari derived its name from 'kal' or banana, translating as 'garden of bananas'. The banana indeed was a wonder tree, every part of it being used for a purpose. The fruit was delicious, the flower and core of the stem too were edible, while the leaves and stems were used to make receptacles for eating food. Salt was scarce in those days, so kala khar was made by burning the skin of the banana fruit and collecting the ashes. Kala khar was used by the people instead of salt.

With a strong Ahom administration at Cheraidai, these were prosperous days. Except in times of war, when some of the men were required to go to battle, not much happened to disturb the peaceful existence of the village folk. Their needs were few and the village was self-sufficient in every way. The farmers grew paddy, pulses, mustard, cotton and sugarcane. Previously, paddy cultivation was done far away from the river because it was prone to severe inundation during the rains; but since the coming of the Ahoms the indigenous communities had learnt the technique of wetland rice cultivation, so nowadays land closer to the river too was utilized.

After the harvest had been reaped, the grains were stored in bhorals or granaries. Expect for seasonal floods and periodic earthquakes, there were no natural disasters to disrupt the placid flow of life. Rivers, streams and other water bodies were filled with fish and aquatic life, which the villagers could catch with nets and bamboo traps. They hunted for meat in the jungles: mostly deer and wild boar, also waterbirds such as wild ducks and geese which roosted in the shallows. The farmers bred cattle for ploughing as well as milk; eating beef was prevalent amongst some of the tribes. The Habung area was famous throughout the realm for the quality of the cattle reared there.

The jungles also provided honey, extracted from the hives of wild bees. Each household grew vegetables in the backyard. Women and children often went to the edge of the jungles to gather edible ferns, shoots and herbs. During winter, people would scour the sandbanks of the river for turtles basking in the sunshine and for turtle eggs, considered a delicacy. Apart from bananas, a variety of fruit trees grew both in household compounds and in the wilds. Coconut and betelnut palms too were aplenty.

A villager did not have to step out of his village to meet his needs. Many non-farming professionals lived in the village. There was even a bipra, or Brahmin, who performed religious ceremonies for the Hindu members of the community and also taught the village children. With the arrival of some Ahom families to settle in Kalabari, a Bailung priest with his family had come along, and he took care of the ceremonial needs of the community. The village had a komar, or blacksmith to fashion iron implements, a kumar or potter to make pots and pans of clay and another craftsman who made utensils of brass. A mukhi, or manufacturer of snail-lime, gathered snails from ponds and paddy fields and burned the shells to extract lime. Snail-lime, of a blackish colour, was pungent, and was used as a medicine for minor cuts and bruises as also to flavour betel-nut and paan. Kalabari had a cane and bamboo weaver who made highly useful items including bamboo murrahs or stools for sitting upon. There was a carpenter, too, who made rudimentary items of furniture, but since precious metals were only for the royalty and aristocrats, Kalabari had no goldsmith.

When ill, the villagers consulted the local bez, or medicine man. He was a venerable individual called Khenkham. He diagnosed disease by examining the navel of his patient, often prescribing talismans instead of medicine as a remedy. However, most of the villagers were familiar with curative herbs for different ailments, and went to the medicine man only as a last recourse.

Every winter when the great river had less water and thus was less turbulent, traders from the capital would come on boats to purchase wares made by the villagers. These included cattle raised by the dwellers, as well as sealing wax, snail-lime, and receptacles and utensils of bamboo, brass and iron. Every household in the village reared silkworms and the womenfolk were expert weavers. Thus, cloth produced in Kalabari was in great demand in the capital. The villagers traded by means of the barter system, exchanging their ware for items brought by the merchants.

At that period of time, life in Kalabari flowed on an even keel. No one was very rich, nor were too many weighed down by poverty. Sons followed their father's calling. No one was envious of others' wealth; there were very few quarrels and almost no crime. In fact, hardly anything happened to ruffle the placidity of the village.

One evening in autumn the bipra of Kalabari sat in the prayer room of his cottage, studying the scriptures by the light from an earthen lamp. The Brahmin was a tall and imposing man, around forty-five years of age, with lean, sharply defined features and a hawk-like nose. His head was clean-shaven, except for a long tuft of hair that, tied at the end in a bow-knot, hung at the back of his head. He wore a dhoti. A sacred thread ran across his bare chest.

The rest of the village was already asleep. The villagers knew how to make best use of daylight hours, rising at the break of dawn and retiring to sleep just after sunset. Fuel for earthen lamps, basically oil from mustard seeds, which was also used for cooking, was precious and no one wanted to waste it for a job which the sun could very well do.

The villagers used ingenious means of keeping fire alive, for getting one lighted was time-consuming and laborious work. The most common was to keep a heap of rice husks smouldering—a fire could be kept alive for months together by this method, though during the rainy season this was less effective. Often a householder would go to a neighbouring cottage to light a flare to be brought back home for igniting the kitchen fire!

The bipra was one of the very few individuals who kept awake after sunset. The quietude was ideal for study and contemplation, and he would sit before his altar, perusing various manuscripts in his possession. Upon the altar was placed clay statues of a number of deities, as well as a stone Laxmi-Narayan Shaligram, indicating that the Brahmin was a devotee of Lord Shiva.

A gust of wind swept into the room, making the flame of the earthen-lamp flicker, disturbing the bipra in his perusal. He looked around and noticed that the bamboo-framed window of the prayer-room was open. As he got up to shut it, his eyes turned towards the river at a distance away. The night, though dark, was clear and he could see a glow from a luminous object bobbing up and down upon the waters.

His curiosity roused, he continued for a while to look at the glow; the wind had grown stiffer, hinting at a thundery, pre-winter squall. It appeared to bring the object closer to the bank upon which the village was sited.

The bipra woke up his eldest son who was sleeping alone in a room of his own, picked up the dao the villagers always carried during the night for protection, and went towards the river to investigate the light. While most of the superstitious villagers were afraid to stir out of their homes at night, the Brahmin was burdened by no such fears. A hint of rain was already in the air as the two of them reached the riverbank and gazed open-mouthed at the sight that met their eyes.

It was a raft made by lashing together tree trunks, but far bigger than the ones the villagers built during the floods. Half of it was covered by a roof made of spliced bamboo, but it had drifted very close to the bank and they could make out what lay within that shelter—a lamp of intricate design, its flame protected from the breeze by a thin, metal chimney. The lamp's light revealed the reclining figure of a woman. The gold bangles on her arms and diamond necklace around her neck glittered.

Wading into the shallows, the bipra and his son pulled at and moored the raft to the riverbank. The Brahmin quickly examined the woman— she appeared to be in a deep swoon, but alive. 'Quick,' he instructed his son. 'Wake up Khenkham, the medicine man, and fetch him here. I think you had better bring along the blacksmith, too.'

The lad returned a half hour later, accompanied by two men carrying flares. Khenkham examined the woman and confirmed what the bipra had concluded. 'She is alive but very weak,' he said. 'The river breeze can be cold and cruel. We need to get her warmed up as quickly as possible.'

'She is no ordinary woman,' said the blacksmith. 'Only the nobility wears such fine clothes embroidered with threads of gold. Just look at her ornaments! Must be worth a fortune!'

'We'll know in good time,' said the Brahmin. 'Let us first get her into my cottage. Stealth is the need of the hour, my friends. Clearly, if a lady such as her has been left to drift upon a raft, she must be in dire danger.'

The bipra's son and the blacksmith quickly set to work, fashioning a makeshift stretcher of bamboo, placing the woman upon it and carrying her to the Brahmin's cottage. Meanwhile, the Brahmin and the medicine man hacked away at the lashings of the raft, dismantling it and setting the logs afloat.

At first the Brahmin's wife was overawed by the sight of a strange woman dressed in such finery. Being highly superstitious, she was terrified that the men had brought an evil spirit into the household. But then she realized that it was merely a woman in distress; experienced enough to observe such things, she at once made out that the woman was pregnant. As Khenkham had said, she needed to be warmed up. With the help of her son, she brought out a thick cotton mattress for the woman to be placed upon, and wrapped her in a coarse cotton shawl, after which she went to the kitchen and returned with an iron pan containing burning charcoal. Spreading mustard oil on her palms, and warming them over the fire, she rubbed the warm oil on the soles of the stranger's feet.

The limbs were ice-cold. She was still as death and for a while it appeared that she could not be revived. But slowly, as the bipra's wife continued with her ministrations, the warmth returned to the woman's limbs and colour to her cheeks. Her eyes flickered open. She gazed at the faces around her with stark terror in her eyes.

'Please, please, don't kill me,' she whimpered. 'If not for my sake ... at least for the unborn child that I carry.'

'Don't be afraid,' said the Brahmin's wife soothingly. 'You're safe with us.'

'Where am I?' the woman asked, no longer fearful. Her voice too was stronger.

'In Kalabari village,' the Brahmin replied. 'It's on the north bank of the Luit River. You'll tell us who you are, won't you?'

'I'm the younger queen of King Tyaokhampthi.'

There was a sudden hush in the room. Everyone appeared startled. They had correctly guessed that the strange woman was of noble birth. But not in their wildest dream could they have imagined that she was a queen of the Ahom kingdom!

Everyone in the room prostrated themselves before the queen. 'Arise,' she commanded, but the sweetness in her voice made it sound more like a request than a command. 'I'm thirsty. May I have some water, please?'

'We're poor folks, Your Highness,' said the Brahmin's wife. 'We don't have utensils befitting a queen.'

The woman smiled gently. 'My sister, does it really matter whether the bowl I drink from is made of gold or clay?'

Greatly relieved, the Brahmin's wife brought her warm water to drink. She also made a broth of vegetables and meat which the queen consumed with obvious relish.

When she had finished eating the Brahmin asked, 'Our lord, King Tyaokhampthi, has two wives, the first being known as bor kuonri or elder queen. You must be the soru kuonri or younger queen, Your Highness?'

'Yes, I was the soru kuonri, but I'm no longer so. Let me tell you my tragic story.'

'King Tyaokhampthi, my lord and husband,' the queen began, 'married the elder queen a long time back, even before the nobles selected him to grace the throne at Cheraidai. He soon discovered that her beauty was skin-deep, for she was a strong-minded, hard-hearted woman, incapable of thinking of anyone else but herself. Though his affection for her waned, she continued to wield great influence upon him and he took no decision without her consent.

'It was, of course, by sheer chance that he was raised to the Ahom throne. His elder brother Sutupha, who had been the king before him, was treacherously killed by the Chutiyas without leaving an heir. The nobles did not trust my husband with the throne and so tried for a few years to rule the kingdom on their own. However, this proved difficult and they were finally compelled to place my husband on the throne. The elder queen was overjoyed at this quirk of fate. She grew more dictatorial than ever, contributing to the increasing unpopularity of my husband with his subjects.

'The elder queen, being barren, could not give birth to a male child to succeed to the throne and thereby continue the lineage of my husband. So, against the wishes of the elder queen but with the consent of his ministers, my lord married again. I was the unfortunate second wife.'

'We learned of this marriage, Your Highness,' said Khenkham, 'through cattle-traders. A year ago, wasn't it?'

'Yes. My lord and king loved me greatly. He spent most of his time with me and showered me with costly gifts. The elder queen felt neglected and grew jealous. She tried to poison my husband's mind against me, but without success. I could understand her plight and felt sympathy. But I could not really judge how vicious she really was. Her antipathy towards me grew more pronounced when it was learnt that I was carrying the king's child. It was like a knife stab to her heart.

'My husband, naturally, was delighted with the news. He summoned the Deodhai head priest of the palace to forecast the child's future. The priest killed a cock and observed that it would be a boy, and was destined to become a king. This made my husband even more happy and loving, while it made the elder queen more determined to destroy me. But she pretended she was concerned about my well-being now that I was carrying the future heir to the throne. She even sent me a herbal tonic through one of my servants to boost up my energy. Innocent that I was, I was about to drink it when the servant snatched away the potion container and threw it away. She told me that the so-called herbal tonic would have actually destroyed the child within me. She paid for her loyalty towards me with her life.'

'Can a human being be so vile?' cried out the Brahmin's wife in horror and disgust.

'As long as the king was by my side, she could not harm a hair on my head. So, she next attempted to send him away from the capital. She called him a coward for not avenging the death of his elder brother and punishing the Chutiyas. Egged on by her, against the judgement of the nobles, my husband led an army on an expedition against the Chutiya chieftain who had murdered his brother. Normally, the ministers would have handled the affairs of the state in his absence. But his disagreement with them on the issue of going to war made him suspect their loyalty. Therefore, he appointed the elder queen as regent to govern the kingdom in his absence.

'This gave her unfettered power. Even the bargohain and buragohain dared not oppose her. Hardly had my lord and husband left the kingdom than she framed false charges against me and ordered that I be executed!'

'A false, deceitful woman,' cried out the bipra and the others nodded their heads in agreement.

'It was the ministers who saved me. The executioner sent to execute me killed a goat instead and showed the blood-spattered dao to the elder queen to confirm I had been beheaded and my body thrown into the river. The nobles arranged that I be instead placed on a raft and left on my own to drift down the Luit. I am fortunate indeed to have drifted towards good people like you.'

The intelligent Brahmin at once understood the implications of the younger queen's story. 'You're in great danger, Your Highness,' he said. 'If the elder queen discovers you've escaped, she will search heaven and earth to find and kill you.'

'I'm not afraid for myself,' the younger-queen said. 'I don't have much to live for. I've lost a husband, I'm queen no longer. But the child within me must be protected at all costs.'

'That's true,' the Brahmin agreed. 'He is the future king of the realm. Your presence in Kalabari must be kept a secret.'

'But how?' asked the blacksmith, a practical fellow. 'You can be assured of the silence of those in this room. But the sudden arrival of a stranger is sure to set tongues wagging in the village.'

'I have a plan,' said the Brahmin. 'Your Highness, can you pretend to be a commoner for a while?'

'I don't need to pretend,' said the younger queen with a wry smile. 'Remember, I'm queen no longer. You all don't need to address me as Your Highness.'

'Yes, that's one thing we must learn to no longer do,' the bipra continued. 'This is my plan. I shall let it be known to our folks that my wife's younger sister, from a village some distance away, has come to live with us. She is a young widow who has no one else to turn to. So, I've taken pity on her and had her brought into our household.'

Khenkham was sceptical. 'I suppose that's the best thing to do under the circumstances. But our folks are no fools. Her beauty, her way of speaking, everything shows her up to be no ordinary villager. They'll suspect something was amiss.'

'That can be taken care of,' the Brahmin said. 'We'll tell them that she's just lost her husband and is in deep mourning. So, she can't be allowed visitors. Also, her health is none too good so she must stay indoors till she can get her mental and physical strength back.'

'Yes,' the blacksmith said enthusiastically. 'Such a plan might work. But secrecy is essential. We must not breathe out a word to anyone.'

The younger queen stood up with an effort. She took off her ornaments one by one and handed them to the Brahmin's wife. 'Keep these well hidden,' she advised.

'We'll bury them,' the blacksmith said.

All the ornaments had been taken off except a ring on her finger. Drawing it off, she gave it to the Brahmin. 'Don't bury this. Guard it with your life, for it is the insignia of royalty. It has the royal symbol carved upon it. If someday the need arises to prove that my child is of royal blood, show this ring.'

She accompanied the bipra's wife into an inner room. The bipra mused for a couple of minutes and, darting into the puja-room, hid the ring under the altar. A little later the queen re-entered the room. Now she was dressed in white and wore no ornaments and looked quite different.

The ploy worked. The villagers did not suspect that the new woman in the Brahmin's household was not his wife's sister. One man, however, was not taken in—Baduli, the village wastrel. Every village has such a pariah or outcast; besides being a lazybones who shirked any sort of work, Baduli was foul-mouthed and hated the villagers. He lived apart at some distance from the village in a ramshackle hut, making do with whatever he could scrounge from the very villagers whom he never tired of verbally abusing.

Baduli would often enter a household uninvited and demand he be fed. The villagers tolerated him, though he was more liable to curse his benefactors than thank them. One day, Baduli had entered the courtyard of the Brahmin's cottage in search of a meal and accidentally sighted the widow. Her beauty and grace caught him by surprise. She looked nothing like the Brahmin's wife.

The more Baduli dwelt on the circumstances of the stranger's presence, the more suspicious he grew. Not only had none of the other village people seen her face, no one in Kalabari had even been witness to her arrival at the village! However, Baduli never shared his secrets with anyone else unless it was for personal gain. So, he kept his suspicions to himself.

Sadly, the ill-fated queen was not destined to live much longer. One cold winter night, a month after her arrival at Kalabari, she gave birth to a male child. But the rigours of the trip on the raft over the Luit had taken its toll on her health. The same night she died post childbirth. The wailings of the Brahmin's wife and children had aroused the village folk and they helped to carry her bier to the nearby cremation ground. A pyre was built and the bipra's eldest son lit it. Soon the flames consumed the mortal remains of the younger queen.

After the villagers left the cremation ground, only the bipra, the blacksmith and Khenkham remained behind. The former had carried an earthen pot with him, which he now began filling with the queen's ashes.

'What are you doing?' asked Khenkham, surprised.

'You, being an Ahom, should be able to guess,' the bipra replied. 'The queen too was an Ahom. It would have been more fitting to have buried her according to Ahom custom.'

'True,' agreed Khenkham. 'But we had no choice. Burying her instead of cremation would have given the game away.'

'That's correct. But we can at least bury her ashes, can't we?'

The three men returned to the Brahmin's house to dig up the ornaments they had buried in the courtyard. Khenkham brought a wooden chest from his home and they put the ashes and ornaments in it. Venturing into the edge of the jungle they buried the chest and piled up earth over it to create a maidam, or burial mound, as was the Ahom custom. Under the circumstances, that was the best they could do for the unfortunate queen.

Then, exhausted, they returned to their respective homes. None of them noticed the shadowy figure of Baduli furtively watching what they were doing.

The years passed. The baby prince grew up to be robust and handsome child. Because of the need to keep up appearances, they named him Gopal. But had the villagers been a curious lot, they would have suspected something amiss about the lad. Well-grown for his age, he was at least a head taller than the other children of the village, and far stronger. To the few who knew the secret of his birth, his royal lineage was evident in his features and build, and the manner in which he carried himself.

The Brahmin couple loved the boy as their own. After his mother's death, they had been in constant dread that someone would uncover who his actual parents were and soldiers would arrive from Cheraidai to kill him. But nothing happened and with passing time, the fear ebbed. The unsuspecting lad treated the Brahmin couple as his real father and mother, and their children as his brothers and sisters.

The bipra was the teacher of the village and taught what he knew to those who came to him. Unfortunately, the villagers were none too impressed with bookish knowledge, so there were very few for him to teach. Gopal was the least serious about studies amongst them. As he grew up, it became apparent that his hunting and fighting skills were far superior to his ability to memorize Sanskrit shlokas.

In an anteroom of the royal palace at Cheraidai, the bor kuonri or elder queen of the Ahom King Tyaokhampthi reclined on a couch. The chamber was luxuriously furnished, the draperies being made of the finest silk and the lamps, betel-nut trays and bowls of gold or silver. Even the spittoon was plated with gold and encrusted with precious stones.

The queen was in a foul mood, which made her face look even harsher. Six years had passed since the younger queen had been beheaded. So, the fire of jealousy within her had died down, or so she thought. Possessing as she did a commanding presence which could strike terror into the stoutest heart, she had imposed her will on her husband when he returned triumphant from the war with the Chutiyas, forcing him through her lies to concede that the younger queen had committed the unpardonable crime of conspiring with the nobles to oust him from the throne. The king, of course, did not believe the elder queen, but he refused to take action against her as advised by his nobles.

The king's inaction had alienated the bargohain and buragohain and they were getting more defiant every day. Then, this morning, a terrible piece of information had been conveyed to her by one of her trusted officers. The chaodang executioner who was supposed to have beheaded the soru kuonri had died of an incurable disease. As he lay on his deathbed, he confided to his younger brother that though he had executed so many, yet he was glad he had spared the life of the younger queen. On being quizzed by his brother, he revealed how the nobles had set her adrift on a raft.

The bor kuonri's face had turned into an ugly mask at the news. Her first thought was that she would summon the nobles and fling her accusations at them. But then she realized if the information was to get to the king, he would learn that the soru kuonri might be alive, perhaps living somewhere secretly with her child. Knowing of his love for her, there was danger that he might search for her and bring her back to the palace.

The need of the moment was to secretly seek out the younger queen and destroy her and the child. She had instructed the officer to identify a spy who could be sent out on a hunt for the wretched woman. Now she awaited his arrival in the antechamber.

Soon the officer returned with the man. The queen was taken aback. The fellow hardly looked like a spy; rather, he had the face of a saint. But that went well with the disguise he normally adopted while seeking information on behalf of the rulers of the kingdom—a wandering minstrel. He also possessed a melodious voice to complement the disguise.

The queen gave him her instructions. He was to scour the kingdom and hunt out the whereabouts of the younger queen. If he found her and her child, he was to return to the capital and inform the elder queen. On no account must he try to kill them on his own, for she might be protected by those around her and the spy himself might be killed if he tried to harm her. In that case, the information would die with him!

The spy had just left when King Tyaokhampthi entered the chamber. He was a tall and handsome man. He had come directly from a conference with his ministers and was dressed in his royal robes. The gems on his clothes glittered as he moved. Seeing the regal manner in his movements and the arrogance upon his face, no one would guess he was merely a puppet in the hands of his queen.

The queen noticed the frown upon his forehead. 'Is anything the matter, my lord?' she asked.

'Yes, it's the ministers. I've been quarrelling with them again. They've given me an ultimatum. Choose who is to help you govern this kingdom, they had the effrontery to order me. The queen ... or us? They've warned me of dire consequences if I do not heed the combined wisdom of the court.'

The elder queen's face had a queer, evil look upon it. 'Destroy them, my lord,' she said. 'You're the descendent of Lengdon, the Lord of Heaven. Invoke your divine sanction and destroy them.'

'That's easier said than done,' the king replied. 'The ministers are united and the people are clearly on their side. Following your advice, I've tried to instill terror into my subjects, executing or imprisoning hundreds, even for petty misdemeanors. But that seems to have made them even more rebellious.'

'Then this is what we must do, my lord. If the people are rebellious, they must be cowed down even further. But we must use guile with the ministers. If they are united, we must divide them. From now on give greater importance to the bargohain, while ignoring and snubbing the buragohain.'

Rivers being the most passable 'roads' in this region, the spy set off in a one-man dinghy, dressed as a wandering minstrel, thrumming a been, the one-stringed instrument commonly carried by such people. Week after week, he wandered around, entertaining village folk with ballads and devotional songs, while keeping his eyes and ears open for news of the soru kuonri. Three months later, having crossed the Luit, he arrived at Kalabari village.

He chose the shade of a large tree to sit and thrum his been. The news of his arrival spread in a matter of minutes throughout the village. There was little entertainment of this kind in Kalabari and the dwellers were not going to miss the opportunity. Villagers, young and old, congregated on the open ground surrounding the tree beneath which the wandering minstrel sat.

The minstrel began singing. With his eyes closed as though in deep devotion, he sang in a melodious voice rich with emotions, celebrating the bounty of nature and the generosity of the gods. After a while he broke out into a popular ballad which everyone knew, so the audience clapped and joined in the singing. With brief pauses in between to sip water and partake of refreshments the villagers had brought, he entertained them for almost two hours even as his eyes probed the audience for telltale clues.

Two individuals stood out amongst the people before him. One was a young boy, inordinately tall for his age, who had features startlingly resembling King Tyaokhampthi. The other was a man, of shabby appearance and clothing, who sat at the very back of the throng, a little apart from others. The villagers were surprised that, when requested to partake of their hospitality for the night, the minstrel chose Baduli as the person in whose house he would like to stay.

Even as a huge smirk appeared on the village wastrel's face, the villagers were appalled, and protested vociferously. But the minstrel said, 'I thank you all, good people. Yet you must remember I'm a deeply pious and humble man. It is my practice to stay with individuals who clearly are the poorest in any village. Apparently, this man is so in this community, and so I chose to stay the night with him.'

The villagers understood. The minstrel was an individual of plain living and high thinking! But Baduli was not as naïve as the villagers. The moment he was alone at his hovel with his guest, he asked belligerently, 'Who are you? What is your motive in coming to this village?'

'Ah, you're a clever one, aren't you?' said the spy with a mocking laugh. 'It's a wonder why you haven't made something more of yourself! But you're right. I come at the directive of Her Highness, the Queen. I am searching for someone.'

'I think I can guess who! These traders from Cheraidai, they give us news from outside. You're searching for the younger queen, aren't you?'

'I told you I consider you clever. So, can you tell me something about her whereabouts?'

'Perhaps, yes. But what's in it for me?'

'There's a substantial reward for any information. If it helps me in my quest, I shall make you rich beyond your wildest dreams.'

Baduli laughed contemptuously. 'Riches do not interest me. But power does! Promise to take me to Cheraidai and make me an officer in the service of His Majesty.'

'But why?' asked the spy, genuinely astonished.

'So that I can come back to the village and show these stupid folks who I really am! Make them grovel at my feet, begging for mercy!'

'Fine. That can be easily arranged. Now tell me, had any strange woman arrived at this village around six years ago?'

Baduli spilled it all—about the woman who had claimed to be the widowed sister of the village Brahmin, how she had died and left behind a son. 'Guess what,' he concluded. 'Though they cremated her corpse, they buried her ashes and built a small mound around that place. If you dig up the mound, you will also find a number of precious ornaments.'

Late that night, while the village was deep in slumber, the spy and Baduli, carrying flares, went into the jungle to the spot where the soru kuonri's ashes were buried. Fast-growing vegetation had completely covered up the maidam and, had not Baduli memorized the location, it might have been difficult to locate it. They dug up the chest containing the ashes and ornaments and the spy emitted a low chuckle as he examined the necklace, bracelets, etc. The precious stones upon them glittered like stars in the light of the flares.

The spy took out a pouch from the folds of his dhoti and carefully placed the ornaments in it. Baduli guessed that the finery would not be returned to the palace but retained by the man himself. This did not bother him, for Baduli sought power and status, not wealth. The two of them made their way back through the jungle but, instead of turning towards the path leading to Baduli's hutment, the spy veered off in the direction of the river-ghat where his boat was moored.

'You aren't staying the night?' Baduli, surprised, asked.

'No need. You've provided me with proof enough and the sooner I carry the news to the queen, the better. You can either choose to stay behind, or you can come with me.'

Baduli smirked smugly. An opportunity had been offered to him to fulfill his dreams. He would be a fool not to seize it.

'Of course, I shall go with you. Remember, you promised to make me an officer of the court.'

"Right. Then come along."

They unfastened the spy's boat from the pier and embarked upon it. Baduli should have been warned by the fact that the dinghy had been built for one person, but so filled was his head with visions of power and revenge that he failed to notice it. He sat near the prow with his back to the spy as the latter expertly guided the craft into the deeper currents of the Brahmaputra.

Once they were far enough from the village, the spy suddenly stopped rowing and, wielding his oar like a mace, savagely struck Baduli on the head, splitting it. The victim toppled into the Luit and was sucked in by the powerful currents.

The spy emitted another chuckle and steered his dinghy towards the south bank of the Luit.

Half-a-dozen grim-faced men had collected in a room deep within the buragohain's abode. The two principal ministers, the buragohain and bargohain, were in the group, as also lesser officials. They had gathered stealthily and spoke in low conspiratorial whispers. There was reason for their caution. The elder queen had her spies everywhere. If she came to know of this gathering, the consequences might be disastrous.

The bargohain opened the discussions. 'We're meeting here today with a common goal,' he said. 'We need to remove Tyaokhampthi and his queen from the throne.'

'How?' asked one of the nobles.

'Kill them!' the buragohain said flatly.

'Can't they be arrested and put in a dungeon?' asked another noble, clearly indicating that to him the crime of regicide was distasteful.

'No,' said the bargohain. 'A king who remains alive would be a constant danger to his successor.'

'But that's precisely my point,' said the noble. 'There's no successor. The elder queen has produced no heir; the younger queen is dead. Perhaps it would be wiser to kill the queen and let the king live.'

'No, that would rather be foolish. By his actions against his subjects, he's proving himself to be a tyrant. The people are growing rebellious, which is bad for the stability of our kingdom. Before anarchy descends, let us get rid of both the king and his consort.'

'But what about a successor?' another noble again posed the crucial question.

'As laid down by the law, we nobles will govern the kingdom till a successor is found,' said the bargohain. 'Just as we had done before we made the mistake of putting Tyaokhampthi on the throne. We strike tonight itself. I've made all the arrangements. The king's official guards at the palace have been replaced by soldiers who owe their loyalty to us.'

The six nobles drew out their hengdangs and brought the blades together. 'Death to the tyrants!' they intoned in chorus. 'Long live the Ahom kingdom!'

The spy reached Cheraidai the same evening the nobles were plotting the death of the royal couple. He was in a jubilant mood. Not only would he be able to pocket the expensive jewellery he had brought back from Kalabari, but surely the queen would reward him for the information he would bring her. He could now retire from his risky job, an immensely wealthy individual.

He hurried to the home of the officer who had recruited him. The latter was effusive in his praise of what the spy had achieved and the duo set off immediately for the palace.

Dusk had fallen by the time they arrived at the palace gate. There was something strange in the air that evening; an ominous tension seemed to wrap the royal palace. The guards at the gate were unfamiliar; moreover, the palace would normally be a hive of activity at this time of the evening; servants would be bustling about; royal guards would be standing in front of every doorway.

But today the corridors were deserted. No guards challenged them. They met a solitary housemaid who informed them that the queen had retired to her chamber and could not be disturbed. The girl seemed to be eager to leave the palace and would not comply with the officer's order that she let the queen know of his arrival. The officer had no alternative but to himself knock loudly on the door of her chamber.

'Come in,' the queen called out, and was surprised to find that it was not one of her servants but her officer who entered the room. However, her rising anger subsided when she saw the man who accompanied the officer.

'It's you!' she cried out eagerly. 'Could you find that wretched witch?'

Quickly and concisely the spy told her about what he had uncovered, without mentioning the ornaments he had acquired. The queen became animated as she heard the spy's tale.

'So, the woman's dead!' she cried out harshly. 'But her son lives! You must leave this very night, officer, for Kalabari village. Take a small group of trusted soldiers with you. Bring his head back to me. I won't be fooled a second time.'

'Your wish is my command, Your Highness,' said the officer, bowing. 'I'll need a formal order stating that I act at your bidding.'

The queen rang the gong to summon her housemaid and ask that paraphernalia for writing out the order be brought. 'Burn the village before you leave,' she told the officer. 'Wipe out the Brahmin and his family. Where is that housemaid? Why isn't she responding? I shall have her flayed alive for her tardiness.'

At that moment, the door of her room burst open and a group of men rushed in with swords drawn. The queen sprang up; there was no fear in her face; her eyes blazed like twin flares. 'How dare you enter my chamber without my permission!' she cried.

The bargohain laughed. 'We've already dealt with the king,' he said. 'Now it's your turn.' He thrust his sword into her heart.

The officer tried to resist, but he was outnumbered and cut down. The spy grovelled on the floor and begged to be spared. But the very fact that he was in the private chamber of the queen was evidence enough of his complicity and he was killed.

Having carried out the assassinations, the nobles left the palace to announce to the subjects that the hated king and queen were dead.

There was rejoicing all over the kingdom. People lit bonfires and danced in the streets. Heralds were sent all around the capital. They beat drums and announced that the court ministers would rule the kingdom till a new king was chosen. Dungeons were thrown open and the elder queen's victims who had been imprisoned were set free.

A few months later, news of the death of the king and queen reached Kalabari. The Brahmin, Khenkham and the blacksmith discussed the new development. Traders had also brought news that the court ministers were searching the kingdom for possible presence of the younger queen and her child.

'Do you think the time has come for us to reveal Gopal's true identity?' the blacksmith asked.

'I feel he is better off where he is,' the Brahmin replied. 'Who knows what new peril lurks for him in the capital? There might be other claimants to the throne at Cheraidai.'

'I agree,' said Khenkham. 'Gopal is but a child. Revealing his identity might put his life at risk.'

Soldiers, led by a petty officer, did indeed visit Kalabari a few months later asking about the possible presence of the soru kuonri and her child, but the ones in the know chose to remain silent. Thus, the prince continued to stay on at Kalabari. The years went by and Gopal, into his fourteenth year now, had grown to be a strong and handsome youth.

The Brahmin was anxious that the boy take up a vocation and settle down. Having grown up in a Brahmin household, it would have been appropriate if he took up priestly work, but the boy showed neither inclination for the scriptures nor for rituals. Hunting, wrestling, archery—such activities were more to his preference! He was adept at setting traps to catch small animals and at killing larger ones, the latter by setting a bow trap. The boy showed no indication that he was ready to embark on a profession, since nothing seemed suitable for him.

Yet, intelligent as he was, he realized the wisdom of his 'father's' advice that he take up a vocation, for he could not live on like this for ever. 'I will give myself another year,' he secretly decided. 'Then I shall leave this village and seek my fortune in the capital Cheraidai.'

Thaokhuncheng was a prosperous merchant from Cheraidai. He traded in almost everything on earth, buying produce cheaply from far-flung villages in the Ahom kingdom as well as neighbouring ones, and selling these at a far higher price in the capital. His biggest profits came from trading in cattle. Being an opulent and respected figure in social circles in Cheraidai, he had deemed it below his dignity to embark on cattle purchase himself, and therefore would send his underlings to negotiate. But lately, he had begun to suspect that his men were shortcharging him and had decided that he himself would be present for the latest deal on cattle in villages of Habung area.

Thus, it was the first time that he had set foot in Kalabari village. It was the end of the spring season and the rains would commence soon. The rainy season was the one which the villagers dreaded most as far as the cattle were concerned, for it brought diseases and death. So, the villagers were willing to dispose of their surplus cattle at whatever they could get. The wily merchant knew that this was the best time to strike a business deal.

He had crossed the Luit on a large trading boat, requiring six able-bodied men to guide it. The boat, carrying small packets of salt, scented wood, trinkets and similar items to be bartered for cattle, moored at the river-ghat at Kalabari. The scene around him, as he moved with an assistant towards the residential part of the village, was typical of rural life in these parts. Some women were washing clothes on the riverbank, but most were with the men in the paddy fields. Children were frolicking upon the sandy bank; a group of youths were engaged in dhopkhel, a game played with a tightly packed cloth-ball.

The merchant, in no hurry, stopped for a while to watch the dhopkhel game. His eyes almost popped out of his head when he saw one of players. Taller than anyone else in that group, the youth had the build of a fine athlete. But of more interest to the merchant was the lad's face. As one who moved in the highest social circles in Cheraidai, Thaokhuncheng had met the late king a number of times and had even spoken to him. Possessing a good memory for faces, he had no doubt in his mind. This youth had the features and mannerisms of Tyaokhampthi!

The merchant tried to control the wild beating of his heart. A purse of a hundred gold counters had been offered by the two chief nobles for information about the boy. A small fortune. The more he looked at the youth, the more Thaokhuncheng grew assured that the purse was for his taking. Always the cautious businessman, he tried to prise out more information from the villagers in order to confirm his suspicions. But the folks were tight-lipped and would not give a clue.

He would have left at once without concluding his business, but he was clever enough to understand that doing so would make the villagers suspicious. However, he took one-fourth of the time he otherwise would have and returned to Cheraidai as soon as possible and requested an audience with the bargohain. On meeting him, he related his impressions about the youth in Kalabari village.

'Ever since the reward was announced, we've had a dozen of people coming to stake their claims. None have proved right so far and were whipped for their greedy lies. So be careful, merchant,' the bargohain warned.

'I'll stake my life on it, my lord,' Thaokhuncheng said with confidence.

'Right, then. We'll set off tomorrow morning on the royal barge.'

The boy whom the villagers knew as Gopal sat alone on the shade of a tree, contemplating his future. His mood was sombre, for he instinctively understood that the day when he would have to leave Kalabari was none too distant. Though it would break his heart to depart from his loved ones and friends, it had to be done, for somehow his temperament did not appear suited for a rustic existence.

Suddenly he heard a commotion from the direction of the river. Soon one of his brothers came running up to him in excitement. 'Come, Gopal,' he shouted. 'Everyone's going to the river-ghat. A beautiful boat is approaching it, one the likes of which we've never ever seen.'

'You go on ahead,' said Gopal mournfully. 'I will catch up with you later.'

He had no intention of going, for the sorrow in his heart had obliterated all other emotions. So he did not see the royal barge moor at the ghat. The craft, an enormous vessel pulled by rows of oarsmen, shone like a jewel in the bright sunshine. The boat's prow was in the shape of a peacock, plated with gold and encrusted with jewels. The villagers stared in awe as soldiers first disembarked to lay down the gangway so that the nobles aboard could reach the riverbank.

The Brahmin had been in his prayer room when his eldest son apprised him of the sighting of the royal barge headed for Kalabari. The bipra understood that the moment for revelation had arrived. There could be no other reason for the boat to come to the insignificant village. Shifting the altar slightly, he picked up the royal ring. Clasping it tightly in one hand, he left for the riverbank.

As soon as the gangway was in place, a herald descended, beating upon a gong. 'Their Excellencies the bargohain and buragohain will descend from the royal barge, as will other nobles.' He proclaimed loudly. 'You will all prostrate yourselves on the ground and not rise till you're bidden.'

As the villagers flung themselves to the ground, the court ministers crossed over to the bank. 'You may all rise now,' the buragohain said. 'Who amongst you is the village Brahmin?'

'I am,' the bipra, rising to his feet, said with dignity. 'Have I offended you in any way, my lord?'

The buragohain smiled. 'No, old man, not at all,' he said. 'All we seek of you are a few answers. Come aside here, so that we can speak in private.'

The villagers murmured amongst themselves, wondering what business the highest dignitaries of the land could have with a poor village Brahmin. The youngsters gaped with awe at the golden barge and the tall and muscular soldiers with their shields and hengdangs.

'You have a son?' the bargohain asked.

'I have eight, my lord,' the bipra replied.

'But one of them is not your own?'

'That is true, my lord. We've named him Gopal.'

'Tell us how he came to live with you. You've no reason to fear our motives. If your Gopal is indeed the boy we seek, you will be doing the realm a great service.'

The Brahmin relaxed. The destined moment had arrived. With great conciseness he related the story, how they had found a woman who turned out to be the younger queen and how she requested before her death that he take care of the newborn baby. They had kept the facts secret because they were afraid the boy's life might be in danger if others had come to know.

'Do you have any proof you're telling the truth?' the buragohain asked.

The Brahmin opened his fist and handed over the royal ring. The bargohain and buragohain examined it closely and then nodded to each other. 'The king has been found,' the buragohain announced loudly. 'Long live the king!'

'Long live the king!' responded the villagers and Kalabari resounded with the cry.

Seated under the tree, the sound reached Gopal. He continued to remain where he was, disinterested. But he could not ignore the noisy procession that was coming towards him. It was led by a few men, dressed in grand regalia, guarded by soldiers. However, reassuringly, his father was with them at the head, as well as a few village elders, while rest of the village folk trailed behind them.

To his great astonishment the procession came right up to him. He looked on, open-mouthed, as everyone, including the important men and soldiers, as also his father, mother, brothers, sisters, friends—in fact, everyone—prostrated themselves before him.

'We salute Your Highness,' the buragohain said. 'Please permit us to rise.'

'Why do you mock me by addressing me as "Your Highness"?' the boy cried. 'Father, tell them that I am your son.'

At a signal from the bargohain, everyone rose. The bipra, overcome with emotion, remained silent. But the buragohain said,

'No, Your Highness. You're not a Brahmin's son. You're a prince, the son of King Tyaokhampthi, and heir to the Ahom throne.'

Almost desperately, the youth turned towards the bipra once again for reassurance.

'Father, this isn't true, is it?' he pleaded.

'It's true, Your Highness,' said the Brahmin, willing himself to speak. 'You're the son of King Tyaokhampthi. I gave shelter to your mother, the younger queen, when she was in danger. She left you in my care before she died.'

The familiar world of the youth crumbled. His father was addressing him as 'Your Highness'; his mother had prostrated herself at his feet! He was bewildered.

The bargohain understood the depth of the boy's shock. 'You'll learn the entire story in due course of time,' he spoke in a gentle tone. 'The throne at Cheraidai lies vacant, awaiting a king. You must leave this village and go to Cheraidai to sit upon that throne.'

'No,' said the boy. 'I'll not leave Kalabari. I'll not leave my family.'

'They can come along,' said the buragohain. 'The royal palace has room enough for them.'

The boy looked at the villagers, the folks who had given him so much love, the youths with whom he had spent such a glorious childhood. But now they cringed before him, fear and awe in their eyes. Nothing would be the same again. He squared his shoulders.

'Right,' he said in a firm voice. 'To Cheraidai I must go. My family will come with me.'

'I'll need a few days to wind up my affairs in Kalabari,' the Brahmin said. Turning to the ministers, he asked, 'May I bring my Laxmi-Narayan Shaligram with me?'

'Of course you can,' said the bargohain. 'We follow our own religion, but do not look upon other religions with unfavourable eyes. We'll build a prayer room for your use.'

When the royal barge left Kalabari, every person in the village was on the riverbank to wave to the boy who would be known as Bamuni-Kuonr or the Brahmin Prince.

Everyone on the barge was sworn to keep the discovery of the new king a secret till he could be tutored in regal ways. On reaching Cheraidai, the boy was quickly conveyed to the palace in a screened palanquin; his rough, rural clothes were discarded for royal robes, while Deodhai and Bailung priests, aided by the chief nobles, taught him Ahom lore. They changed his name from Gopal to Sudang and taught him the Tai language because he had only learnt to speak in Assamese at Kalabari. Sudang proved to be the quickest of learners; regal mannerisms came naturally to him and he was swift and firm in taking decisions—within a month of his arrival at Cheraidai, the nobles could announce to the public that a king had been found and the throne at Cheraidai would no longer be empty.

The intelligent Brahmin, however, could sense that all was not well in the air of the palace. The Ahom priests were hostile towards him, but that was understandable and could be tolerated. What worried him was the fact that some members of the royal family secretly begrudged the elevation of Sudang to the Ahom throne. The boy, after all, was merely a country bumpkin who had to be taught the ways of royalty! The bipra, in one of those rare moments when he could speak to the prince, told him:

'Your Highness, you need to exercise extreme caution. You appear to have some enemies in the court.'

'You too have sensed that, have you?'

"Yes, Your Highness. This is what you must do. Stamp your authority upon the realm and everyone in it. First, you need to get away from Cheraidai. Build a new capital using your royal prerogative. Your officials, who are quite settled at Cheraidai, might not like the idea but you must hold your ground. Second, you must have a grand coronation to drive home to your subjects, as well as your enemies, that you are the king.'

'Thank you,' said Sudang with genuine gratitude. 'I feel uncomfortable not addressing you as father, but I suppose that I shall have to get used to it. But feel free to give me advice on every occasion, even if you have to keep your words away from eavesdroppers. Above all, please pray for my well-being before your shaligram as you used to do at Kalabari.'

Sudang told his principal ministers that he would like to speak to his subjects. The people gathered at the open ground beside the northern rampart of the palace, as Sudang, looking resplendent in his royal robes and ornaments, flanked by the nobles, stood upon the rampart and waved to his subjects. Then he began to speak in a resonant voice which carried even to those at the farthest end of the field. Women broke into tears as he related how unjustly his mother had been treated and made to suffer, how the good people of Kalabari, in particular the Brahmin family, had helped raise him up.

'I have given my Brahmin foster father rooms in the palace so that he can worship in his own manner and his own gods,' he announced. 'I have made his sons, my foster brothers, provincial officials as token of my gratitude.'

'Yes, yes!' the people responded. 'They deserve it!'

'This palace and this city hold sad memories for me,' the new king continued. 'Therefore, I have decided that I shall build another capital for our kingdom at Charguya. I realize that Cheraidai, established by our great ancestor Chowlung Sukapha, whose hallowed memory we shall always cherish, has been our capital for almost one hundred and forty years. It will always remain a special centre for business but the time has come for us Shans, who the people of this valley have given the name of Ahoms, to make changes and move on. We must expand our realm and extend our influence in this beautiful valley. Yes, I shall build a new capital at Charguya and revive the custom of ascending the singorighar to be crowned king as did our ancestors at Mungmau. Are you with me, my people?'

'Yes, yes!' cried the throng, obviously impressed by the confidence of their new king.

The new capital at Charguya on the bank of the Dihing River, patterned on Cheraidai, was built in record time. Thousands of men were conscripted to construct the wood, bamboo and cane structures needed to house the royal entourage, and the nobles and numerous officials. A spacious and separate complex was made for the priests as well as for the safekeeping of the Somdeo. A small complex, along with a prayer room, was constructed to house the Brahman and his wife. Most of the traders and citizens of Cheraidai chose to stay back in the former capital, so Charguya had the look of an administrative township when Prince Sudang shifted there to be crowned the king.

The day and time had been chosen by the royal head priest. Three chang-type houses, made entirely of the wood and leaves from the singori tree, had been constructed. The word 'singori' was derived from the Tai word 'cheng', which meant god, and 'ri' meant abode or temple. Thus, a singorighar was a temple of god, the concept being taken from Shan traditions and scriptures, and coronation in a singorighar was in accordance with Shan customs. The two lesser structures were called paatghar and holonghar. Since the singori tree was considered sacred, the Ahoms never made residential or other buildings out of the wood of this particular tree.

Prior to the new king ascending the singorighar, the priests had to perform another important ritual—this was to ensure the formal release of the spirit of the previous king from the throne before a new monarch could sit upon it. For this the golden throne upon which King Tyaokhampthi used to sit had been transported from Cheraidai and placed in a room in the Charguya royal palace. The Deodhai head priest made a petty palace official sit on the throne and, using him as a medium, summoned through incantations the 'deo' or spirit of Tyaokhampthi. A strange transformation occurred in the man; his voice assumed a regal timbre as he, in sepulchral tones, made a brief prediction about the new king's future: it would be propitious, the voice said. Then Prince Sudang, under instructions from the priest, touched the officer's feet and bid farewell to the spirit of Tyaokhampthi. Even as the priests muttered incantations, the petty officer, whose eyes had been closed, now opened them as though waking from a trance and immediately got down from the throne. He was rewarded with a basket of gold and silver nuggets and the throne was carried ceremonially to the singorighar.

The very next day, Prince Sudang rode on an elephant to Cheraidai, bearing the Somdeo with him. At the maidams of Sukapha and the kings who followed the founder of the Ahom dynasty, the prince paid homage to his forefathers. He offered prayers to the Supreme God Lengdon by worshipping the Somdeo, and performing Saipha, Ompha and Sompha pujas. Then he rode back to his new capital where arrangements for the coronation had been completed. People thronged in huge numbers to watch the crowning of the new monarch; a special enclosure had been built for subordinate kings and chieftains of tributary states, owing allegiance to the Ahom monarchy; they sat within it in pomp and finery, bearing costly gifts. The nobles and important officers and their families too had separate enclosures. There was a great deal of noise and bustle; the atmosphere was of a carnival. A huge roar went up as the young prince rode upon his elephant to the coronation venue.

First, under instruction from the priests, he ascended the paatghar wearing the Somdeo hung over his chest. He was divested of his outer raiment, turmeric paste was rubbed upon his body and he was bathed with holy water even as the Ahom priests continued to utter incantations. Had he been married, the queen too would have had to undergo the coronation rituals but, of course, this was not the case with Sudang. The king walked to the holonghar and ascended the steps to the upper chamber where he was ritualistically bathed once again by the priests. However, on this occasion a man and a variety of wild animals in cages had been placed beneath the floor of the chang-house and the water made to fall upon them. The animals were taken to the jungles and released. The man was gifted a casket full of gold and jewels and exiled from the kingdom. This part of the ritual was called neucha niya. Having been bathed and dried, the prince was dressed in the finest clothes the realm could produce and adorned with unmatched jewellery.

Next came the grisliest part of the coronation. At the bottom of the steps of the holonghar, a man, heavily manacled and with two soldiers guarding him, stood with bowed head. As the prince descended, another soldier marched up, saluted, and handed him a sharp-edged, gleaming hengdang. A collective gasp arose from the watching congregation when Sudang, with one powerful swing of the sword, cut off the man's head. So clean had been the blow that not a drop of blood fell upon the prince's clothing.

Finally, the prince ascended the singorighar, which was wide open in front so that the multitude could see the happenings inside. Nine gilded steps led to the golden throne which was encrusted with precious jewels and had gold-and-silver-plated lion heads as its feet. The resplendent throne had soft silken cushions and was sheltered at the top by a large chandratap. The bargohain and buragohain came up from their seats amongst the audience and stood in a deep bow on either side of the lowest step. Placing his hands on the heads of his principal ministers, Sudang urged them to climb up the first step, a symbolic gesture to show how he depended on them for support to rule the kingdom. They straightened, climbed up a step and stood with folded hands. He climbed the next few steps on his own and, to the roar of the crowd and ululations from the women, seated himself upon the throne.

The priests continued to sprinkle holy water upon him while two maidens standing behind the throne waved fans made from the feathers of exotic birds. The chief priest wrote upon a bark parchment with golden paint the name the prince would be invested with after the coronation: King Sudangpha. The roar of the crowd grew deafening as the bargohain made this announcement to the subjects and the buragohain ceremonially placed the silk-and-diamond crown upon the prince's head. One by one the tributary kings and chiefs of the Ahom kingdom, its nobles and officers came up to prostrate themselves before His Majesty, solemnly pledged their continued loyalty and then offered the gifts they had brought along, which were immediately carted off by waiting slaves.

Seated upon the throne, wearing the royal crown with the Somdeo slung across his chest, waving to his vassals and officers in acknowledgement, the lad from Kalabari looked every inch a king!

THE NARRATOR

'That, my people, is the strange tale of King Sudangpha. Sometimes truth can be stranger than fiction, isn't it? Because he was born and brought up by a Brahmin, he is known in Ahom history as Bamuni-Kuonr or the Brahmin Prince.'

The bonfire burned brightly, continuing to ward off the winter mist. The faces of the audience, upturned towards the Narrator, continued to remain enthralled.

'Sudangpha reigned for but a decade,' the compelling voice, resonant and tireless, continued to speak. 'He ascended the throne in 1397 and died in 1407. Yet his reign was eventful and in many ways one of the most important in Ahom history. For one thing, it was the first time that the Hinduism, which in those days was the predominant religion outside the Ahom realm, penetrated into it right at the very top. The Brahmin foster father was an important advisor, while Hindu rituals, including worship of the Laxmi-Narayan Shaligram in addition to the Shan idol Somdeo, began to be performed at the royal palace. So pervasive and dominant was Hinduism becoming amongst the common people as well that, in course of time, it wielded greater influence upon the royal house than the religion of the Ahoms themselves, resulting in the lessening of importance of the Deodhai and Bailung priests. Later the Hindu god Indra supplanted Lengdon in Ahom estimate and Ahom kings began to adopt Hindu names in addition to the Shan titles.

'Sudangpha's reign also marked a signal moment when the Ahoms stepped out of the shadows of their founder Sukapha, changed the capital and began an aggressive campaign of action against neighbours. For instance, the chiefs in the Tipam area had become restive and thought that, because the new king was so young and inexperienced, he would fail to retain Ahom influence over the Tipamia tribes. Sudangpha feigned ignorance of their designs to rebel, invited them to a kheddah or elephant-trapping operation and, during the feasting and merriment that followed a successful operation, killed the entire group of Tipam chiefs and put their heads in a heap for display.

'You might feel that this was barbaric—but those, my people, were different times! Take the practice of beheading a man during the coronation ceremony, for example. That was to show that the person who would be gracing the Ahom throne had the strength and heart to slay a man in cold blood. Of course, only a criminal of the worst kind was chosen to be the one to be beheaded, but that doesn't rob the action of its barbarity. Later, in a more enlightened era, the Ahom king Rudrasingha changed this custom to the ritualistic beheading of a buffalo instead of a man during the coronation ceremony.

'The reign of Sudangpha does not lack for its share of other interesting tales! Having instilled terror into the Tipamia tribes by his savagery, he next made an essay at conciliation by marrying the daughter of a Tipamia chief named Khuntai. But the new queen had a secret paramour called Tai Sulai, who was discovered to be continuing the liaison even after she was married to Sudangpha. When the liaison was exposed, Tai Sulai, aware of the consequences, fled to Mungkang and asked its king, Surumpha, to shelter him. This led to a battle between the armies of the two kings, with Sudangpha leading his own army and even being injured in the battle. The triumphant Ahom army pursued Surumpha's forces right up to Daikaorang or the place where nine mountains met. Surumpha pleaded for an end to the hostilities and a treaty between the bargohains of the two armies was signed at Nongnyang Lake, at the very spot through which Sukapha had passed! By this formal treaty of 1401, Daikaorang was fixed as the boundary of the two kingdoms. The statues of the bargohains were carved on the rocks of the mountain and a cock was killed to consecrate the vows of amity. As I had earlier told you, from then onwards the name Daikaorang changed to the Patkai Mountains.

'Sudangpha rekindled the martial spirit amongst the group of Shans whom the world now called the Ahoms—the rest of his reign, till he died in 1407, being spent subjugating the tribes of Tipam, Khamjang, Aiton and so on, reasserting Ahom hegemony over them. However, the kings who immediately followed him appear to have harboured no expansionist ambitions. The reigns of his son, Sujangpha, between 1407 and 1422, and of his grandson Suphakpha, between 1422 and 1439, were marked by no conflict with neighbours. However, during the reign of Susenpha—ruling from 1439 to 1488 for a period of forty-nine years, one of the longest-serving Ahom kings—trouble brewed with some of the Naga tribes. These hostilities intensified during the reign of Susenpha's son Suhenpha, when open war broke out between the Ahoms and Tangsu Nagas. The Nagas were fierce warriors and adept at launching sudden and unexpected ambush on their enemies; in fact, in the initial stages it was they who achieved success, defeating the Ahom soldiers sent against them, capturing the bargohain and cutting off his head.

'Thus, for a while, a period of darkness and defeat settled over the Ahom kingdom. In 1490, conflict commenced with the Kachari tribe, with the Ahom army suffering heavy losses and Suhenpha having to sue for peace. He had to send an Ahom princess to the Kachari king along with a sizeable dowry which included two elephants and twelve female slaves. This too was a time when conspiracy in the palace was rife and the nobles forsook their tradition of loyalty to king and country. Suhenpha himself was murdered in 1493 by some palace workers, allegedly being instigated by his buragohain.

'His enraged son Supimpha, who ascended to the throne, tried to take action against the buragohain, resulting in open revolt by the latter. Though the matter was apparently resolved, actually it was not, and it is suspected that Supimpha was murdered by the nobles in 1497 after just four years on the throne. One interesting incident took place during Supimpha's short rule. One of his queens was heard by the king praising the handsomeness of a Naga chief who had come to pay tribute, even though she was carrying the king's child at that time. So angry was Supimpha that he exiled her to the village of that Naga chief. I shall not reveal to you what happened to the son she gave birth to in the Naga village ... have to keep you in suspense every now and again, don't I?

'But every dark cloud has a silver lining. You must bear in mind that almost two-and-a-half centuries had elapsed since Sukapha first laid the foundations of the Ahom kingdom in the land they called Mungdunsukham and built his capital at Cheraidai. The fertility of the soil and the languorous air had made the once fierce Shan warriors complacent and lazy. Decadence had set in. It required an individual of extraordinary character and competence to jolt his people out of their stupor and reinvigorate them. Such a man of the moment was Suhungmung, the son of Supimpha, who ascended the throne at Charguya in 1497 after his father's death ...'

Tiger of a Famous Country

~⌒

ONCE AGAIN, A NEW AHOM MONARCH ASCENDED THE singorighar and was crowned the king. As so many times before, a paatghar and a holonghar had been built; the new king, resplendent in royal robes, had ascended these one by one. As so many times before, he had decapitated a man with his hengdang prior to climbing the steps of the singorighar. However, there was a difference to this coronation. Earlier it had been Ahom priests who had guided the new monarch through the entire ceremony. But, on this occasion, a Brahmin was present along with the Deodhai priest in each of the stages—in fact, two sets of rituals were being observed simultaneously, the traditional Ahom ceremony as well as a Brahmin one, testifying to the inroads made by the Hindu religion into the Ahom way of life since the days of Sudangpha.

Tall, well-built and imposing, the king sat regally, back erect, legs spread, hands resting upon the arms of the golden throne. The Somdeo hung by a golden chain over his chest, but the vermillion marks upon his forehead had been impressed by the Brahmin priest. The open ground before the singorighar was crowded with the realm's subjects; a phalanx of soldiers kept them apart from the august gathering seated in the very front—the buragohain and bargohain, known collectively as the patra-mantris, and their families, high-ranking nobles and officials

90

with their families, and tributary rajas and tribal chieftains with their minions bearing gifts.

The new king's queens and children sat in the very first row. His four sons, Sukleng, Sureng, Sukhreng and Suting, were amongst them. Curiously enough, a handsome youth in Naga tribal dress sat with the queens and princes. The courtiers and others not in the know threw curious glances at this youth. He was none other than Konseng, whose mother, Supimpha, had been sent to the Naga village as punishment. So fair and farsighted was the new king that, as soon as his father was dead, he had brought his stepbrother Konseng back to the palace on this coronation day and embraced him within the fold of his family.

After the Deodhai head priest and the Brahmin priest signalled the end of the religious rituals, the two patra-mantris stood up and solemnly approached the holy men. The Deodhai priest had written the name of the new king in golden letters upon a piece of bark and this he handed to the buragohain. Similarly, the Brahmin priest wrote out a name on a piece of bark and handed it over to the bargohain. The two patra-mantris next approached the monarch and consulted with him. The buragohain raised his right hand and the boisterous crowd slowly subsided into silence.

'Good people, our lord the king has decided to take on the name of Suhungmung, or Tiger from a Famous Country. Long live Suhungmung, our new king!'

An enormous clamour arose from the enthusiastic crowd, wishing the new king a long and prosperous reign. Next, the bargohain raised his right hand and called out for silence.

'Since our lord the king has also adopted Hinduism which had been the religion of this land before our people came here. He has also decided to take on the Hindu name Swarganarayana or King of Heaven. He, let me remind you, is the first of our kings to do so. Befitting this change, no longer will our lord the king be referred to as Chaopha. From now on our monarchs will be addressed as Swargadeo, or God of Heaven. Long live Swargadeo Swarganarayana, our new king.'

For a few moments this new development was greeted with stunned silence on the part of the gathering, but soon those at the front, recovering quickly from their surprise, stood up and raised cheers for Swargadeo Swarganarayana. The crowd at the back, thereupon, followed suit and cheered. The king next stood up to address the gathering.

'Honoured patra-mantris, dangarias, officers and their families, our guest rajas and chieftains, and, above all, my people! I will not beat about the bush. We Shans, whom our great ancestor Chaolung Sukapha had led to this land and whose descendents are now called Ahom by the entire world, have lost our good name. As our written records will show, our royal house is riven by strife, jealousy, greed for power in the recent decades. My own father, Chao Supimpha, was treacherously slain by internal enemies. Our dangarias have grown arrogant, our officers undisciplined. But, above all, our people have become indolent and lost the warrior blood in our veins.

'The time has come to redeem our race and that will be my main objective. Seeing our weakened status, our enemies, the Nagas to our south, the Chutiyas to our east, and the Kacharis, Barbhuyans and Kamatas to our west, have begun eyeing our kingdom like tigers a herd of deer. The time has come to show them that we, instead, are the tigers and I, indeed, am a tiger of a famous land! As Swargadeo Suhungmung, it will be my sworn duty to restore the glory of the kingdom that Chaolung Sukapha had established. I shall ruthlessly quell any challenge to my authority; let me promise you that.

'The key to enhancing the glory of our kingdom is discipline. Also, reintroducing the systematic manner of governance our Shan ancestors were known for. At the same time, I, as your monarch, need to know of your problems and requirements. This I propose to do in two ways. Firstly, after due preparation, we shall embark on a census of the people and take stock of their economic condition. With that knowledge, we shall be in a position to help the needy and ensure that every citizen enjoys the fruits of progress of the kingdom.

'Secondly, I shall make myself and my officers accessible to the common multitude. You, my people, can petition me through my officers for any hardship you are facing or any injustice you have suffered. As for good and effective governance, it is common knowledge that power has been for too long been concentrated in a couple of hands. As you are all aware, my father himself had to try and discipline one of the patra-mantris and was treacherously slain. I shall not allow such a thing to happen during my kingship. For this I shall introduce decentralization of power, so that officers at every level of our governing hierarchy have both power as well as responsibility.

'As for the patra-mantris, I propose to create an additional post equivalent in the power wielded by the bargohain and buragohain. This post shall be designated as barpatragohain. My stepbrother, Konseng, who grew up in a Naga village, I have brought back. I am happy to announce that he will be the first barpatragohain and will be invested with the authority the post carries.' The youth named Konseng stood up, bowed to the king, swivelled round and bowed to the audience. While cheers broke out at this gesture, the faces of the bargohain and buragohain hardened.

'Progress, my people, implies keeping an eye on the past, yet also making a break from it and taking a new direction. As a symbolic gesture I have decided to build a new capital at Bagata on the bank of the Dihing River. Yes, yes, I realize the Dihing can be treacherous during the rains, overflowing its banks and causing floods. But, my people, we will work together to erect embankments upon this river and raise palaces and houses and crops and cattle on the fertile soil that lies by its side.

'As another symbolic break with the past, I am decreeing that from henceforth our priests and writers of buranjis shall discard the lakli system, whereby we count the taosinga or cycle of time as every sixty laklis or years. Instead, we shall adopt the Sak calendar of the Hindus, whereby each cycle is completed every 100 years. In the course of my rule, I shall bring in more such reforms to our administrative and customary systems. Do I have your support for this, my people?'

In truth, few amongst the multitude understood the implications of discarding the Lakli system, but blind obedience to the ruler made it mandatory that they express their support as vocally as possible. The new king appeared pleased with the response.

'Yes, my people, with your support and under the guidance of my patra-mantris and me, we shall restore the Ahom kingdom to its former glory. Be assured that I shall amply reward those who help me in my mission and come down in wrath like Lengdon's bolt of lightning upon those who dare oppose me.'

Swargadeo Suhungmung, who had taken on the additional title of Swarganarayan, sat upon a cushioned wooden throne within the intimacy of a small hall in the royal palace at Charguya. The room contained additional wooden chairs, but these were smaller and lower than the one upon which the king sat, so that those who occupied them had to look up when they addressed him. That very afternoon, following the morning's coronation ceremony, two of these chairs were occupied by the bargohain and the buragohain, expressions of displeasure writ large upon their faces.

'We are not pleased,' Khunlungkhampeng Buragohain spoke up, looking the king straight in the eye. 'You did not deem it necessary to consult your patra-mantris before creating the new post of barpatragohain, with powers that are equivalent to the bargohain's and mine.'

Chaophrachengmung Bargohain nodded in agreement. 'You must bear in mind, Your Majesty,' he said, 'that the Shan, now Ahom, tradition has provision for only two patra-mantris. Even the king must stick to tradition. Acting as one pleases on the spur of a moment is sure prescription for anarchy.'

'I am Swargadeo Swarganarayan, of the lineage of Indra the God of Heaven, descendent of Chaolung Sukapha, the founder of the Ahom race.' The king's voice was not raised; yet, though flat and even, the words were pregnant with authority. 'I am invested with the power to change our administrative structure to keep up with the changing times.'

'That's a matter for debate,' the buragohain persisted. 'Also, you need to be practical. One of your forbears, Chaopha Subinpha, had divided the Ahom realm administratively into two halves, investing me with the authority to govern the upper half, and the bargohain the lower half. At the same time, the subjects of the realm were apportioned equally between me and the bargohain. We're not willing to share with the new patra-mantri an inch of the kingdom nor a single subject. So, what will you apportion to the barpatragohain, may I ask?'

The king's voice remained calm, but the undertones of menace were palpable. 'What had been given can be taken back, Buragohain dangoriya! Yet I'll not do that … I'll not take an inch of the land that you both govern on my behalf, nor any of the subjects you've been allotted. For the time being, I shall bestow upon the new minister the group of Moran, Chutiya and Barahi people who in recent years have become a part of our own race and who yet remain unallotted. Also, bear in mind that the realm that we possess at this moment will expand beyond your wildest dream by the time I join my forebears in Heaven. You can rest assured that the additional land that we shall conquer will not be bestowed upon you!'

The two patra-mantris were rendered mute by the unmistakable threat in the king's voice. Suhungmung struck a small gong by his side and an attendant entered. 'Summon Konseng to my presence,' the king said shortly. 'Also, summon the recorder of court affairs.'

The handsome youth in Naga attire who had attracted such curiosity during the coronation ceremony entered and bowed before the king. The court recorder, a Brahmin, entered silently after him and, flitting to a spot behind the monarch, seated himself on a mat upon the floor, ready to record all that would be pronounced by Swargadeo Suhungmung.

'Come, brother,' the king, without rising, said, the obvious affection rubbing away the cutting edge of menace from his voice. 'Be seated. Henceforth, you'll be a part of our family and advise us in your new role as barpatragohain, which is equivalent to the Shan title of chaosenglung, or god-holy-great. The buragohain and bargohain completely approve of this arrangement. Also, henceforth you will bear the Ahom name of Tyaosungrin.'

Suhungmung smiled sardonically and turned towards the other two ministers. 'You do approve of this arrangement, don't you, Khunlungkhampeng and Chaophrachengmung dangoriyas?'

The two ministers nodded, but their sullen faces betrayed their true feelings.

As Kongsen seated himself, the king once more struck the gong and summoned the attendant. 'My four sons may join us now,' he ordered.

Four young men strode into the chamber and prostrated themselves before Suhungmung. From their demeanour, as also that of the king, it could hardly be made out that they were father and sons. Rather, their formal behaviour made them appear to be a king and his vassals.

'Come, Suklen, Sureng, Sukhreng and Suting, take your places in the room. I'm allotting certain parts of my kingdom to each of you. Though you'll be invested with the title of raja of specific areas, you'll be subject to my and the ministers' authority. Patra-mantris, bear witness to the fact that I give to my eldest son Suklen the area around the new capital Bakata on the bank of the Dihing River. Members of my family who will shift with him will henceforth be known as the Dihingiya phaid. Similarly, I will allot areas around Charing to Sureng, around Tipam to Sukhreng and that around Tungkhung to Suting. They'll head the Charingiya, Tipamiya and Tungkhungia phaids respectively.'

The four sons rose, bowed with utmost gravity and seated themselves. 'To which phaid will Your Majesty belong?' the bargohain asked.

'I'll belong to the Dihingiya phaid. Let it be recorded that in future it is from Suklen's progeny that an Ahom king must first be chosen. Only if none from the Dihingiya phaid is deemed fit to reign may a king from another phaid be selected.'

Everyone in the room nodded in acquiescence. The court recorder scribbled furiously with a quill dipped in ink upon a bark sheet of the sanchi plant, scripting the king's wishes for posterity.

The king continued: 'I'd hinted during my coronation that my main mission in life would be to rejuvenate the Ahom race and take them towards greater glory. Our tiny kingdom can no longer contain our burgeoning populace. To our east and west lie relatively unpopulated areas, but outside our control. The Chutiya people occupy the swathe of land to our east. We shall seize any opportunity offered by their king to wage war against them and incorporate their land into our kingdom. Next will be the turn of the Kacharis to our west on the south bank of the Luit, and the Barabhuyans upon the north bank. It would, of course, be unwise to on take all of them simultaneously. We shall proceed against each of our adversaries turn by turn. Our immediate concern would be the Aitoniya Nagas who have of late become increasingly defiant. Buragohain and Bargohain dangoriyas, prepare yourself to lead our forces against the Nagas and subjugate them.'

'What about our new barpatragohain?' the buragohain asked, not hesitating to put sarcasm into his words. 'Will he not be participating in this skirmish? Or have you taken him in merely as a decorative piece?'

Swargadeo Suhungmung kept his rising temper under tight leash. 'You need not worry on that account,' he replied suavely. 'I'm saving him for far greater things!'

The two paiks, Lukhring and Kedung, were seated around a small fire on the bank of the Dihing River, relaxing after a day's hard manual labour. They were from the same village and friends from childhood. They puffed upon a lighted clay chillum which contained a tiny amount of opium. This they passed to each other in turn.

'Life has become far more vigorous since the Dihingiya raja ascended the throne at Charguya,' Lukhring observed.

'You're telling me!' Kedung said, nodding his head in agreement. 'Half of the men from our village have been conscripted for public duty. Not that our womenfolk and children have been spared either. We've had to leave the village our forebears had lived in for many laklis, and shift bag and baggage to this spot on the banks of the river Dihing.'

This was true enough. King Suhungmung had by royal decree relocated quite a few Ahom villages to lands close to the new capital at Bagata. Since the river Dihing, which flowed close by, was prone to flooding during the rainy season, many able-bodied men from the relocated villages had been conscripted to build embankments to contain the floods expected in a few months' time. For the past fortnight, Lukhring and Kedung, summoned for embankment-building duty, had been living in makeshift cane, bamboo and thatch hutments erected close to the riverbank, digging and carting earth from a distance and heaping it upon the riverbank to raise it. Similarly, men were working on the opposite bank to create high embankments as a defence against flooding. This, however, had created a problem. Wetland rice cultivation was rendered easier in the fertile land created by the alluvial deposits left behind by the floods; now the farmers would have to dig artificial ponds and reservoirs, and narrow ditches to convey water for irrigating their paddy fields.

Their lives, after King Suhungmung ascended the Ahom throne, had indeed become hectic. First had come the order for the shifting of their village to Bagata; no sooner had they, along with fellow villagers, finished building cottages and clearing jungle land for cultivation, and settled down to their lives as farmers in that new place, a herald accompanied by soldiers had come to their village to conscript workers for the embankments as also for military duty. Those chosen for the army were imparted a brief stint of military training before being sent back to their families to resume their farming and other professional activities. Whenever required, they would be summoned for military duty—thus, just like in the time of his forefathers, the Ahom ruler had a large body of able-bodied men which could be converted into a relatively trained army in a matter of days. The realm, therefore, did not need to retain a full-fledged army and was thus spared the heavy expenditure this would have involved. However, the administration at Charguya was careful in their selection: only one individual from each family of paiks was required to serve the realm when required; thus it was ensured that agriculture, the main occupation of the populace, did not suffer. Also, professionals such as kumars and bezes were never conscripted for military duty.

'It's our bad luck that we've been chosen for civil work duty,' Kedung continued. 'I'd rather fight for our swargadeo than dig earth like a common slave!'

'Ah!' retorted Lukhring. 'You'll have to admit that it's not a bad system. The king is the possessor of all the land of the realm. Logically, when he grants us land, we're required to pay for being allowed to use it for farming. I'm told in other realms they have to pay in kind, or cattle. But here all we have to do is serve our raja for a while in some capacity or the other. Not a bad system, oh yes, not bad at all!'

'Be that as it may,' grumbled his companion, taking a puff on the chillum and passing it back. 'I'd still rather be in the army fighting on behalf of the Dihingiya raja than digging trenches.'

'And risk life and limb? No, friend, I myself am content in doing what I'm doing! Happy that here there is less chance of me making my wife a widow and my children fatherless. Many of our fellow villagers are at this very moment fighting against the Aitoniya Nagas, who have once again risen up in rebellion. I've heard that the Nagas have been suppressed, though at a great cost to our people—many were injured or killed. There are rumours that one of the patra-mantris who led the war against the Aitoniya Nagas has been wounded. It's only a rumour, mind you!'

'Yes, I've heard of it too. They say the Naga chief gifted one of his daughters to our Dihingiya raja as a token of servitude. Also, a few elephants. He has also agreed to pay an annual tribute. You know what's great about all this? Our Dihingiya raja and patra-mantris are at the forefront of every skirmish, as has been our Ahom tradition. They don't sit on their thrones and let underlings and paiks do their fighting for them! His daughter, eh? Pity it's always the raja and not his foot soldiers who get the spoils of war!'

'Don't let your wife hear you speak like that, ha, ha!'

'Ha, ha! But seriously, these are exciting times. The Dihingiya raja's army has also crossed the Luit into Habung territory and taken possession of that region. Only yesterday some passing boatmen brought news that Panbari has been occupied and a town is being built at Haldhibari.'

'So, more lives and limbs at risk, eh? Our Dihingiya raja has certainly woken up the kingdom! The news is that training camps have been set up all over the realm and hundreds of young men are being trained. Our forges are kept busy night and day, making swords and spears. River banks are crammed with the hulls of war boats being built.'

'Yes, great things are in the offing while we dig dirt!'

Lukhring spat in the ground to ward off any ill luck Kedung's words may have brought and they continued to puff at the chillum.

'You must admit,' he observed, 'it's not all war with the Dihingiya raja—he's concerned with the welfare of his subjects too. Just after he ascended the singorighar at Charguya, he undertook a family-to-family survey of his subjects, remember? The officers he sent for the survey took note of the economic condition of the people. But not merely for the record. If you recall, he gave additional land grants to those having less, as also other forms of assistance. How many kings have bothered to show such concern for the welfare of their subjects, I ask you?'

'Yes, he's a great man, the lord of our realm, I concede,' said Kedung. 'But do you notice Lukhring that it's only us village folk who refer to our king as the Dihingiya raja. When his minions come to our village, they refer to him as Swargadeo Suhungmung, also known as Swarganarayan.'

'Big words, Kedung ... those are big words that get twisted on our common tongues! He might be the Lord of Heaven for all those fine folks at Charguya, but since he has sought to shift his capital to Bagata on the bank of the Dihing River, he'll always be the Dihingiya raja to us, his humble but loyal subjects.'

The king of the Chutiya tribe, Jongmung, along with his prime minister Kachitara, was in conference with a spy in one of the rooms of his palace in the capital town of Sadiya.

The Chutiyas, a tribe from southwestern China, had migrated to the valley far earlier than the Ahoms, and set up their kingdom in its upper part, upon the area east of the river Subansiri on the north bank of the Luit and the south bank of the river Disang. The Chutiya kings had adopted Brahmanical Hinduism and become adherents of the Sakta sect of that religion. Thus, Jongmung was also known by the name of Dhirnarayan or Chandranarayan given to him by his Brahmin priests to impart divine sanction to his kingship. Dhirnarayan was also called Nitipal by a section of the Chutiya populace. Naturally, the chief Brahmin priest, who was also the chief advisor to the king, was present as Jongmung and Kachitara listened to the spy.

'It's clear that the Ahoms are preparing for war, Your Majesty,' the elderly spy spoke urgently. 'I've been in your service as a spy for two decades now ... in fact, have lived amongst them and can pass myself as an Ahom ... but never have I seen war preparations on so large a scale. Thousands of young men are being trained ... a huge fleet of boats is being built ... something big is in the offing, Your Majesty!'

Jongung knew this spy well and trusted him fully. 'The question is why,' he mused aloud. 'For all we know it may be defensive preparations. Traders who have come by the Luit route on their way to China have brought news of attacks by armies from distant lands that lie far to the west. These people, the Mussulmans, belong to a different faith. It is possible that the Ahoms fear an attack from the west and thus are gearing themselves for battle.'

'Yet we must not discount the possibility we might be the target,' Prime Minister Kachitara cautioned.

'I'm not blind, am I, Kachitara, nor a fool? Yet I find it difficult to concede that the Ahoms might actually attack us after all these years of peace. Oh yes, we've had our occasional differences ... for instance, long, long back their Chaopha Sutupha was accidentally gored by a runaway bull while a guest of our king, inducing his son Tyaokhamphti to launch a campaign against us. But, on the whole, we've learned to coexist side by side for over two centuries. Would the Ahoms now dare disturb this harmony?'

'There's a strong possibility they might do so,' said the spy. 'I'd already told you that when the Dihingiya raja ascended the singorighar some years ago, he had talked of showing us Chutiyas who the real tigers were.'

'That may have been mere hyperbole—words spoken during a ceremonial occasion to cement his place in the hearts of the rabble.' Jongmung remained unconvinced.

'Forgive me, Your Majesty,' the Brahmin advisor interjected. 'But I too am convinced that we're the target of that Ahom upstart who has had the impertinence to take on the name of Swarganarayan. I suspect that he's after the treasure gifted to our race by no less a person than Lord Kubera, the treasure-keeper to the gods. You need to keep in mind that the existence of this treasure is now known in all corners of the world.'

Legend had it that King Birpal, the founder of the Chutiya dynasty, had a wife named Rupavali, who had been a devout worshipper of Lord Kubera. In return, the Hindu god of wealth had gifted her with certain items made of gold, including a sceptre, shield, sword, elephant, umbrella and cat. It was said that as long as the Chutiyas could retain 'Kubera's treasure', they would remain invincible.

At the mention of the treasure gifted by Kubera, a frown of indecision appeared on Jongmung's face. The Brahmin advisor pressed home his point.

'The wise man doesn't wait stoically for adversity to strike,' he said. 'He takes steps to ward off misfortune. In my humble opinion, sire, we Chutiyas must strike at the Ahoms first. Take advantage of a surprise assault—destroy their boats and army.'

'That would be the best course of action,' Kachitara advised, convinced by the Brahmin's words.

'All right, then,' said Jongmung. 'The destiny of the Chutiya race is linked to Kubera's treasure. We must nip in the bud any attempt by anyone to seize our treasure. Kachitara, prepare our forces. We must attack the Ahoms when they least expect it.'

With the new capital at Bagata not yet ready, and the embankments on the river Dihing yet to be completed, Suhungmung was at Charguya when news of the Chutiya attack reached him. Messengers sent by Ahom military officers at border outposts had rushed to the royal palace to inform the king that a sizeable force under Jongmung, his prime minister Kachitara and the Chutiya chief's eldest son was on its way towards Dikhowmukh, the point where the river Dikhow met the Luit. The force comprised a flotilla of war boats, as well as a land army, which had marched down the south bank of the Luit. The Chutiya plan, according to the messages, was to travel up the Dikhow and strike at the very heart of the Ahom territory.

The months of preparation now bore fruit for the Ahoms. War boats raced down the Dikhow under the command of Khunlungkhampeng Buragohain, while a quickly mobilized army of foot soldiers under Chaophrachengmung Bargohain marched across a land route to meet the advancing Chutiyas. Jongmung had clearly underestimated Ahom strength and preparation, as also their efficient system of spies and intelligence gathering, which totally neutralized any element of surprise his assault might have carried. The Ahom counterattack was overwhelming; many of Jongmung's war boats, which had proceeded up the Dikhow, were destroyed and many soldiers were slain—the Chutiyas were forced to beat a hasty retreat. Jongmung now built temporary fortifications first at Dikhowmukh, the mouth of the Dikhow, and next at the mouth of the Dihing and tried to put up a stand—but the Ahom forces dislodged him from both the spots and forced him to flee up the Luit. The Chutiya land army too was routed close to Dikhowmukh and had to retreat. The Ahom monarch, informed of the defeat handed out to his adversary, himself came to the battlefront and took possession of Chutiya territory around Mungkhrang and Namdang, erecting small townships at both the spots. He placed a garrison at the Mungkhrang fort under a trusted officer and, since the rains were approaching, suspended the campaign against the aggressor. This was a deliberate strategy; he would next proceed against the Chutiyas only on his own terms and when fully prepared.

But the Chutiyas appeared to be bent on self-destruction. Smarting under the previous defeat, Jongmung, some years later, launched yet another surprise attack, but this time to regain lost territory around Mungkhrang. The Ahom fort there was the target. The soldiers there were outnumbered; their commanding officer was killed and they had to abandon the fort and retreat. Pressing home their assault, the Chutiyas in the space of months, ousted the Ahoms from what had earlier been Chutiya territory. However, by now cognizant of the martial superiority of the Ahoms on their home ground, Jongmung wisely chose to remain content with regaining his territory and refrained from further attacks against the Ahoms.

Suhungmung, on the other hand, was not willing to sit idly. He conferred with his patra-mantris and eldest son Suklen, and devised a strategy to defeat the Chutiyas once and for all, and establish Ahom dominance over them. The Chutiyas within their own realm were familiar with the lie of the land, thereby giving them an advantage. Thus, the most important thing to do was to send spies into their country to scout the terrain and acquire as much knowledge as possible, particularly on defensive positions of the enemy. Such a strategy took time but finally the campaign was ready and Suhungmung's land and river forces moved against the Chutiyas. It was a swift and lethal strike; the Chutiyas were first defeated at the point where the river Sessa met the Luit and the land ceded in the earlier strike by them was wrested back. A fort was erected at Tiphaomukh where the Ahom forces took a temporary breather.

The Chutiya king, Jongmung, fearful that the Ahoms were in such close proximity that his capital Sadiya itself was under threat, launched an almost desperate attack on the Tiphaomukh fortress. Coincidentally, Suhungmung, who had been none too happy at the tardy progress the campaign against the Chutiyas was making and now wanted to lead it himself, arrived at the fort on the very same day the enemy laid siege to it. The Ahom garrison, reinforced by the force Suhungmung had brought, utterly routed the Chutiyas, inflicting defeat after defeat upon them at various spots while they were in retreat, finally forcing them back into the Chutiya capital at Sadiya.

A wide river was the only obstacle between Suhungmung and Sadiya. The Ahom king did not know its name, but then, this was alien territory, and there were many things he did not know of this place. All he knew was that ramparts had been erected on the other side; he could see the movement of the enemy at a distance. The western bank of the river was cluttered with his own war boats; hundreds of tents made of animal hide had sprung up on this side of the river. With cooking fires burning for miles on end, the assault force presented a fearful face at night.

Perhaps Jongmung was rendered afraid by the vastness of Suhungmung's army and disheartened by the repeated defeats he had suffered at its hand. Early next morning, as Suhungmung reclined upon an improvised divan in the royal tent, news was delivered to him that a boat had traversed the span of the river, bearing a crew of unarmed men led by one who claimed he was an emissary of the Chutiya king.

'Admit him to my presence,' Suhungmung ordered.

A swarthy, stocky individual entered the tent and prostrated himself full-length upon the ground at Suhungmung's feet. 'Rise,' the Ahom king commanded. 'Tell me the nature of your business.'

'I've been dispatched by my lord, King Jongmung, also known as Chandranarayan. His Majesty sues for peace and implores that you return to your own kingdom.'

'He does, does he? And what does your lord who presumes to call himself a descendent of the moon god, have to offer me if I were to accede to his request?'

'I carry what he has to offer in my boat, Your Majesty. A chest full of gold ornaments and shawls beautified with exotic embroidery. King Jongmung also pledges fealty to Your Majesty and promises to pay an annual tribute.'

Suhungmung emitted a scornful, mirthless laugh. 'A chest full of ornaments and shawls! Who does your lord, who presumes to be of celestial lineage, think I am? A bride being decked for a wedding? Take back your king's chest and fling it on his face. Note, these are what he must cede if he wants to save himself and his capital. I want that his chief queen be sent to me for my pleasure, as also ten elephants. Also, above all, I want the sceptre, umbrella and the rest of the golden stuff that comprises what you people call the treasure of Kubera. And remind the impostor who passes for your king that it was not Suhungmung who first sounded the battle cry.'

'I shall carry back your demand, Your Majesty ... and be back as soon as I am able with my lord Jongmung's reply.'

'Don't be too long,' Suhungmung said shortly. 'Patience is not one of my virtues!'

The emissary was back that very afternoon. 'King Jongmung, also known as Chandranarayan, throws himself at your mercy,' he told Suhungmung. 'He has agreed to send his chief queen to join your harem, and to gift you ten elephants along with their mahouts. But on no account can he part with Kubera's treasure. That is his family's heirloom, the loss of which will spell doom for the entire Chutiya people. He will, however, have replicas of the items made in gold by his goldsmiths and gift them to you. But to do this, he will require more time.'

Suhungmung was bubbling with inner laughter, though he did not allow this to be reflected upon his face, which remained stern and unforgiving. The treasure of Kubera had been only a pretext—he was well aware that the Chutiya king would never part with the heirloom. So, the continuation of the conflict was inevitable and the destruction of the Chutiyas as an independent race a fait accompli, which had been his real objective from the very beginning.

'That is unfortunate,' he said. 'Tell your king that Swargadeo Suhungmung, also known as Swarganarayan, will wreak vengeance on the Chutiyas and heap destruction upon them. No treasure of Kubera will be able to save your king and his subjects from such a fate!'

The fighting resumed from early next morning. While in retreat, the Chutiya army had been destroying communications infrastructure to impede the Ahom advance; expectedly, the river that now stood between Suhungmung's force and the Chutiya capital of Sadiya had no bridge. But the Ahoms were well prepared for such a contingency and had practised the drill numerous times. Boats, in pairs, were so manoeuvred as to be positioned prow to prow and then lashed with bamboo poles and coir ropes. The double row of boats gradually extended till it reached the opposite bank, and thus a bridge of boats was formed. Suhungmung's mighty army, weapons, equipment and all, clambered over the makeshift bridge and, when the last of them had crossed the river, the boats were unlashed and rowed to be moored upon the other side.

The ensuing fight was fierce. The Chutiyas knew that it was a do-or-die battle for them and fought with utmost courage and tenacity. But the Ahom force, spurred on by the presence of the king, his sons and the patra-mantris, was unstoppable. It sliced its way through all resistance, captured and sacked Sadiya, forcing Jongmung, Kachitara and what remained of the Chutiya army into the Kaitara hills. Pursued relentlessly, they had to cede their defensive positions there too and make another stand at Chandangiri hill where they had a fortification. This was strategically an advantageous structure; the rear of the fort was perched atop what seemed to be sheer, unassailable cliffs, thus there was little possibility of attack from that direction. The approach to the front of the fort, too, was steep; the Chutiyas had stockpiled large rocks within the fort; as the Ahom soldiers attempted to attack the fort from the front, they were effectively kept at bay by the Chutiyas who rolled down the heavy stones against them. A frontal attack appeared impractical and Suhungmung decided that a stealthy assault from the rear had to be attempted, no matter how precipitous the climb was.

For this hazardous enterprise, he chose a small, hand-picked group of men and, placing them under one of his most able and trusted junior officers, sent them up the cliff face. It was a bold move. The small band, by dint of holding on to creepers and hacking out hand and footholds on the sheer mountainside, performed the unimaginable—inch by inch, they climbed till they finally reached the top without being detected. Their rear exposed, the Chutiya defenders were taken completely by surprise; the fierce attack from the back was complemented by an equally fierce charge from the front; King Jongmung and his few remaining men were forced to flee their advantageous position to another fortress at Mathadang nearby. But there was no holding back the Ahom soldiers; the Chutiya king and his men had nowhere else to run and had to make their final stand. An arrow pierced King Jongmung in the heart; his eldest son who rushed forward to avenge his father's death was struck down. Chaophrachengmung Bargohain himself pursued Prime Minister Kachitara as the latter made a desperate attempt to flee, and cut off his head.

Scores of prisoners were taken, including members of the royal family. But Sati Sadhini, the principal queen of King Jongmung and a brave woman, rather than be captured and enslaved by the Ahoms, chose to inflict death upon herself by falling upon a sword.

The lineage of the Chutiya king was irrevocably ended; under no circumstances would Suhungmung appoint any of Jongmung's kinsmen as a titular chief of the Chutiyas, for this might lead to rebellions in the future. In order to thoroughly end the Chutiya realm and incorporate it as an integral component of the Ahom Empire, Suhungmung created a new post designated as the Sadiyakhowa Gohain to administer the area, investing upon Chaophrachengmung Bargohain this additional title as well as the responsibility it carried. To augment Ahom presence in the newly acquired region, their king also ordered the relocation of a number of families belonging to the Gharphaliya clan from Garhgaon to Sadiya. The Ahom kingdom now extended eastward to encompass the entire upper area of the Luit Valley on the south bank and parts of the north bank.

As the Ahom king and his men returned in triumph after totally obliterating the Chutiya kingdom and dynasty, they carried with them the spoils of victory. These included thirty elephants, gold and silver utensils, cattle, palanquins and much more. But the most significant trophy was the treasure of Kubera; indeed, the loss of this had led to the end of the Chutiyas as a sovereign people! A number of Brahmins, sniffing new opportunities, voluntarily joined Suhungmung's entourage, as also artisans from former Chutiya territory. The victors also carried back some grisly trophies—the severed heads of King Jongmung and Prime Minister Kachitara. These two heads were buried beneath the steps leading to the deoghar or temple at Charaidai so that Ahom kings would be able to step on them every time they climbed the stairs to the temple—an unequivocal assertion of the fate that awaited anyone who might henceforth dare to act against a resurgent Ahom kingdom.

Having subjugated the Chutiyas and annexed their kingdom, Swargadeo Suhungmung performed the Rikkhvan ceremony. This was an ancient Shan ritual performed on important occasions, such as in periods of great danger to the realm, after the coronation of a new ruler or to celebrate a great victory. 'Rik' in Tai meant 'revive' or 'rejuvenate' and 'khvan' meant 'life'. Thus, the Rikkhvan ceremony was designed to rejuvenate the monarch, which, because he was the indisputable symbol of the Ahom State, also implied rejuvenation of the entire kingdom and its people after battle and bloodshed. None of the kings after Sukapha had deemed it necessary to perform the Rikkhvan ceremony, primarily because none of them had been made of the mettle Suhungmung was and had not embarked on a fierce, expansionist campaign as the current Ahom monarch had. Till then, the Ahom descendents of Sukapha had been content to remain within the limited area taken over by Sukapha and wage war only to protect the realm from external aggression or to subjugate unruly chieftains owing allegiance to the Ahom king. But Suhungmung harboured far more ambitious designs. The defeat of the rebellious Aitoniya Nagas and the annexation of the Chutiya kingdom had only whetted his appetite for more conquests—he was now setting his sights westward. But he knew that the Ahom race, because they had remained sedentary for so long, had lost some of their warrior zeal; the Rikkhvan ceremony would revive their martial spirit, put heat into their blood, readying them to rise up to the challenges in store for them in the near future.

Because it was designed to inspire the people as a whole, the Rikkhvan ceremony was performed at a public place so that members of the public, as also the palace guards, could witness it. Word of mouth would carry the news of the ceremony to all parts of the kingdom, unleashing the sought-for rejuvenation of the Shan spirit. A huge platform on stilts was erected on a piece of open land at the ancient and sacred city of Charaidai. A small hole was cut out at the very centre and a throne placed over it. The king, who with his entourage had camped overnight at the palace at Charaidai, set off in a procession atop his favourite elephant early in the morning, waving imperiously at the people who thronged the sides of Charaidai's broad avenues. Reaching the site of the ceremony, already crowded with such a large swarm of people that the guards had difficulty controlling them, the king halted and dismounted, and walked with measured steps up the platform. Deodhai, Bailung and Mohan priests were already assembled on the platform; curiously enough, the chief of the Deodhai priests did not stand with the others atop the platform but sat semi-naked upon a chair placed beneath the hole that had been cut on the stage.

King Suhungmung was ceremonially escorted onto the platform by the Ahom priests and astrologers, and requested to be seated on the throne. This being a purely Shan ritual, the esoteric incantations handed down orally generation to generation known only to the Ahom priests, the Brahmin priests could not participate and thus were absent from the group on the stage. No sooner had the monarch, looking magnificent in his royal robes, marched to the throne and sat down upon it, to the horror of the crowd with the aid of wooden ladles the priests began to pour water on his head, though he was fully dressed. The priests muttered incantations and periodically ululated even while pouring the consecrated water, which trickled down the king's raiment and through the whole, to fall upon the chief of the Deodhai priests seated underneath the platform.

The crowd stopped cheering, overwhelmed by the stark simplicity of the ritual into silence. They continued to watch in muted fascination as the Ahom priests kept on pouring ladlefuls of holy water while mouthing age-old incantations. The spectators had never before witnessed a Rikkhvan ceremony before but understood the implications. The water had been purified and rendered holy by the priests; it in turn was washing away all misfortune and ailment from the self of the king, thereby blessing him with good fortune and long life, while rejuvenating him in mind and spirit. But the misfortune could not be discarded into emptiness; these were therefore being transferred to the self of the chief Deodhai. But he was an all-knowing, all-powerful being, armed against the forces of evil; misfortunes could not touch him.

The simplicity of the symbolic ritual communicated the powerful message effectively as no elaborate ceremony could. Finally, with a flourish of movements, the final incantations, ululations and clanging of gongs brought the ceremony to its close; a screen was placed around the king so that he could dry himself, take off his wet garments and don dry ones even more ostentatious and magnificent than the previous; one of the priests gathered the wet raiment and took it to the Deodhai chief waiting below the rostrum who put them on in affirmation of the fact that he was now bearing upon himself all the misfortune marked by the gods in Heaven for Swargadeo Suhungmung also known as Swarganarayan.

The rejuvenated monarch descended the steps and marched determinedly towards his pachyderm awaiting him at some distance, while the ululations and the beating of drums by the priests reached a cacophony. Sensing that the ceremony had ended the crowd, which had been stunned as though frozen into a trance, now stirred and burst out into deafening cheers.

'Long live Swargadeo Suhungmung,' they cried. 'Long live Swargadeo Swarganarayan!'

Lukhring and Kedung, friends from childhood, had served their term as paiks chosen for civil construction work—the embankment on the river Dihing where the capital at Bagata was built had been completed, and the duo were now back in their village, working in their fields. But, as had become a habit of long standing with them, every evening they shared a chillum of opium alternately at each other's courtyard before retiring to bed.

'You didn't get your wish, did you now, Kedung?' Lukhring said playfully one winter evening. 'These days, with the Dihingiya raja on the throne at Bagata—a place, bear in mind, we helped build—life is but one military campaign after another. Each boat which travels up or down the Dihing brings fresh tidings every day. But you didn't get a slice of the excitement, did you now, Kedung?'

'Not so far, no,' conceded Kedung, allowing the languor caused by the opium fumes to wash over his senses. 'But there is time yet. I might get my call any day, what say you, Lukhring?'

'Oh, time has passed you by, my friend. Don't you get it? It has been many years since we worked at that embankment. The Dihingiya raja has been out of Bagata most of the time, quelling uprisings amongst the Nagas. The Chutiyas have been worsted; didn't the boatmen tell you how that campaign ended?'

'There are other campaigns ahead,' remarked Kedung, unwilling to accept the reality that he might never see active military service. 'Those folks that dwell in the mountains, they're rebelling all the time and the Dihingiya raja has been kept busy. Why, just a few months back they attacked the Sadiyakhowa Gohain's encampment and killed an officer!'

'Ah, but you forget that the chieftain himself was killed and his head displayed on a pole for all to see. Had results, I tell you. We hear that so cowed down were the mountain folks that another chieftain on his own submitted to the Dihingiya raja and even sent one of his daughters to be the raja's wife.'

'Be that as it may, but there's more action ahead, I tell you. This raja is not one to sit on his backside warming the throne. Why, even as we speak, he's touring the northern and eastern borders of his realm, supervising the erection of forts, placing garrisons to guard localities such as Habung and Banlung, and appointing officers to command them.'

'You aren't wrong on that account,' Lukhring agreed. 'The land of this valley, towards the north, east and south of the kingdom our lord Chaolung Sukapha established is under our occupation. Now the west remains. They say the Dihingiya raja is eyeing the land of the Kachari folks ... and perhaps the Barabhuyans and Kamatapur realms beyond.'

When, in 1253, the founder of the Ahom dynasty Chaolung Sukapha set up his capital at Charaidai, to the immediate west lay the vast Kachari Kingdom, encompassing the area between the river Dikhow and the river Kolong, even extending southward to another valley through which the river Barak flowed. Sukapha had been careful not to antagonize the powerful Kacharis but, as was inevitable, friction gradually began to develop between the two races. But hostilities had been localized, being confined mainly to the strip of land between the Dikhow and the Namdang rivers, which passed alternately between the Kacharis and the Ahoms. But Suhungmung was determined to end the self-imposed restraint and extend Ahom hegemony over the Kacharis, just as he had done with the Chutiyas.

The Kacharis, belonging to the Bodo ethnic group, had at that precise period attained cultural and technological sophistication more advanced than the Ahoms, having imbibed influences from the west through the Koch Kingdom and beyond. For instance, the staple material for construction for the Ahoms till then had remained bamboo, cane and thatch, while the Kacharis had learnt the art of making bricks and erecting concrete structures. However, as far as martial activities were concerned, the Ahoms under Suhungmung were far superior, the enterprise and organizing capacity shown by their leader making its army a formidable force.

Suhungmung began his campaign against the Kacharis in 1526, himself at the head of his army. The initial objective was to annex a part of the Kachari Kingdom and to reduce the Kachari monarch to the status of a vassal owing subservience to the Ahom king. The Ahom army ascended up the river Dhansiri to Barduar, where a defensive rampart was erected; and then onto Marangi, where a fort was built. Suhungmung appointed one of his nobles as Marangikhowa Gohain to rule over the occupied Kachari land. So rapid had been his advance and so seemingly weak the Kachari resistance that the Ahom officers grew complacent; thus when, on reaching Maiham or Kathkatia, a fierce attack was launched by the Kacharis at the rear of the Ahom army, the latter was caught off-guard and, suffering the loss of at least two score men, forced to retreat. Soon, however, their training and discipline reasserted itself and the Ahoms, regrouping, began advancing again with greater caution and alertness. There was a fierce engagement near Kathkatia; the preferred weapon of the Kacharis was the bow; being expert archers they could deal decisive blows against the enemy with their arrows. Such resistance from the Kacharis called for a different strategy involving more effective use of shields against the rain of arrows. Also, previously the Ahom officers were mounted on elephants which made them easier targets; now they began to lead their men on foot, with the pachyderms being used as buffers as also to clear the jungles as they advanced. The ensuing fight was the fiercest in Ahom history till that date; by the time the Kacharis fled, over 17,000 corpses littered the battleground.

However, the desire for vengeance continued to burn in the hearts of the Kacharis at the fact that a part of their kingdom had been occupied by the Ahoms, and they bided their time to retaliate. In the year 1527, the Ahom forces were being tested from two directions: for the first time in their history, they were being assailed by the Muslim rulers of Bengal in the west; in the eastern front a section of the Chutiyas was rising in revolt and had to be suppressed. The Kachari king, Khunkhara, thought he could take advantage of such a situation to wrest back lost territory. He sent his brother Detcha to oust the intruders from the Kachari Kingdom. But not only did the well-entrenched Ahoms repulse the attack upon the fort at Marangi, they also counterattacked, pursued the fleeing enemy and entered in triumph the Kachari capital of Dimapur, which they sacked and looted. Detcha himself was captured and publicly executed as a warning to anyone who might challenge the authority of the Ahoms.

The savagery of Ahom retaliation had the desired effect; though Khunkhara himself had fled from Dimapur along with his loved ones, many members of the royal family had been trapped at Dimapur. A prince named Detsung was the first to make his submission before Suhungmung and proffer gifts to him, including one of his sisters. The Ahom king in return made Detsung the titular king of the Kacharis owing allegiance to the Ahoms and placed him upon the throne at Dimapur. However, this arrangement was not to last very long; the Kacharis were a proud and independent people and could not bear to remain under Ahom dominance. In 1536 Detsung rebelled and attempted to throw off the Ahom yoke. Suhungmung's brilliance as a leader now came to the fore: despite being hamstrung through having to deal with revolts by the Naga tribes and the Chutiyas in other parts of the kingdom, as well as meeting headlong the onslaught of the armies from Bengal, Suhungmung managed to muster up a powerful army and dispatched it after Detsung. Setting up his base at Marangi on the south side of the valley of the river Dhansiri, Suhungmung sent his army up the river Doyang to a place named Banphu, the Ahom warriors proceeding both by boat and on foot along the banks. There was fierce resistance from the Kacharis but finally they had to concede defeat and were hotly pursued by Ahom soldiers. Detsung, who himself had led the Kachari army, fell back, first to a place named Lengur and then to his capital at Dimapur.

The Ahom pursuit proved relentless; even as it swept once again into the Kachari capital, Detsung had to flee the city, leaving behind his mother and daughter. The matriarch was put to the sword and the princess sent back to Bagata to be a member of the king's harem. Suhungmung's emissaries took orders to the generals at the battlefront that under no circumstance was Detsung allowed to escape—the unfortunate Kachari king was pursued to a place called Jangmarang, captured, brought back to Dimapur and publicly executed. Suhungmung ordained that his head be brought to Charaidai and buried there so that Ahom monarchs could step upon it while on their way to the temple to worship their ancestors.

The defeat of Detsung spelt the end of the age-old Kachari dominion of the central part of the Brahmaputra Valley; the Ahom realm now extended westward up to the river Kolong on the south bank of the Luit and river Bharalu on the north bank. Having ceded the Doyang-Dhansiri Valley to the Ahoms as also their capital at Dimapur, the Kacharis retreated further south and built a new capital at Maibong, where they had a respite from the Ahom onslaught.

The man slid like a shadow through the fringes of the enemy camp. The Ahoms were heavily dependent upon intelligence gathered about the strength of their adversaries; spies were specially trained to infiltrate camps of the opponents and garner information. This man was such a spy, sent by Suhungmung to learn about the alien invading force which had intruded into Ahom territory. The king's own army lay in wait a few miles east, anxious for news about the invaders.

Highly skilled at blending with the background as to be almost invisible, the spy had undertaken similar dangerous night missions before—against the Chutiyas and the Kacharis. But his experience this night was of a different nature altogether. First, the features of the previous enemy soldiers had not been much different from that of the spy, both being of Sino-Tibetan stock, so it had been easier to blend in, especially if one had taken the trouble of learning their dialect. But the men who guarded this force and slept in the tents appeared to be from a different clime, if their features were any indication; thus, the spy would stick out like a sore thumb if detected.

Secondly, this was a vast force, the likes of which the spy had never encountered before. The camps, raised on both banks of the Luit, stretched for many miles. The river itself was crammed with hundreds of sturdy war vessels, each having a cannon mounted at the prow. The spy had seen such cannons before; intercourse with the Kamata and Koch Kingdoms had ensured that specimens of cannons, cannonballs and gunpowder had been brought earlier before the Ahom swargadeo, while the Kacharis too had used this weapon in their defence of Dimapur. But neither had the Ahoms become proficient in its use, nor could their armament manufacturers till then succeed in duplicating their design for mass production. But the invading army appeared to possess many, those on land being equipped with wheels so that they could be pulled along when the army was on the move. Other than the cannons, the enemy was armed with familiar, conventional weaponry: swords, spears and the like. The spy also noted that the enemy had brought horses with them, which would not be of much use given the thick growth of jungle that extended almost up to the river bank. Having made his survey and mentally mapped the enemy camp throughout that night, the spy left it stealthily just before daybreak, clambered aboard a small boat which he had moored a little ahead, and rowed his way upstream, back to his own camp. He was taken directly to Suhungmung.

'They're neither from the Koch Kingdom, Your Majesty,' the spy told his master, 'nor from Kamatapur. I've never seen such soldiers before. They are tall and strong and bearded. They speak to each other in a language I've never heard. They must be from foreign parts.'

'Mussulmans, Your Majesty,' the chief Brahmin advisor spoke up, 'in all likelihood from Bengal. I've spoken to Hindu proselytizers who have passed through our kingdom on their way to lands which lie further east. They spoke with fear about the Mussulmans' invasions.'

'What about our brethren amongst the Koches and Kamatas? Could they not repel this army of strangers? Or have they been subjugated? Is that why this force has been able to come so close to our kingdom?'

'We've no means of knowing, Your Majesty,' said the buragohain. 'They may have traversed the Luit, bypassing the others, to strike directly at us.'

Suhungmung nodded. 'What's the measure of their strength?' he asked the spy.

'It is a vast army, Your Majesty, commanded by an individual who is called the Great Vazir. The boats are big and have filled up the Luit bank to bank. They have cannons mounted upon them. The soldiers run into thousands ... they can't be counted, so many are they! They have elephants and horses and a strange animal with a hump and long neck. Believe me, Your Majesty, I've never seen such a huge army before!'

'It will call for a different strategy, that's all,' Suhungmung said, almost nonchalantly. 'We'll lie recumbent during the daytime, retreating as they advance, and strike only at night. They've come to this region for the very first time. We, on the other hand, know the lay of the land and water, and can move swiftly even in the dark of night ...'

Not only were the Ahoms fierce warriors, they were master strategists, too. The Great Vazir Sultan Allauddin Hussain Shah's army, which had been advancing slowly but with impunity up the river that outsiders called the Brahmaputra, renewed their advance the very next day. The rowers being unable to propel the boats upstream against the powerful currents of the mighty river, these had to be pulled along by men walking on the banks, which slowed down the expedition further. Because of the dense foliage, the cavalry was almost reduced to being foot soldiers. Also, the humid weather did not suit these men who apparently belonged to drier climes, and many had fallen ill and had to be left behind.

But that was the last day of advance for the army of the Great Vazir. Advance scouts had informed their general that the opposing force was retreating even as they moved forward, which aroused a sense of complacency in the general. This was rudely shattered as darkness settled in; the invaders did not know what hit them!

War boats, which had been craftily camouflaged in many of the tributaries of the river Luit, emerged stealthily and attacked with deadly effect the invading flotilla from behind. Their cannons being mounted at the prow, by the time the invading boats could be turned against the Ahom vessels, at least a third of their strength had been rammed into and sunk. The land army was startled at being attacked from the front, sides and rear; it was an effective ambush; hundreds of flares tied to arrows shot from bows rained down on the enemy vessels at the front, setting them on fire and forcing the men aboard to jump into the powerful flow, either to drown or to be cut down by Ahom soldiers. A thick cloud cover had helped in carrying out the ambush; it was no coincidence; Suhungmung's astrologers had kept their eyes on the sky even as they killed a rooster and examined it to foretell the best time for the assault.

Though many Ahom warriors sacrificed their lives, the invaders' casualties were ten times that number. Before the night was over, the advancing army of the Great Vazir was in inglorious retreat, having lost most of their war vessels and at least one-fourth of their men, animals and materials. The invading army fled, taking along with them their dead and wounded. The Ahoms chased them beyond the river Burai; not much booty was taken since this was an invading army and did not carry with it any valuables; but a number of cannons were taken, as also prisoners who knew how to make these and the powder needed to fire them. Also, riderless elephants and horses were seized.

Suhungmung had a permanent fort constructed at the point where the Burai debouched into the Luit; for strategic reasons he also annexed the area around Duimunisila and set up another encampment at Phulbari. Having posted a guard at Narayanpur, the Ahom monarch returned to his capital to focus on suppressing rebellious factions of Chutiyas and concluding the campaign against the Kacharis. But, shrewd campaigner that he was, he knew that the tussle against the invaders from the west was far from ended and they would be returning, perhaps in greater numbers.

He was not wrong. Sultan Allauddin Hussain and his generals, smarting from the initial rout, launched attack after attack from 1531. The next force, equipped with merely fifty war vessels, was easily defeated by the Ahom forces under the leadership of Konseng Barpatragohain at Temani, with its commander being forced to abandon his war boat and escape on horseback. On Suhungmung's instructions, the defensive positions in and around Sala on the bank of the river Bharali were reinforced, while new positions were constructed at Singri. None too soon, as it proved. Even as ramparts were being constructed, a mammoth army, led by a commander-in-chief named Bit Malik, approached Singri.

Emboldened by their earlier success, and realizing that the invaders were not the great warriors they had imagined them to be, the Ahoms met them headlong, defeated them and forced them to flee beyond Khagarijan, killing Bit Malik in the process. A huge number of horses, cannons and prisoners were taken and presented to Suhungmung. So pleased was the Ahom swargadeo that he ordered a Rikkhvan ceremony to be performed for his brother Konseng and presented him with a bride. But the most severe Muslim assault during Suhungmung's reign was yet to come. It was led by a commander named Turbak, accompanied by reputed generals such as Bangal, Taaju. Hussain Khan and others. The mammoth army consisted of numerous elephants and horses, war boats, cannons, cavalry and foot soldiers. Apparently, previous encounters with the Ahoms had made the invaders more aware of the former's prowess in warfare, thus they were taking no chances in this expedition. The huge force made its way unresisted to Singri and encamped at a little distance from the fort the Ahoms had constructed there.

On learning of the approaching army, Suhungmung sent a strong force under his eldest son Suklen to reinforce the garrison stationed at Singri, while he himself led another army to Sala. The two opponents at Singri stood in eyeball-to-eyeball confrontation, though neither made the first move.

Suklen was the first to blink. 'This waiting game is getting on my nerves,' he told his advisors. 'We need to strike at the enemy before they are strengthened more by the arrival of fresh forces.'

'No, my prince,' said the eldest of the advisors. 'Their ploy is apparent. The ramparts of our fort give us a great advantage. They're obviously testing our patience so that we might be tempted to venture out and attack them.'

'Are we cowards to hide behind the safety of ramparts?' Suklen, young and hot-blooded, thundered.

'Certainly not!' retorted another advisor. 'But we must also heed our Deodhai and Brahmin astrologers. Both have deemed this moment inauspicious for launching an attack.'

This was true. The Brahmin astrologers had consulted their almanacs and declared that the dates were inauspicious. The Deodhai priests had cut a rooster and examined the position of its legs and shape of its entrails and come to the same conclusion.

'If we cross the ramparts and venture outside, we are doomed to be defeated,' was their universal conclusion.

'Superstitious balderdash,' said the headstrong prince. 'If the moment is inauspicious, tell our men of magic to make it auspicious. They've rituals for that too, don't they?'

Sensing that the prince would not budge, a strange ritual to ward off misfortune and ensure victory was performed. A slave was beheaded, as were a dog, cat, horse, pig, goat, monkey and pigeon, and their heads were floated down the Luit on a plantain raft along with a bunch of bananas, betel nuts and paan leaves, incense, rice cakes coloured red, yellow and green, cotton seeds, mustard oil, ghee and vermillion.

Unfortunately, such magic did not come to the aid of the Ahoms. The astrologers' prediction came true—the moment his army ventured out of the fort, the enemy set off a barrage of cannon fire, while enemy cavalrymen rushed the foot soldiers with long lances and swords. It was a terrible massacre; eight senior section commanders were killed along with hundreds of common soldiers; the fort at Singri had to be abandoned and Suklen, himself badly wounded, had to retreat with what remained of his force to Sala where his father was.

Suhungmung was furious. 'You went against the advice of our wise men and priests, you fool?' he castigated his son. 'You've disgraced our race and emboldened our enemy. Now go and get yourself treated so that you can recover to fight another day. Meanwhile, I am putting Konseng Barpatragohain at the head of our army.'

Suklen turned around and left the king's presence. His taut face mirrored the anger he felt towards his father for rebuking him before others. In the course of time, this anger was to harden into cruel resolve, but for the time being all he felt was shame and helplessness.

The rainy season arrived and Turbak's advance was halted for a while due to the slushy impassability of the terrain. Meanwhile, Suklen had recovered; bowing to his importunities Suhungmung made him the commander again. Having learnt from previous experience, Suklen did not venture out of the fort, but directed hit-and-run guerilla attacks upon Turbak's army by bands of Ahom soldiers hidden in the nearby hills. This time it was Turbak who lost patience and stormed the fortress at Sala, first pillaging and burning the small settlement that had mushroomed around it. The Ahom defenders were ready for such an eventuality, warding off the soldiers who attempted to scale the fortress walls by pouring boiling water over them.

But Turbak's forces were not to be repulsed that easily and their commander threw everything he had at the opponent; while the cannons engaged in an unrelenting fusillade, soldiers on elephants were attempting to batter down the main gate and side walls. Fearful that if the fort was breached, the confined space would prove to be a handicap for his warriors, Suklen was forced into the open, and had to suffer another defeat as Turbak's cavalry rode like a whirlwind amongst his army, throwing the elephants into confusion and terror. Once again Suklen was forced back into the fortress even as emissaries were sent to the Ahom capital for reinforcement.

No matter how many sorties Suklen sent against the enemy, his soldiers tasted defeat every time. Thinking that the morale of his soldiers might be raised if his elders led the attacks, Suklen requested Chaophrachengmung Bargohain to lead the next assault.

'I beg you not to go to battle today,' Chaophrachengmung's wife pleaded with her husband. She was a tall, beautiful woman, as courageous as any Ahom male warrior.

'But why not, my dear Mula Gabharoo?' asked the bargohain.

'The cloth is not ready,' Mula Gabharoo replied.

It was the custom amongst the Ahoms that whenever a commander went out to battle, his wife or wives gave him a piece of battle cloth as a talisman for good fortune. The cloth had to be woven by the women themselves; the cotton had to be cleaned and fluffed, spun into threads and woven into cloth upon the handloom, all in the space of a single night. The universal superstition was that the commander who wore such a piece of cloth would not come to harm.

Unfortunately, Suklen had made his request that the bargohain lead the next assault very late in the night and, hard as she tried, there had been no time for Mula Gabharoo to finish weaving the piece of battle cloth.

'I understand the reason,' the bargohain said lovingly. 'You did not get sufficient time. Yet I have to go. If I were to hold back on the importunities of my wife, my honour would be stained forever.'

'But our astrologers too have deemed this day to be not propitious. Prince Suklen had always been a rash one ... he allows his passion to rule over his head. You must tell him that you'll not go to battle on this morning!'

'You, dear Mula Gabharoo, more than anyone else know that I can't do that! My good name is at stake here—cloth or no cloth, good prediction or ill, I need to go.'

The skirmish that morning was fierce. Inspired by the bargohain who led from the front atop an elephant, the Ahom warriors went hard at the enemy, forcing them on the back foot. However, an unfortunate incident suddenly altered the course of the battle. A lance flung by one of Turbak's foot soldiers pierced through the bargohain's armour and struck his heart. As the commander slumped upon the howdah, the mahout turned his mount and began moving to the rear of the advancing Ahom troops. His intentions were good—to try to take his master to safety and, if possible, get medical assistance. But the Ahom soldiers misunderstood this as a signal for retreat—the outcome was disastrous, for the hard-pressed bangals, sensing an opportunity, fought back savagely, putting their adversary to flight. Hundreds were killed, though the mahout did succeed in taking his elephant into the fort. But it was too late. Chaophrachengmung Bargohain was dead.

In courage and enterprise, Ahom women were no less than their male counterparts. Warrior blood ran in their veins too and Mula Gabharoo was determined to prove that. The next rnorning, donning battle dress and mounted atop an elephant, this brave lady stepped out of the fort, searching for Turbak whom she considered to be the culprit, bent on wreaking revenge for the killing of her husband. Though the Ahom warriors were inspired by her heroic action, it was merely a symbolic act on her part, since she was not trained for warfare. Within hours of the battle, she was cut down and the Ahom soldiers once again beat a retreat.

The martyrdom of Mula Gabharoo for the cause of her husband and her country forms one of the most inspiring episodes in Ahom history.

Suhungmung decided it was time that, though he was growing old, he himself had to lead the campaign. The threat from the Sultan of Bengal was of a serious nature such as never confronted by the Ahoms before; it had even emboldened tribes within the Ahom realm to begin to rebel and try to wrest independence for themselves. Suhungmung decided that he would deal with them later; the first priority was to end once and for all the threat from the bangals and he had to throw the entire might of the Ahoms against this adversary.

Since it was not possible for him to actively engage in combat, and his son Suklen proving to be less effective as a commander, Konseng Barpatragohain was once more deputed to lead the Ahom forces. For a while, hostilities had halted because of the onset of rains, but as soon as they ceased towards the autumn of 1532, these resumed. The Ahoms, bolstered by reinforcement sent from other parts of the kingdom, soon gained the upper hand. Their biggest victory came in March 1533 in the naval battle of Duimunisila, where they succeeded in killing two of Turbak's dreaded commanders, Bangal and Taju. By Ahom estimate, at least 2,000 of the enemy soldiers were killed in that battle and over two dozen war boats were sunk.

The beleaguered Turbak retreated to the point where the river Dikrai met the Luit and set up defensive positions. There he was joined by his lieutenant Husain Khan who brought with him a sizeable force. But

Turbak in his heart knew it was a lost cause. When the Ahom assault came, his soldiers did not display the zeal they once had, his cannons had rusted and his gunpowder grown damp. With extreme valour, Turbak endeavoured to galvanize his forces by mounting a horse and leading his cavalry in person, but he was killed by an Ahom soldier with his spear.

There was no stopping the Ahoms after this. The Bengal Sultan's army fled in disarray, Hussain Khan was captured and executed, and a huge booty of armaments and animals was taken. The victorious Ahoms chased their enemy beyond the river Karatoya, which from then onwards was pronounced as the western extremity of the Ahom realm. In order to reinforce this claim Konseng Barpatragohain built a large tank and erected a temple to celebrate the victory.

As was the custom, the severed head of Turbak was brought back and buried at Charaidai. Once again Suhungmung performed the Rikkhvan ceremony to rejuvenate his race after the long and gruelling war. The Ahom army had captured a number of Muslim prisoners and Suhungmung ordained that their lives be spared and they be made members of the broader Ahom community. These prisoners were professional soldiers and thus unfit for any other occupation. They were first employed as grass cutters who fed the elephants but proved inept, nor could they be settled as farmers because they knew nothing of agriculture. Finally, however, these men of Pathan stock were trained employed as makers of brassware such as mugs, urns, etc., and were collectively called Moriyas. Since they were believed to have originally come from the state of Gaur in Bengal, they were also called Goriyas.

Age was catching up with Suhungmung. He had never hesitated to lead his own armed forces; the scars were showing upon his aged body. But now he was the monarch in ceremonial sense only; the martial side of the kingdom he was leaving his son Suklen and the patra-mantris to take care of. The fame of the Ahoms had spread far and wide. Even the monarch of the mighty Koch Kingdom, Biswa Singha, had travelled by boat all the way to the Ahom capital of Bagata to pay a courtesy visit and bring gifts. Suhungmung, clever strategist that he was, understood the actual reason behind the Koch king's gesture. He himself was being threatened by the attacks from Gaur and other aliens from Delhi; it was in his interest to befriend the mighty Ahoms and ensure that at least the eastern flank of the Koch Kingdom remain safe from attack.

But Suhungmung had kept his thoughts to himself. He realized that the Ahom kingdom had expanded enormously and it would be difficult for his progeny to keep the various communities subjugated unless allies were made. So, he received Biswa Singha with the utmost courtesy and gifted him presents in return. He also offered a conciliatory hand to others such as the king of Manipur, sending him gifts through emissaries.

While his lieutenants were ensuring that the Ahom kingdom was kept from rebellion, all was not well within the king's own household. Day by day his oldest son Suklen was growing openly rebellious. Petty issues such as who was the winner in a cockfight, or to whom a princess gifted by the Kachari chief should belong, exacerbated the friction between father and son. The latter was still smarting from the presumed humiliation he suffered during the war with the invaders from Bengal; his defiance made the king fear the worst, and he summoned Suklen's mother and made her promise that her son would do nothing rash.

Suhungmung's fears proved to be well founded. In January 1539 Suklen bribed one of his father's trusted servants to steal into his chamber while Suhungmung was sleeping and pierce him through the heart with his sword.

THE NARRATOR

'This, my people,' said the Narrator, 'was the ignominious end of an individual whom many historians deem to be the greatest amongst Ahom monarchs. I've told you before and I tell you again. The corridors of power are stained with the blood of betrayal!

'Swargadeo Suhungmung, also known as Swarganarayan or Dihingiya raja, was indeed a fearless campaigner and administrator without peer.

Having subdued the Chutiyas and Kacharis, and defeated the Bengal sultan's armies, his empire grew far bigger than the one originally erected by our progenitor Chaolung Sukapha. He understood that the existing administrative structure was insufficient to govern the larger area and far greater population, so he created new official posts and delegated duties. He always kept the welfare of his subjects in mind despite his preoccupation with his enemies.

'It was during his reign that the Ahoms learnt the use of firearms and how to build cannons and cannonballs and make gunpowder, knowledge they gradually perfected and which came of great use in future campaigns by later Ahom monarchs. From the Kacharis was learnt the building of brick structures and this king brought in artisans from far-off places to enrich his kingdom with their constructions.

'If there was one shortcoming during his reign, it was in the inordinate importance he gave to his Brahmin priests at the expense of traditional Ahom Deodhais and Bailungs. Due to this he also ignored one of the most significant changes that occurred in the Brahmaputra Valley during his reign, one that was to completely alter the religious and cultural face of the region. I am speaking, of course, of the birth of the great saint Mahapurush Sankardev and the Ekasarana Namadharma faith that he preached.

'As you are no doubt aware, Mahapurush Sankardev was born in October 1449 at Bardowa in today's Nowgong District, into a powerful family of Bhuyans. He studied under the tutorship of a noted Brahmin teacher named Mahendra Kandali and grew well-versed in the Vedas, Upanishads, Puranas and Sanskrit epics. In 1481, Sankardev went on a pilgrimage to north India and there came under the influence of the neo-Vaishnav renaissance that was sweeping across the region. This movement was in reaction against the degeneration that had gradually been taking place in Hinduism and Buddhism, which was pushing these faiths away from the common people, and complicating worship with excessive and ostentatious ritualism. Also known as the Bhakti movement, this all-India faith, led by saints such as Ramanuj, Namdev, Tukaram, Ramananda, Kabir, Chaitanyadev, Mirabai and Vidyapati, forsook idol worship, and deemed meditation and community chanting of prayers to be the best way to offer obeisance to God.

'Nowhere had Hinduism and Buddhism become more debased than in medieval Assam, where Tantrik Saktism had become a dominant cult and rituals like human sacrifice were practised. The fact that overt importance was given to sensual enjoyment of worldly pleasures, had brought bad repute to the land, which had become synonymous with sorcery, witchcraft and other vile practices. Sankardev, the reformist, was determined to fight the degeneration of Hinduism and formulated his own version of neo-Vaishnavism, which he called Ekasarana Namadharma. It was a simple religion with three articles of faith: Ekasarana, or obeisance to one God; Satsanga, or a congregation of bhaktas or faithfuls; and Nama, or chanting, as a means of prayer. The common man could attain God by adhering to these three articles. In reducing rituals to a minimum and placing emphasis on prayer through community chanting in congregation halls called Namghars or private prayer rooms called Kirtanghars, Sankardev offered to the people a creed that was in total contrast with the prevalent esoteric Hinduism.

'Moreover, in the Vaishnava fraternity, everyone was considered equal, so everyone could be a member, no matter which tribe they belonging to. This egalitarian ethos made people flock to his faith and soon Ekasarana Namadharma, also called Mahapurushiya Dharma, spread like wildfire. In order to help proselytize the new faith, Sankardev and his staunch disciples like Madhavdev, set up monastic institutions called Sattras, and since its followers used literary and artistic modes such as music, dance and drama, these institutions became hubs for bringing about a cultural renaissance to the region.

'The great King Suhungmung, unfortunately, was under the spell of the Brahmin priests, who were soon up in arms against this new faith that threatened to rob them of their own priestly influence. They poisoned the mind of the king; he discarded the spirit of tolerance that his great forebear Sukapha had displayed, and ordered persecution of Sankardev and his followers, even having his son-in-law Haridev charged with treason and executed. Sankardev and some of his followers fled the Ahom territory and took shelter in the kingdom of the Koch; but within the Ahom realm the Vaishnavites continued to be persecuted, in particular, one of their sects called the Moamarias. It is indeed ironic that the uprising of this sect in the nineteenth century brought about an end to the Ahom rule. Truly, the persecution of the Vaishnavites was the one blot in the otherwise glorious reign of Swargadeo Suhungmung.

'After the treacherous assassination of this great monarch, his eldest son Suklen ascended the Ahom throne. His father had confronted hostilities from Bengal, but his immediate descendents had to face danger from another direction—that of the Koch Kingdom. As I had mentioned, Biswa Singha, the founder of the Koch dynasty, had paid a courtesy call on the Ahom monarch. Assailed by the Sultan of Bengal on their western flank, the Koches had grown wary of Ahom expansion under Suhungmung and wanted to maintain friendly relations so as to keep their eastern flank free of strife. But, once the Koch Kingdom itself became vaster and their armies stronger, it was actually they who now sought to usurp land under Ahom dominion. Thus, Suklen's reign, though free of attacks from Bengal, was marked by the assault of a new enemy, the Koch.

'The Koch tribe was one of the earliest Mongoloid migrants into the lower Brahmaputra Valley and adjoining areas. In the early sixteenth century, under the dynamic leadership of Biswa Singha, the Koch Kingdom came into being and expanded into a powerful empire that embraced parts of Lower Assam as well as Bengal. Biswa Singha set up his capital at Kochbehar and even made advances eastward to test the possibility of attacking the Ahoms, but when he realized the difficulty of this, he instead extended a hand of friendship in order to maintain peace.

'The kingdom he erected embraced the territory of erstwhile Kamarupa. Legend has it that once when he was advancing across the river Brahmaputra, he got cut off from his own troops. Wandering alone, he stumbled upon the ruins of the ancient temple called Kamakhya on top of the Nilachal Hills. He prayed at the decrepit temple, promising Goddess Kamakhya that he would rebuild the structure if she reunited him with his army. Later, after his wish had been granted, he fulfilled his promising by building a new temple at Kamakhya atop the foundations of the old one.

'Biswa Singha was followed to the throne by the greatest of the Koch kings, Malladeva, who took up the Hindu name of Naranarayan after he ascended the throne. During his period of kingship, the Koches became the most powerful entity in the northeastern part of India. Naranarayan was a great patron of the arts and learning, and peopled his court with men of erudition and culture. As I had told you before, it was this king who gave Mahapurush Sankardev shelter, despite the machinations of his Brahmin priests who too were against the neo-Vaishnav religion. It was under his patronage that Sankardev could compose almost all of his major literary works, including the *Kirtan Ghosa*, the doctrinal thesis *Bhakti Ratnakar*, and plays such as *Rukmini Haran*, *Parijat Haran*, *Kaliya Daman* and *Keli Gopal*. Thus, it can be said that the Koches, like the Ahoms, were also instrumental in forming the Assamese identity by helping in bringing about a cultural renaissance through Sankardev and his disciples like Madhavdev and Ananta Kandali, the translator of the Ramayana into Assamese and author of *Kumar Haran*, as also through other intellectuals such as Ramsaraswati who translated the Mahabharata into Assamese.

'If the Koch realm attained magnificence in terms of size, stature and power, much of the credit must also go to Naranarayan's brother, Sukladhvaj, who had been appointed as the general of the Koch army. Sukladhvaj was so swift in action that the popular imagination compared him to a kite, and he was known as Chilarai or Lord of the Kites. The general's dynamism ensured that within years of Naranarayan's ascension, the Koches brought under their suzerainty the Kacharis, the Jaiantias, the Manipuris, and the kingdoms of Tippera, Sylhet, Bhutan, etc. Very soon the eyes of the Kite-king fell upon the Ahoms, and thus, my people, was it that we Ahoms were soon on the verge of being obliterated as a race ...'

Dark Clouds

Prince Suklen conferred with his close advisors in one of the inner sanctums of the palace at Bagata. Taophrongdam, the newly appointed buragohain, was present, as was Aikhek, the new bargohain. Konjang Barpatragohain, son of the renowned Konseng, who had inherited his father's office, made up the third member of the patra-mantris present in the chamber.

His ministers were visibly angry and agitated. 'The late Swargadeo Suhungmung was a very popular monarch,' Taophrongdam Buragohain said. 'The entire Ahom realm is in mourning at his tragic demise. The people are growing restive. They're not satisfied with the explanation that he died a natural death. Somehow word has leaked out of the palace that he was treacherously slain.'

'They think it is you who planned and executed the assassination,' Konjang Barpatragohain, who was not one to mince his words, said. 'We also think the same.'

'The name of the assassin was Lehetia,' added Aikhek Bargohain. 'He was caught by the palace guards after the assassination. He confessed he was acting under direct orders from you before one of the guards decapitated him with his sword.'

'You believe him?' Prince Suklen spoke forcefully. 'I swear on the name of my mother I had nothing to do with the killing. The people must be made to understand that I stand unjustly accused. In order to prove that I am innocent, I am ordering that all Lehetia's relatives who can be found in the kingdom be put to the hul.'

Hulat diya, or being put to the hul, was a barbaric punishment awarded to the worst offenders. A large pit was dug and bamboo spikes with their pointed ends facing upwards were fixed at the bottom of the hole. The offender was flung into the hole and impaled by the bamboo stakes, often taking days to die.

'Yes,' said the buragohain, 'we know of it. Dozens of innocent creatures are being caught by your henchmen and thrown onto the huls. Unfortunately, far from proving your innocence, these mindless killings have only made you more unpopular.'

'Your own brothers accuse you of patricide,' the bargohain pointed out. 'They're thirsting for revenge.'

'I've already set some of my officers after them. They've been ordered to put my brothers under house arrest and ensure that they don't embark on any mischief. I say again, I'm totally innocent. As the eldest son of my father, I assert my right to the throne.'

'It was stupid of the chaodang guard to have killed the assassin, for alive and under interrogation, he would have revealed everything,' the buragohain said. 'Yes, according to Ahom tradition you're entitled to sit on the vacant throne. Also, we have to obey you, though we know well what you've done.'

'That's right, isn't it, my dear Buragohain?' Prince Suklen said with a wicked leer. 'You've to obey me, like it or not. But don't think I'm stupid. I know from past examples what our patra-mantris are capable of. So, I've taken the precaution of increasing my security. I shall also come down harshly upon anyone contemplating harm towards me. But, most important, I shall not stay here in Bagata which has become too dangerous for me. Instead, I shall build a new capital at Hemanabari and shift as soon as possible to that place. And believe me, dear dangoriyas, it will be the most protected capital you will ever live to see!'

Prince Suklen was true to his word. Work commenced on the building of a new capital at Hemanabari, at the centre of which the royal palace was built. At first, a cluster of villages was chosen, and tall, earthen defensive ramparts were built all around them, extending many miles. While in capitals like Bagata, there had been only two gates, at the east and west, upon the ramparts or garhs, here four immense wooden gates were erected, guarded round the clock by well-armed soldiers who would not allow entry without some proof of identity. The ramparts had niches upon them, wherein sat Ahom sentries and archers who maintained vigil day and night. The palace was almost equidistant from the four entry gates, the roads leading to it being about six miles long. It was a magnificent, sprawling structure made of wood, cane and thatch, which was set upon stilts; though the Ahoms had become familiar with the art of constructing brick structures, there were not enough masons in the realm to be able to build an entire palace of bricks. Thus, there were only a few brick structures; the enormous entry gates and the two temples of the palaces housing the Laxminarayan Shaligram and the Somdeo were made of concrete.

Records have it that 12,000 paiks toiled for a year in order to construct the palace, which was beautifully decorated and grand to behold. The entire palace compound was set within a circle of densely planted bamboo through which no living creature could cross, so as to provide a natural defensive shield. Augmenting its defences was a deep moat perennially filled with water, which ran all around the palace, with just a single wooden drawbridge allowing entry. Suklen had taken the precaution of having the residences of his patra-mantris and other nobles and officers constructed outside the perimeter of the palace; these too were chang-type structures set on stilts.

Indeed, as work on it commenced, the capital began to resemble a well-guarded fortress and the people began to call it Garhgaon or village within ramparts rather than Hemanabari. The name stuck and Garhgaon remained the capital of the Ahom kingdom for a century and a half. Because Prince Suklen shifted to Garhgaon as soon as it was constructed and ascended the singorighar there, he was also known as the Garhgoyan raja. After his coronation, having learnt of the practice of Koch and other monarchs, King Suklenmung also struck coins commemorating the occasion, being the first Ahom ruler to do so.

Chilarai, the Kite-king, was chafing at the dithering on the part of his brother, the Koch monarch Naranarayan, on arriving at a decision to attack the Ahom kingdom.

'This is an opportune moment,' Chilarai said. 'We have extended our influence as far as Manipur in the east and parts of Bengal in the west. Even the Nawab of Gaur is fearful of offending us and has given up all thoughts of hostility. Only the Ahoms remain. They would continue to be a threat to us unless we take steps to bring them under our suzerainty.'

'I'm not too certain,' King Naranarayan said sagely. 'If you recall, our father the late Biswa Singha had initially thought of attacking the Ahoms. But soon he realized that the land around the Luit was too difficult for an army to traverse, so he strove at a peace treaty with the Ahoms instead.'

'I will take care of any obstacles which come in the way,' Sukladhvaj the Chilarai spoke with confidence. 'We have received intelligence through our informants. His subjects suspect that the new Ahom king, Suklenmung had murdered his father. They are rebellious. There is disaffection amongst the nobles and the officers, too. Also, subjugated tribes within his kingdom, like the Bhuyans in the Kopili Valley and the Chutiyas in the east, are engaged in armed uprisings. Allow me to repeat, brother, this is the proper moment to strike. The Ahoms might prove to be a thorn in the flesh for us in the future. It is time to remove this thorn once and for all.'

'You're the strategist, dear brother,' said Naranarayan, speaking from the heart. 'You, through your glorious martial feats, have proven your loyalty to our kingdom. Do what you think is best. I shall give you every support and assistance.'

The Kite-king wasted no time in raising a powerful army and proceeding in 1546 along the north bank of the Luit till he reached the Dikrai River. The going had indeed been difficult because of the marshy terrain and the thick jungles growing close to the riverbank. Chilarai took the precaution of building a passable road as his army moved along at what seemed to him to be the slowest of paces. Suklenmung, underestimating the extent of the threat, made the mistake of remaining behind at Garhgaon and dispatching an army under some officers to meet the invading forces. The officers themselves were none too loyal to the new king while the forces under them were none too keen to fight; when the two forces met near the mouth of the Dikrai, the outcome was inevitable. Many of the Ahom officers were shot dead by Koch archers, while some surrendered. The soldiers fled, with the Koches pursuing them and slaughtering them in hundreds.

As the Koches advanced, the Ahoms retreated to fortified positions initially at Kharanga and next at Kaliabor, but their adversary was relentless, defeating them at both the places, and even at Sala, where they had stout defences. Despite his unpopularity, Suklenmung had fought alongside his father the great Suhungmung and knew the ins and outs of warfare. Discovering that the Koch army was undefeatable, but was proceeding across the north bank of the Luit, he ordered his army to pull back and allow the former to progress unhindered. He waited till the Koch army had reached Narayanpur at the eastern extreme of the Brahmaputra Valley, where they built a fort. With himself at the head, Suklenmung now took his forces down the south bank of the Luit and attacked the flank of Chilarai's army on the bank of the river Pichala, thereby cutting off his supply route. Too late the Kite-king realized that the Ahom monarch had outwitted him; his soldiers, with their supply of food and arms cut off, fought ferociously, but were thoroughly routed. With at least 5,000 of his men killed, Chilarai was forced into an undisciplined and ignominious retreat to Kochbehar, while Suklenmung returned in triumph to Garhgaon. Having regained some of his lost popularity with his subjects, he performed the Rikkhvan ceremony in imitation of his illustrious father.

Thus far, the dark clouds ominously threatening the Ahom kingdom had been warded off, but not for long. The Great Earthquake of 1548, which wreaked havoc in the Brahmaputra Valley, was perhaps an indication of this. Having defeated the Koches, Suklenmung was content to rest on his oars, sending his senior officers to suppress the occasional rebellions in his realm. He had always been of unhealthy physical disposition, thereby earning another sobriquet: the Nariya or the Ailing Raja. By 1452, his health declined irreversibly and he died the same year, though not too many of his subjects mourned the loss.

The jungle was dense, dark and filled with nocturnal noises. It was a night of the full moon, but the thick overhead canopy of foliage prevented the rays from pouring in, wrapping the jungle in a weird gloom. Had these men not been on the backs of sure-footed elephants they would not have been able to proceed.

There were six elephants in the party; with two men on the back of each pachyderm; there were a dozen men in all.

But, clearly, the elephant leading the group was all-important, and it would be the two individuals upon that beast who would be responsible for the night's action. One of them was a mahout; though his mount normally was decked with an ornate howdah, tonight it only had a cotton padding upon its back. The man who sat upon it carried a rope, one end of which was fashioned into a lasso, the other being wound thrice round the elephant's torso and securely tied. He, obviously, was a phandi, or trapper, and the group was on a mela shikar for wild elephants.

The Ahoms adopted two methods of capturing wild elephants. The most common was kheda shikar, or trapping elephants by building a large stockade of cut tree trunks firmly lashed with cane and driving a herd of wild elephants into it. During mela shikar, an elephant trapper or phandi seated upon a domesticated and trained elephant enters a herd of wild elephants and traps a calf by noosing it with the phand or rope lasso. The latter method is fraught with risk.

The phandi on the back of the lead elephant did not really need to undertake this mela shikar merely to trap a beast. He, in fact, was a thrill addict and was engaged in the hunt for the excitement and risk. For two nights his men had camped in the jungle on the lookout for an elephant herd. This evening they had spotted one, and the phandi on the lead elephant had immediately set out on the hunt.

As they moved ahead, the foliage became slightly less dense and suddenly they were out in the open, beside a river which was almost dry because the rainy season was long over. Not too far away was the elephant herd, spread over the pebbled surface of the river bed. The moonlight which now bathed the landscape because there was no overhead foliage to shield it, reflected upon the wet, black skins of the animals. There were two dozen elephants in the herd, including sub-adults and calves; an aged female elephant was the leader of the group, while there were a few bull tuskers that stood as guards.

The trapping party slowed its pace, careful to ensure that it was downwind and the smell of human beings would not carry to the herd. At a signal from the phandi upon the lead elephant, the rest of the party stopped, while his mahout urged his beast ahead. The animal, swathed with ropes, moved extremely slowly, closing the distance separating it from the herd, even as the mahout and the phandi crouched flat upon its back to reduce visibility of their presence. The domestic elephant pushed ahead, imitating a feeding wild elephant, pausing to grip a clutch of leaves with its trunk and then walking a few more paces forward in an unhurried gait. In all appearance, it was a member of the herd, grazing, moving forward, and again stopping to graze.

Cunningly imitating a wild elephant as it was, the herd had no inkling about its approach, and fed and bathed unwarily on. The phandi, still flat upon the elephant's back, gripped the lasso tightly as he surveyed the herd. His eyes fixed upon a four-year-old grazing barely a few feet away. The phandi silently signalled to the mahout that it was to be the target and the latter directed his own mount towards it.

Then, without warning, the direction of the wind changed. The female leader scented the danger and trumpeted out a warning. Bull tuskers took up her refrain and urged the herd to flee.

Too late! Even as the herd swivelled to escape the mahout pushed his mount to a run and placed it alongside the calf. The phandi's eyes never strayed from the targeted animal. He stretched himself almost perpendicularly and flung the lasso across the calf's neck. Its immediate reaction was to curl its trunk inwards; the phandi dexterously slipped the noose over the coiled trunk and round the beast's neck. The mahout gradually brought his charge to a stop, thereby tightening the noose and bringing the calf to an unwilling halt.

It wheeled around and began struggling backwards, unable to shake off the noose trap. Even as the phandi signalled the rest of the party waiting at some distance to advance, the inevitable happened. The female leader of the herd swept upon his beast in a mighty rush, intent upon rescuing her trapped ward. For a split second it seemed that a collision of the two huge pachyderms was inevitable. But the domestic elephant stood its ground and at the very last moment the herd leader came to an abrupt stop, trumpeting a challenge.

The rest of the party now rushed towards the site, men beating gongs and making a racket with their voices. Startled, the herd-leader was in two minds, when the unexpected happened. A bull elephant charged the domesticated mount from another direction, its mouth biting at the rope tethering the calf in an effort to sever it.

Though highly trained, the domesticated animal was momentarily unnerved at such an unprecedented attack on both flanks, and rocked back a few steps. The phandi, caught unawares, slipped from his seat and tumbled heavily to the ground. Fearful that the man would be trampled to death by his own beast, the mahout did what to him was the safest thing to do. He quickly plucked out a dao from his waistband and cut the rope tying his animal to the calf. The animal, finding itself free, wheeled around and disappeared in the jungle up ahead, followed closely by the bull tusker and herd-leader.

The phandi lay unconscious in a heap on the ground, severely injured. The others in the party dismounted quickly; one of the elephants had carried a stretcher of woven bamboo for just such an emergency; this was brought forth and the phandi placed and strapped upon it. Then, having lifted the stretcher upon the back of the lead elephant, the group turned around and headed at a rapid clip towards the camp that had been set up in a clearing in the jungle.

The royal bez or physician was urgently summoned into the temporary bamboo, cane and thatch structure into which the stretcher was taken. The man on the stretcher, clearly, was no ordinary phandi. On the contrary, he was Swargadeo Sukhampha, son of King Suklenmung, who had ascended the Ahom throne at Garhgaon after his father's death. Very adventurous and fond of elephant-trapping, he had been indulging in his favourite pastime when the accident had taken place.

The bez examined the unconscious man and turned to the three patra-mantris who had been part of the trapping group. 'He has taken a blow to his head,' he told them. 'But he will recover consciousness within the hour. He's lucky indeed, for apart from a broken leg he has suffered no serious injury. I'll try and reset the bone and apply a herbal plaster. But, from what I can make out, he will remain lame forever.'

'It is fortunate that this accident happened after his crowning,' Konjang Barpatragohain observed acidly, 'else his lameness would have deprived him of the throne despite him being the eldest son.'

This was an ancient Shan tradition carried on by the Ahoms. Only an heir who was completely without physical blemish was eligible to become a king. A prince who was lame would be rejected outright by the ministers for a claim to the throne.

'That's true,' agreed Taophrongdam Buragohain. 'As it is, his brothers and cousins are already up in arms against him, and it took all our persuasion to ensure that they were not put to death. Had he been lame, he stood no chance at becoming the king.'

The prediction of the royal physician proved true. Even though he recovered from the accident Sukhampha became lame, thereby earning himself the name of Khora Raja or Lame King.

The buragohain, Aikhek, was summoned by the king. He entered
the royal antechamber with some trepidation. Elements opposing the
ascension of Sukhampha were active and the king might harbour the
idea that he was involved. In the past, even high functionaries such as
the buragohain had been put to the sword on suspicion of complicity
in plots against kings.

But then, he had repeatedly proved his mettle, first against the
rebellious Aitoniya Papuk and Khamteng Nagas, then against the
Bhuyan chieftain Pratap Raj, who had been defeated in a battle fought
at Dikhowmukh. Perhaps he was worried needlessly, for surely the Lame
King understood that he needed men like Aikhek all the more at such
a time.

This proved to be the case. 'I'm happy with the manner you've
conducted martial operations against my enemies as well as those of
the Ahoms,' Sukhampha had told him after he had made obeisance
before the king. 'Since my infirmity prevents me from taking active part
in battles, I am pleased to appoint you the commander-in-chief of our
army. We have intelligence that the Koch General Chilarai is eying our
kingdom once again. We need someone of your calibre to prepare our
defences against possible attacks from our west.'

'We're already taking precautions, Your Majesty. As you know, the
Koches under a general named Tipu had launched an assault against us,
which was repulsed. I believe that was merely a test, to gauge our defences
and get a feel of the problems which a full-scale attack might confront.
Yes, we need to strengthen our defensive positions. I've ordered forts
be erected at Boka and Sala, and garrisons of our forces permanently
stationed there.'

'The Kite-king has been crafty,' Sukhampha observed, nodding his
head in agreement. 'Under his guidance, Gohainkamal, a brother of
Koch King Naranarayan, has completed construction of a road on the
north bank of the Luit, which connects their capital Kochbehar with
Narayanpur. Not on the south bank, mind you, since that would bring
him into conflict with us far in advance. The Gohainkamal road will

facilitate a direct attack on our kingdom, a sure sign that such an attack is being contemplated.'

'I too think an attack is imminent,' Aikhek Buragohain said. 'The Koch army is powerful, so we must use subterfuge. Our informants tell us that there are two things an ordinary Koch bestows total reverence upon—Brahmins and cows. So, may I suggest a strategy, Your Majesty ...'

Indeed, the Koch army now under the command of Chilarai was a mighty one. It comprised hundreds of war boats with cannons, as well as thousands of soldiers travelling over the Gohainkamal road on foot and horseback. Advance scouts had warned them that the Ahoms awaited them a few miles ahead and the order to meet them headlong had already been given.

But what was this? The Koch general rubbed his eyes, as did his lieutenants and men. Before them stood the weirdest army they had ever seen! The Ahom war boats were not manned by soldiers but by Brahmins—the sacred thread on their bare chests, the lock of hair hanging like a pony's tail from their shaved heads and the vermillion marks on their foreheads marking them as such. Stranger still, the land army which confronted them was also comprised entirely of Brahmins, some of whom rode not on horses, but on the back of cows!

As soon as they sighted the advancing Koch forces, the Brahmin army emitted blood-curdling yells and rushed towards the enemy. Chilarai's men, not knowing what to do, turned tail and fled. The general himself was confused: how could he wage war against revered Brahmins who rode upon equally sacred cows? He at once ordered his boat to turn around and retreat. The call for retreat was sounded amongst the land forces and the Koch army fell back.

The Brahmin army fell upon the rear of the fleeing Koches, slaughtering as many as possible. They chased the enemy beyond the boundary of the Ahom realm, rousing the very heavens with their cries of victory!

Back in Kochbehar, Chilarai, on reflection, understood he had been tricked. His brother Naranarayan had actually laughed at his discomfiture! The Ahoms had dressed up their soldiers like Brahmins, knowing well how the Koch held the caste in high esteem. The Kite-king was enraged. He would launch another assault on the Ahoms, the likes of which his adversary had never seen. He would go and conquer the Ahom capital—only this time he would not allow himself to be fooled by fake Brahmins!

Within the royal palace complex at Garhgaon, there was a large pool for the king and members of royalty to swim in. It being summer, Sukhampha fancied a swim and went with his immediate entourage to this pool. He took off his robes and ornaments one by one, handing them over to an attendant who laid them carefully on the bank of the pool. The king, dressed in only a loincloth, lowered himself into the water and began to swim.

Then something unforeseen happened. Suddenly, out of nowhere, a kite swooped down and, picking up the king's gem-encrusted necklace which lay glittering in the sunlight, flew off with it!

That ended the king's swim for the day. Distraught and not even bothering to dry himself and put on his clothes, he headed for the abode of his chief astrologer in quest for a meaning to this omen.

'An ill omen, Your Majesty,' the astrologer replied unhesitatingly. 'The Kite-king from the west is marching towards your territory. A kite has stolen one of your precious ornaments. You are doomed to lose something precious to the Kite-king.'

Sukhampha was crestfallen. It did indeed prove to be an ill omen. The news of the incident, first related by the king's attendants, soon spread like wildfire across the entire kingdom. It demoralized the common soldiers and affected the spirit of their commanders, who now considered that defeat at the hands of the King of Kites was inevitable.

Thus, Chilarai was astonished at the ease with which he advanced through the Ahom territory; he had come prepared for subterfuges as he had been subjected to on the previous occasion, but there were none. He had heard that the Ahoms were fierce warriors, but the ease with which his army vanquished the enemy in spot after spot filled him with nothing but contempt.

Dark clouds had indeed been cast over the Ahom realm. The capital Garhgaon was in the throes of panic; much before the Koches were knocking on its western door, Sukhampha gave the orders for its evacuation—never before had the proud Ahoms undergone the humiliation of having to let their capital be captured by outsiders! The road leading out of the eastern gate was crowded with the fleeing residents of Garhgaon. Wild rumours fuelled the panic and confusion.

By the time Chilarai entered Garhgaon, it was a ghost city. The king and his nobles had fled to Charaikharang in Namrup, leaving the capital to be occupied by Chilarai and his men. The Ahom villagers outside the city suffered greatly at the hands of the pillaging Koches, having been abandoned by their king and with nowhere else they could run to.

But even greater humiliation was in store for Sukhampha. As he cowered in a makeshift camp at Charaikharang, an emissary was sent to him asking that he arrive at a treaty with Chilarai and accept the latter's terms and conditions if the Ahom throne was to be his again. In truth the Kite-king himself was eager to return to his own kingdom, for news had been conveyed to him that the Padshah of Gaur was making preparations to attack it. But Sukhampha, who had given up all hopes of regaining his capital with his depleted forces, did not know of this and took up Chilarai on his offer as an utterly unexpected and welcome development. He sent his commander Aikhek Buragohain to Garhgaon to negotiate the treaty.

Expectedly, the conditions imposed were tough. Chilarai, in a position to make demands, stipulated that the Ahom cede the entire part of the Brahmaputra Valley on the north bank wrested from the Koches by the Ahoms. In addition, the Ahom king would have to pay a punitive tribute of sixty elephants, sixty pieces of cloth and an enormous treasure in the form of gold, silver and precious gems.

Sukhampha agreed to the terms but humbly requested that he be given some time to raise the demanded war indemnity. This was granted by Chilarai on the condition that some sons of the patra-mantris were offered as hostages, to be taken along to the Koch empire and released only when the entire amount was paid. Thus it was that after the end of the rainy season, Chilarai left Garhgaon along with the hostages, after having posted a garrison at Narayanpur, while Sukhampha returned to a sullen and hostile reception of the citizenry who had not fled the capital. The shame he had suffered demanded scapegoats—the first to suffer was Aikhek Buragohain, who was divested of his rank for gross negligence in erecting the infrastructure required to defend the realm, and was replaced by a noble named Kankham.

Sukhampha also understood that quick action was needed if he were to redeem himself from the ignominy suffered by his people. Thus, when the indemnity had been paid and the conditions for release of the hostages complied with, Kankham Buragohain was instructed first to repair the forts and strengthen defensive positions, and then to embark on an essay at regaining lost Ahom territory. Stronger forts, manned by greater number of soldiers, were erected at strategic places such as Dikhowmukh. The Ahom forces next crossed the Luit River upon a flotilla of boats, attacked the Koch garrison at Narayanpur and dislodged them. Sala too was recovered and its fortification strengthened.

To say that Sukhampha was surprised by the ease with which he drove the Koches from the bounds of Ahom territory would be an understatement. His surprise was all the greater when the sons of the nobles who had been taken as hostages were returned by the Koch King Naranarayan safely to their families.

Sukhampha summoned Sundargohain, one of the young men taken as hostage and the brightest of the lot, to try find out the answer to the puzzle as to why he and the others were released despite the fact that the Ahoms were wresting back territory occupied by the Koches.

'There are many reasons, Your Majesty,' Sundargohain explained. 'First and foremost, the Koch King Naranarayan is a man of principles. Chilarai had promised to release us once the war indemnity had been paid. Naranarayan has kept true to that promise, irrespective of the fact that we have resumed hostility.'

'You spoke of many reasons?'

'Yes, Your Majesty. The most compelling is the fact that the Koch kingdom is under assault from the Badshah of Gaur, who apparently has achieved some success against the forces of the former. The Koch king and his commander-in-chief face pressure on the western flank and thus are willing to remain on amicable terms with us in order to secure peace on their eastern flank. Our release was a gesture on the part of Naranarayan to signal the same.'

'I'll send emissaries to his court to tell him that I'm willing to maintain peace. We've regained all our land anyway, and have no designs for conquest of their territory.'

'Another thing, Your Majesty,' added the observant young man. 'The Koches worship a goddess rather than Lord Shiva whom you worship. Every year, around autumn, they hold a grand and prolonged session of worship centred round a clay idol of this goddess.'

'A female deity? Our Brahmins worship the male deity called Shiva. They might laugh at the thought of having to worship a female goddess.'

'You need not worry on that account, Your Majesty. I know that in private our Brahmins worship that deity too, though they may not have communicated this to you. Her name is Durga. She represents Shakti, or power. It's my earnest belief that worship of Goddess Durga gives the Koches special power in battle. Perhaps she might bestow the same upon us Ahoms if we worship her.'

The king was more than pleased with young Sundargohain. 'I shall do as you advise,' he said. 'An emissary will be dispatched at once to King

Naranarayan with gifts and a message desiring peace. I shall send some of our own craftsmen with him so that they can learn how to make out of clay an idol of this mighty goddess. When they return, Durga Puja will be performed in the Ahom land, though only in the royal palace.'

THE NARRATOR

'So it was that Durga Puja came to be annually performed in the Ahom realm,' said the Narrator. His audience had not wearied of his voice; though the night had grown old, they continued to listen enraptured as he spoke. In their imagination, they tried to visualize what Durga Puja may have been like over four centuries ago. The flames of the bonfire continued to fight the gloom of the misty night.

'Though Sukhampha ruled for fifty-one years from 1552 to 1603, he is not counted as an Ahom monarch of the stature of, say, Suhungmung. On the contrary, it had been during his reign that the Ahom kingdom was almost destroyed! Just imagine what would have happened if Chilarai had not decided to enter into a treaty and leave the Ahom capital Garhgaon. The history of the Brahmaputra Valley may have been totally different then. The Ahoms had conquered the Chutiyas and the Kacharis; having been themselves conquered, they would have been reduced to the status of being subservient to the Koches!

'As I had said, it was the desire of the Koch King Naranarayan to safeguard his eastern flank by extending a hand of friendship to the Ahom monarch, which induced him to enter into a treaty with the latter. Not that this marked a complete end to the strife between these two major entities present during those days in the Brahmaputra Valley. Twice more during the reign of Sukhampha, the Koches, under the generalship of Tipu, engaged the Ahom troops in battle. On both occasions, however, they were repulsed with heavy losses on their side.

'The Koches were not the sole threats. The Chutiyas and Tipamias, too, rose up occasionally in arms and had to be suppressed. In 1563, one Dhekeri raja, in all probability a petty chieftain, dared to pit himself against the Ahom king and was soundly beaten. However, the most significant threat came in 1576 from unexpected quarters—the Nara king of Mungkang in today's Myanmar showed a sudden inclination to expand his sphere of influence westward and made a foray into Ahom territory. Not wishing to add yet another point of confrontation in a kingdom beset on every quarter, Sukhampha entered into a treaty with the Mungkang king, whereby he would pay a princely sum to the latter and in turn would be offered the king's daughter in marriage.

'Though the money was paid, the Mungkang king, rather than send his daughter, instead sent his sister. So offended was Sukhampha with this breach of promise that he dispatched a group of men to abduct the daughter. They were caught and put to death, while the Mungkang king, considering the attempted kidnapping to be an affront, once again advanced with his army into Ahom territory. However, he was beaten thoroughly and had to retreat ingloriously to his own kingdom.

'Know you this, my people, history is like a rolling wave, with periodic highs and lows; no matter how low a wave might sink, it will rise again to the crest. No doubt the period following the death of Suhungmung marked one of the lowest points in the history of our people. But then came a mighty one once again: Susengpha, the son of Sukhampha, who also called himself by the Hindu name of Buddha Swarganarain. His wisdom and enterprise, and the public service he rendered, also earned for him the title of Pratap Singha, or the mighty one, while in popular perception he was the Burha Raja, or the 'Old King' because he had ascended the Ahom throne so late in his life.

'By the time this wise and old monarch ascended the throne at around fifty years of age, the Ahom realm had changed beyond belief. During Sukapha's times, it was a tiny kingdom. It needed the enterprise of Suhungmung to have broadened Ahom horizons and heightened Ahom aspirations. The major principalities, the Chutiyas to the east and Kacharis to the west, had been subjugated; the Koches too had understood what a powerful adversary the Ahoms could be and maintained a broader peace with them. The Ahoms now controlled the entire central and eastern part of the Brahmaputra Valley on both the north and south banks.

'More important, greater exposure to the outside world, particularly to the two ancient civilizations of China and India, had opened up Ahom society. Sankardev had ushered in a religious, social and cultural renaissance; intercourse with the enlightened Koch society during the days of Naranarayan and Chilarai had added to the number of intellectuals and artisans who visited and settled in Ahom land. We, the Ahoms, as we have throughout seen, are highly adaptable. We had given up our language and religion to embrace those of the land we had chosen to migrate to. With changing times, we too adapted. Slowly, brickwork replaced our bamboo, cane and thatch structures, though at first only the royalty was permitted to use it. New techniques of war, particularly naval engagements upon the Brahmaputra and its tributaries, were incorporated and bigger war vessels constructed. From past experience the Ahoms had learned how important the mighty Brahmaputra and its tributaries were to the security of their kingdom and they not only erected defensive forts and ramparts at strategic places, but also built up a formidable armada of war boats. Picking up the art of manufacturing gunpowder, hiloi or cannons and round stone balls from elsewhere to arm them, they took these arts to perfection and grew proficient in their use.

'The stage was thus set for further expansion of the Ahom realm and greater intercourse, not necessarily peaceful, with the rest of Hindustan. This expansion brought about inevitable and direct conflict with the followers of Islam who were bent on conquest of the Brahmaputra Valley with a number of objectives. One was, of course, economic—the control of a historical trade route across the Brahmaputra reaching up to China and other Asian countries. Another was extension of the Mughal empire, with the fertile valley of the Luit being a jewel in its crown. But the most important objective was to disseminate their faith and enlarge its influence through conquest and domination. It is a coincidence, of course, that the indomitable Ahoms were present in the Valley to stem the tide of expansionist Islam, which, in that period, had become a global phenomenon. One consequence of such expansionism had been the conversion of Hindustan from a Hindu- to a Mussulman-ruled nation. To understand this, you must be told a little bit of history of northern India.

'Towards the end of the twelfth century, a Sultan named Mohammed Ghori entered north India from his Ghazni kingdom in Afghanistan, defeated the Hindu ruler Prithvi Raj Chauhan, and captured the throne of Delhi. From then on, till the coming of the British, Delhi was occupied by Mussulman monarchs. Ghori returned to Ghazni, leaving a general named Qutb ud-Din Aibak to rule over the newly conquered territory. During the latter's reign, the Mussulman empire expanded significantly, with one of his commanders named Ibn Bukhtiar moving eastward to conquer Bihar and Bengal and being invested with governorship of this region, then known as Gaur.

'After the death of Ghori his empire disintegrated, with Qutb ud-Din declaring himself the Sultan of Delhi and founding what is known as the slave dynasty. Throughout its reign there were attempts to expand east of Gaur and conquer the land then known as Kamarupa, but the invaders were successfully repulsed. In the mid-fourteenth century, the governor of Gaur, taking advantage of a weak ruler in Delhi, declared his independence and set himself up as a sultan. While, in the early stages, there were amicable relations between Gaur and Kamrup (which was a portion of the erstwhile Kamarupa and was later called Kamatapur), towards the end of the fifteenth century, Sultan Hussein Khan of Gaur conquered Lower Assam and set up a subsidiary kingdom with Hajo as its capital, making his own son the sultan.

'But the new kingdom did not last long, passing through many hands till finally the Koches, whom I have already spoken of, rose to prominence. Though during the time of Ahom King Suhungmung, there had been attacks from Gaur, the brunt of the Mussulman assault was borne by the Koch kingdom. The break-up of the Koch kingdom and occupation of part of it by both the sultan of Gaur as well as the Ahoms finally resulted in direct confrontation between the two.

'It had been utter miscalculation on the part of the good King Naranarayan, who wanted to be fair! Because he was childless, he wished that Raghudev, the son of his brother and close associate Chilarai, inherit the throne at Kochbehar. But at an advanced age, a son was born to Naranarayan. Not wanting that Raghudev be deprived of his due, Naranarayan made the mistake of dividing his kingdom in two, giving half each to Raghudev and his own son Laxminarayan.

'This weakened the Koch empire and provided an opportunity to both the nawab of Gaur and the Ahom King Susengpha to take over the once-powerful kingdom. Meanwhile, in 1526, after the Battle of Panipat, the Mughal dynasty had come to power in Delhi. In the course of the years, the Mughals conquered the Gaur kingdom. Now there was no buffer between the Islamic expansionists and the doughty Ahoms. The next century-and-a-half witnessed repeated conflicts between the Mughals and the Ahoms, leading to some of the most glorious exploits on the part of our race ...'

Lord of a Thousand Elephants

❧

THAT BEEL, A KIND OF RESERVOIR OR LAKE, WAS SITUATED DEEP IN the heart of Ahom territory. It contained one of the largest nao-sals or boat-making facilities in the kingdom. Having as it did a large channel which flowed directly into the Luit, the beel was strategically positioned, for boats built upon it could be rowed directly to the main river. It also possessed another major advantage during naval engagements—the inland beel, surrounded by vegetation, could be used to conceal a fleet of boats which would steal out after an enemy armada had passed and attack it from behind. There were numerous similar beels within the Ahom ruled areas and many of them were used as boatyards to manufacture or moor boats.

Having realized that the Brahmaputra or Luit River was key to the realm's defence, the industrious and enterprising Ahoms lost little time in perfecting their skill in the art of making boats, not only simple dugout canoes, but also complex and elaborate vessels for the purposes of war, trade, recreation and racing. These were constructed by joining together planks of wood, with the two ends raised very high over the water level. Lac and beeswax were used to caulk the gaps between planks, which were welded together by use of a special resin bartered from the Apatani hill tribe. Called Ahom etha, this resin-glue never came unstuck after it was applied and also provided waterproof coating to a vessel.

Another adhesive, consisting of a mixture of snail-lime, molasses and a seed called kenduguti, was also occasionally used.

The enormous variety of boats made in those days testified to the skill of the boatbuilders of the Ahom kingdom. There was the choranao, used for pleasure cruises and racing; the kochanao, or passenger boat, which was a large, flat-bottomed vessel capable of traversing the shallowest of waters while carrying hundreds of passengers; the bojoranao, a luxury boat with overhead covering for affluent passengers; the maarnaos, or two-hulled cargo boat and many others. However, this particular boatyard manufactured only war vessels such as the gochnao, bharinao, gerapnao and sulupnao. The specialty of the craftsmen here was the building of the most fearsome war vessel of them all, the hiloichoranao, which had cannons mounted at the prow.

The scores of craftsmen working in the yard were particularly active and energetic this morning; petty officers were barking out commands, asking the men to look sharp. The reason for such alacrity became evident soon enough; a long caravan of elephants with colourful howdahs affixed to their backs was approaching from a distance, raising a trail of dust. It was Swargadeo Susengpha, the Burha Raja, coming to the boatyard for an inspection.

This king was renowned across the realm for his love of elephants and the thrill he derived from trapping them. It was said that his ambition had been to be the proud owner of 1,000 elephants, which he had succeeded in becoming, thereby earning him another name, Gajapati, or Lord of Elephants! He was also well known for traversing large tracts of his kingdom on such elephant caravans to ensure that defence preparations were up to the mark and his men were as alert and active as their king.

At the head of the procession came the elephant carrying the senior officer titled Naoboicha Phukan, one who was invested with the all-important task of building and maintaining the various fleets of the Ahom kingdom. Behind him on elephants came the patra-mantris, Chowpret Buragohain, Khamsin Bargohain and Laku Barpatragohain, as well as lesser officers, with the king's elephant wedged exactly at the centre, alert soldiers on elephants before and behind him.

Having arrived at the beel and dismounted, the king was shown around the boat-building yard, with the Naoboicha Phukan escorting him and reeling out facts and figures about the construction activities going on throughout the kingdom. As they walked around, the king waving and nodding agreeably at the awestruck workers, other officers filled him in about ancillary activities—the training of soldiers in the manoeuvring of war boats and the handling of cannons, the manufacture of cannons and so on. A temporary canopy had been constructed at a little distance from the water and, after the inspection was over, the king and his senior ministers moved under it and seated themselves on cane chairs.

Susengpha appeared to be satisfied with the war preparations. 'The way things are shaping up, war on an enormous scale is inevitable,' he said, digging into the refreshments that were being served. 'I'm not referring to the kind of skirmish we recently had with the Jaiantias or the Kacharis. They are small fry and no match for the might of us Ahoms. I am referring to the followers of Islam, the generals of the rulers of far-off Delhi, who are known as the Mughals. They are formidable foes who have conquered the eastern parts of Hindustan as also the Koch kingdom. Their henchmen rule Bengal as its subahdars. The good King Naranarayan was ill-advised to have split his kingdom; as our spies inform us, the Mughals have taken over both the parts and are present in great strength as close as Hajo. The Koch kings of both parts of the kingdom have been taken prisoner and carted off to Delhi.'

'True, Your Majesty,' said the buragohain. 'These bangals from far off pose a grave threat.' The term was used to denote the people in the army from Bengal; one of its generals had been named Bangal as well.

'The threat has become graver since we gave shelter to Balinarayan, the brother of the captured Koch King Parikshit. The Mughals have annexed Parikshit's realm, but Balinarayan has given them the slip and sought shelter with us.'

'We can send him back to the Mughals and make peace with them,' Khamsin Bargohain suggested.

'Are we, the descendants of Sukapha, cowards?' retorted Susengpha, visibly angry. 'Should we sue for peace by sacrificing someone who has come to us for succour? How would history treat us, Bargohain dangoriya? No, we will resist the Mughals if they dare to advance towards us.'

The bargohain bowed his head in acknowledgment of the rebuke. Laku Barpatragohain pointed out a salient fact: 'Having captured the eastern part of the Koch kingdom, the Mughal army is now massed on our borders. It would need just one pretext for them to advance into our lands.'

'Let them come. Ever since I, eldest son of Sukhampha, known earlier as Langi Gohain, ascended the singorighar and took on the name of Susengpha, I've been preparing for such a conflict. Why else do you think I've been touring the length and breadth of my realm, personally supervising the training of soldiers and augmentation of our war arsenal? Let the drums of war be sounded and we'll be ready.'

The spark for the prolonged conflict between the Ahoms and the mighty Mughals, which forms the most glorious chapter in the former's history, was lit in the guise of a seemingly minor incident in 1615.

Two maarnaos were making their laborious way up the river Luit inside the Ahom realm. These were laden with cargo from the Indian mainland, particularly salt, and bound for the Ahom capital of Garhgaon. On their return journey, they would carry mainly a cargo of precious agar wood from which perfume was extracted. Since the huge boats were travelling upstream against the currents, although it was the dry season, the going was both slow and difficult. A group of men walked along the shoals on the right bank, pulling ropes tethered to the vessels and towing them on. One man stood at the helm of each boat with a bamboo pole in hand, to gauge the depth of the waters as well as to provide limited steerage.

The owner of the boat was Ratan Shah, a trader from Bengal. Trading vessels entering Ahom territory, which at that point of time was marked by the river Bharali, a north-bank tributary of the Luit, had to acquire permission in writing from the authorities; the long-time trader was equipped with the permission letter. But, on this particular trip, trading was not the sole motive. Under instructions from Sheikh Qasim, the subahdar or governor of Bengal, Ratan Shah was engaged on a spying mission in Ahom territory. The majhis or mudois who pulled and guided the boats upstream were actually soldiers in civil dress; spies lay concealed within the awnings, which provided shelter from the elements, making notes about the lay of the land and extent of Ahom fortifications. Underneath the salt, tobacco and other items were concealed weapons for defence in case freebooters attempted to loot the vessels on the way.

However, impediment came from official quarters. Ratan Shah had underestimated the intelligence-gathering machinery of the Ahoms. From the moment the two maarnaos had entered Ahom territory, they had been under close observation. The manner in which the boatmen were guiding the boats had aroused suspicion, for these men lacked the dexterity experienced mudois show. Near Kaliabor, where the Ahoms had fortifications and encampment, a fleet of hiloichoranaos, led by an Ahom officer designated as Chengdhara Neog, swept in swiftly upon the two vessels. A quick search revealed that it was no ordinary trading trip; retribution was swift and deadly; Ratan Shah and the spies inside the boats were slaughtered and the cargo seized; but the soldiers masquerading as the boatmen were allowed to return and carry a stern message to the governor of Bengal not to attempt similar spying missions again.

The Chengdhara Neog carried the captured goods as well as news of the attempted spying to King Susengpha. The latter at once realized the implications of such a provocation, though secretly pleased at the opportunity this offered. Nor was he wrong. The Governor of Bengal Sheikh Qasim, whose territory by then had extended right up to

Guwahati after the annexation of the erstwhile Koch Hajo kingdom, sent a huge army on a punitive expedition. It consisted of 400 war vessels and 10,000 cavalry and infantry soldiers and was led by two imperial officers named Syed Hakim and Syed Aba Bakr. They were accompanied by a factotum of the Mughals named Sattarjit, who had been made a petty official of Koch Hajo after the Mughals had captured that kingdom.

It was deep in the night. Though the two armies, the one sent by the subahdar of Bengal and that of the Ahoms who lay in wait for them, were encamped on opposite sides at the mouth of the Bharali River, there were no flares, for a strict lights-out was being observed by both. Anyway, the fog was so thick that any light would have been obscured; it was inconceivable that an attack would be launched in conditions that made it impossible for one to see beyond a foot ahead; so, the Ahom camp, aware that the army of strangers would be unfamiliar with the terrain, was complacent and the sentries placed to guard it were sleeping soundly.

Syed Hakim, however, was crafty. He had been told of the Ahom dread of cavalry and understood that a small group would be sufficient to put his adversary to flight. He had chosen the best of his boatmen and the best amongst his cavalry; the small band of horsemen were transported through the fog and silently landed on the shore just yards away from the Ahom camp at the mouth of the Bharali. The attack was swift and accompanied by blood-curdling yells; though it was a pitch-black night, the trained cavalrymen had no difficulty swiping fleeing foot soldiers with their swords. Dozens were killed; the Ahom camp, caught by surprise, fled directionless through the fog.

The Burha Raja was angry. It was said in the palace that when the Burha Raja was angry, all Garhgaon trembled. 'Useless nincompoops!' he thundered. 'To allow themselves to be caught by surprise! Apprehend the garrison commander at Bharali and throw him into the dungeons. I want him replaced by Akhek Gohain.'

Chowpret Buragohain cried out in consternation. 'Surely that cannot be, Your Majesty! Akhek is a renegade who betrayed the confidence you had shown in him when you appointed him commander of the garrison at Dikhowmukh. He not only tried to poison the minds of local chieftains against you, but had also hobnobbed with the enemy by fleeing to Sheikh Qasim, the subahdar of Bengal.'

'He is a habitual betrayer, Your Majesty,' Khamsin Bargohain nodded his head to denote that he concurred with the buragohain. 'We realize that he has now turned his back on the sheikh and has once again pledged allegiance to you. But we doubt if he can be trusted. It's only the promise of a pardon which has brought him back to you.'

'Yes, I've accepted him into our fold,' Susengpha said. 'Incentive enough, don't you think, for him to give his all in battle? But my memory is like that of my beloved elephants—I don't forget. So, it's another matter what I do with Akhek afterwards.'

The three patra-mantris smiled, quick to understand the hint thrown by the king. The king spelt out what needed to be done, the court scribe writing his orders on a piece of sanchi bark.

'This is the moment we've been waiting for,' Swargadeo Pratap Singha said. 'Ever since I became king, I've anticipated this moment and prepared for it. Put our plan in action. Akhek must take up the leadership of the frontline of the Ahom forces and begin counter-attacking. We need to send him reinforcements ... I, myself, will take them to him.'

The Burha Raja had been right. Akhek Gohain was highly intelligent and efficient. Moreover, because he was beholden to the king, he gave all he had, taking a cue from the Bengal subahdar's army and attacking the enemy at night, both on land and water. What followed was total rout of the latter; over 5,000 of the sheikh's soldiers were slaughtered,

9,000 captured and the rest had to be rescued by a fleet of boats sent for the purpose by the Bengal governor. Hakim and Aba Bakr, the two commanders, were killed in action. Akhek Gohain picked out the lesser officers, led them chained to the Kamakhya temple rebuilt by King Naranarayan, and sacrificed them to the goddess. Amongst those beheaded was the son of Sattarjit.

A broad swathe of land to the west of the Bharali now came under Ahom occupation. Balinarayan, the brother of the Koch King Parikshit, who had sought protection under Pratap Singha, was made ruler of this new territory and given the title of Raja of Darrang. The spoils of the well-coordinated counterattack on the Bengal army were ample— hundreds of war vessels and cannons, elephants and horses—the Ahom king, accompanied by Akhek, marched back to his capital with his trophies and performed the Rikkhvan ceremony.

Swargadeo Susengpha's words were true. Like an elephant, he never forgot. As soon as he got back to his capital, he revoked the pardon on Akhek and put him to the sword. In Bengal, Sheikh Qasim Khan was deprived of his post of subahdar.

Susengpha was always on the move and rarely confined himself to his capital at Garhgaon. The wise monarch understood that this was the best way to keep himself in touch with his people and comprehend their needs and aspirations. This morning, his elephant train had been making its way through a hamlet in the Nazira area, when something caught the king's eyes.

It was the cottage of a petty official who, though he dwelt at Garhgaon, retained his family at Nazira. Perched upon the back of his pachyderm, Susengpha had a broad view of the compound of the cottage and was impressed by the neat and orderly manner in which the gardens at the front and rear had been maintained. A smartly trimmed hedge ran around the entire perimeter of the cottage. Flowering shrubs and plants, as also medicinal herbs, were planted in perfect rows in the front garden. The back garden had been retained exclusively for vegetables.

The Burha Raja had a knack for sniffing out the qualities of an individual, as people like Akhek had realized to their misfortune. The person who had raised the gardens was industrious, for in the wet climate of Assam, where greenery grew fast and thick, maintaining such spick-and-span gardens required capacity for hard toil. Moreover, the man had an orderly and utilitarian mind, as mirrored by the manner in which the plants and vegetables had been placed.

The king signalled to his elephant train to stop and descended. Not merely the members of the particular household, but also scores of villagers, ran towards the visitors and prostrated themselves.

'Arise,' the king commanded. 'Who is the head of this household?'

A man stepped up and bowed his head.

'Let me congratulate you on the neat and orderly manner in which you've maintained your compound,' the king said with a smile.

Clearly, lying did not come easily to the head of the household. 'It's not my doing, Your Majesty,' he acknowledged. 'It's my momai's.'

'That's strange,' the king commented with curiosity. 'You call yourself the head of the household yet you have an uncle, who must be older, living with you!'

'It's not strange at all, Your Majesty. My momai, whose real name is Sukoti, had borrowed my bulls to plough his land, but they died of some disease. He has agreed to work as my servant to pay off his debt. It is he who can take credit for keeping my compound so neat.'

The king guffawed. 'An uncle willingly becoming a slave to his own nephew!' the Burha Raja said. 'Strange indeed are the ways of men! Where's this uncle of yours? Let him stand before me.'

A grave-featured man, tall and imposing, strode up to the king and prostrated himself.

'You are Sukoti?' the Burha Raja asked, impressed by the demeanour of the man.

'Yes, Your Majesty.'

'I not only admire your handiwork in creating such lovely gardens,' said the king, 'but also your sense of ethical values in agreeing to work as a slave for your own nephew so that you can clear your debt. What say you, after your debt is cleared, come to my palace at Garhgaon and work for me?'

'He can go today itself, Your Majesty,' cried the nephew, surprised and flustered, yet pleased. 'He has been working for me despite my protestations. He has long since repaid what he considers to be a debt.'

'In that case, collect your belongings and hop on to one of my elephants,' the king ordered. 'I shall make you the barichoa tamuli, the officer who looks after the gardens in the royal palace.'

Momai Tamuli, as Sukoti came to be known in the course of time, did not remain the caretaker of the royal gardens for long. The Burha Raja, correctly judging the character and industriousness of the man, soon began to rely upon him for advice in matters regarding the governance of the kingdom. This elicited protesting comments from his patra-mantris. 'Such interference from one who has no official standing is unacceptable, Your Majesty,' the bargohain commented petulantly one day.

'Well,' said the king shortly, 'in that case, I'll bestow upon him the necessary "official standing"! From today I'm creating a new post, to be termed as barbarua. The person who graces this will assist me and future monarchs in administering the realm. This is a much-needed post, for I myself, as well as you three, are mostly engaged in armed conflict. But a good and wise king does not neglect the welfare of his subjects even while he is defending the kingdom or enlarging its extent.

'I appoint Momai Tamuli as the first barbarua. Although, as a token of my trust, I bestow upon him the newly conquered land east of Koliabor not belonging to the patra-mantris; his primary duty will be to assist me in carrying out reformative measures for the welfare of my subjects, as also to strengthen the Ahom realm.'

From then onwards, the Burha Raja and his barbarua embarked on a series of welfare measures and administrative reforms the likes of which the kingdom had never seen before. 'The rivers are the roads of our realm, no doubt, Your Majesty,' Momai Tamuli Barbarua said to his liege, 'but during the rainy season they swell and grow treacherous. We need a chain of land routes crisscrossing the kingdom, which will be safer modes of communication no matter which season.'

The officer, in a planned way, built up a system of roads, some of which simultaneously served as embankments against floods, as well as defensive ramparts. This proved to be a catalyst to greater intercourse and trade between various communities. In order to broaden the range of barter trade, a number of haats or periodic but permanent markets were set up at strategic places. Monitored trade with neighbours was encouraged and special attention was paid to the export of products of the cottage industries in villages. Through reallocation of resources and restructuring of the demographic and professional structure, villages were rendered self-sufficient. Momai Tamuli made it compulsory for every adult male to learn how to make bamboo and cane implements and every woman how to work at the loom. By deftly utilizing the latent energy of the masses, he ensured that the Ahom kingdom enjoyed a level of prosperity never attained before, despite a serious outbreak of cattle disease in 1618 and a famine in 1641 due to a locust invasion.

Though the monarch was away on martial expeditions much of the time, his absence did not see deferment of welfare measures, for Momai Tamuli Barbarua enjoyed his full confidence and could embark on projects without prior approval. He understood that many of the prevailing ailments amongst the subjects were waterborne diseases; so, in many places he built large tanks, protected by earthen ramparts from pollution by flood water, to provide fresh drinking water to villagers. Nor were the spiritual needs of the subjects neglected—in consultation with the king, Momai Tamuli supervised the construction of a number of dols or temples, two of the larger Sivadols being built at Biswanath and Dergaon.

'May I make a suggestion, Your Majesty?' said Momai Tamuli Barbarua to Swargadeo Susengpha when they were alone in the king's antechamber.

'It must be something important,' the king observed with a twinkle in his eyes. 'The timing and the place, my dear Barbarua! Here you're alone with me in my inner sanctum. The patra-mantris are nowhere in sight!'

'You're all-seeing, Your majesty! Yes, it is a suggestion for a momentous change, one which might transform the destiny of the Valley. As you may have observed, Asamiya has become the common language of the diverse ethnic groups who constitute your subjects. Our own Tai language is the official language of the court and you speak in that language with your nobles. But the language of the people is Asamiya!'

'So, what do you suggest?'

'Proclaim Asamiya to be the court language along with Tai, Your Majesty. This language has become an instrument for bringing about unity amongst the people. It is but apt that it should be the official language. And one more thing ... it is time we began to record our buranjis in Asamiya.'

The monarch's brows were furrowed with thought. 'A momentous change, indeed! Yet there is logic to what you suggest. No longer are our subjects exclusively Ahoms—today, apart from so many tribes, we even have Mussulman subjects whom we had captured and allowed to settle here. A new identity is being slowly but surely formed—the sense of belonging to one nationality. Adopting Asamiya as the court language and writing our buranjis in it would enhance the nationalistic spirit.'

'I'm glad you think so, Your Majesty. But would you be able to carry your patra-mantris with you if you agree with my proposal?'

'Tush! They would not dare to go against my wishes! But I'm more concerned about our Ahom priests, the Deodhais, Bailungs and the rest. They consider themselves to be the guardians of our native language and might oppose it.'

'Our priests no longer carry any weight with the masses, Your Majesty. They listen to the Brahmin priests instead, as do you. I recall that when the tank at Misagarh was completed, you had Brahmin priests rather than Ahom ones consecrate it.'

'That's true. But what about Mahapurushiya, the cult begun by Sankardev? This new faith seems to be spreading like wildfire. On the advice of my Brahmin priests, I've arrested and put to death many of their gosains and adherents. But that hasn't stemmed the spread. Would not adopting Asamiya as the official language help the cause of these Vaishnavites?'

'One cannot deter the course of any movement through mere persecution, Your Majesty. After all, one adopts the faith with which one is comfortable. It is my belief, Your Majesty, that no man should be persecuted for his faith. This only proves to be a hurdle on the path of nationalism and unity.'

'All right. I'm convinced. Asamiya shall be the official language of the court, along with Tai.'

'Thank you, Your Majesty. Your name shall be written in golden letters a thousand years from now for the decision you've made. Now we come to another matter. There is a dire need to usher in administrative reforms ...'

Indeed, as Momai Tamuli Barbarua rose in power and stature, momentous changes began to be effected in the administrative and social structure, their tangible benefits delighting the king. Knowledge was the key to social transformation—this was a tenet by which the barbarua swore. Prior to the commencement of his reforms, therefore, he had a census conducted of the entire kingdom—one room in the palace was reserved exclusively to the placement and analysis of the census data. Momai Tamuli had a palace artist sketch a rough map of the kingdom upon the floor of that room; small figurines of different colours were used to denote the density of population as well as the presence of specific tribes. Based upon his estimates, the barbarua began dispersal of the population, serving specific needs and with utilitarian objectives. For instance, the frontier with the Kachari kingdom required martial men who could resist possible incursions—thus 400 Ahom families were taken from Abhayapur, Dihing and Namdang, and settled at Marangi. Similarly, hundreds of families from the more thickly populated parts of Lower Assam were shifted to parts of Upper Assam where there was thin population in order to strike a balance. Also, for the first time, the concept of townships as different from villages was introduced, and two of the former, Abhayapur and Mathurapur, primarily trading centres, were built. Momai Tamuli also introduced the concept of grouping families following similar professions together in a single village, which then became renowned for the particular product it produced. For example, in the later phase of Swargadeo Pratap Singha's reign, when the region came under Ahom suzerainty, Momai Tamuli created the Sualkuchi village which soon grew famous for its silk weaving.

Next, around 1609, the barbarua began a reformation of the paik system. The obvious benefits of the system had been somewhat diluted by arbitrariness and disorganization; he sought to bring about order by straitjacketing the system within a rigorous framework. As before, every male between the age of fifteen and fifty was required to work in different capacities in lieu of agricultural land. Momai Tamuli organized the paiks by the nature of the work they were to do into khels; paiks belonging to the same tribe or profession were grouped into a single khel, each having from 1,000 to 5,000 paiks. In order to prevent injustice or discrimination, officers were appointed to monitor the paiks: an officer with twenty paiks under him was called a bora; one having control of 100 paiks was a saikia; 1,000 paiks, a hazarika; 3,000 paiks, a rajkhowa; and 10,000 paiks, a phukan. Starting from Pratap Singha, if the Ahom monarchs were able to successfully resist the onslaught of the Mughals while the kingdom attained peaks of prosperity and self-sufficiency, much of the credit went to this systematic reorganization of the subjects. The streamlining, while enabling the conscription of fighting men in quick time for a military campaign, gave a boost to the manufacture of local cottage-industry products as also to trade.

Apart from khels, Momai Tamuli also established the pancha system. The hills to the north and east of the Ahom kingdom were peopled by martial hill tribes who would occasionally descend into the valley and carry out acts of depredation upon villages in the plains, looting crops and cattle, more often than not also capturing village folk to be made their slaves. It being well-nigh impossible to provide security to each and every village, the barbarua initiated the pancha system whereby each family of villages on the border would give a part of its annual produce to a community fund, which would then be given to the hill tribes. This system not only reduced the depredation upon the people of the plains, but also brought about greater intercourse between the hills and the valley, with Asamiya emerging as a common lingua franca.

Cognizant of the organizing capacity of the barbarua, the Burha Raja, in consultation with his army generals, also made him oversee the defence infrastructure. Numerous ramparts, embankments and forts were constructed at strategic places such as Samdhara, Safrai and Sita. The Naga tribes had been a recurrent headache—a well-guarded rampart called Dhopgarh was constructed and Nagas were ordered on the pain of death not to cross it unless accompanied by an Ahom katoki or peon. Momai Tamuli fashioned an intricate network of spies and katokis to keep an eye on other hill tribes and alert villagers to resist any raids.

Momai Tamuli Barbarua was indubitably one of the most capable administrators the Ahom era produced. However, he would not have been able to bring about the far-reaching social and economic changes had he not had an authoritarian Ahom ruler at the helm. Swargadeo Pratap Singha was notorious for the severity with which he came down upon individuals who transgressed his orders. For instance, he had totally subjugated the group of petty chiefs known as Bhuyans and resettled them on the south bank of the Luit, forbidding them to cross the river and return to their original homes. When some silkworm rearers amongst the Bhuyans crossed the Luit simply to breed cocoons, they were arrested and executed on the spot. Even the highest of nobles quaked at his name for he did not let power or reputation deter him when pronouncing punishment; a Bharalibarua who was a close confidant of the king was ordered to be beheaded on discovering that the man was putting his hands into the royal till.

The year was 1617; the month, November. A conclave of chiefs was gathered at a spot on the south bank of the river Luit. Amongst the dignitaries were representatives of Jashamanik, the king of the Jaiantias, whose daughter Pratap Singha had married, as also those of the Kachari king. The Koch prince, Balinarayan, whom Pratap Singha had made the raja of Darrang and who after ascension had changed his name to Dharmanarayan, too was there, as were a dozen petty chiefs owing allegiance to the Ahom swargadeo, including the rajas of Dimarua, Rani, Luki, Beltola, Hojai, etc. But the star of the conclave was indubitably the towering personality of Swargadeo Pratap Singha himself, accompanied by his officials, including Momai Tamuli.

'Honoured chiefs,' said Pratap Singha addressing the gathering, 'the bangals are at our doorstep. Though for a while they have not stepped out, we will never be fully secure as long as they are there. They are bent on conquering our territory and thrusting their religion upon us.'

There was a concurring murmur. 'Their intentions are hostile,' said one of the chiefs brusquely. 'There can be no arguing that.'

'Yet they are strong,' resumed the swargadeo. 'They have infinite resources. It is not only the subahdar of Bengal or that nawab of Dhaka who have soldiers and armaments; they can draw on resources all the way from the king they call the Badshah in distant Dilli.'

'True, they are strong,' said another chief. 'Compared to them we are but weaklings.'

'That's where you're wrong,' said the Ahom king firmly. 'If we put our resources together, we can outstrip theirs many times over. I myself believe that attack is the best form of defence. So, I am going to launch an all-out war against these Mughals and bangals. Honoured chiefs, I ask you to join me in my campaign. Your presence would strengthen my army and raise the morale of my soldiers. What say you, will you join me?'

'Yes, yes,' the chiefs at the gathering spoke in a chorus. 'Though we owe allegiance to you, we enjoy a great deal of freedom. But these bangals will destroy our freedom. Yes, yes, we're with you.'

'It will be a prolonged war, let me warn you,' the swargadeo said. 'But we need to persevere and fling the intruders from our doorsteps. In unity lies our strength. So here is to our unity!'

The Ahom swargadeo raised his hengdang. All the chiefs gathered at the conclave raised their swords and the battle cry, 'Death to the bangals!' filled the air.

This was the first memorable occasion when the tribes of the hills and valleys of the region now universally known as Assam joined hands against an external enemy. Such a political compulsion, together with the spiritual and cultural unification by Sankardev and his disciples, as also the development and growing eminence of a common Assamese language, reinforced the feeling of Assamese nationalism and strengthened the sense of unity in diversity.

It was an army as was never beheld before. Traditional adversaries, Ahoms, Koches, Kacharis, Chutiyas, Bhuyans and Nagas now sank their earlier differences to battle a common foe. The Mughals had never encountered such a diverse army; attacked at their advance position at Agiathuri, they were forced to retreat to the well-fortified and heavily manned Hajo. But the assault by Pratap Singha and his men was fierce indeed and Hajo was in dire peril of falling into their hands, so much so that the Mughal commander, Abdussalam, had to beg the assistance of the nawab of Dhaka. The latter sent a huge force, under the command of his brother Muhiuddin, comprising 1,000 matchlock men, a 1,000-strong cavalry and over 200 war boats.

Pratap Singha had instructed the garrison manning the frontlines to stay put in their newly fortified positions till he could formulate a plan of action to attack Hajo. Unfortunately, their success in battle so far had fired up the blood of soldiers and when they saw a few Mughal soldiers on a sortie at a distance, they could not resist the temptation to come out from their fortification and give chase right up to Hajo. Other chiefs presumed this to be a signal to attack and Hajo was assaulted from all sides, the Ahoms taking on the front, and Dharmanarayan's men as also the Kacharis, Chutiyas, etc. attacking the rear and flanks. But the attack was disorganized and the sizeable body of Mughal defenders was not only able to ward off the challengers but pursue them right up to Srighat. Time and again Pratap Singha's army stopped to resist the Mughal forces, but were defeated each time with heavy losses. The buragohain was captured, thousands of soldiers were killed, and elephants and boats taken.

Swargadeo Pratap Singha trembled with rage. His officers seated with him within a makeshift tent were also trembling, but in fear.

'It speaks ill of our discipline,' the monarch thundered, 'that our officers and soldiers cannot wait for the king's orders and strike out on their own. I will make an example of some of them. Momai Tamuli, select the ones that you deem most guilty and behead or starve them to death. Arrest the bargohain and the Saring raja and have them put in a pigsty to make them realize who they really are!'

'Your will be done, Your Majesty,' replied the barbarua, though his demeanour clearly showed that he was none too happy at being assigned to the task.

'Send out emissaries to the forces now stuck at different spots and ask them to rally at Samdhara. I shall send reinforcements there and stem the enemy's advance.'

'The problem, Your Majesty,' observed the barbarua, 'is that each group of troops is led by different chiefs. In your absence, there is no one to coordinate the attacks. May I suggest that you create a new post, the holder of which will be overall commander in your absence.'

'A good suggestion, Barbarua. I hereby decree that a new post of Barphukan be created. Not only will he be the overall commander of our assault forces, but he would also act as the governor of all the newly conquered land under us west of Kaliabor.'

'May I also suggest, Your Majesty, that Commander Langi Panisiya, who has proved himself worthy by regrouping our disorganized forces, be made the first barphukan,' the barbarua said.

'Let that be so. Once we have regrouped and reinforced our forces, we shall show these Mughals what stuff we are made of.'

Beginning from September 1619, a series of hostilities commenced between the combined forces led by Pratap Singha and the Mughals, the results veering this way and that. The dogs of war were let loose during the decades that followed, with no decisive wins on either side. The Mughals soon realized that their expansionist designs were being thwarted by a formidable foe, while the Ahoms and the tribal chiefs fiercely defended whatever land they could regain. There were betrayals and treachery on either side, too numerous for brief encapsulation, and many Ahom nobles lost their lives because of this. There were long periods of truce, particularly during the period of heavy rains which hindered warfare. At the same time there were numerous skirmishes; for instance the Nawab of Dhaka sent a retaliatory force in 1635 to seize one of his allies who had defected to the Ahom camp as well as to avenge the slaughter of some Mughal soldiers but the Ahoms met it on the banks of the Bharali river and forced it to retreat.

It was not always defensive strategy on the part of Pratap Singha—aided by the chiefs of Dimarua, Hojai, Barduar and other places, and also conscripting 10,000 paiks actually settled within the Mughal territory, he launched an attack on the latter's forts in places like Banikot, Chamaria and Nagarbera, even advancing to the Kulsi river, inflicting heavy defeats and capturing elephants, cannons and war boats, and taking hundreds of prisoners who were transported to be resettled in Ahom territory. Hajo itself was assailed and the Mughal governor there had to request Nawab Islam Khan for help. A cavalry of 1,000 men and another 1,000 foot soldiers were dispatched and the Ahom army was coerced to retreat in the ensuing engagements. In one of these engagements, the Ahoms took prisoner a white bangal, or a European in the employ of the Mughals, who aroused great curiosity amongst his captors, the first such individual to have set foot in Assam.

Later, taking advantage of the dry season which made operating the Mughal war boats impossible, the Ahom-led army counterattacked and inflicted a crushing defeat on the advancing enemy, killing Commander Muhammad Salih and capturing 300 cannons and an equal number of war boats. Hajo was once more put under siege and, due to the lack of supplies and consequent starvation, its inmates were forced to surrender. Governor Abdussalam was brought before Pratap Singha, who ordered that he and his soldiers be taken to Upper Assam and settled there. One faction of the Mughal army under Syed Zainul-abidin, however, refused to give up and was defeated and slaughtered.

The capture of Hajo marked the high point of Pratap Singha's campaign against the Mughal. It yielded a huge booty, including 2,000 guns and 700 horses. The Goalpara area was cleared of Mughal presence. A large swathe of land in Kamrup was given to some of the chiefs who had assisted the Ahoms in the campaign.

However, the Ahom dominance of Lower Assam was not to last long. Earlier the nawab of Dhaka had dispatched under Mir Zainuddin a large army to aid his men at Hajo, but the place had been captured by the Ahoms and their allies before it could get there. On reaching the ceded territory, Zainuddin at once set about retrieving it. His soldiers were fresh and equipped with ample supplies, while his opponents were exhausted after a bitter campaign in which thousands of lives had been lost. Despite this, the latter stood their ground at Jogighopa on the north bank of the Luit River and at Hirapur on the south bank, with the stretch of the river in between being blocked by their armada.

It was, at best, an unequal battle; the Ahoms and their allies were defeated and forced to retreat. Local chieftains, sensing which way the wind was blowing, switched sides and vowed allegiance to the Mughal force, augmenting it. At the end of the rainy season in 1637, Mir Zainuddin had inflicted one crushing defeat after another on his adversary, recapturing Hajo, Pandu, Agiathuri and Saraighat. After a campaign of attrition Pratap Singha's forces were forced to retreat to Kaliabor, where they had a firmer foothold.

On the advice of his patra-mantris, Pratap Singha had gone back to Garhgaon and direct operations from there rather than from Kaliabor. The news being periodically brought by couriers was not heartening, and the king was understandably alarmed. Two chieftains, Dimarua Raja and Hari Deka, who had assisted him in his confrontation with the Mughals and were entrusted with the task of defending the Kajali fort at the mouth of the river Kollong, had been forced to leave that bastion and join the rest of the Ahom forces at Kaliabor. Equally disheartening had been treacherous action on the part of Panisiya Barphukan, the first officer to have been invested that post, who had had to be executed because of the serious nature of his offence. Given the ferocity and speed of the Mughal advance, it might be merely a matter of time till Garhgaon fell into the hands of Mir Zainuddin.

The Burha Raja, whose habit of planning ahead for contingencies was well known, immediately ordered the populace of Garhgaon to prepare for possible evacuation of the capital. All the valuables in the royal palace and the houses of the nobles were packed and readied for transportation towards the shelter of the hills if required. The previous occupation of Garhgaon by the Koch army of Chilarai had not been forgotten and the Ahom monarch had a plan of action in mind in case his capital fell once again. At the same time, as a kind of warning to the invading forces, he publicly executed some Muslims who had been made prisoner in previous battles.

However, much to his relief, the Mughal forces did not progress further for the time being and instead embarked on a process of consolidation of their hold on the recaptured areas. A Mughal commander named Mir Nurullah was appointed Thanedar of Kamrup with his headquarters at Guwahati. He immediately introduced the Mughal system of administration and effected financial settlement of the region, signifying that they sought to retain jurisdiction for a long time to come.

It was only after the end of the rainy season of the year 1638 that the Mughal forces renewed their advance, sending a huge armada up the Brahmaputra to engage the Ahom forces. The delay was a blessing for Pratap Singha, for it enabled him to restructure and strengthen his forces for a do-or-die battle against the invaders. Momai Tamuli Barbarua was put in overall command and, apart from erecting defensive ramparts at strategic places and framing a plan of action, the crafty statesman bought additional time by pretending to offer an olive branch to the Mughals and promising to pay annual tribute. As negotiations were being concluded, so were the defensive preparations; once the barbarua felt confident enough of his defences, he abruptly called off the truce and challenged his adversary to battle.

The Ahoms gained the upper hand in the ensuing conflict and drove the Mughal forces beyond Kajali. The sagacious barbarua knew when enough was enough, so he advised Pratap Singha to end the hostilities and arrive at a peace accord. The Mughals too appeared weary of the campaign; they readily agreed to a treaty being drafted, thereby ending their attempt at advance towards the Ahom kingdom for some years to come.

The two individuals engaged in hammering out this path-breaking treaty were Nawab Allah Yar Khan on behalf of the Mughals and Momai Tamuli Barbarua for the Ahoms. By the terms of the treaty the Bar Nadi on the north bank of the river Brahmaputra and the Asurar Ali on the south bank were demarcated as the dividing boundary between the Ahom realm and that of the nawab of Dhaka. Though for the next two decades, Kamrup remained under Mughal administration with their headquarters in Guwahati, the treaty was the biggest achievement for Pratap Singha, for he became the unchallenged monarch of the biggest realm ruled over thus far by an Ahom swargadeo. Momai Tamuli Barbarua stationed himself at the Kajoli fort at the western border of the Ahom territory for the next twelve years to ensure that the Ahom boundary was protected from Mughal aggression, the latter's outpost being situated further west at Rangamati.

The year was 1641 and although the rainy spell had not ended, a small fleet of pleasure boats sailed down the river Dikhow. The royal barge, resplendent in all its glory, glided along at the centre; it carried a bed upon which reclined Swargadeo Pratap Singha. His queens were in an adjacent section of the royal barge, screened from view; but the nobles were seated on cane chairs beside the bed. Hundreds of villagers stood upon the bank waving at the royal fleet as it progressed in a stately manner down the river Dikhow.

A pall of gloom had settled upon the three patra-mantris, as well as the barbarua. The Deodhai medicine men in the palace, as well as the royal bezbarua or physician, had diagnosed that the king did not have many more months to live. Swargadeo Pratap Singha had taken the news with a smile. 'No one,' he told his close confidants, 'is immortal, not even the swargadeo! Prepare the royal barge. I will sail upon it across my entire kingdom and cast a final look upon my beloved subjects.'

Three months later, back in Garhgaon, the Burha Raja died in his sleep.

The entire realm mourned the death of the great monarch who not only defended it from being overrun by a powerful enemy from the west, but also through administrative and economic reforms brought about unprecedented prosperity to its people. He was given a ceremonial burial and an elaborate mausoleum befitting a monarch of his stature was built at Cheraidai to mark his grave.

THE NARRATOR

'Yes,' said the Narrator, 'Swargadeo Susengpha, also known as Swarganarain, Burha Raja and Pratap Singha, was one of the greatest monarchs to have graced the Ahom throne at Garhgaon. It was due to his foresight as well as of his chosen administrator Momai Tamuli Barbarua that the spirit of Assamese nationalism was born. Confronted with grave external danger, the people of the valley and hills came together in a rare bond of unity to repel the invaders. The patronage by the royal court of a common Asomiya language furthered the sense of a unique identity, further reinforced at the religious and cultural levels by the Vaishnav saint Mahapurush Sankardev and his disciples such as Madhavdev. No doubt, at the instigation of the Brahmin priests who by then commanded total sway in the royal palace, the proponents of Ekasaran Namadharma continued to be persecuted, but this could not prevent the religion from taking a widespread hold over the minds and hearts of the common masses.

'But the darkness of night always follows the brightness of day, as I never tire of repeating. Great eras of a great race's history have shameful periods in between. Such a period followed the death of Swargadeo Susengpha in 1641. As I said, the corridors of power are shadowed by dark niches where perfidy and treachery lurk. The period immediately following the demise of the great monarch was darkened by conspiracies and betrayals.

'Susengpha had three sons, Surampha, Sutyinpha and Sai. By the laws established by the progenitor of the Ahoms, Chaolung Sukapha, the eldest son Surampha should have automatically been chosen as the next king. But the patra-mantris were all too aware of the immoral character of the eldest prince, a stark contrast to that of his illustrious father. Thus, they were keener to make the second son, Sutyinpha, ascend the throne at Garhgaon.

'But the youngest son Sai, driven by innate ambition, wanted to stake his claim. He knew that to a section of the younger nobles as well as officers of the army, neither of his elder brothers was acceptable, for

Sutyinpha was sickly of disposition and would prove to be a weakling of a king. Gathering a small band of conspirators, Sai attempted to take over the royal palace—this forced the two elder brothers into acting jointly with the aid of the chief nobles. Surampha pledged that since he was childless the throne would be handed over to Sutyinpha after his death; the two brothers took immediate charge of the army, ordered that the gates of Garhgaon be closed and no one allowed to enter or leave the capital. Then they swooped in upon Sai and his followers, who were hunted down within the palace and on the streets till the entire band including its leader was decimated.

'So, the morally weak Surampha was made king. That he was an unworthy inheritor of his father's crown was made evident soon enough, since he was less interested in the welfare of his subjects and more in satisfying his own needs. He grew infatuated with the wife of one of his vassals, had the husband wickedly poisoned and brought her to the palace as the chief queen of his harem. She brought along with her a nephew, son of her ex-husband's elder brother, and convinced her new husband to declare him the heir to the throne, thereby betraying the pledge made to Sutyinpha.

'Instigated by his chief queen, Surampha went berserk after the newly declared heir-apparent died under mysterious circumstances. He accused Sutyinpha's elder son of poisoning the boy and ordered that both father and son be executed and his brother's property confiscated. By then the nobles had had enough—their fury was heightened by a strange order from Surampha, who decreed that a son of each of the patra-mantris was to be buried alive in the maidam designed for the nephew! The nobles lost little time in wielding the power bestowed upon them by the adopted system of governance, deposing Surampha, imprisoning him in a remote location and finally assassinating him, thereby bestowing him with the title Bhaga Raja or Deposed King in popular nomenclature.

'However, Sutyinpha, who next ascended the singorighar in 1644 with great pomp and ceremony, was no more fit to be the monarch of the Ahom realm. Afflicted with various illnesses from childhood, he earned the sobriquet of Nariya Raja or Sickly King amongst the people, who due to this very reason did not hold him in the high esteem they had done his father the Burha Raja. Worse still, he suffered from curvature of his spine as well, which made people call him the Kekora Raja or the Crab King or the Crooked King and laugh behind his back. Perhaps awareness of his own adequacies and the knowledge that he was mocked by his own people had hardened his heart, for Sutyinpha betrayed a streak of cruelty that ill became a king. No sooner were the powers of the Ahom throne invested with him, he began arresting and executing every official he suspected of being against his being made the king. His vindictive nature made him easily persuaded by allegations, however ill-founded— for instance, a sister of the buragohain, who had his ear, persuaded him to murder the barpatragohain and his son.

'The sense of unbridled power apparently went to his head, for his vindictiveness seemed to embrace everyone, no matter how high in the hierarchy. In 1646, an expedition he had sent to subjugate a hill tribe returned defeated. Not only did Sutyinpha dismiss the buragohain and barpatragohain who had led his troops, but also dressed them in female garb and paraded them in public. Other petty officers who enjoyed his patronage also began to behave in a high-handed manner to all and sundry; for instance, the son of his chief queen alienated the higher nobility by his insulting behaviour towards them. Laughed at by his subjects and disowned by his own nobles, no wonder the reign of Sutyinpha was prematurely cut short—in November 1648, he was deposed by the nobles and replaced by his son Sutamla.

'Those who swear by violence die by violence. Some of the chronicles have it that Sutyinpha was poisoned a few days after he was deposed and that his chief queen was buried alive with him in the maidam built on his grave ...'

Monarch of Ambition

～

THE BRAHMIN HEAD PRIEST'S FACE WAS INSCRUTABLE, THOUGH HE trembled inside. Swargadeo Sutamla had already shown how ruthless he could be. The king who was earlier designated as Khahuagohain had been coroneted with great pomp and display of power, and had taken on the Hindu title of Jayadhwaj Singha. Immediately afterwards he had placed in chains individuals he considered to be inimical to his status as undisputed king and had them executed. The head priest knew that the ruthlessness was in order; it ran in the blood of the son of Sutyinpha who had been renowned for his cruel nature; the royal lineage was in disfavour with the populace and conspiracies were being hatched to depose the monarch. The new king had to act without mercy and consolidate his hold upon his throne. Neither the grandiose ascension of the singorighar nor the week-long festivities organized amongst the people at the behest of the royal palace could conceal the reality that in the near anarchic environment created after the demise of the Burha Raja, no one could claim to be safely seated upon the throne at Garhgaon.

Thus, when the swargadeo had summoned him, the Brahmin head priest could not but feel a twinge of fear shoot through his heart. But, as it turned out, he had been afraid without reason, for the king had something else in mind rather than the fact that the head priest had been bestowing land and favours upon his kith and kin in the absence of a strong royal authority.

'Evil tidings have fallen upon my ears,' Swargadeo Sutamla said from his throne. 'Apparently, during my grandfather's days, a Brahmin named Mishrabapu had been falsely accused of conspiracy and executed. You priests are of the opinion that is the cause of the anarchy which descended upon our realm in the past decade?'

A surge of relief washed over the head priest but his face remained impassive. 'That's true, Your Majesty. Not only the Brahmin priests, but your Deodhai, Bailung and Mohan priests too have opined the same. The murder of a Brahmin is the worst crime a monarch can commit. That is the cause of the cattle disease which killed so many of our cows and bulls two years ago, as also why the earth shakes so frequently, causing damage to your palaces.'

Sutamla nodded. 'I need you to perform rituals to ward off the evil so caused. Know you this, I am a man with ambition and plan to wage war with the bangals who bark at our doorstep.'

The Brahmin head priest well knew from where 'the evil tidings' that had fallen upon Sutamla's ears emanated—to spread the rumour had been all too easy, though he had been kept in suspense as to the kind of reaction it would evoke in the king. Apparently, his reading of the highly superstitious nature of the swargadeo had been correct and the results were even better than he had expected.

'Mere rituals would not be enough, Your Majesty. You need to recompense Mishrabapu's family with a grant of land as well as gold and silver.'

'I'll do that. Arrange to have the eldest son of Mishrabapu brought to me.'

The head priest lost no time in sending soldiers to the village where Mishrabapu's widow and her two sons lived. However, the arrival of soldiers at her doorsteps terrified the woman and, concealing her sons, she instead sent a follower of Sankardev named Chandra Niranjandev to pose as her son. In the meantime, another rumour had been floated that a great saint had been born in Ahom territory. When Niranjandev was presented before the king, he was impressed with the saintly appearance of the man and identified him as the great saint—Sutamla became a disciple of Niranjandev and bestowed upon him a grant of land to set up the Auniati Sattra or monastery, becoming the first king in Ahom history to formally accept the Vaishnava tenets. Also, for the first time in Ahom history, copper plates were inscribed upon to commemorate the land grants. Later the highly devout Sutamla set up more sattras, including the famous Dakhinpat Sattra.

Though he had taken every precaution to ward off evil, Jayadhwaj Singha could not immediately embark on fulfilling his ambition of wresting back ceded land from the Mughals. The lack of good governance in the preceding years had emboldened some vassals to try and shake off the Ahom yoke and the swargadeo was kept occupied subduing them. The Lakma Nagas as well as the Dafla tribe rose up in rebellion in 1650; no sooner were these quelled than the Jaiantia raja tried to shake off the Ahom hold over his domain and had to be subjugated. In 1655, the Mishing tribe rose up; in the ensuing Ahom campaign hundreds of tribals were killed and dozens of villages burnt before their chief sued for peace. There were conflicts too with the Kacharis and other chieftains, distractions that prevented Jayadhwaj Singha from embarking on his principal goal.

However, the minor skirmishes did not hinder him from continuing his preparations; a shrewd judge of human character, he had picked a nobleman for this task. This was none other than an individual named Atan, belonging to an illustrious family of nobles whose ancestors had come with Sukapha during his conquest of the Brahmaputra Valley, who was to later play an even bigger role in forging the destiny of the Ahoms. Impressed with the man's intelligence and strength of character, Jayadhwaj Singha appointed him as the Khanikar Barua, entrusted with building and reinforcing forts and ramparts throughout the realm. Such was the loyalty and sense of service that in 1662, in the midst of the war against the Mughals, Atan was appointed the buragohain and served in that capacity till 1679.

It was well that the Ahom monarch had not neglected preparations for, in 1658, the opportunity he had waited for suddenly presented itself. It had been during the reign of the Mughal Emperor Shah Jahan that the Bengal subahdar had wrested back Lower Assam from the Ahoms in 1639 and fixed the outer bounds of the latter's realm at Barnadi on the north bank and Asurar Ali in the south. In 1657, Shah Jahan fell gravely ill and a tussle broke out between his four sons, Dara, Shuja, Murad and Aurangzeb. At that time, Prince Shuja was the subahdar of Bengal. As soon as the news of his father's illness reached him, he gathered a large army and marched towards Agra to lay stake to the Mughal throne. Not only was Bengal left leaderless, but also their fortifications on the eastern edges of Bengal became very thinly manned and without their flotilla of war boats.

The wolves moved swiftly in. The first off the block was Prananarayan, the raja of Kochbehar, under vassalage to the Mughal emperor, who asserted his independence and attacked the Mughal faujdar at Guwahati, advancing as far as Hajo. At the same time Jayadhwaj Singha made his move, pushing forward with a huge army and flotilla towards Guwahati. Caught in a pincer, the Mughal faujdar Mir Lutfulla Shiraji deemed discretion to be the better part of valour, and escaped to Dhaka without offering any resistance. The result was that the Ahoms and the Koches came face to face; the latter were no match for the mighty Ahom army and were forthwith dispatched from the bounds of Kamrup beyond the river Sankoch.

Thus, for the first time in Ahom history, the entire Brahmaputra Valley came under their suzerainty. Chengmun Rajasahur Barphukan was put in charge of the newly conquered territory with headquarters in Guwahati. In the next couple of years, the Ahoms ordered the inhabitants of Lower Assam to shift bag and baggage to Upper Assam, so that Kamrup was soon reduced to barren wilderness. This was in the supposition that the Mughals, after they had recovered from the shock of this assault, would not be tempted to try and recover territory that would yield no revenue. The Ahoms also made forays beyond Kamrup towards the south, plundering and depredating any settlements they came across. Under the leadership of Baduli Phukan, Lapeti Phukan and Phulbarua Phukan they reached Hatichola, which was a mere five days' march from Dhaka, and brought a number of Mughal soldiers and civilians as captives and sent them to Upper Assam. The historian Ghulam Hussain Salim in his chronicle *Riyaz-us-Salatin* recorded the extent of Ahom depredation. 'The Assamese,' he wrote, 'raised the standard of daring and insurrection, and without contest, they conquered the province of Kamrup, swept it with the broom of plunder, carried by force to their own country all and everything, including the moveable and immoveable effects of the people, pulled down the edifices, left no trace of fertility, and reduced the whole province to one plain level ground.'*

In the meanwhile, at Delhi, the crafty Aurangzeb triumphed in the tussle over his brothers; Shah Jahan was incarcerated at Agra while Prince Shuja was forced to flee to the Arakans. The new emperor lost no time in appointing one of his most powerful nobles, Mir Jumlah, as the governor of Bengal and urging him to recapture territory currently occupied by the Ahoms. Mir Jumlah had already testified to his allegiance towards Aurangzeb by assisting him in the subjugation of Golconda and also financing him in his tussle against his brothers. But Aurangzeb was the kind of ruler who trusted no one; he understood the power and wealth commanded by a man like Mir Jumlah, whose friendship was sought by rulers as far off as Persia, and the magnificence of whose palaces rivalled those of the Mughal emperor himself. In making him the governor of Bengal, Aurangzeb was taking a calculated gamble, for the powerful noble could well declare his independence without the emperor being able to do anything. Thus, the accompanying order to proceed against the Ahoms was intended to keep the powerful man busy, with the hope that the myth that individuals who entered

---

* This passage translated into English by A. Salam (1904) is quoted by Sir Edward Gait in his book *A History of Assam* (1905) from where it has been taken.

the forbidden kingdom of the Ahoms never returned would prove true in the case of a potential rival.

Mir Jumlah's ambitions reached even higher—to teach the upstart Ahoms a lesson and capture their entire domain. This noble had risen from humble beginnings as an attendant of an oil merchant to become one of the most eminent individuals in Hindustan; he was, by nature, ambitious and even dreamed of conquering China once he had dealt with the Ahoms. However, he was willing to adopt peaceful means to attain his objective. Therefore, when the Ahom monarch Jayadhwaja Singh sent an emissary informing him that he had taken possession of Lower Assam only to protect it from the Koches, and was prepared to return the territory to any officer whom the governor might send, he dispatched Rashid Khan to receive back the land.

As the Mughal general advanced with a small force, the Ahoms abandoned Dhubri and fell back to Jogighopa. This was in direct opposition to their king's orders; the commanding officers of the Ahom troops were removed and Baduli Phukan was appointed as commander-in-chief. On the other hand, the easy passage he was given made Rashid Khan suspicious that he was being led into a trap—he halted and requested reinforcements. At the time, Mir Jumlah was leading another campaign in an offensive against the remnants of the Koch army; he had captured Kochbehar when Rashid Khan's request reached him. Leaving a sufficiently manned garrison at Kochbehar to defend the territory, Mir Jumlah with a huge army, comprising 12,000 cavalry and 30,000 infantry, set out on 4 January 1662 to meet his lieutenant. There was also a mammoth armada with him of 323 war boats called ghrabs, huge vessels capable of carrying at least fourteen cannons and fifty to sixty men, each towed by smaller kasahs or lighter boats manned by oarsmen.

The fort at Jogighopa, like all Ahom fortifications in advance outposts, was made of mud and emanated the air of a temporary encampment. It was built high on a hillock on the banks of the river Luit or Brahmaputra so as to command a view of both an invading armada on the river and an advancing land army. Pits had been dug across a broad swathe of land and camouflaged—traps for horses to fall into, the upturned bamboo spikes at the bottom ensuring impalement. A ditch full of bamboo stakes was the next line of defence, at a sufficient distance from the fort so that Mughal artillery could not reach it. More such ditches, behind which the defenders could begin the initial process of resisting invaders, lay on the way before the ramparts of the fort could be reached.

However, on this occasion neither the strategic location of the fort nor its ingenious defences could save the Jogighopa fort from the onslaught. Firstly, the Ahom garrison of 12,000 was heavily outnumbered. Second, it was at that point of time stricken by a deadly pestilence, in all probability cholera, and many of the soldiers were in no condition to fight. As soon as advance scouts hastily returned to apprise the commander of the enormous scale of the enemy force, he ordered evacuation. Leaving their armaments and provisions behind, the Ahoms slipped out of the rear, boarded vessels moored on the Brahmaputra, and retreated towards the garrisons at Saraighat and Pandu.

The inputs provided by the retreating soldiers as to the size and strength of the invading forces served to lower the morale of those at these two strategic positions. News of the Jogighopa debacle reached Garhgaon and reinforcements were hastily sent by Jayadhwaj Singha to augment his defences. But before these could reach their intended positions, Mir Jumlah, who had divided his land army into two and had them simultaneously advance both on the south and north banks of the Brahmaputra, with the flotilla in the middle, reached Saraighat and Pandu. The defenders in these two forts also declined to engage the enemy; in fact, the commanding officer with the rank of parvatiya phukan defected to the enemy; the disorganized rank and files fled, those on the north bank fleeing to Kajali while the unfortunate hordes on the south bank were mowed down by Mir Jumlah's cavalry and war boats. Mir Jumlah's army demolished the fort at Saraighat and captured Guwahati on 4 February 1662, completely decimating the garrison of the Beltola fort.

The Ahom forces retreated to their next stronghold, the fort at Samdhara, on the Bhomoraguri hills near Tezpur. Atan was now appointed as the buragohain and entrusted with the task of preventing the Mughals from making further inroads into Ahom territory. He prepared his forces to make a final stand at Samdhara against Mir Jumlah's wing of the army moving across the north bank of the Brahmaputra, and at Simalugarh on the south bank. The latter fort, situated on a high hill beside the river and surrounded by defensive moats armed with bamboo spikes, was considered to be almost impregnable. Rather than storm both the forts, the Mughals decided to lay siege to them, a time-wasting move which later proved to be costly.

The Ahoms fought bravely, but there was no stopping the Mughal juggernaut. The mighty army soon wore down the resistance offered at Samdhara and Simalugarh, aided by some miscalculations on the part of Langichang Bargohain, who failed to dispatch the reinforcements requested by the defenders on the south bank, with the consequence that Simalugarh ran out of ammunition. That fort having been overrun, with Mir Jumlah himself entering it on 26 February 1662, the garrison at Samdhara lost heart, and fled to Kaliabor after destroying their stock of gunpowder. Despite the legendary valour displayed by commanders such as Lecham Hatibarua, the mighty Mughal army could not be halted; having taken Kaliabor, Mir Jumlah rested his army for a few days and then proceeded with speed up the Brahmaputra. A little while later an Ahom fleet of around 800 boats met that of the Mughals head on, but had to retreat due to the superior firepower of the invaders. Jayadhwaj Singha, sensing total defeat, sent emissaries asking for peace, but Mir Jumlah rejected the overtures.

He pressed on to Lakhau at the confluence of the river Dihing and the Brahmaputra, where he moored his fleet. The Mughal army marched on foot through Gajpur and Tiromani, meeting with little or no resistance; news was brought that the Ahom king had gathered 1,000 boats close to the capital Garhgaon to remove his personal effects from the city; it meant that the monarch was bent on decamping the capital bag and baggage and Mir Jumlah dispatched a flying column to intercept the evacuation and seize properties not yet removed. On entering the capital Garhgaon on 17 March 1662, Mir Jumlah was delighted to discover that not everything had been removed due to the shortage of time and his ploy of sending a flying column had worked to some extent. Eighty-two elephants yet remained in the palace, along with a quantity of gold and silver, as also granaries full of thousands of maunds of rice.

Thus far it had been an extraordinarily successful campaign. Apart from causing heavy losses of Ahom soldiers, the Mughal forces had succeeded in capturing hundreds of cannons and thousands of matchlocks, a huge quantity of gunpowder and over 1,000 war boats. The Mughal commander appointed a task force to carry back the booty to Dhaka. Now the beautiful city of Garhgaon too was in his grasp. But the rainy season was upon them. Mir Jumlah decided to wait out the rains and pursue the fleeing Ahom monarch once the dry season recommenced. In the meanwhile, he set up administrative sub-headquarters at different places such as Mathurapur, Ramdang, Trimohini, Gajpur, Silpani and Abhaypur. From Lakhau westwards, posts were also established along the Brahmaputra right up to Guwahati.

The Ahom nobles and their families, as also officers, had fled along with their king. Though the ordinary subjects chafed under the new rulers, they had no recourse but to obey. So confident was Mir Jumlah of not only strengthening his grip over the newly conquered territory but also pressing onwards during the autumn season that he established a mint at Garhgaon and struck coins in the name of the emperor at Delhi!

Then the heavens opened up in full fury and Mir Jumlah felt the force of the rains in Assam. It rained continuously for months together, cramping mobility, cutting off communications, suddenly tilting the balance in favour of the Ahoms.

Swargadeo Sutamla, also known as Jayadhwaj Singha, reclined wearily upon a couch made of cane within a temporary encampment at Chorai-khorong at Namrup in the foothills of the Naga Hills. He had reasons to be tired. In the nick of time, he had escaped from Garhgaon along with his family, some nobles and 5,000 men; it had taken him and his entourage many days of continuous and hard travel to reach Chorai-khorong; his bargohain had fled to Tira; other senior officials took shelter in the sattras of Majuli; his forces were disorganized and there were rumours rather than hard information upon which he could act. The worst part of his humiliation was that the populace had begun to call him Bhaganiya Raja or the King Who Fled from His Realm!

His hopes now rested with Atan Buragohain, of whose ability and loyalty he had no doubt. 'It is my fault,' he conceded to the buragohain. 'I had become over ambitious. If we had let the sleeping dog lie, all this would not have happened and we would not have been reduced to such dire straits.'

'It's not wrong to be ambitious, Your Majesty,' Atan Buragohain spoke with conviction. 'Also, if you recall, we have been attacked before by these surrogates of Delhi, although we had then done nothing to rouse their hostility. So, clearly, they have their own agenda—they would have attacked us whether we were ambitious or not. But all is not lost yet. These bangals come from dry lands. They have never encountered the rains that we have in Assam. I have sent spies to report directly to me from Garhgaon. Only a week of heavy rains and already the bangals are finding it difficult to cope. Their oarsmen cannot steer smaller crafts through the swollen river waters. Apparently, their commander had sent some boats to Lakhau to bring in supplies from the ships moored there. But the boats sank and the men inside saved themselves with some difficulty.'

'Ah, but the rains will pass,' said the king despondently. 'Then this devil incarnate, who calls himself Mir Jumlah will begin moving again. Where can I run to next, I ask you?'

Atan Buragohain's voice continued to be strong. 'My spies bring back more good news,' he said. 'The bellies of the bangals are unused to this weather and the water. Already fever and stomach ailments have gripped many of the men. Their situation would worsen in the coming months.'

Sutamla remained unconvinced. 'No,' he said. 'We must plead with these conquerors and work out a treaty whereby they are induced to leave my beloved Garhgaon. I am willing to pay any amount of indemnity as well as future tribute to get my throne back.'

The buragohain's heart swelled with contempt at such display of weakness on the part of his king, but he kept his voice even and dispassionate. 'We shall sue for peace, indeed, Your Majesty, but from a position of greater strength than we are in now. Let them taste a few months more of our rains. Meanwhile, we'll engage them with guerilla tactics, hitting their outposts, cutting off their supply route.'

Sutamla in his heart did not agree but, in his difficult position he could hardly contradict a buragohain who had shown such loyalty. 'All right, Buragohain dangoriya,' he said. 'Do as you deem fit. I suppose a few months will not make any difference, seeing that the rains will keep the bangals stuck to their camps. But be cautious; do not alienate them to an extent that they would seek vengeance rather than peace!'

History was repeating itself. Years back, the redoubtable Koch Prince Chilarai had discovered how inimical the Ahom realm could be especially during the rainy season; Mir Jumlah was to experience it now. Making matters worse was the hit-and-run tactics adopted by the Ahoms under the leadership of Atan Buragohain. They would slip, ghostlike, into a Mughal outpost under the cover of the rain and darkness, and silently slit the throats of any sentry they came across; these were slung on top of bamboo posts so as to strike terror in the hearts of those who beheld the corpses the following morning. Even sentries guarding the capital city were not spared; so many of his forces were killed and such grew the difficulty of communicating with his outposts that Mir Jumlah was forced to order the closure of many of the remoter outposts and bring back his men to the safety of the capital. The Ahoms now openly attacked the isolated posts that were still kept operational; Gajpur was reclaimed and its commander and his men were put to the sword; Murkata was retaken next by a force with the buragohain himself in the lead. So effective was the Ahom campaign that within a few weeks all strategic spots in the area were freed of Mughal occupancy except Garhgaon and Mathurapur.

Taking a leaf out of the book of the Ahom campaign against Chilarai, the buragohain simultaneously focused on cutting off provisions to the capital by attacking and disrupting the supply lines. Unfortunately for Mir Jumlah, that year there was a famine in the Dhaka area, so there was a shortfall in the foodstuffs being sent to the frontlines; even this had trouble reaching its destination because boats and caravans carrying them were attacked and destroyed by marauding Ahom forces. Assamese villages closer to the capital disappeared almost overnight, their inhabitants taking away all their stock of foodstuff to far-off places so that the occupying forces could not get at them. Mathurapur had to be abandoned; an epidemic of fever swept through Diler Khan's detachment stationed there; the 1,500 horses were soon reduced to less than 500; Mir Jumlah's own nephew was struck down by the fever.

Incessant rain, slush, floods, fever and dysentery; the travails of Mir Jumlah's starving forces were exacerbated by the continuous guerilla warfare being waged by the Ahoms, who were familiar with the terrain and at home in the wet conditions. The now emboldened Ahom king left Chorai-khorong and set up a new encampment at Solaguri relatively closer to Garhgaon. The spies' reports were becoming more optimistic day by day. The alien invaders, due to lack of food and supplies, were being compelled to kill their horses and camels for food.

The scholarly looking man sat within a room in the palace, a quill in his hand. Upon the wooden table before him were a sheet of parchment and a phial of ink. His name was Shihabuddin Talish. He was a chronicler of events, who had accompanied Mir Jumlah on this campaign.

'A similar case had never happened before in the history of Delhi,' dipping his quill in the ink, he began writing. 'Here were 12,000 horses and numerous infantry locked in for six months, prevented by the rains from continuing operations, yet scarcely attacked by the enemies that surround them. Nor did during this time provisions arrive. The amirs turned their eyes longingly to Delhi and the soldiers yearned for their wives and children ...'

But Shihabuddin was not quite right in stating that those within Garhgaon were safe from attack by the enemy. In fact, taking advantage of the demoralization of the Mughal forces trapped within, the Ahoms made several assaults on the capital, on one occasion almost occupying half of the city, though they were finally evicted with great difficulty. Atan Buragohain now considered that the moment was ripe for forging a treaty and made overtures to the Mughal general. But there were differences on certain terms and conditions, and a treaty was not arrived at.

The rains finally ceased around September and communications with the fleet stationed at Lakhau could be restored. This also meant the restoration of supplies and with it the restoration of the morale of the occupying forces. Sensing trouble, Jayadhwaj Singha and his retinue once again fled to Namrup, while Mir Jumlah again set out to capture the king. An Ahom officer entrusted by the king to repulse the Mughal advance, Baduli Phukan, instead laid down arms and submitted to the Mughal general, who installed him as the subahdar of the area between Garhgaon and Namrup, and entrusted him with the task of capturing the Ahom king.

However, before this plan could be set in motion, Mir Jumlah fell ill; rebellious mutterings amongst his officers and men who were loath to go to Namrup at the risk of having to spend another rainy season in the Brahmaputra Valley further handicapped him. The adverse circumstances made Mir Jumlah give up his plans of further conquest and leave the Ahom realm along with his troops. His chronicler records the relief and joy amongst his officers and men when he announced his decision in no less than two pages of his diary!

However, Mir Jumlah was all too aware of the risks his troops faced while retreating to Guwahati; they could well be decimated on the way unless some kind of agreement was reached with the Ahom monarch. The Ahoms had been making overtures for a treaty—he now sent emissaries to inform them that given honourable terms, he was willing to hand over the kingdom back to the Ahom king. Atan Buragohain immediately grasped the offer and himself handled the negotiations to arrive at a treaty.

No doubt the buragohain was aware of the difficulties confronting the Mughals and that, given a few more months, Mir Jumlah would have been forced to leave without concluding a treaty. But he could not risk the fate of his motherland on what might happen; it could well be that Mir Jumlah might change his mind, ask for reinforcements from Dhaka to augment his forces and decide to press on. Moreover, the weak Ahom king was growing impatient; he was persisting with his request for a treaty no matter how humiliating to his own race; he was also threatening to leave Assam for good and settle down in the Nara kingdom.

Thus it was that Atan Buragohain found himself under compulsion to be present at Ghiladharighat in Tipam on 23 January 1663, or 9 Magh 1584 Saka era, to sign a treaty with the Mughal generals. He was accompanied by the barpatragohain and the rajmantri phukan. The most humiliating aspect of the treaty was that the Ahom king had to send his one and only daughter to the imperial harem at Delhi. This six-year-old princess was Ramani Gabharu, also known as Langchen Gabharu, whose mother was the king's younger queen Pakhari Gabharu, daughter of the renowned Ahom officer Momai Tamuli Barbarua of the Pratap Singha era. Later, on 2 May 1668, she was married to Sultan Muhammad Azam, the third son of Aurangzeb and her name was changed to Rahmat Banu Begum. The Ahom king had also to send Mohini Aideu, the daughter of the Tipam raja, to Delhi.

Jayadhwaj Singha also was required to immediately pay 20,000 tolas of gold, 1,20,000 tolas of silver and 40 elephants. Within a year another

300 tolas of silver and 90 elephants were to be given and 20 elephants to be supplied annually. In exchange, Mir Jumla and his forces would withdraw to Guwahati, though the Ahoms would have to cede to the Delhi emperor the land west of the river Bharali on the north and river Kalang on the south. At the same time, all Mughal prisoners taken captive by the Ahoms, as also the renegade Baduli Phukan and his family were to be handed over to the Mughals. The condition of the annual tribute of twenty elephants was inserted to drive home the point that the Ahom monarch was a vassal of the emperor of Delhi. To ensure that the conditions of the treaty were fully implemented, the Mughals took with them some young men as hostages, including Ramrai, a nephew of the buragohain; Dhala Gohain, son of the bargohain; Langi Gohain, son of the barpatragohain; and Maupia, son of the rajmantri phukan.

Mir Jumlah's retreat was a sorry spectacle. His war-weary troops headed home on 25 January 1663, having little food to carry back with them, thereby having to subsist on grass and water for much of the way to Guwahati. The Ahoms tactic of cutting off supplies also involved the scorched-earth technique whereby villages on the route were summarily removed and all cultivation destroyed. To make matters worse, while the troops were resting at Kajali, they were first struck by a fierce storm followed by a severe and terrifying earthquake! Somehow, they managed to reach Guwahati where finally they found succour from their travails.

Gravely ill, Mir Jumlah himself could not ride on elephant-back and had to be carried on a palki from Garhgaon to Lakhau and thence by ship to Kaliabor and then again by palki. At Garhgaon he had been suffering from chest pains and asthma, but his personal doctors were unable to diagnose what exactly was the cause of the ailment and had tried various medications without visible alleviation. The lay soldiers, however, were unanimous in their opinion that sorcerers in this land of witchery and black magic had cast an evil spell on their leader and that was the cause of his suffering!

Despite his illness, Mir Jumlah halted for two weeks at Guwahati setting up the mechanism through which to govern the new territory. Rashid Khan had to be persuaded to become the faujdar of Guwahati and his reluctance later secured him a reprimand from the Mughal emperor Aurangzeb, while Muhammad Beg was made the thanadar of Kajali. Mir Jumla then continued on his passage to Dhaka but his health deteriorated rapidly and, on 30 March 1663, he died aboard his ship at a short distance from Dhaka. Historians are unanimous in their opinion that it was the Brahmaputra Valley which was responsible for the inglorious end of this great commander, who had risen from a humble background to become the greatest personality in India next only to the Mughal emperor; the man who had once possessed the famous Kohinoor diamond, which he had gifted to Emperor Shah Jahan.

In a room in the governor's impressive palace in Dhaka sat Shihabuddin Talish, giving the finishing touches to his chronicle of the ill-fated campaign of Mir Jumlah against the Ahoms. Every now and again, he consulted the copious notes he had made during that campaign:

'Assam is a wild and dreadful country,' he wrote, 'abounding in danger ... The river Brahmaputra flows through it from the east towards the west. The length of Assam from west to east, Guwahati to Sadiya, is about 200 kos ... The land on the north bank of the Brahmaputra is called Uttarkol, and on the southern bank Dakhinkol ... From Kaliabor to Garhgaon, houses and orchards full of fruit trees stretch in an unbroken line; and on both sides of the road, shady bamboo groves raise their heads to the sky. Many varieties of sweet scented wild and garden flowers bloom here and from the rear of the bamboo groves up to the foot of the hills there are cultivated fields and gardens. From Lakhugarh to Garhgaon also there are roads, houses and farms in the same style; and a lofty and wide embanked road has been constructed up to Garhgaon for traffic.

'In this country they make the surface of fields and gardens so level that the eye cannot find the least elevation in it up to the extreme horizon. Uttarkol has greater abundance of population and cultivation, but as there are more inaccessible strongholds and defensible central places in Dakhinkol, the kings of Assam have fixed their abode in the latter.

'The climate on the parts on the banks of the Brahmaputra suits natives and strangers alike. But at a distance from the river, though the climate agrees with the natives, it is rank poison to foreigners. It rains for eight months in the year and even the four months of winter are not free from rain. In the cold weather, the diseases of cold and moisture affect foreigners with greater severity than natives, while in summer excessive secretion of bile grasps foreigners more violently than natives. The people of this country are free from certain fatal and loathsome diseases such as leprosy, white leprosy, elephantiasis, cutaneous eruptions, goitre and hydrocele which prevail in Bengal ...

'The trees of its hills and plains are exceedingly tall, thick and strong. Its streams are deep and wide, and both those that contain pools and those that do not are beyond the range of numbering. Many kinds of odorous fruits and herbs of Bengal and Hindustan grow in Assam. We saw here certain varieties of flowers and fruits, both wild and cultivated, which are not to be met with elsewhere in the whole of India. The coconut and neem trees are rare; but pepper, spikenard and many species of lemon are abundant ... The chief crop of the country is rice but the thin and long varieties of the grain are rare. Wheat, barley and lentils are not grown. The soil is fertile; whatever they sow or plant grows well. Salt is very dear and difficult to procure. It is found in the skirts of certain hills, but is very bitter and pungent. Some of the people of this country cut bananas to pieces, dry them in the sun and burn them. Then they put the ashes on a piece of fine linen which they tie to four rods fixed in the ground, place a pot underneath and gradually sprinkle water on the cloth; and they use the drippings, which are extremely brackish and bitter, as a substitute for salt ...

'Gold is washed from the sand of the Brahmaputra. Ten to twelve thousand Assamese are engaged in this employment, and they pay to the raja's government one tola of gold per head per year. But this gold is of a low standard of purity; a tola of it fetches only eight or nine rupees. It is said that gold can be procured from the sand at all places on the bank of the Brahmaputra, but the only people who know how to gather it are those Assamese. The currency of the kingdom consists of cowries and rupees and gold coins stamped with the stamp of the raja. Copper coins are not current ...

'If this country were administered like the imperial dominions, it is very likely that forty to forty-five lakhs of rupees would be collected from the revenue paid by the raiyats, the price of elephants caught in the jungles and other sources. It is not the custom here to take any land tax from the cultivators; but in every house one man out of three has to render service to the raja, and if there is any delay in doing what he orders, not other punishment than death is inflicted. Hence the most complete obedience is rendered by the people to the bidding of their raja.

'In all past ages, no foreign king could lay the hand of conquest on the skirts of this country, and no foreigner could treat it with the foot of invasion. Narrow are the gates by which outsiders can enter or issue from this country and lame are the feet on which its natives can go to other countries. Their kings neither allow foreigners to enter their land, nor permit any of their own subjects to go out of it. Formerly, once a year, by the order of the raja, a party used to go for trade to their frontier near Guwahati; they gave gold, musk, aloe wood, pepper, spikenard and silk cloth in exchange for salt, saltpetre, sulphur and certain other products of Hindustan which the people of Guwahati used to take thither. In short, every army that entered this country made its exit from the realm of life; every caravan that set foot on this land deposited its baggage of residence in the halting place of death. In former times, whenever an army turned towards this country for raid and conquest, as soon as it reached the frontier, the wretches made night attacks on it. If success did not dawn on the night of their enterprise, they used to drive away to the hills the peasantry along the route of invasion, leaving not a man to inhabit a house or kindle a fire in that tract. The invaders, neglecting caution and watchfulness, reached the centre of the country after passing unobstructed roads full of danger, raging torrents and frightful valleys covered with deadly forests. And by reason of the distance, the winter expired on the way and the rainy season began. The wretches, descending from the hilltops like a flood, invested the army on all sides ... So that imprudent army on being besieged, had no power left to confront and repel the enemy and grew weaker through failure to procure supplies of food and was exterminated or taken prisoner ... As no one who entered this country ever returned and the manners of its natives were never made known to outsiders, the people of Hindustan used to call the inhabitants of Assam sorcerers and magicians, and considered them as standing outside the human species. They say that whoever enters this country is overcome by charms and never comes out of it.

'The rajas of this country have always been self-confident and proud by reason of the large number of their followers and attendants, and the abundance of their property, treasure and armed force; and they have always maintained vast bodies of fighting men and mountain-like ferocious-looking elephants ... And all the people of this country, not placing their necks in the yoke of any faith, eat whatever they get from the hand of any man, regardless of his caste, and undertake every kind of labour that appears proper to their defective sights. They do not abstain from eating food, regardless if it was cooked by Mussulmans or non-Mussulmans, and partake of every kind of meat, whether of dead or slaughtered animals, except human flesh ... Their language differs entirely from that of all the peoples of eastern India. Strength and heroism are apparent in the people of this country; they are able to undertake hard tasks; all of them are warlike and bloodthirsty, fearless in slaying and being slain, unrivalled in cruelty, treachery and rudeness unique in the world of deception, lying and breach of faith. The persons of their women are marked by beauty and delicacy of features, blackness and length of hair, softness of body, fairness of complexion and loveliness of hands and feet ... The wives of the rajas and peasants alike never veil their faces before anybody and they move about in the market places with bare heads ...

'Asses, camels and horses are rare and difficult to procure in this country ... They are greatly frightened by horses, and if they catch one, they hamstring it. If a single trooper charges a hundred well-armed Assamese, they all throw down their arms and run away, and if they cannot flee, they put their hands up to be chained as prisoners. But if one of them encounters ten Mussalman infantrymen, he fearlessly tries to slay them and succeeds in defeating them. The Assamese considers the sale of an elephant as the most disgraceful of acts and never commits it.

'The raja and phukans ride on sinhasans, and the chiefs and rich men in dulis, which are constructed with poles and planks in a ridiculous fashion ... It is not their custom to tie turbans round their heads, to wear coats, trousers or shoes or to sleep in bedsteads. They only wrap a piece of fine linen round the head, and a waistband round the middle, and place a chaddar on the shoulders. Some of their rich men in winter put on a half-coat like a jacket. Those who can afford it sleep on a plank which serves as a bedstead. They chew large quantities of betel leaves with unripe areca nuts. Flowered silk, velvet, tat-band and other kinds of silk stuff are excellently woven here. They make very nice and neat trays, chests, thrones and chairs, each carved out of a single piece of wood ...

'They build war boats like the kosahs of Bengal and call them bacharis. There are no other differences between the two than this that the prow and stern of the kosah have two projecting horns, while those of the bachari consist of only one leveled plank; and as, aiming solely at strength, they build these boats with the heart-wood of timber, they are slower than kosahs. So numerous are the boats, large and small, in this country that on one occasion the news-writer of Guwahati reported in the month of Ramzan that up to the date of his writing, 32,000 bachari and kosah boats had reached that place or passed it ... They build most of their boats of chambal wood; and such vessels, however heavily they may be loaded, on being swamped do not sink in the water.

'They cast excellent matchlocks and bachadar artillery, and show great skill in this craft. They make first-rate gunpowder, of which they procure the material from imperial dominions. In the whole of Assam there is no building of brick, stone or mud, with the exception of the gates of Garhgaon and a few temples. Rich and poor alike construct their houses with wood, bamboo and straw ... The weapons of war are matchlocks, cannons, arrows with and without iron heads, short swords, spears and long crossbows. In times of war, all the inhabitants of the kingdom have to go to battle, whether they wish it or not ...

'The common people bury their dead with some of the property of the diseased, placing the head towards the east and the feet towards the west. The chiefs build vaults for their dead, and place therein the wives and servants of the deceased, after killing them, together with necessary articles for a few years, including various kinds of gold and silver vessels, carpets, cloths and foodstuffs. They cover the head of the dead very strongly with stout poles, and bury in the vault a lamp with plenty of oil and one living lamp attendant to remain engaged in the work of trimming the lamp. From the ten vaults which were opened by the Mughals, property worth nearly 90,000 rupees was recovered ...

'The city of Garhgaon has four gates of stone set in mud, from each of which to the raja's palace, for a distance of three kos, an extremely strong, high and wide embankment has been constructed for the passage of men. Around the city, in the place of a wall, there is an encompassing bamboo plantation running continuously, two kos or more in width. But in the city, the habitations are not regularly laid out ... Near the raja's palace, on both banks of the Dikhow River, the houses are numerous and there is a narrow bazaar road. The only traders who sit in the bazaar are betel-leaf sellers. It is not their practice to buy and sell articles of food in the market place. The inhabitants store in their houses one year's supply of food of all kinds, and are under no necessity to buy or sell any eatable.

'In short, the village of Garhgaon appeared to us to be circular, wide and an aggregation of villages. Round the raja's house an embankment has been made and strong bamboos have been planted on it close together to serve as a wall. Round it a moat has been dug, which is deeper than a man's height in most places and is always full of water. The enclosure is one kos and fourteen chains in circumference. Inside it high and spacious thatched houses have been built.

'The raja's audience hall, called solang, is 120 cubits long and 30 cubits broad, measured on the inside. It stands on sixty-six pillars, each of them about four cubits round ... Perhaps nowhere else in the world can wooden houses be built with such decorations and figure carvings as by the people of this country. The sides of this palace have been partitioned with wooden lattices of various designs carved in relief and adorned, both within and without, with mirrors of brass, polished so finely that when the sunbeams fall on them, the eye is dazzled by the flashing back of light ...

'Owing to the excess of damp, it is not the custom in this country to make the courtyards of houses on the surface of the ground; they build their houses on platforms resting on wooden pillars.'

'The gods punish those who overreach themselves,' Jayadhwaj Singha told his courtiers. 'I was ambitious, I repeat. Had I known that the emperor of Delhi would send such a huge army and fleet against us, I would perhaps have thought twice about provoking the bangals. Now I weep inside for the misfortune I've heaped upon my realm and my subjects.'

On learning of the departure of Mir Jumlah from the Ahom kingdom, Jayadhwaj Singha had left his retreat at Namrup. He wanted to immediately reoccupy his capital at Garhgaon but his loyalists, as also the Brahmin and Ahom priestly advisors, counselled against it. The infidels had defiled the city, they said. It needed to be cleansed and purified before the king could once again dwell within it. Therefore, Jayadhwaj Singha had stationed himself at Bakata about five miles away from Garhgaon. Now, as he conferred with his nobles, his shoulders were stooped and the torment within him was visible upon his face. His posture mirrored the demoralization that had swept across the entire Ahom kingdom.

'Please do not lose heart, Your Majesty,' Atan Buragohain said gently. 'You have got back your kingdom ...'

'True. But how much truncated! We have lost every inch of land west of the Bharali and Kalang, and Darrang and Kamrup and the all-important centre of Guwahati have been taken away from us. We've also suffered the humiliation of having to pay a bangal ruler war indemnity and tribute. Many of my officers turned traitors and, thinking the bangals were here to rule permanently, offered their allegiance to them. No less a person than my bargohain deserted me.'

Turning to a personal officer standing next to him, he asked, 'Has Barukial Langi Bargohain been put in chains and brought here?'

'Yes, Your Majesty.'

'Fetch him. I want to make an example of him.'

The wretched patra-mantri was dragged by some chaodangs and flung at the monarch's feet. The terror-stricken onlookers were sure that the king would decapitate the prisoner. But the king, taking out his hengdang, simply struck the man a few times with the flat of his sword before ordering that he be dragged out of his sight.

'You've acted wisely,' Atan Buragohain said approvingly. 'Now is not the time to take revenge but to effect reconciliation. The most important thing is to win back the trust of our subjects.'

'Deal similarly with all the other traitors that we have taken prisoners. Let them wallow in their own shame and guilt. I'm giving you a free hand in restoring order and discipline in our devastated land. Above all, we must show the bangals that we're the descendents of Chaolung Sukapha and bow before no man.'

Within a matter of weeks, Atan Buragohain began taking steps towards the revival of the Ahom kingdom and its people. The Mughal campaign had depopulated the country since many villagers had fled the valley to take shelter in the surrounding hills. These were persuaded to return and set up villages and begin the process of attaining self-sufficiency again. In fact, they were urged to cultivate crops on wider swathes of agricultural land so as to create a surplus. The training of young men in the martial arts was begun with renewed vigour, with the buragohain touring the length and breadth of the country to orate and instil nationalistic pride in them. Weapons were manufactured in huge numbers while the realm's defences at strategic points were strengthened once more.

Everything pointed towards the fact that the Ahoms were preparing to take back what they had lost to Mir Jumlah and his army.

However, the Ahom leaders took great pains to keep this a secret from outside eyes and rouse not an iota of suspicion. This entailed that the war indemnity, which was to be paid in instalments, was regularly sent to Guwahati, though in lesser amounts, with the Ahom king sending emissaries to explain how he was finding it difficult to raise resources in a war-ravaged area. Simultaneously, emissaries were being sent secretly to other rajas and chieftains, apprising them of a possible attack against the outsiders and seeking their help. Prananarain, the Koch prince, on being attacked by the Mughals, had fled to the shelter of the king of Bhutan; when contacted, he was all too ready to offer his services. Others, such as the Jaiantia raja Jasamatta Rai, too agreed to help the Ahoms when the time was ripe.

The king was gravely ill. He had, in fact, been ill at Namrup itself, and it had only been sheer willpower which had kept him alive to try and redeem himself after the Mughal debacle. But slowly this willpower began to fail him—it deserted him completely when news arrived that further humiliation awaited him. Two imperial couriers sent by Emperor Aurangzeb had reached Guwahati and would be proceeding in due course to Bakata. They were carrying with them a gift—a robe! Jayadhwaj Singha understood the significance of that robe. The one who wore it, by doing so, acknowledged the supremacy of the Mughal emperor and admitted to being a mere vassal.

'I shall rather die than wear that robe, Buragohain dangoriya,' he told his principal minister. 'I may prove a prophet yet, for I feel the shadow of death falling over me. I know you have advised me not to visit Garhgaon, for its reconstruction has not yet commenced. But my soul will not rest in peace if I do not have a final glimpse of my beloved city.'

Atan Buragohain nodded his head understandingly. The next morning the ailing king was borne on a palki to Garhgaon. He stood

before a gate and looked through it at the ravaged capital. Tears came
to his eyes and flowed down his cheeks.

Nine days later, Swargadeo Sutamla, also known as Jayadhwaj Singha,
died of his illness.

THE NARRATOR

The old Deodhai priest took a break. Clay bowls of tea were being passed
round. Someone handed him a bowl. He sat upon a murrah placed for
him and sipped his tea.

The babies and toddlers had fallen asleep in their parents' arms. But
there was no trace of sleep in the eyes of many of the youngsters, nor
amongst the men and women. Up above in the cloudless sky the stars
were brilliant clusters. The bonfire continued to burn and, beyond the
range of the flame light, fireflies twinkled in the deepened gloom.

The old man finished his tea, stood up, and resumed his narration.

'Those, indeed, were sad days for the Ahom race. Mir Jumlah was one
of the Mussulmans who had advanced the furthest up the river Luit. A
few days more of marching and he could have breached the border that
separated the Ahom kingdom from the land of the Naras, which today
we call Burma and Myanmar. Who knows where the Mughals would
have gone on then?

'But, since the first encounter near Dhubri, the Ahoms had fought
Jumla's mammoth army all the way, draining it of its blood and stamina.
Even though he occupied the Ahom capital, his adversary fought him
with guerilla tactics, cutting off supply lines and forcing him to turn
back. Yes, my people, even in those sad times we displayed our valour
and ability to frame strategy. In our defeat lay our glory too.

'But then, as I had said before and will say again, power is a tempting
bait and can make people do the weirdest things. Amongst his wives
Jayadhwaj Singha had two sisters, daughters of an influential nobleman
named Khamun Rajmantri Phukan. Jayadhwaj Singha had no children
of his own. Thus, while on his deathbed, these two sisters pressed upon
the king to nominate Kalia Gohain, son of the elder sister by a previous

marriage, as the heir to the throne. This he refused to do, naming instead the Saring raja, who had shown enormous gallantry in the campaign against Mir Jumlah, as the next occupant of the Ahom throne.

'But Khamun Phukan would have none of it. The very moment Jayadhwaj Singha breathed his last, he and his brothers tried to grab the throne for themselves, but were warded off by the patra-mantris led by Atan Buragohain. In deference to the dead king's wishes they brought the Saring raja to Bakata in the middle of the night and placed him upon the Ahom throne. Taking on the Ahom name of Supungmung and the Hindu title of Chakradhwaj Singha, the new king, backed by the ministers, immediately asserted his royal authority and dealt severely with those who had tried to usurp the royal seat.

'Most of the vassals of the Ahom monarch accepted the new king but, as it often happens in periods of transition, some of the tribes attempted to take advantage of the discord and rebelled. These included the Banpara Nagas as well as the Mishing, Dafla and Deuri Chutiya tribes, but each of them was subdued. Also, in 1665, occurred a drought which brought on a severe famine, a rare occasion in a region known for its rains and fertility of its soil.

'Meanwhile, the two couriers of Aurangzeb, who had brought gifts for Jayadhwaj Singha, reached Bakata. The new king was unwilling to receive them but the patra-mantris advised against opposing them. They pointed out that the realm was still in the process of recovery and it would be inadvisable to give offence to the Mughal emperor, thereby inviting possible retaliation. King Chakradhwaj Singha listened to the wise advice and sent through the couriers an epistle to Aurangzeb expressing his desire to remain on cordial terms ...'

Saraighat

～

THE YEAR WAS 1667. KING CHAKRADHWAJ SINGHA WAS entrenched firmly on the throne and had shifted from the temporary camp at Bakata to the refurbished capital at Garhgaon. With the help of his ministers, he had continued the efforts to restore confidence in the people of his kingdom regarding their own prowess, training up the paiks in the art of warfare as well as intensive cultivation so that they would be ready for battle and there would be surplus food in the kingdom. The armaments industry too was in full swing, as was boat-making. Also, like his predecessors, the new king made overtures to other chiefs and rajas to come to his aid if the need arose.

'I think the time for action has arrived,' he told his top council of ministers. 'As advised by you, I've been very patient, paying instalments of the remaining war indemnity ... though not as frequently as I am supposed to, making excuses for the delay so as not to offend the Mughal faujdar at Guwahati or arouse suspicion of our intentions. But I'm at the end of my patience now. The Mughal emissaries coming here to demand quicker payment of tributes are becoming more insulting on each visit, even threatening to take their Ahom hostages at Guwahati to Dhaka for punishment.'

'We have to be careful, Your Majesty,' advised the barpatragohain. 'Our defences are not yet complete. We also need to make more war boats and ammunition.'

'No, I shall not wait any longer. Enough is enough, I say. The latest request from Guwahati is the ultimate humiliation. They want some beautiful women from my realm to grace their seraglio. Would any of my predecessors tolerate such insult, I ask you?'

'Yes,' agreed Atan Buragohain. 'Such an insulting request is hurtful to our pride.'

'I'm of the opinion that the time is ripe to wrest back the land we've lost. Rashid Khan has had enough of Assam and is relinquishing his post as faujdar. He's being replaced by Syed Firoz Khan. The missives I've received from the new official are even more demanding and abusive. But he's yet to make his presence felt amongst his officers and troops, and take full stock of the situation. An attack now would be striking the iron while it is hot.'

'You seem to have someone in mind to lead the expedition,' the buragohain observed astutely.

'Yes. A diamond stands out amongst a handful of other gemstones. I think I've found the right man for the job. He has been put to various tests and emerged from them with flying high. His name is Lachit Deka. As you're all aware, he is the son of the great warrior-statesman Momai Tamuli Barbarua. I shall immediately appoint him the Barphukan to lead our army against the bangals.'

A huge armada of Ahom war boats lay ready to set sail down the river Luit. Upon the vast open field just outside the capital city of Garhgaon stood thousands of Ahom soldiers, their swords, spears, matchlocks and shields glinting in the sun. It was an impressive gathering despite consisting mainly of infantry, but there were a few horsemen mounted on their steeds too. On one of these sat Lachit Barphukan, tall and handsome, endowed with a nervous energy which hinted at the dynamism of the man. King Chakradhwaj Singha sat upon a throne on an improvised podium, a shamiana shielding him from the autumn sun. Close by, the traditional Ahom priests were performing rituals to ensure victory for the expedition, while Brahmin priests performed a yagna.

The Ahom monarch gestured to Lachit to approach him. The barphukan guided his horse towards the podium. Other Ahom army officers, including several phukans and rajkhowas, who would be leading the various divisions of the army, rode beside him. They all dismounted on reaching the king's presence and knelt on the ground, heads bowed. The Deodhais and Brahmins sprinkled holy water on them and placed spots of vermilion on their foreheads.

'Foreigners have usurped our holy motherland,' King Chakradhwaj Singha said loudly, addressing Lachit and his officers. 'They have overrun the realm and defiled our capital. They continue to taunt and insult us. We, who have Shan blood in our veins, will no longer tolerate the rudeness of the bangals. I have entrusted you with the task of redeeming the pride of our motherland and the prestige of the Ahom throne and people. Go and drive these infidels from our land. If you succeed in this enterprise, any reward that you ask will be yours. But if you do not succeed, do not come back at all to Garhgaon!'

Lachit Barphukan raised his hengdang. 'We shall restore the glory of our motherland!' he proclaimed. 'We shall destroy the bangals and restore the prestige of the Ahom throne and people.'

Thousands of soldiers raised their swords and spears and took up the refrain. Lachit saluted his monarch, mounted his steed, and led his army towards the ships waiting to convey them towards the enemy. The day was Thursday, 3 Bhada, 1589 Saka era, or 20 August 1667 CE.

The barphukan understood too well the need to keep up the momentum of his army, as also the requirement for quick action. He split his force to attack the Mughal outposts at Kajali on the south bank and Bahnbari on the north; the small garrisons within fought back with ferocity but were soon overwhelmed. Leaving a few of his men to repair and reinforce the forts for their own use later, the Ahom general continued his assault, the momentum of the advance ensuring that Mughal forts at Sonapur, Panikhaiti and Tatimara were overrun and Guwahati, the principal target, was within reach.

The Mughals had strongly fortified this river-port city. The main fort was located on the banks of the Luit at Itakhuli, but the city itself was guarded by smaller detachments of the army at various fortified locations. Lachit Barphukan studied the position and, consulting with his second in command, arrived at a decision. The Itakhuli fort being almost impregnable, those within it would have to be flushed out through a siege. This meant that an attack only across the riverfront would be meaningless; so other fortified locations would have to be overrun so that the Itakhuli fort could be surrounded from all sides.

Mooring their war boats on the south bank of the river Luit at a little distance away from Guwahati, Lachit ordered a large body of soldiers to disembark and, placing Pelan Phukan in charge with orders to breach the city's defences and surround the Itakhuli fort, he himself proceeded up the river with an armada to assail it from the riverside. The breaching of the city's defences was effected at Jaiduar; the Mughal forces retreated into the main fort, which could now be laid under siege. Pelan Phukan observed with apprehension how well guarded the fort was and communicated its seeming impregnability to his commander. Much to everyone's surprise some days later, even as the siege was in progress, a packet sent by Chakradhwaj Singha arrived at the Ahom camp. The packet contained garments worn by women. The letter was an order from the Ahom monarch that if Pelan had made such defeatist comments, he should be executed, and his soldiers made to wear the female garments! Pelan and his fellow officers swore that such a comment had never been made, a reply which satisfied the Ahom king.

But that message served as a warning to expedite the taking of Itakhuli fort. Two months had passed since its siege had begun, but there was no sign that the Mughals inside were ready to surrender. Adding to the danger was the possibility that news of the Ahom assault had reached

Dhaka and reinforcements might already be on their way. Thus, a frontal attack became inevitable. But the Ahoms had always been cunning in their warfare; a couple of their men scaled the walls of the fort at night without being seen and poured water into the cannons. Then, on the night of 4 November 1667, their forces launched an attack in the dead of the night. Even as the cannons from their war boats pounded the Itakhuli fort from one side, warriors scaled the walls of the fortress with the help of ladders and went on a killing spree. Hundreds of Mughal warriors were slaughtered, no prisoners taken and the few who managed to escape from the fort and fled on boats were chased beyond the river Manas.

The storming of the Itakhuli fort and the wresting back of Guwahati and parts of Lower Assam, which caused huge delight to the Ahom monarch, had come none too soon, for indeed, days later, a number of ships carrying soldiers and supplies arrived from Dhaka. The Mughal army made another stand at the point where the Manas met the Brahmaputra; but the impetus and advantage lay with the Ahoms who, fired by the taste of success, fell upon their adversary and decimated them. Only the officers, including the faujdar Syed Firoz Khan and his mirbukshi Syed Sala, were taken prisoner and sent to Garhgaon, while the common soldiers were killed. In Guwahati itself the Ahoms acquired a huge treasure trove belonging to the Mughals—cannons, matchlocks and ammunition, weapons, boats, horses, elephants, camels, bullocks, buffaloes and asses, as also a huge quantity of gold, silver, brass and copper, which were carried back to Garhgaon.

In what had proved to be a relatively swift campaign, the Ahoms had taken back the Kamrup region extending up to Manas. There could be little doubt that the Mughal emperor in Delhi would react to the developments and send a sizeable force to regain lost territory. But this time the Ahoms were determined that the 'success' of Mir Jumlah should not be repeated and their territory no more truncated. Lachit Barphukan and Atan Buragohain, in order to ensure this, began strengthening the fortifications at Guwahati, which appeared to be strategically the most advantageous position from where to repulse the Mughals. There were hillocks close to both banks of the Brahmaputra, providing the defenders with the advantage of height in launching a barrage of artillery at enemy war boats coming up the Brahmaputra, or troops advancing by land. There were also numerous water bodies with channels which opened out to the Brahmaputra; Ahom ships could lurk in them and then emerge stealthily after enemy ships had passed to attack the latter from the rear.

However, there were gaps between the hillocks; if these were closed with earthen ramparts, the hills would provide a protective ring about twenty-five miles in circumference. Therefore, work was immediately commenced on erecting such ramparts and watchtowers placed upon them at regular intervals so that the enemy could be sighted from a long distance, thereby complementing news garnered by spies. An arms and ammunition factory was set up on a hill so as to facilitate quick availability, the hill later coming to be called Kharguli or the place where gun powder and cannonballs were made. Some of the best and brightest army and civil officers were sent to Guwahati to help in the preparations; in Kamrup the zamindari system employed by the Mughals was retained, the revenue to be collected by appointed officials as also by vassal chiefs.

The defensive preparations proved adequate to repulse another attack by the Mughals in 1668 at Rangamati; the Ahoms made a tactical retreat from their forward positions to allow the nawab of Dhaka's troops to advance to Saraighat, where they were set upon and comprehensively routed. This relatively low-scale assault was actually a blessing in disguise, for it showed up some of the lacunae in the defences at Guwahati, which might have fallen before an assault by a bigger army. Lachit set up his headquarters at Itakhuli, while Atan Buragohain had his at Lathia Parvat on the opposite bank, and together they began further defensive preparations. These covered a potential war zone extending from Pandu to Asurar Ali on the south bank and Agiyathuri to Kurua on the north.

Lachit also made his naval troops practise and perfect the art of building bridges of boats which could span the Brahmaputra from one bank to the other, necessary when troops from one side had to quickly cross over to assist their brethren upon the other. One of the most striking features of the defences on the Brahmaputra River itself was the construction of wooden stockades within the waters, a skill not known to any other people in India. Such stockades were made possible by the fact that the Luit or the Brahmaputra was a braided river, flowing in numerous channels with sandbanks in between. So, tree trunks could be driven into the riverbed from one sandbank to another, thereby forming a kind of wooden bridge across the flow. Such river stockades proved effective barriers against enemy vessels, and also provided vantage points from where to fight them. So skilled were the Assamese workmen at building such stockades that these weathered the fury of the river's currents even during the monsoons when it was in full flow. They had gate-like passages which could be opened to allow their own boats through.

Even as the shortcomings in defences were being rectified, news reached the Ahom leaders at Guwahati—Aurangzeb, seeking revenge, had sent an enormous force which was fast approaching Guwahati! A new sense of urgency gripped the Ahoms at this information. The ramparts which remained to be built had to be completed in record time.

The enemy was at the gate! There was little time to be lost. Work on completing the defence preparations was going on day and night. Lachit Barphukan himself supervised these, riding from one position to another on his horse, making surprise visits.

On this night, he and his horse, accompanied by other officials, had crossed over by boat to the north bank at Saraighat. A rampart was being erected there; since it was of vital importance, Lachit had put his own uncle in charge of the workers building it, with instructions that it be completed by dawn.

But what was this? Riding up the slight incline, Lachit came upon a sight that infuriated him. Rather than being busy at work piling up earth, all the workers were recumbent on the ground, fast asleep! His uncle too was amongst them, as deep in sleep as his charges.

The sound of horse hooves and the light of the flares borne by the party startled awake his uncle as well as the workers, and everyone clambered to their feet.

'Sleeping, are you?' Lachit thundered, 'when you should be putting your heart and soul putting up this rampart in time! I demand an explanation, uncle. This rampart is not even half complete.'

'My apologies, nephew,' said the uncle nonchalantly. 'These men have been toiling at it without a break since morning. They're dog-tired. I have given them a break for rest.'

'But my instructions were to have it completed before dawn. It is past midnight, yet a lot remains to be done.'

'Oh, we've time enough,' replied the uncle in the same nonchalant tone. 'A few more hours of rest for the men will make no difference.'

'Perhaps so. But orders are orders and must not be flouted. That is the tenet which keeps an army disciplined. Uncle, you imagine that you're beyond reproach just because you're my relative. But remember, an uncle is not greater than one's motherland!'

Saying this, Lachit raised his hengdang and beheaded the unfortunate man. Seeing this, the terrified workers lost their tiredness and began working frantically.

That rampart, popularly known as Momai-kota Garh, or the rampart where the uncle was slain, was completed before the cock crowed next! Although only the king was empowered to give orders for such a type of execution, Chakradhwaj Singha condoned Lachit's action, because this kind of strictness was essential for motivating and disciplining the men in times of war.

News of the Mughal defeat had reached Emperor Aurangzeb in Delhi in December 1667. He had been told of the sufferings undergone by his army under Mir Jumlah in order to secure the territory of Lower Assam. It was no longer a question of imperialist expansion of Islam—it was more a question of prestige now. These upstart Ahoms needed to be taught a lesson.

The cunning emperor planned to kill two birds with one stone. He had under him the valiant Rajput Raja Ram Singh of the famous Kuchhwaha clan and son of Raja Jai Singh of Amber. Ram Singh had been implicated in the escape of Chatrapati Shivaji, the Maratha king, from captivity in Delhi, and was thus in disgrace with the imperial court. But Aurangzeb knew that Ram Singh with his Rajput loyalists remained a perpetual threat to the Mughals. By revoking his disgraced status, restoring to him all his royal privileges and making him the commander-in-chief of the campaign against the Ahoms, the Mughal emperor sought to remove a potential thorn in the flesh. If the great Mir Jumlah had been killed by the treacherous air of Assam, could Raja Ram Singh return alive?

Raja Ram Singh was aware of Aurangzeb's stratagem, but could do nothing to check the latter's designs. On his family's advice, he consulted Guru Teg Bahadur. 'It is certain death to command the invading army,' he told the guru, 'but it would be equally fatal to me to disobey the emperor's orders.'

'Have faith in God,' Guru Teg Bahadur replied. 'You will return from this campaign to Assam alive and well. I myself will accompany you.'

It took some time for the emperor in Delhi to raise the kind of army that would be able to inflict a crushing defeat on the Assamese, and Raja Ram Singh could set out in his campaign only a few months later and reach Rangamati, the eastern-most Mughal outpost, in February 1669. His army initially comprised Rajput chiefs, his own troopers and 500 artillery men; but when reinforcements from Bengal joined him, it was enhanced to 30,000 infantry, 18,000 Turkish cavalry and 15,000 Koch archers, as also numerous war boats. In order to keep watch over him, Aurangzeb sent along Rashid Khan, who was a part of the Mir Jumlah campaign and had served for four years as the faujdar of Guwahati.

As promised, Guru Teg Bahadur, as also five Muslim pirs, accompanied Ram Singh in order to protect the army from the sorcery and black magic of the people of Kamarupa, whose 'evil powers' the

Mughal soldiers were terrified of. The Sikh guru built the first gurudwara in Assam at Dhubri on the bank of the Brahmaputra. Known as Gurudwara Damdama Sahib, it later became a holy pilgrimage shrine for Sikhs.

The spies having brought advance news of the enormous size of the approaching Mughal army, Lachit Barphukan and Atan Buragohain at once understood that they would have to further strengthen their defences to confront it. Therefore, they adopted tactics that would delay the Mughals from reaching Guwahati. One of these was to order the Ahom outposts near the river Manas to involve the imperial army in skirmishes so as to distract it from the primary target of Guwahati. The small detachments, adopting guerilla hit-and-run tactics, were easily defeated though they did help to delay the advance. To their horror, the Ahom soldiers who had engaged the imperial army discovered that the Mughals had brought along with them ferocious hounds that would go for their throats and tear them to death.

By April 1669, the Mughals had reached Sualkuchi on the north bank and encamped. The rains would be arriving soon and would hamper the Mughals by making communications difficult as they had done in the past. Thus, in order to further delay the inevitable conflict, the Ahoms sent an emissary to Ram Singh's camp carrying an epistle for the raja, questioning his motive for coming to the Ahom kingdom with such a strong and hostile army. The letter also stated that if there was any dispute between Delhi and Garhgaon, it could be settled amicably through peaceful negotiations rather than through needless conflict. Ram Singh was of the old school of warriors for whom adherence to the code of warfare was as important as the battle itself. He could not see through the subterfuges of the wily Ahoms and took their missive seriously. He replied that there was no need for war and that his was not an army of conquest. All that the Ahom king needed to do was to get his forces to retreat to Barnadi on the north and Asurar Ali on the south bank, which had been the western limits for his realm by the earlier treaty. Raja Ram Singh even offered to have one hour of 'battle' to show both monarchs that force had been used—if the Assamese army did not have sufficient ammunition, the Mughals would be happy to supply them with the same!

Correspondence on the part of the commanders of the two forces continued for some time; to show that he meant business, Raja Ram Singh advanced further and camped at Hajo, close to the outer bounds of the Ahom fortifications. He sent an emissary reiterating his demand that the Assamese leave Guwahati; along with a letter he also sent a bag of poppy seeds indicating that the number of soldiers under him were as numerous as those seeds. However, by then Lachit and Atan had completed their defensive measures; they now sent their reply that they would rather fight than yield an inch of territory which they had wrested from the Koches. They also sent a bamboo tube filled with sand along with the letter to denote the numbers of their own army!

Despite the size of his army, there was demoralization in Raja Ram Singh's camp, particularly with regard to the effective fortification of the area, which hinted at the fighting calibre of the Ahom leadership. Moreover, friction between the Raja and Rashid Khan had been growing over who wielded greater authority. Raja Ram Singh, provoked by Khan's refusal to follow his order to be present at a war-strategy conference, finally settled matters by slashing the ropes of the Mughal commander's tent and driving him out of the encampment!

Clearly, Raja Ram Singh's heart was not in the campaign, and he was keener to try and fulfil his mandate through negotiations and show of force rather than actual use of force. Thus, even after the passing of the rains, his force could not make much progress despite a series of victories on land. He even challenged the Ahom king to single combat and asserted, that if he lost, he would return with his army to Bengal, a challenge which Chakradhwaj Singha declined. On their part, the Ahoms understood the danger of trying to attack the vast enemy force head-on until an opportune moment arrived. They were quite content to remain within the safety of their highly fortified position and harass the Mughal army by using guerrilla hit-and-run tactics. They used the most ingenious means of harassment, including playing on the fears of the Mughal soldiers that Assam was the land of sorcery and black magic!

The eyes of the sentry at the riverside post of the Mughal encampment popped wide. He wanted to yell out a warning, but no sound emerged from his throat.

The river bank was filled with dancing skeletons!

There were hundreds of them on the small stretch of land separating the waters from the perimeter of the camp, their skulls and bones glowing weirdly in the dark. Then they began to wail, a prolonged, terrible keening that chilled the heart. Others too heard that dreadful noise and joined the sentry in watching the devilish dance of the dead. So paralysed were they with fear that they did not even consider attacking the skeletal force with bared swords! They simply gaped at the spectacle, convinced that the rumours they had heard about Assam being a land of sorcery were absolutely true.

One of them turned his eyes away and ran to a camp to alert his superior. Soon that section of the camp grew alive with voices shouting out commands and men holding aloft lighted flares. At that precise moment, as if by magic, the dancing skeletons disappeared.

It had been, of course, a trick played by the wily Ahoms to further demoralize the Mughal soldiers. The 'skeletons' were men from an Ahom group which had been hiding on top of a hillock. The Ahoms had many such secret groups hidden at strategic places, to observe enemy movement, launch surprise attacks, or play pranks like the one just witnessed by the Mughal sentries.

Two dozen of these men in four sloops had rowed their way to that point in the river. The night had been carefully chosen. Being moonless, with clouds covering the sky, it was a pitch-black night. Scrambling on to the riverbank, the group had donned black shirts, pajamas and caps on which skulls, rib-cages and bones had been drawn with luminous paint made from secret but natural ingredients known only to the Ahom priests. It had been an awe-inspiring, convincing performance—however, the flares and burst of activity within the camp alerted the group that the show should be concluded! Turning their backs to the camp, the men had taken off the clothes, which caused the skeletons to mysteriously vanish. Moments later they were in their boats and rowing swiftly away to their hideouts.

The very same night, taking advantage of the darkness and the river mist, a group of Ahom warriors silently slid into the enemy camp. Their padded feet made no noise as they slid ghost-like through gaps between the lookout posts and entered the tents where the soldiers slept. Knives sliced through throats and the smell of warm human blood filled the tents.

Just three tents, nine cavalry soldiers—a token attack, to show how easy it was for the Ahoms to slip into the enemy encampments. Their job done, the group left the camp as silently and unseen as they had entered, making a swift escape in their boats.

The emissary sent by Raja Ram Singh to Lachit Barphukan did not bother to hide his contemptuous anger. 'Do you know what our commander-in-chief calls such dirty tricks?' he asked the Ahom general. 'He calls them "thieves' affairs". Only thieves steal into a house at night to commit mischief.'

'Ah, that is our way of fighting, tell the raja that,' Lachit Barphukan laughed and replied. "You see, only tigers fight at night! Also, your raja too is not averse to dipping into his own bag of tricks. His soldiers tried to infiltrate into our fort at Amingaon by digging a tunnel! Had we not been alert and flooded the tunnel, we might have been in some amount of discomfort. Now what would you call that? A hero's affair? If he desires to fight, confront us directly.'

But there was no single, direct confrontation, since neither party desired one. Instead, numerous sporadic, limited engagements continued through 1669 and 1670, none giving either of the adversaries the upper hand. Unable to make any headway from Sualkuchi, the Mughals endeavoured to march across the north bank and try to breach Ahom defences at Guwahati through Darrang, thereby extending the theatre of war right up to Tezpur. Timely warning of the attempt by the vassal raja of Rani enabled Lachit and his men to thwart the attempt. Ram Singh defeated his adversary at Sessa close to Agiathuri, but his men suffered a loss at Rangmahal on the north bank.

Pressure was being applied by Delhi and Garhgaon on both the combatants to engage in more decisive action. It had been an aspect of Lachit and Atan's strategy to lure Ram Singh into the trap at Guwahati and defeat him in a naval battle, which needed patience on the part of the Ahoms. But, in Garhgaon, Chakradhwaj Singha was losing his patience at the seeming inaction, mistaking the delay in repulsing the Mughals to be hesitancy on the part of his generals. He threatened his barphukan and buragohain with dire consequences if they delayed things further, thereby forcing the duo to make a false move that they were otherwise not willing to do.

At that precise period of, a large detachment of the Mughal forces sent by Ram Singh were encamped upon a stretch of open land near the river Sessa close to the Alaboi Mountains. Lachit was against a direct confrontation on such open ground, but given orders by his king, he had no other course but to obey. A sizeable force of 40,000 infantrymen was dispatched by him to attack the encamped Mughal army; it succeeded in inflicting heavy casualties on the imperial troops and captured Mir Nawab, who was the commander of the outpost, and took prisoners and booty. However, as they were returning to their camps with their captives and booty, they were charged by the imperial cavalry with Ram Singh himself in the lead. What followed was carnage. Lachit's misgivings had proved right; at the end of the day, 10,000 corpses of Ahom warriors lay strewn upon the Alaboi plains, the biggest loss suffered by the Ahoms in any campaign.

Lachit was disheartened by the death of such a huge number of his men and by the inability of those ensconced safely at Garhgaon to comprehend the ground realities on the battlefront. 'Each of our soldiers is a pillar of strength,' he told Atan Buragohain. 'That we've lost ten thousand such stalwarts at Alaboi pains me.' The buragohain asked the barphukan not to lose heart. 'We have an advantage over Raja Ram Singh,' he pointed out. 'The Mughal commander is fighting under compulsion. We can note by the nature of his war tactics that his heart is not in this campaign. You and I, on the other hand, are fighting for king and country, as are our officers and men. Our passion will give us ultimate victory.'

The Rajput prince, hopeful that the disaster at Alaboi might persuade the Ahom commanders to accede to his demands, again sent emissaries with the pledge to return with his army to Delhi if the Ahoms accepted Asurar Ali and Barnadi as the western edge of their realm. In fact, the Mughal commander used every subterfuge in his arsenal to convince the barphukan, including bribery in the form of gifts, as well as allegations of perfidy in the Ahom ranks and demoralization amongst the men. A priceless necklace of gold studded with gems was disdainfully sent back to the Mughal camp by Lachit Barphukan, with a request that such blatant attempts at bribery be no longer made in future. Also, almost every day, arrows would be shot into the Itakhuli fort, the messages wrapped around them hinting that some of the lower-ranked Ahom officers were hobnobbing with the Mughals in expectation of favours.

Lachit Barphukan and Atan Buragohain ignored all such efforts to accede to Ram Singh's offer. However, conscious of the military superiority of the Mughals, especially of their cavalry and artillery, the barphukan was sorely tempted, and even sent a message to Chakradhwaj Singha informing him of Ram Singh's offer. It was at this time that Chakradhwaj Singha fell ill and died in April 1670, and his brother Maju Gohain, who took on the Ahom name of Sunyatpha and the Hindu title of Udayaditya Singha, succeeded him. The new king sought Atan Buragohain's views as to the Mughal offer. The latter pointed out that ceding ground after so many of their soldiers had laid down their lives would be demoralizing for the entire Ahom community. Also, Ram Singh might not be content with the acquired region and, like Mir Jumlah before him, aspire to attack Garhgaon itself. Udayaditya agreed and instructed Lachit to embark on an all-out campaign to rid the realm of the bangals once and for all.

Coincidentally, at the same time pressure was being imposed upon Ram Singh to end his dilatory tactics and take concrete steps to drive the Ahoms out of Guwahati. As though to drive home his wishes, Aurangzeb sent reinforcements to the Rajput chief, as also a sarcastic message through Rashid Khan that read: 'I have sent Ram Singh to fight with the Assamese, not to make friends with them.' To this Ram Singh replied: 'I have not refrained from fighting but it has proved useless. As there are no fields, fighting by spears, shields and guns is an impossible affair. The Assamese have erected an impenetrable wall of defences on both banks. The only possibility is a naval fight.'

Ram Singh had come to know from the men who arrived with the reinforcements that his son had been maltreated by Aurangzeb. This made his aversion to fight on behalf of the Mughal emperor even deeper. Yet there was no help for it—as a Rajput, he was oath-bound to the pledge made to Aurangzeb and had to attempt to bring this campaign to an end and oust the Ahoms from Guwahati.

Thus commenced the final battle of Saraighat in March 1671—one in which the Ahoms under the leadership of Lachit Barphukan and Atan Buragohain dealt a mortal blow to Mughal expansionist ambitions. As predicted by Ram Singh, it was a naval battle. This put the Mughals at a disadvantage, for their war-vessels had to move upstream against the mighty Brahmaputra currents while the Assamese boats could move in swiftly upon them. But then, Ram Singh had been heartened by the news that Lachit was gravely ill, and could not lead the Ahoms against his forces.

Ram Singh's huge flotilla of boats swept in on the Assamese with all guns blazing, attacking the first of the opponent's war boats at Saraighat, a little downstream of Guwahati. Simultaneously, some of the boats carried Mughal cavalry to a sandbank named Andharubali, the rampart at which spot had broken, as informed by spies, thereby having an opening for a land attack on the Itakhuli fort. But the Ahoms guessed his tactics and defended the waters near the sandbank fiercely even as the rampart was quickly repaired, and the cavalry had to turn back.

It was a river battle the likes of which the hoary Luit had never seen. The whole of the Brahmaputra at the triangle between Kamakhya, Itakhuli and Aswakranta grew cluttered with boats; the flashes and thunderclaps of cannons being fired filled the air; drowning out the cries for help of men struggling in the waters. The red waters of the Brahmaputra turned even redder with human blood. Though, on the north bank, the men under Atan Buragohain were gaining the upper hand, those towards the south bank had been demoralized at not finding Lachit at the head. Soon the results of this demoralization began to unfurl against the Ahoms; one after another their boats gave way before the Mughal onslaught and then turned and fled. With the reek of impending defeat befouling the air, boatmen at Itakhuli began transferring the barphukan's personal effects to their crafts for the inevitable departure for Kaliabor.

News of the looming defeat reached the ears of the gravely ill barphukan. He barked out instructions, and his attendants carried the entire bed onto a war-boat which rowed swiftly towards the enemy. A miracle occurred. At the sight of Lachit coming to lead them, the soldiers were energized with new courage and hope. The Assamese boats once again turned to confront the enemy. Patriotic cries rent the air as the fight to defend king and country was resumed; the Mughals could not resist the renewed Assamese onslaught and began to escape from the watery arena after heavy casualties. It was a decisive victory. Lachit himself chased the Mughals up to Pandu from where his boat returned, but his forces continued the pursuit till Ram Singh's forces had been sent packing beyond the river Manas. The full extent of Ahom territory was once more in their king's possession.

Even in defeat the chivalrous Ram Singh praised his adversary. 'Every Assamese soldier is an expert in rowing boats, in shooting arrows, in digging trenches and in wielding guns and cannons,' he remarked. 'I have not seen such specimens of versatility in any other part of India.'

Lachit Barphukan did not recover from his illness and died a few months later, at the age of fifty-nine.

Lachit's elder brother Laluksola was appointed as the new barphukan. Once again, the river Manas became the western boundary of the Ahom realm. At a place called Hadira on the bank of the river, an Ahom army outpost as well as a trading centre was set up and it began to be called the Hadirachowki by the local people. Since it marked the outer bounds of the Ahom empire, people from outside began calling it the Assamchowki, and it soon developed into an important trading centre. During the rainy season, the garrison stationed there would shift to a fort built upon a hill nearby. A functionary was appointed to administer the area and also keep an eye on trading activities.

Having been comprehensively defeated, Ram Singh and his force retired to the traditional Mughal outpost at Rangamati and camped there, waiting for an opportunity to renew the campaign. From then on Rangamati became the acknowledged Mughal administrative headquarters for the region.

THE NARRATOR

'The Battle of Saraighat marked the pinnacle of military achievement of the Ahom kings and dealt a death blow to imperialistic Mughal aspirations of conquering the Valley of the Luit and perhaps marching into China. This was not the ultimate battle between the two adversaries—as we shall learn, there was to be another fight, but that was one of subterfuge rather than of martial valour. The hearts of the Mughals were really not in it and they were repulsed easily by the Assamese.

'The crushing defeat at Saraighat crushed Mughal spirits. It proved that Lachit Barphukan and Atan Buragohain were master strategists who could be compared with great generals in any part of India. They employed every strategy in the book to stem the advance of a far more powerful Mughal army— erecting strong fortifications at carefully chosen spots, especially beside the Brahmaputra which had always acted as a highway for invaders; getting Ahom forces to show themselves to the enemy and then pretending to flee and enticing them towards well-fortified traps to be ambushed; using the evil reputation of their land outside to instill terror into the hearts of Mughal soldiers by kindling their superstitious streak regarding magic and sorcery; not confronting the enemy on open ground but adopting hit-and-run tactics; taking advantage of the dark to launch night attacks; concealing war boats and troops at strategic places which could launch guerilla attacks on the enemy from the flanks and the rear; undertaking marvels of engineering construction, such as wooden stockades on the mighty Brahmaputra that could withstand powerful currents—few battles fought on the soil of Hindustan could match the complex but successful strategy employed at Saraighat. It is a pity indeed that magnificent leaders of men like Lachit and Atan are not known outside our state and the great battle of Saraighat is ignored by Indian historians.

'Unfortunately, as I had said before, the height of glory is almost invariably followed by a descent into nightmare ... this was the case immediately following the defeat of the Mughal forces at Saraighat and the death of Lachit Barphukan. After the passing away of Chakradhwaj Singha in 1670, there was a power struggle of the most reprehensible kind and, within the space of eleven years, no less than seven kings were enthroned and then murdered! Anarchy gripped what had been a well-ordered system of government; personal ambition was placed before national pride; senior patra-mantris, whose wishes had once been commands, were not only defied by ambitious underlings, but also imprisoned and murdered.* No less a patriot than Atan Buragohain suffered such a fate!

'Yes, my people, the 1670s were a nightmare. Conspiracies, killings, betrayals—one could hardly imagine that the race of Chaolung Sukapha was ruling at Garhgaon! The main reason for such decay of moral authority was that the ablest ministers and army commanders were all at Guwahati battling the Mughals—thus only the petty officials were ruling the realm at Garhgaon and advising the king. These insignificant men were afraid that once the higher ministers returned to Garhgaon, the authority and affluence attained by them would be removed; thus some amongst them tried to play kingmaker in order to empower themselves. This was the reason why when Atan Buragohain returned to Garhgaon, he discovered that his counsel did not have the former influence over the new king, Udayaditya Singha. For instance, the king wanted a campaign launched against the Dafala mountain tribe since they were harassing the subjects living in the valley. Atan Buragohain advised against such a campaign, pointing out that it would be very difficult to fight the Dafalas within the difficult mountainous terrain which they were familiar with, but the king did not listen to his counsel. The campaign was a total disaster for the Ahom army but Udayaditya Singha, rather than acknowledge his error, held the Barbarua, who had led the campaign, responsible, and had him dismissed and banished from the realm.

'One particular episode that set the senior ministers as well as the subjects against Udayaditya Singha was his infatuation for a holy man, described variously in different accounts as a Vaishnav saint named Chakrapani, a descendent of Mahapurush Sankardev, or a sanyasi or a roving ascetic named Paramananda who hailed from Gakulpur near Brindaban and had wandered into the Ahom kingdom. Whatever be the case, the weak-willed and deeply superstitious Udayaditya Singha became infatuated with this man and was greatly influenced by him.

---

* Please refer to Ahom buranjis; Bhuyan, *Atan Buragohain and His Times* (2010); Gait, *A History of Assam* (1905).

This incensed a section of the nobles as well as the Vaishnav monks of the sattras, with the former determined to remove Udayaditya from the throne. While the principal ministers were not a part of the conspiracy, a petty officer named Lechai Debera Dakhinpatia Hazarika, with the blessings of the monks and assistance from Sarugohain, the king's brother, attacked the royal palace with a band of men. They overpowered the royal guards, killed a number of officers loyal to the king and put Udayaditya under house arrest in his bedchamber.

'In the middle of the night itself, the usurper Sarugohain summoned the patra-mantris and the priests, sat in the audience hall and declared himself the new king, taking on the Ahom name of Suklampha and the Hindu name of Ramdhvaj Singha. The next day Udayaditya Singha was taken as a captive to Charaideo where he was administered poison and killed, while his three wives were executed. The holy man who had been the immediate cause of the fratricide was impaled to death and his corpse floated down the river Dikhow.

'Suklampha became king in November 1672. His guilty conscience at having murdered his brother to attain the throne made him afraid of shadows; a number of innocent officials were suspected of treason and put to the sword. He also tried to atone for his crime by having his Brahmin priests perform sacrificial rites and the Vaishnav devotees chant prayers at their naamghars.

'However, Lechai Debera, who had been the principal person in elevating Suklampha to the throne, grew dissatisfied that he was not being rewarded. After all, a post of hazarika, or an officer in charge of a thousand paiks, was hardly apt for what he had done. He coveted the post of barbarua, but discovered that the man gracing the post at the time, Ghorakonwar Barbarua, enjoyed the full confidence of the king. Using devilish cunning, Debera slowly poisoned the mind of the monarch against Ghorakonwar as being involved in a conspiracy against him and succeeded in having him removed from that office. A grateful king made Debera the barbarua. Simultaneously, this totally unprincipled officer brought charges before the monarch against patra-mantris such as Langichang Barukial Bargohain and had them executed, thereby making himself the closest confidant of the newly crowned king.

'By then the air within the royal palace had grown very poisonous indeed! Not only did Debera appoint his own kith and kin as officers, he also began killing many who had objected to a mere hazarika suddenly playing the role of kingmaker. The principal ministers being involved in insurrections by the Deori Chutiyas and the Mishmis, Debera took full advantage of the situation to become all-powerful. However, by then Swargadeo Suklampha began realizing that he had created a monster. Also, he was very ill with a number of ailments including dropsy, and felt he did not have much time to live. There was no telling who Debera would appoint as the king if he died. To forestall such a possibility, the monarch summoned his top officials and suggested that either his two brothers, or else Kalia Gohain who was the son of Udayaditya Singha, be made the king after his death.

'There was no unanimity amongst the nobles as to who should be made the king, different officials supporting any one of the three. But Debera Barbarua was determined to act before power slipped out of his hands. The evil officer, using the authority commanded by his office, summoned those opposed to him one by one on the pretext that the king wanted them, and on a single night slaughtered no less than twenty-four hazarikas and all the phukans attached to the palace. When he learned of the massacre, Ramdhvaj Singha grew alarmed; he did not believe Debera's assertion that all these men were his enemies and understood that he needed to get rid of the barbarua before that man turned against him. The king entrusted a phukan with the task of killing Debera.

'He had underestimated the barbarua! His residence complex adjacent to the royal palace was well guarded by his trusted men; he also had informers in his pay amongst the menials who served the royal family. One of the chambermaids eavesdropped and overheard the king give the order for the execution of Debera and conveyed this to him. So, the barbarua was quite prepared when two phukans from the palace came to his house to deliver a 'message' from the king. Even before the phukans could unsheathe their swords, they were overpowered and killed. Then Debera and a band of armed men roamed the streets of Garhgaon, cutting down each and every individual they thought to be their enemy and could lay hands on. Oh, my people, never had so much blood been split on the streets of glorious Garhgaon!

'The swargadeo did not know what to do. Debera Barbarua was running amok and there was no one to stop him. Even as he was planning as to what could be done, the fiend struck. Threatening the royal physician Kharmaju bez with annihilation of his entire family if he did not do as ordered, poison was mixed with the medicine the king was being given and in November 1674, just three days after the second massacre, Swargadeo Suklampha was dead. Such was the cruelty of Debera that he buried alive with the king his chief queen as also the widowed queen of Swargadeo Jayadhwaj Singha because she had refused to become his mistress.

'There was fear and suspicion everywhere; Debera Barbarua, slayer of hundreds, was the most feared of the lot. Some of the nobles did try to place the son of Swargadeo Udayaditya upon the throne, but were thwarted by Debera and his cohorts. Instead, Debera chose a man named Suhung, an Ahom prince who resided at Samaguri. This insignificant candidate had been chosen by Debera because he could be easily controlled. In reality, he could not be termed as a swargadeo because none of the patra-mantris had given concurrence to his anointment, as Ahom rules demanded, and thus many of the buranjis omit his name. The Tipam raja, brother of Swargadeo Suklampha, marched with his men towards Garhgaon to lay his claim to the throne, but was defeated by the barbarua, captured and executed.

'Debera Barbarua, having eliminated his enemies in the capital, in order to further consolidate his hold, now began summoning top Ahom officials based at Guwahati, who were not fully aware of the goings-on at Garhgaon, on the pretext that their counsel was required, and had them murdered. But resistance to his authoritarian ways came from unexpected quarters. Immediately after being placed on the throne, Suhung realized that he was being made use of and, in fact, was a mere

puppet in the hands of his barbarua. He decided to have Debera arrested
and executed and gave instructions to this effect. But, as before, the wily
officer was alerted by his informants and he immediately sent assassins
to kill Suhung who, with merely twenty-one days of rule, became the
shortest-reigning monarch in Ahom history.

'Do not think, my people, that Debera Barbarua the monster was
an exception. If you study the history of every dynasty in the world,
you will find such Deberas everywhere, individuals without morality or
compunction, greedy for power and drunk with it. He slew the entire
family of Udayaditya Singha except for one daughter. He then placed
a Tungkhungiya prince by the name of Gobar Gohain on the throne.
But nemesis was soon to overtake this murderous thug who brought
such disgrace to the fair name of the Ahom race. Laluksola Barphukan,
who had assumed that office after the death of Lachit Barphukan, and
Atan Buragohain, were still at Guwahati; disquieting news had reached
their ears as to the happenings at Garhgaon, but, with Ram Singh still
stationed at Rangamati with his troops thereby posing a perpetual danger
to the extended Ahom realm, they had not been in a position to rectify
matters at the capital. But soon the tidings became very grim indeed.
Simultaneously, towards the beginning of 1675, Ram Singh began
preparations to depart back to Delhi, so the senior Ahom nobles could
turn their eyes towards Garhgaon.

'Atan Buragohain and Laluksola Barphukan, accompanied by some
of the most valiant Ahom commanders who had fought so well during
the campaign at Guwahati, set off in April 1675 for Garhgaon at the
head of a large force, having deputed Guimela Gohain-Phukan to
manage the affairs of the river-port city. Debera Barbarua understood the
implications, and made preparations to meet the formidable opponents.
But suddenly he discovered that his soldiers had deserted him; he tried
to placate the advancing nobles by sending them costly gifts, which
were scornfully spurned. You must understand, my people, that the one
who is the cruellest is also a coward at heart. Faced with the prospect
of confronting his adversaries with a handful of men, Debera fled—the
advancing nobles, who entered Garhgaon without any resistance,

discovered him hiding in a hut in Thukubil near Dilih. Brought back in a cage and humiliated and insulted by the multitude all the way, the barbarua was tried and found guilty.

'He was put to death in the most gruesome manner. Thus ended the life of one of the archvillains in Ahom history, who in the space of two-and-a-half years struck such terror amongst the nobles and the subjects! I never tire of repeating, my people, that power makes quirky creatures of men. Debera rose to prominence because he was seen as a champion of the Vaishnav monks of the sattras in their fight against the undue influence of a holy man. But his success and the power he suddenly commanded turned his head, and he was transformed into an ogre.

'The king appointed by him, Gobar Gohain, was tried and executed on the 23 May 1675, the period of his "reign" lasting barely a month. Many nobles and officers who had been adherents of Debera were summarily killed. The buragohain spent some time in putting back into place the administrative structure of long standing, which had suddenly been disrupted by the actions of Debera. Since there was no occupant on the Ahom throne, and the experience of installing princes of unknown calibre upon it being none too good, the nobles importuned Atan Buragohain to take up the mantle of kingship. But the great man refused, reminding the nobles that it had been Chaolung Sukapha's wish that only someone of his blood become a king of his people. Since he did not have royal blood, he could not accept the offer of kingship—a sacrifice rare in the annals of human history!

'In consultation with the other patra-mantris, a new king named Sujinpha, a descendent of Swargadeo Suhungmung, the Dihingiya raja, was placed on the Ahom throne. Having seen order restored, Laluksola Barphukan and his commanders returned to Guwahati. But peace was not to remain for very long at Garhgaon or, for that matter, in the Ahom realm. Sujinpha was not of the same mettle as his illustrious ancestor, the Dihingiya raja. He had been witness to the fate of the kings just preceding him and was anxious not to share the same. He sniffed conspiracy and treachery everywhere; additional security was placed within and without Garhgaon; cannons were mounted at the capital's gates and its streets guarded night and day by soldiers. But the new king caused even greater disaffection amongst the nobles by having them come one by one to his presence and swear fealty to him. Also, against the advice of the buragohain, he had princes of competing Ahom clans secretly murdered to ensure that his own sons would succeed him to the throne.

'To cut a long story short, Atan Buragohain soon discovered that Sujinpha was not an ideal king. Some nobles in the court, who had earlier enjoyed great privileges under Debera but were now deprived of the same, poisoned the mind of the chief queen, who had great influence over the monarch, against the buragohain. So grave did the situation become that Atan was forced to escape from Garhgaon to Lakhau. There he was joined by other nobles and commanders dismayed by the goings-on in the royal palace and together they defeated the army sent against them by Sujinpha. The king himself was put to the sword. Once again, the nobles requested Atan Buragohain to become the king and once again he refused.

'Instead, he chose a prince from the Parvatiya clan, named Khamcheo, had him brought from Cheraidai to Garhgaon, and placed him on the Ahom throne, giving him the name Sudaipha. He gave his own daughter in marriage to the new king to ensure that the latter took heed of his counsel. But the forces inimical to the buragohain, who was an upright and honourable man, were continuously at work in the Ahom court. Nobles who were jealous of the power commanded by the buragohain, who sometimes could even take decisions without informing the king, recommenced their rumour-mongering to poison the mind of the monarch.

'Also, certain trivial incidents served to drive a wedge between Sudaipha and his principal minister. For instance, it was customary in the court for the nobles to prostrate themselves before the monarch whenever they entered the hall and approached. Whenever the senior queen, the buragohain's daughter, was seated beside the monarch and her father entered, she quickly left the hall because she did not like to see her father prostrate himself before her. The buragohain's detractors poisoned the mind of the king by telling him that she was showing disrespect to him at the instigation of her father!

'Atan Buragohain deemed it proper that he nip such mischief in the bud and began taking action against offenders. This prompted some of the nobles to attack the king himself because he was the buragohain's nominee. A petty officer named Chikon Tamuli was assigned to creep into the palace at night and murder the sleeping Sudaipha. However, in the darkness, the officer mistook the king's mother for the king and killed her instead! Knowing that he would now be the target of both the king's allies and enemies because of the botched attempt at assassination, Chikon fled from Garhgaon, along with some other confederates of the conspiracy, to Guwahati, where they sought the protection of Laluksola Barphukan.

'Meanwhile, news had reached the buragohain that Laluksola Barphukan was displaying a friendly disposition towards the Mughal commanders stationed at Rangamati. Now, having learned that the barphukan had given shelter to those who had carried out the attempt on the life of King Sudaipha, Laluksola was requested to return the fugitives to the capital, which he refused to do. You must remember, my people, that communication in those days was extremely difficult and time-consuming; the distance from Garhgaon to Guwahati was the same as it is now, but oh, what a difference! It was almost as though Guwahati was situated in another realm! If those stationed there did not obey instructions sent from the capital, nothing much could be done.

'It became clear to the buragohain that the barphukan at Guwahati had designs of his own, and the Ahom kingdom would suffer for it. Nor was he wrong. The barphukan had become envious of the power the buragohain commanded and was determined to grab that power for himself. Atan Buragohain was overwhelmed with his own impotency to quash the ambitions of the barphukan. The stark fact was that the bulk of Ahom standing armed forces, as also the cream amongst the officers, were posted at Guwahati to repulse any attempt by the Mughals to retake the port city. Recent communications from the Mughal Thanadar

at Rangamati to King Sudaipha also indicated that the possibility of
another offensive aimed at taking Guwahati was all too real. An epistle
from Sultan Azamtara from Dhaka to Laluksola Barphukan giving an
ultimatum to the Ahoms to go back to the old boundaries enhanced the
possibility. Thus, the question of recalling at least a part of the soldiers
and boats from Guwahati to bolster the defences at Garhgaon could not
even be contemplated.

'Then, on 26 February 1679, Atan Buragohain's worst nightmare
came true! Just imagine, my people, how two siblings emerging from the
same womb can behave in such a different manner! Lachit Barphukan,
the hero of Assam, gave his life in the service of his motherland. His
elder brother, Laluksola Barphukan, proved to be a traitor who, to
further his own ambition to attain power, on that fateful day undid
an achievement for which thousands of Assamese soldiers died, and
returned Guwahati and adjacent areas to the Mughals. On behalf of the
emperor at Delhi, Mansur Khan entered Guwahati with a small fleet and
occupied the city vacated by the Ahoms.

'Three days earlier, Laluksola and his band of loyal officers,
accompanied by the entire Assamese force and flotilla assigned to guard
the realm from Mughal assault, sailed up the Brahmaputra, its offensive
now directed against Garhgaon itself. The resistance offered by Atan
Buragohain was feeble; soon he and his men were overpowered by
the traitor and arrested. King Sudaipha was executed and replaced by
a prince named Sulikpha handpicked by Laluk. His first act on being
enthroned was to order the execution of the buragohain.

'Thus ended the life of the great statesman and patriot, Atan
Buragohain: he was taken from incarceration at Duimunisila to a place
in Kaliabor, and strangled. Now there was no stopping Laluk Barphukan,
who discarded that title, and designated himself rajmantri phukan or
prime minister. It is said that so filled with a sense of power was this
man that sometimes he dressed himself in royal robes and ornaments
that, according to Ahom laws, only the king could wear. Indeed, he was
all-powerful in the realm—Sulikpha, who belonged to the royal clan of
Samaguri, was only fourteen years old when he was placed on the throne.

Laluk had intentionally chosen a child as king so that he could wield total control over him, even marrying off his five-year-old daughter to the lad so as to further strengthen his grip on the reins. Sulikpha, on ascension, had taken on the name of Ratnadhwaj Singha, but because of his tender years, he was called the Lora Raja or Boy King by his subjects.

'His actions, however, were hardly those of a child. Over four centuries of Ahom rule had seen the spread of the family tree of the progenitor, Chaolung Sukapha. You will recall that Swargadeo Suhungmung had classified ruling clans as Charingiya, Dihingiya, Tipamia and Tungkhungiya, and allotted territories to them. Since then, other clans had sprouted: Samaguriya, Namrupiya, Parvatiya and so on. Thus, there were royal families spread throughout the kingdom and the land was full of princes who could lay claim to the Ahom throne or around whom rebellions could take place.

'Laluk Rajmantri Phukan well realized that each of these princes could in the future jeopardize the new king, as well as his own position. Since ancient times Shan laws had decreed that one who aspired to be a king must be perfect physically and of sound mind. Even if a prince had scars or marks left after measles or chickenpox, he was deemed to be unfit to grace the Ahom throne. Thus far, in the kingdom founded by Sukapha, this rule was not strictly observed. For instance, Swargadeo Sukhampha, who had ruled between 1552 and 1603, was lame but not deemed unfit to be the king.

'However, now, instigated by Laluk, the Lora Raja embarked on a brutal spree of violence the likes of which the kingdom founded by Chaolung Sukapha had never before seen. Chaodang soldiers scoured the land hunting for princes and when caught, either killing or maiming them. Eyes were gouged out, ears and noses cut, and such injuries were afflicted on some that they would have been better off dead. The object was to eliminate each and every possible rival claimant to the throne, no matter how innocent. Soon the intentions of the rulers in Garhgaon spread like wildfire across the realm. Princes who were forewarned tried their best to escape from the kingdom, travelling incognito or hiding in some secret place. A few were successful, but all too many were caught

and killed or mutilated. It was a macabre drama that was being enacted
by Laluk and Lora Raja.

'One of their principal targets was a prince named Gadapani of the
Tungkhungiya clan. He was the son of Gobar who had sat for a brief
while on the Ahom throne, and thus could lay greater claim to the
throne than most others. Also, Gadapani had the reputation of being a
dynamic and resourceful person, and thus loomed as one of the biggest
threats to the Lora Raja ...'

Wielder of the Mace

~

'RACE YOU TO THE OTHER BANK AND BACK?' THE FATHER challenged his two sons.

'Sure,' replied one. 'But what do we get as prize if we win?'

'A trip to a friendly Naga village,' replied the father laughingly. 'They make the most delicious pork dishes there!'

The family had come to the bank of the wide stream, a tributary of the river Darika, which marked the boundary of their princely estate, for a picnic. A retinue of menials had accompanied them, carrying bamboo murrahs and tables, as also cane baskets containing victuals for the picnic. They were in the process of laying these out under the supervision of the mother, while the father and the two sons ran towards the stream's edge for a swim.

The man, tall and strong of physique, was Langi Panisiya Gadapani, Saring raja of the Tungkhungiya clan. He was of legendary fame throughout the realm for his heroic nature as well as courage; he had been able to take an elephant on his own for shikar when just into his teens and had hunted tigers with his spear. He was equally well known for his wisdom and judgement, and for his belief that the Ahoms should erase the differences that separated one clan from another and present a united front.

His wife, stately and beautiful, was Jaimati, daughter of Laithepena Bargohain, a noble who had once been of the highest rank. She was endowed with a dulcet voice that had once charmed her toddler sons with lullabies to sleep. But the years had passed and the two sons had grown up; the elder named Lai was fourteen while the younger named Lechai was twelve. She looked fondly at the three loves of her life as they prepared to jump into the stream.

'It's not fair, father,' said Lechai. 'You're far taller than me and the reach of your arms is longer. I might be able to take on Lai, but not you.'

'All right,' said the father and laughed. 'Tell you what, I'll give both of you a headstart, and jump in only when you have reached the middle of the waters.'

'Right then,' said Lechai and, without waiting for his brother, jumped into the stream and began swimming.

'That's fair, is it now?' said Lai grimly, and swam after his brother. Gadapani waited till they had just crossed half the width of the stream and then set off. He had crossed and was back even as his sons were at quite a distance.

Lai and Lechai climbed on to the bank, dried themselves and changed into clothes a retainer handed to them. 'There goes the Naga village and the pork!' said Lai ruefully.

They seated themselves on the murrahs and began tucking into the food. The scene was quiet and rustic, the ambience loving. That was to be the last moment this family was to eat together. Suddenly the peace of the afternoon was shattered by the sound of running feet. Two men came racing through the orchard in which they were seated—one a retainer in their household, other a kataki or courier.

'I've been sent by a handique from the royal palace at Garhgaon,' the courier spoke hurriedly. 'I shall not tell who has sent me, for the less you know the better, else you might be captured and tortured into divulging his name.'

'Come, man, control yourself,' said Gadapani impatiently. 'What are you babbling about?'

'Here, my good man, be seated, and have a drink of water,' Jaimati said kindly, realizing that the man was exhausted from running. 'Then tell us what you've to tell.'

But the courier remained standing and agitated. 'His Majesty, Swargadeo Sulikpha, has gone utterly mad. He's given orders that all young men of royal blood be either killed or mutilated so that they may not become a rival to the throne. This handique, who is your kinsman, has sent me to warn you that you're on the top of the king's list. You must save yourself, Gadapani dangoriya. Even as we speak chaodang soldiers are on their way to harm you.'

'Thank you,' said Gadapani calmly. 'You yourself need to get away at once. If the soldiers meet you while you're on your way back, they'll surely kill you. My boats are moored on the bank a little way ahead. Take one and row away to safety.'

That was typical of the man. Even though he himself was in mortal danger, his thoughts were for the welfare of the messenger.

Leaving their retainers to collect the picnic stuff, the four of them hurried back to their home, a huge complex entirely constructed upon wooden stilts. The urgency of the situation was not lost upon them. 'We'll leave at once for the Naga village I had told you about,' Gadapani told his family when no one was within earshot. 'The headman is a good friend of mine. I once saved his life when we were hunting together. But we need to travel light. That way we can reach safety faster.'

'No,' said Jaimati. 'The three of you go. If I go with you, I'll only delay you. On the other hand, I can direct them towards a false direction which will give you more time to effect an escape. After all, that madman is only out to kill or mutilate princes of royal blood. They will not touch me.'

That was a sound argument, for Jaimati indeed would have slowed them down. Gadapani's concern was less about his own safety than that of his two sons. Quickly conceding that his wife was right, they gathered together the minimum requirements, and set off towards the hills from back of the estate.

Not a minute too soon. A troop of chaodang soldiers marched up the path leading to the house. Jaimati walked boldly towards them and asked what the object of their visit was.

'We need to speak with your husband,' the officer who led the troop, named Gidagathi Hazarika of Dakhinapath, and deputed specifically by the Lora Raja to hunt out Gadapani, said with severity.

'Oh, he's not here at the moment. What is it that you want of him?'

'His Majesty Swargadeo Sulikpha has an offer of a royal office for him at Garhgaon. We've come to escort him to the capital.'

'Oh, it's all right, then,' said Jaimati with a completely straight face. 'In fact, he is on his way to Garhgaon. You can meet him there and convey the news to him.'

'But we would have encountered him on our way here if he was going to Garhgaon,' Dakhinpatia Hazarika said, more in puzzlement than suspicion.

'Oh, you must've come on foot,' said Jaimati. 'You see, my husband is travelling by boat. But don't worry; you're sure to meet him in the capital.'

Gadapani and his two sons, accompanied by a trusted retainer, moved swiftly over the ascending trail. This was a familiar path which they had traversed many a times before, though not many knew about this narrow track leading to the land of the Nagas. Towards sunset they hurriedly ate some cooked food they had carried with them, and then climbed on to the branches of tall trees to snatch some hours of sleep. This was dense jungle territory, so sleeping on the ground was not safe. They woke at dawn and were once more on their way, not slackening their pace; the youngster Lechai had the stamina to keep up with the others. Towards sunset they encountered the first of the Naga villages; this was not a friendly one so they pressed on, skirting another village till they reached the one the chief of which was Gadapani's friend.

They were warmly welcomed and allowed to eat and rest. The boys slept in the community hut where all the unmarried young men of the village lived; in the morning, they made friends with them while the elders discussed the reason for the unexpected visit. Gadapani told the Naga chief about all that was happening in the Ahom kingdom and how his life and those of his sons were in dire danger.

'It's bad business,' he said. 'I've been told that scores of princes like me have either been killed or mutilated. By now they must have been to my house and discovered I have fled. I am more concerned about Lai and Lechai ... I would never forgive myself if anything happened to them.'

'Have no fear, my friend,' his friend replied. 'You'll enjoy my hospitality for as long as you deem fit. My warriors will guard your sons as if they were their own. Also, it would require a more venturesome Assamese king than that wretched Lora Raja to venture into our territory.'

Gadapani sent the retainer back to his home to apprise his wife Jaimati that he and his two sons were safely ensconced in the village of his Naga friend. But rapidly developing events entailed his early departure from the village, though his sons Lai and Lechai stayed on, passing their days as though they were Naga youngsters and even dressing like them.

Scrawny and short, with lean features which wore a perpetually hungry look, nervous of manners, Swargadeo Sulikhpha hardly had the air of a king. His thinness was emphasized by the huge throne in the palace hall upon which he sat; that he was in a furious rage made him appear comical rather than threatening. He had a thin, reedy voice which hardly inspired fear, though by now everyone knew how dangerous and brutal he could really be.

The man who had once been designated as Laluk Barphukan, instrumental in enthroning the Lora Raja, sat on his right, significantly upon a throne as large and grand as the monarch's. He was a huge figure of a man, tall and barrel-chested, with a grim face and a harsh voice.

The entire kingdom knew who the real 'king' was; steeped in delusions of grandeur and power, Laluk no longer called himself Barphukan or Rajmantri Phukan. That had been a dilemma; there was no designation of nobility which would fit one as powerful as he. So he had seized on another, grander title; now he was addressed as Rajmantri Laluk Buraphukan.

'You stupid moron,' the Lora Raja screamed at the officer lying prostrate before him. 'You say you haven't been able to catch hold of Gadapani?'

'We rushed to his home but he was not there. His wife Jaimati informed us that he had sailed for Garhgaon. After we returned, we have scoured the city, but he is not to be found. Obviously, someone is sheltering him here.'

'Moron is the right word for this officer here,' it was Rajmantri Laluk Buraphukan who now spoke. 'Couldn't you tell that was a lie? Gadapani coming to Garhgaon ... The goat coming to the lion's den? A likely story! Bought him time, hasn't it? He must be far away by now.'

'Ah,' exclaimed the king, comprehension dawning upon his stupid face. 'So the wife told a lie to throw us off the track, did she? Go and bring her before me. I'll get her to reveal where her husband is hiding.'

Gidagathi Hazarika leapt up from his prostrate position with alacrity. 'Is that also Rajmantri Buraphukan's desire?' he asked.

Laluk said nothing, but nodded. The hazarika left hurriedly to gather a unit to go and fetch Jaimati. She or her retainers were hardly in a position to resist. Her hands were bound and she was dragged to a waiting boat and taken straight to the palace to the royal audience hall. Her ruse had delayed the authorities by days in their search for her beloved husband Gadapani. Gidagathi Hazarika pushed his captive so hard that she fell to the floor at the feet of the king and his mentor. Since she was bound, she could not protect herself from injury during the fall. Her head hit the wooden floor and blood oozed out of a gash on her forehead.

Neither the Lora Raja nor Rajmantri Laluk Buraphukan was bothered by her plight. 'So, you're the hussy that's married to Gadapani?' the Lora Raja squeaked. 'Where is your husband?'

Jaimati raised herself to a kneeling position with difficulty. 'Is this the way you address a princess of the Tungkhungiya family?' she asked defiantly.

It was Laluk who answered. 'You're fortunate we haven't beheaded you for misleading us! Tell us where he is or suffer the consequences.'

'I do not know,' replied Jaimati. 'I would not tell you even if I knew.'

'She's lying, she's lying,' screeched the king. 'She knows. She knows.'

'So be it,' said Laluk. 'Hazarika, take her to the open field at Jerenga and do whatever you must to get the information of her husband's whereabouts.'

Gidhagati Hazarika dragged Jaimati through the streets of Garhgaon like he would a slave. She was carted off to the field called Jerenga Pathar, some distance from the city. He had a wooden stake driven in the centre of the open ground and tied Jaimati to it. She was exposed to the harsh sun of the day and the chill of night. Hazarika left her for twenty-four hours, expecting that simply being tied up would be enough to cow her into letting out information about her husband. But the lady was made of different mettle; she remained defiant despite the threats and abuses flung at her by the Hazarika and his henchmen; that she was not given food or water did not serve to change her resolve.

The officer realized that stronger inducements were required; he began with light punishment, having her face and exposed limbs hit with nettle plants. Red, itchy welts covered her skin; she could not scratch them since her hands were tied. But she bore her punishment with fortitude. Gidhagati next ordered a chaodang to whip her. Lash after lash broke the skin of her body and tears rolled down Jaimati's eyes. But her lips remained closed and not a whimper emerged from her throat.

A crowd had gathered on the fringes of Jerenga Pathar to watch the torture being inflicted on a helpless woman. It consisted almost entirely of ordinary people of Garhgaon; there were tears in the eyes of the women and some men muttered rebellious exclamations under their breaths. Clearly, the sympathy of the public lay with Jaimati, though such was the terror inspired by the palace amongst the ordinary folks that none dared to even voice aloud a word of protest.

Jaimati proving adamant and pressure from his superiors becoming greater as the days passed, the hazarika now used even more painful methods of torture. Salt was fetched from the royal kitchen and applied to the bleeding wounds of the lady. Weakened by lack of food, water and sleep, as also the excruciating pain wracking her body, Jaimati fainted. Her tormentors doused her with water to bring her back to consciousness so that she could feel the pain again. The crowd gasped with loathing and consternation as the cycle of torture commenced again.

A tall man, dressed in the garb of a bairagi or a wandering minstrel, stood amongst the gathering. Age had lined his face; his hair and beard were white. He carried a been, a one-stringed musical instrument, in his hand. Such wandering minstrels were a common feature in the Ahom realm. They roamed from village to village singing ballads in praise of past Ahom monarchs and heroes, and devotional songs, dependent on the hospitality of the villagers to feed and sustain themselves. Because of the familiarity of the common people with bairagis, spies sent by the palace to gauge the mood of the subjects often adopted such a disguise. This particular man too was not a genuine bairagi but simply disguised as one.

But he was no spy. The tears in his eyes were too real. The man, in fact, was none other than Prince Gadapani, husband of the unfortunate woman being tortured on Jerenga Pathar.

Gadapani had returned a few days ago to the Naga village where his children were in hiding. A youth sent by the chief to get the latest information on the search for the prince, had returned with terrible tidings. Jaimati had been arrested and was being tortured to try and find out about the whereabouts of her husband Gadapani!

'I must leave at once,' the prince told his friend the Naga chief. 'It's not that I fear she will betray us. I know her too well for that. But I must attempt to get her out of the clutches of those devils.'

'That will be difficult, you realize that, don't you?' his friend advised. 'Please do not do anything rash or it will defeat the very purpose of her deeds. You are destined for greatness, my friend. Do not flirt with your destiny in trying to achieve what is not possible.'

'I'll not do that, I pledge you. But I must make the attempt or else be deemed a coward. Please take care of Lai and Lechai.'

'I'll guard them with my life. You must not worry. They've already made friends with our youngsters and would be happy here.'

'Thank you, my friend,' Gadapani spoke from the heart. The two embraced and then the prince set off alone from the Naga village.

Now, standing amongst the onlookers as his wife was being subjected to excruciating agony, there were tears in the prince's eyes and the fire of hatred in his heart. He felt utterly helpless. Jaimati was well guarded. To try and rescue her would be akin to committing suicide. He had to control himself, at least for the sake of their two sons. But then, the desire to rescue her and be close to her at least once more was strong.

Jaimati had been made to suffer for many days. Even from a distance it could be made out that she was almost at her final breath. The chaodangs who had been torturing her also realized the futility of inflicting further pain upon their victim. Gidhagati Hazarika spat in disgust and went to report to Laluk Buraphukan his inability to extract information from the woman.

Laluk took the information impassively. 'Then we'll have to trace him by our own means, won't we?' he said. 'Commence a manhunt as this land has never seen before. Catching Gadapani is priority number one for us at this moment. Put all our spies into prising out information about this wretched man; have batches of soldiers scour the realm high and low for him. He can't evade us forever, unless he leaves the kingdom and slips into alien territory.'

Gidhagati Hazarika assured the rajmantri that he would leave no stone unturned in his quest for the elusive prince.

At Jerenga Pathar, with the departure of the hazarika, the watch on Jaimati slackened. The onlookers plucked up courage to approach her one by one, but the guards did nothing to stop them. Some tried to make her sip water, but she choked. An aged woman stroked her head and said, 'Sati Jaimati, you're the bravest of women our realm has produced. You will become a legend.'

Gadapani, dressed as a bairagi, approached her. Since a bairagi also carried saintly associations, those near the dying woman made way for him.

'My beloved Jaimati,' Gadapani whispered, 'I'll carry you away in the darkness of the night.'

At his words, the eyes of the princess opened and a new light shone from them. 'Is it really you, my beloved husband?' she gasped, her voice so low that he could barely understand the words.

'Yes, it is me, dear Jaimati. A few hours more ... and I'll carry you away.'

'It's of no use, my beloved husband. I'll not survive those hours. Are Lai and Lechai safe?'

'Yes. You must make yourself strong, dear Jaimati, for their sake.'

'No,' said Jaimati, her voice sinking. 'I'll never see them again. You've taken too much of a risk coming here. Please go away at once for their sake.'

She breathed a long sigh and passed away from life into legend.

The onlookers close to her began to wail and those further understood that the brave Jaimati was dead. They too began to wail. Gadapani wiped the tears from his eyes and unwillingly left the spot.

Outside the walls of Garhgaon, he was joined by a Naga youth in traditional garb; within the shelter of a jungle, Gadapani too changed into Naga dress complete with face paint and a dao. It took them five days to return to the village.

'I'm sorry about your loss,' said the Naga chief.

'You've learned of her death already?' Gadapani, surprised, asked.

'We've long ears, my friend,' said his friend, but without humour.

'Do my sons know?'

'Yes, they do. But the same ears have heard that this area is no longer safe for you. Lai and Lechai will be all right ... they've blended in so well it would be impossible to recognize them. But you, friend, must leave for your own safety.'

'I've made up my mind. I shall head west towards Kaliabar. My sister is married to Bandar Barphukan who is in charge there. Maybe, my brother-in-law will protect me.'

It was no use tarrying any further. Prince Gadapani hugged his two sons. 'We'll meet again in the not-too-distant future,' he said. 'Your mother has not died in vain. I feel it in my bones.'

A quick farewell to his host, and Gadapani left the village alone.

The next few months were a cat-and-mouse game. The hazarika had been true to his pledge and had used every resource commanded by the buraphukan to find out the whereabouts of his quarry and hunt him down. Meanwhile, the few times Gadapani tried to leave the bounds of the land of the Nagas, he ran into soldiers on the lookout for him, and had to retreat. For a while he lived within the dense jungles, living off the land; or he would spend a night or two in any of the isolated Naga villages where he was welcomed because he knew the dialect. Once, while roaming in the jungle on the Tablung Hills, he discovered that he had been surrounded by the Lora Raja's soldiers—he had been betrayed and someone had informed them about his location. He was trapped; there seemed to be no way to escape the net cast by the soldiers. Gadapani fell to his knees and prayed to the deity of the forest: 'O, Mother, save me!' A moment later he caught sight of a rock with a narrow opening that led to a cave within it. He wriggled into the cave, having concealed the opening behind him with creepers. Later, at night, when he emerged, there was no sign of the soldiers.

However, as the days passed, the search for him slackened to some extent, and Gadapani was able leave the safety of the Naga Hills and slip into the Valley to try and make his way to Kaliabar. Now that he was on open ground, amongst his own people, the danger had grown ten-fold; he could no longer dress as a Naga for that might draw unwanted attention. Once more he changed into the disguise of a minstrel. An unfortunate occurrence made him realize how dangerous such a disguise could be.

All rivers and their tributaries lead to the main river Luit; it had been his plan to hitch a ride on a trading vessel over the river route and sail downstream to Kaliabar. He had considered himself lucky that on the bank of the Dikhow he had come across a large maarnao carrying a cargo of supplies for the nobles stationed at Kaliabar; the crew was more than willing to take the bairagi abroad and offer him their hospitality.

Soldiers had been posted on the banks of the Dikhow and there were boatloads of them patrolling the waters too. Because the boat he was hitching a ride upon was on official duty and carried the ensign of the Barphukan, it was subjected only to cursory stoppages and was not searched; concealed under the shade of the soi on one of the two hulls of the maarnao, the bairagi was seemingly asleep on the wooden floor, and no one took much notice of him. But problems rose from an unexpected quarter; towards evening the cargo-boat reached Dikhowmukh and moored for the night. The crew was a convivial lot; plenty of food was cooked, home-brewed beer was brought out, and they feasted with Gadapani, who had a hearty appetite, digging into the repast with gusto. Then, after the meal was over, the crew requested the bairagi to entertain them with a ballad. One that celebrated the adventures of Chaolung Sukapha, they suggested!

Gadapani's been was merely a prop to his disguise; he had no idea how to play it! While his beloved Jaimati's voice had been mellifluous, his was hardly so. He knew that the moment he opened his mouth, his disguise would fall apart!

Much to the disappointment of the crew, the bairagi made various excuses for not being able to entertain them that evening. He had had a long trek, he explained, and was dog-tired, never mind the fact that just a few minutes earlier he had been eating and drinking with zest. Also, during the trek he had slept in the open air, he said, and the cold and the dust had made his voice hoarse. He promised to entertain them the following evening after he had had some rest.

In the morning, the crew discovered that the bairagi had vanished in the night!

Discarding his disguise of a bairagi, Gadapani donned the dhoti of an ordinary farmer, a jhanpi or wide-brimmed bamboo hat on his head supposedly sheltering him from the rays of the sun, but actually assisting in casting a shadow over his features. Often, he encountered soldiers who questioned him about his identity; he replied in the tones of a simpleton, eliciting guffaws from his inquisitors. Many a night he was offered food and a rude bed to sleep on by ordinary folks; he discovered that the subjects of the realm quietly seethed in rage at the goings-on in the royal palace; they were disgusted with the killings and conspiracies, the wholesale slaughter of princes who might pose a challenge to the Boy King; they were especially furious at the murder of the statesman Atan Buragohain, who had fought off the bangals and brought order to Garhgaon, and the brutal torture and killing of Sati Jaimati. He was informed that the hopes of the people rested with Prince Gadapani who had not yet been captured despite an award of gold being offered for information on him. If reputation was anything to go by, Gadapani seemed to be fit to be the swargadeo, he was told, so even if folks had information on him, they would not go to the officials no matter how much gold was offered.

There were many close shaves. For instance, a fortnight after he had left the Naga Hills, he spent the night in the house of a widow named Aghoni Bai. Somehow news that a stranger was spending the night at the widow's house reached official ears and a platoon of soldiers was dispatched to investigate. The flares carried by them alerted the widow and she confessed to Gadapani that she knew who he really was, and would protect him. She sent her youngest daughter to her neighbours; soon two ladies, Randoi, originally from Raha, and Bhadoi, originally from Tipam, hurried to her cottage. They made Gadapani lie down upon the ground and covered him with a sheet; then the three women set loose their hair, and began beating their breasts and wailing. When the soldiers arrived, they were told that the women were mourning the death of a dear relative who had died of a contagious disease—and the soldiers beat a hasty retreat!

Finally, two months after he had set off on his wanderings, Gadapani reached Kaliabar. He hailed the sentry manning the entrance of the spacious residence of the barphukan and asked to meet his chief wife. 'Please tell her that her brother sends her a message,' he requested. Soon the lady of the household herself came to the entrance and, giving no sign that she recognized Gadapani, signalled to him to follow her. She took him to a cottage at the rear of the sprawling compound and, once inside, embraced him.

'You cannot imagine how happy I'm to see you, Gada,' she cried. 'I was so afraid you had already been killed.'

'Well, it would take more than a mere stripling to kill me,' Gadapani smiled. He went on in sombre tones: 'But my dearest Jaimati is dead, brutally tortured at Garhgaon. I shall avenge her death.'

'We need to proceed cautiously, Gada,' his elder sister said. 'I'll have to judge my husband's mind, though from his words I'm sure he is dismayed at what's happening at Garhgaon and in the kingdom. But I've to be sure, so that you're not put in peril. Meanwhile, you can take shelter in this cottage. Lie low for a while till I have more news for you.'

A development at Garhgaon ensured that Gadapani did not have to hide for very long in Bandar Barphukan's residence. Rajmantri Laluk Buraphukan, who had armed himself with the powers of a king, and dressed and behaved like one, was assassinated in the month of November 1680.

Laluk was all too aware that, in assuming powers akin to an Ahom monarch and rendering the actual king a puppet manipulated by him, he had transgressed Shan laws and made powerful enemies amongst the other nobles. Equally worrisome was the concern expressed by the Deodhai, Bailung and Moran priests. The Brahmin priests, being less involved and more cunning, kept their views to themselves, but their Ahom counterparts openly told the Lora Raja and the buraphukan that they have had very pessimistic visions of the future of the kingdom and its ruler.

The subjects, too, were restive. It was not merely the violence that was sweeping the kingdom and the murder of Atan Buragohain and Sati Jaimati, which had raised murmurs amongst the multitude. What also rankled was the fact that Laluk had returned Guwahati to the Mughals—to acquire which so many of their sons had given their lives. The crafty Laluk felt the pulse of the people and the underlying anger heating up the kingdom's air. He kept himself well guarded and was careful to ensure that whenever any of the patra-mantris called upon the teenage king, he too was present. His downfall, however, came in an indirect way. When the Ahom priests voiced their apprehensions about the future of the kingdom, Laluk had asked them what was needed to be done to counteract the ill omens. They replied that a human must be sacrificed at the Kechaikhati temple at Sadiya to appease the gods.

This was an age-old custom; in fact, a class of people named bhogis had been created to be sacrificial material! Young men were chosen and allowed to eat, drink and make merry to their hearts' desire for an entire year before being sacrificed at the altar of the goddess Shakti. So, Laluk agreed at once to the priests' advice. The only problem was to choose the individual to be beheaded; the priests had said that it must not be an ordinary bhogi, but a hero of extraordinary courage and ability.

There was one such man in the capital named Bhotai Deka Saikia, who had earlier shown his mettle by killing a monstrous bear that had strayed into a residential area of Garhgaon and wreaked havoc. Laluk secretly chose Bhotai as the one to be sacrificed and ordered that he be apprehended and brought to the palace. But evil plans have a way of taking quirky turns; just as Laluk had bribed numerous menials in the palace and households of the nobles to provide him with confidential information, similar spies bribed by others flourished in his household too. Bhotai soon learned of the plans of the rajmantri. In order to save himself, he in turn conspired with disaffected nobles to put an end to Laluk's tyranny.

On the night of Tuesday, 24 November 1680, Bhotai with fellow conspirators Madha Tamuli and Aghona Kachari, taking the help of retainers owing allegiance to them, stealthily entered Laluk's residence, silently slit the throats of the household guards and murdered the buraphukan in his bedroom. Along with Laluk, his three sons were killed, though the ladies were spared. That night saw the end of the power-hungry traitor who had bartered away Guwahati to the Mughals in pursuit of his personal ambitions; with his death, his dream of establishing a dynasty with himself as the progenitor came to an end. His assassins received such accolades from the general public that Lora Raja had to spare their lives, but they were sent into exile from Garhgaon.

The killing of the all-powerful Laluk encouraged the section of higher nobles who had been disgusted with the behaviour of the Lora Raja and wanted to remove him from the throne. This included the commander of the Ahom forces at Kaliabar, Bandar barphukan, who however remained totally unaware that Prince Gadapani was in hiding within his estate. The barphukan was as worried about the developments at Guwahati as he was of the goings-on within the Ahom kingdom. Not only had the Mughals committed excesses in the territories regained by them, even undercutting the authority of the Darrang raja, but there was a distinct possibility that they might proceed once again on an attempt to capture Garhgaon and make a vassal of the Ahom king.

The immaturity and inefficiency of the Boy King, as well as the disaffection amongst the nobles and subjects because of the excesses committed by him, had eroded monarchial authority and weakened the Ahom leadership. News of this had no doubt percolated to Mansur Khan at Guwahati, and spies there had reported to Kaliabar preparations for a possible assault by the Mughals. It was imperative that Lora Raja be replaced by a more imposing monarch and a sense of nationalistic unity brought about amongst the nobles and officials.

Feelers sent out by the barphukan showed that many of the nobles were willing to act against the Ahom king; but to meet at Garhgaon, which was so riddled with treachery, might have alerted the palace. Thus, the chief nobles secretly sailed to Kaliabar and met at the barphukan's house. The conclave included, apart from Bandar Barphukan, two other patra-mantris, Dighala Buragohain and Laithepena Bargohain, as well as a number of phukans, rajkhowas, baruas and hazarikas.

'We have a weak king and a weak administration,' the barphukan said, opening the discussions. 'I'm afraid that the bangals who now occupy Guwahati, gifted to them by the treacherous Laluk, might be planning to attack our realm.'

'We're of the same mind,' agreed Dighala Buragohain. 'The Lora Raja has to be deposed and someone stronger and more efficient needs to be installed as the swargadeo.'

As the discussions progressed, it grew apparent that there was unanimity amongst those gathered that a new king was the need of the hour. 'But whom do we install?' Laithepena Bargohain posed the crucial question. 'Laluk and the present swargadeo have killed or maimed almost all eligible princes. There is hardly anyone left in the kingdom to be presented as an alternative to the king.'

As the conclave mulled over this, an official named Chenkak Phukan asked permission to suggest a possible name. 'May I suggest the name of Langi Panisiya Gadapani of the Tungkhungiya clan? Thanks to the sacrifice made by his valiant wife Jaimati, he has managed to evade the swargadeo's men. He is reputed to be a man of strength and courage.'

'I agree with Chenkak Phukan,' said another official named Khamrak Phukan. 'Prince Gadapani has testified to his astuteness by escaping capture for so long.'

The name entailed more and prolonged discussions. Once again, the gathering came to a unanimous conclusion. Indeed, Gadapani would be the ideal substitute for the Lora Raja.

'Do any of you know where he is hiding right now?' Bandar Barphukan asked. No one present in the hall, however, had an answer to this all-important query.

At that moment, a retainer of the household entered the room and whispered a message into the barphukan's ears. 'I'm surprised,' the officer told the others with a bemused expression on his face. 'But, apparently, the chief amongst my wives is privy to important information and seeks permission to confide in us.'

Permission being granted, the lady entered and bowed to the gathering. 'I've been told you've decided to elevate Prince Gadapani to the throne. I know where he is.'

The room burst out in an excited buzz. 'Where? Where? Tell us where!' a chorus of voice spoke.

'Here,' said the lady. 'On this very estate!'

As Prince Gadapani entered the hall, physically imposing and impressive of bearing, any doubt that had remained in the minds of those gathered quickly evaporated. Dighala Buragohain formally apprised the prince of the deliberations and asked if Gadapani would agree to ascend the singorighar and accept the Ahom throne. With matching gravity, the prince tersely replied that he would.

'You must go at once to the Dakhinpat Sattra and take the blessings as well as permission of the head of that monastery, Banamali Bapu, the sattradhikar gossain. This is imperative, for the Lora Raja too is a disciple of the gossain,' Bandar Barphukan told Gadapani.

This was true. It had been Swargadeo Jayadhwaj Singha who had given land to Banamali Gossain to set up the Dakhinpat monastery and had become his disciple. That monarch had realized that the Ekasarana Namadharma religion, also called the Mahapurushiya dharma, propagated by Mahapurush Sankardev had swept like wildfire throughout the realm, a reality which needed to be acknowledged if the royalty had to keep in tune with the spiritual leanings of the subjects. This was done in the face of objections from the Brahmin priests at the palace, though their influence was in no way lessened by the monarch's display of fealty to an additional faith. Subsequent monarchs had continued the tradition of taking the blessings of the Dakhinpat sattradhikar, for they too realized that he commanded a widespread religious following.

Accordingly, Gadapani, accompanied by some officers as well as a strong guard for his protection, travelled to the Dakhinpat Sattra, but Banamali Gossain refused to give his permission since he had already bestowed his blessings upon the Lora Raja. Deeply offended at this refusal as also the shabby treatment meted out to him during his stay at the monastery, Gadapani returned to Kaliabar to begin his campaign against the Lora Raja. However, a complication arose. Bandar Barphukan, having learned about the sattradhikar's refusal, now backed out of supporting Gadapani's quest for the Ahom throne. It required a great deal of persuasion by his chief wife, and threats from Gadapani loyalists, to turn the barphukan around, though he joined the expedition with marked reluctance.

The gathered nobles knelt before the designated king on 15 August 1681 and, accompanied by a large force, they sailed up the Luit and reached Garhgaon on 22 August. Lora Raja attempted to resist but, discovering to his dismay that his soldiers were not willing to fight on his behalf and had deserted him in huge numbers, attempted to flee. He was caught and taken in chains to Namrup where he was put to death.

During the past decade, the administration had been reduced to a shambles; ambitious officers had indulged in conspiracies and broken every Shan law to grab power; kings had been killed and princes mutilated; the reek of anarchy pervaded the very air. Gadapani was determined to restore the authority of the throne and the rule of law to the land. Therefore, his coronation ceremony in March 1682 was marked less with pomp and pageantry and more with solemnity. On occupying the throne, he assumed the Ahom title of Supatpha and the Hindu name of Gadadhar Singha, which translates as Wielder of the Mace. Also, Garhgaon held unpleasant memories for him; so, having brought back his two sons, Lai and Lechai, and sent gifts to his saviour the Naga chief, Gadadhar Singha shifted his capital to nearby Barkola. However, soon he realized that the move was a mistake; from all aspects including security, Garhgaon was a far superior location, so the administration returned to that city. He married daughters of some of the nobles, including that of Laithepena Buragohain, whom he made his bor kuonri or chief queen. This was a strategic move to ensure that he commanded the loyalty of his important functionaries and to prevent them from indulging in their favourite pastime of conspiring.

Apart from the capabilities he himself possessed, Swargadeo Supatpha had an additional qualification to be a great monarch. During the period when he was a fugitive, he had roamed around the country evading capture, often taking shelter in the humblest of households. This made him familiar with the living conditions of the people, which had degraded because of the unsavoury goings-on at the helm of the realm's affairs. Like Atan Buragohain before him, he too understood that the key to bringing about prosperity amongst his people and earning their loyalty was to provide a good administration that would attend to their needs.

For this, a cleansing process had to be carried out and Gadapani undertook one with an iron hand. A thorough enquiry was launched about the conduct of various officials and those who were guilty of underhand or treacherous conduct were arrested and punished. Any member of the royalty or the nobility who might hold a grudge against the new king was killed, including kinsmen of Laluk Buraphukan and Debera Barbarua. At the same time, he sought out and rewarded individuals who had helped him during the period he was a fugitive and appointed a Brahmin called Arjun Daivjana, who had met the prince during his wanderings and predicted that he would be the king one day, as his chief astrologer.

However, his primary preoccupation during the early days of his reign was the recovery of Guwahati and the territories around it, lost due to the perfidy of Laluk. The knowledge gained through a study of the reigns of earlier kings apprised him of the need to raise the strength and morale of his armed forces and he took a personal interest in this. In March 1682, he summoned a conference of nobles where he announced his intentions of recapturing Guwahati, which was greeted with great nationalistic fervour. War preparations now reached fever-pitch.

Towards the end of August 1682, the Ahoms began their final campaign against the Mughals. Their forces were arrayed for a three-pronged attack—a huge flotilla of war boats, with Bandar Barphukan and Champa Paniphukan at the lead, moved down the Brahmaputra; another flotilla led by Sandikoi Phukan and Khamrak Phukan swept down a branch of a river called Kolong; while a land force led by Halou Deka Phukan and Namdangia Phukan progressed down the south bank.

The Mughals at Guwahati were aware of the war preparations as well as the advancing forces. But Mansur Khan, the Mughal faujdar at Guwahati, found himself incapable of effective resistance. The nawab at Dhaka being gravely ill, his forces at the outposts had not been paid their salaries. A small delegation had gone to Dhaka to air their grievances but were not paid heed to and returned without any assurances. Not only did Mansur Khan have to deal with a rebellious army, he himself was in danger of being killed.

Before Mansur Khan could organize some sort of resistance, the Mughal-occupied forts at Bansbari and Kajali fell. A flotilla sent by him clashed with that of the Ahoms at the mouth of the river Barnadi and suffered a decisive defeat, almost the entire Mughal fleet stationed in that region fell to the Ahoms, dealing a mortal blow to any thoughts of effective resistance by them. They did try to resist at Itakhuli in Guwahati, mounting cannons both at the fort and Umananda Island and launching a volley of shots at the approaching armada. But on the whole, it was a weak and ineffectual resistance; there was no stopping the Ahom forces who, with nationalist cries, continued their relentless advance. Finally, in September 1682, Ali Akbar, the commander at

Itakhuli, deserted his forces and fled; Mansur Khan had already left Guwahati for Rangamati.

Having reoccupied Guwahati, the Ahoms pursued the Mughals right up to the Manas River, which once again became the western-most boundary of the Ahom empire. A vast booty was captured along with numerous war vessels—gold and silver, elephants, horses, bullocks and buffaloes, cannons, guns, swords and spears—far in excess of what had been acquired by the Ahoms at Guwahati on previous occasions. These were taken back to Garhgaon where the Ahom monarch made a fine, loyalty-inspiring gesture of distributing them amongst the officers who had participated in the campaign. Some of the cannons were inscribed with the words, 'King Gadadhar Singha, in the year 1604 Saka, obtained this war weapon after having vanquished the Mussulmans.'

Bhatdhara Phukan, a brother of the infamous Laluk, who had earlier fled for his life to Guwahati and taken shelter amongst the Mughals, had been captured along with his family when the city was taken. Carted back to Garhgaon, he and his son were subjected to the most horrible punishment before being put to death. At Guwahati itself, once again an infrastructure was put in place to make the area impregnable; for a while Nawab Shaista Khan of Dhaka did contemplate an assault to wrest back lost territory, as testified to by records of his confabulations with William Hedges, governor of the English factories at Bengal; but by then the sun was on the verge of setting on the Mughal dynasty, and ultimately the nawab decided not to embark on a fresh campaign.

Thus it was that, after periodic attempts to conquer the Brahmaputra Valley through the centuries, the Muslim rulers finally gave up the attempt. This, in turn, prevented the followers of Islam from colonizing and converting the populace of lands east of the Brahmaputra by a land route. Though they did take the sea route and attained success in some parts of Southeast Asia, their influence might have been far wider had they been able to proceed by a land route. By successfully resisting them, the Ahoms left an abiding imprint upon the politico-religious profile of Asia.

The recapture of Guwahati was the catalyst that was to transform the spirit of a disheartened people and bring an end to the decade-long degeneration that was taking place in the Ahom realm. A new era of relative peace and development was ushered in and the Ahom Empire reached its pinnacle of economic prosperity and cultural achievements in the course of the next century.

Endowed as he was with intimate knowledge of the problems of his subjects, such as the need for access to unpolluted water, which affected health, and the lack of good roads, which hindered communication, Gadadhar Singha set in motion a concerted effort to create an infrastructure to tackle these. A number of large pukhuris or water tanks were dug in various places; these were situated on higher ground so that floodwaters would not enter and contaminate them; these included the Barkola pukhuri, Rohdoi pukhuri, Mitha pukhuri, Bhogdoi pukhuri and many more. Being a devout Shakta, or adherent of the Shakti religion, Gadapani erected a number of temples, the most exotic being the one dedicated to Shiva on the peacock-island of Umananda upon the Brahmaputra near Guwahati, built under the supervision of Sandikoi Barphukan.

In order to improve land communication, a number of alis or roads were constructed. There is an amusing anecdote concerning the construction of the longest of these roads, called Dhodar Ali or the 'road built by lazybones'. Earlier, by royal decree, it had been ordered that the monks of the Vaishnav sattras or monasteries were exempt from performing civic duties such as providing manual labour to the state or being inducted into the army. This had resulted in hundreds of paiks, to avoid service to the state, taking to monkhood and living in a sattra. Gadapani abolished the special privilege enjoyed by the monks and conscripted many of them to build the Dhodar Ali, which resulted in its earning the name that suggested it was built by idlers!

Another detailed survey of the kingdom and its subjects was taken. Land holdings were measured, but this time with the type of measurement introduced by the Mughals in Lower Assam, with surveyors from Bengal being brought in for the purpose. The land area was measured with the aid of a twelve-foot-long bamboo pole called nal and multiplying the length and breadth, the standard unit being a bigha, with four bighas making a pura.

There were, however, undercurrents of tension beneath the seeming placidity, now that a strong and stern ruler was at the helm of the nation's affairs. A section of the nobles, having tasted what it felt to have power over the king, could not discard their conspiratorial habits and adapt themselves to the changed circumstances. No less than a person than his brother-in-law Bandar Barphukan, who had helped him attain the Ahom kingship, led one of the conspiracies to unseat him. Ever since the Dakhinpat sattradhikar had rejected Gadapani's request for support, the barphukan had been a reluctant backer for the prince's bid for kingship; when Bandar discovered that on being made king, Gadapani had struck out on his own and could no longer be influenced, the barphukan with the help of a few fellow officers conspired to unseat him. The plot to overthrow the monarch was discovered soon enough and Bandar Barphukan and his cohorts were arrested at Kaliabar and brought in chains to Garhgaon. The king wanted to make an example of the captives by executing them, but with the other nobles interceding on their behalf, and reminding Gadapani about the role played by the barphukan in placing him upon the throne, the prisoners were condemned to be exiled. Chenak Sandikoi Phukan was appointed as the new barphukan.

The participants of yet another conspiracy to dethrone the monarch were not as fortunate; these were a group of middle-level officers based in Guwahati. The king's spies had brought information that these phukans were planning to sail with a group of elite troops towards Upper Assam in order to place another prince on the throne. The king, realizing the gravity of the situation, himself went to Kaliabar and, through a stratagem, lured some of the conspiring officer there and had them arrested. Soon enough the fellow conspirators too were arrested and all of them executed.

The king now realized that a thorough overhaul of the nobles and officials was essential if the spectre of conspiracy was to be eradicated for good. He set up a searching enquiry; many officials, including surprisingly Dighala Buragohain, were proven to be implicated; while the latter was simply dismissed, severe punishment or execution was meted out to others. Gadadhar Singha understood that, at the time he had ascended the throne, the office of the king had reached rock-bottom, and the real power had been usurped by the nobles. Thus, he had to be harsh while dealing with culprits if he was to break the power of the nobles and restore to the king the traditionally sanctioned authority.

Also, taking advantage of the fact that a new and inexperienced king was on the throne while the realm itself was embarking on a campaign against the Mughals, some hills and plains tribes rebelled to try and get rid of the Ahom yoke. Timely intervention resulted in all such uprisings being subdued and none of them could flare up into a major challenge to Ahom authority over the heterogeneous populace.

From a prince to a vagabond fugitive to the monarch of a vast empire—Gadadhar Singha had seen it all, but not lost his sense of justice or his concern for the common people. Unfortunately, one blot on his record during his fifteen years of rule was his ill treatment of the Assamese Vaishnav community, the followers of the precepts laid down by the founder, Mahapurush Sankardev. His teachings were propagated so well by his disciples such as Madhavdev, Damodardev and Gopaldev that the religion had supplanted Brahmanical Hinduism in the Brahmaputra Valley. The appeal of the Eksarana Namadharma faith was its simplicity; worship was devoid of the complicated rituals which marked Brahmanical Hinduism; the principal tenets were communicated not merely through sermons, but also through cultural vehicles such as literature, music, drama, dance and paintings.

Cognizant of the powerful appeal of this comparatively new religion, previous monarchs had proclaimed their adherence to it in addition to Shakta Hinduism and the Ahom religion. However, Gadadhar Singha's encounters with the community had never been pleasant. During his wanderings as a fugitive, he had once taken shelter at a sattra, but was treated very rudely, the monks being unaware that he was a prince and considering him to be vagabond. When he complained about this to the sattradhikar, the latter, rather than set things right, had abused him.

Also, the refusal of Banamali Bapu, the sattradhikar of Dakhinpat Sattra, to extend support to him when he was seeking kingship, still rankled with Gadadhar Singha. Though the head priest had died in 1683 and his nephew Ramadev Goswami had been appointed in his place, the king had not forgotten or forgiven. During his visit to that sattra, he had been overcome by the grand manner in which the head priest lived, the unquestioned loyalty of the acolytes he commanded and the opulence of the sattras. The sattradhikar, with his hierarchy of servitors, was a monarch in miniature, while the wealth of the sattras duplicated to some extent the wealth of the kingdom. Though the way of life amongst the monks was starkly simple, the articles used by them in the naamghars or prayer halls, the pomp of their processions and the numerousness of their followers made the sattradhikars powerful forces indeed. Gadadhar Singha wondered whether such miniature centres of power and wealth should be allowed to mushroom in the kingdom and whether these did not distract subjects from giving their allegiance and devotion solely to the king.

Learning of his abhorrence of the followers of this faith, the Brahmin priests of the court, as well as some officers, fuelled the animosity, and urged him to take stringent action against the religion. But the pragmatic king had certain practical concerns too. The Vaishnav religion forbade the consumption of meat and alcohol; Gadadhar Singha, who was known to be a voracious eater and imbiber of drink, grew concerned that the mildness of the diet prescribed by the Vaishnavs would deprive the Ahoms of their martial vigour and make them unmanly. Also, the humility and submissiveness which lay at the core of Vaishnav doctrine was, the king thought, not appropriate for a Shan race which sought to dominate others. Equally pertinent, as the new faith spread, new sattras were sprouting up everywhere and drawing acolytes. Some of these were outrageously spurious, set up only to enable the members to avoid their civic duties as paiks, since bhakats or monks were exempted from such service. The opponents of the faith poisoned the mind of the king by alleging that this was causing a dearth of paiks in the realm and public work was suffering.

These were, of course, false assumptions; the Vaishnav movement had been the dominant religion of the Valley when Raja Ram Singh had launched his campaign; this had not prevented the people of Assam from successfully repelling the invaders. There had been large-scale public construction of roads, water tanks and temples during Gadadhar Singh's reign, thus the scarcity of paiks had been exaggerated. But the urgings of his courtiers and Brahmin priests were insistent enough to subdue the sense of fairness of Gadadhar the man, and enhance his antipathy, making him try to destroy the Vaishnavs once and for all.

One officer who had incited the king was Rangacharan Bhandari Barua; he was sent with a detachment of soldiers to arrest the sattradhikars of various sattras and confiscate their property. The Dakhinpat Sattra was a primary target; its sattradhikar Ramdev Gossain was taken prisoner and his eyes gouged out. The golden articles of the monastery were seized and melted to be made into a koloshi and placed on the top of an Ahom temple at Cheraidai. Though Keshavdev Gossain of Auniati Sattra succeeded in eluding the king's men by hiding amongst the Chutiyas, his entire property was confiscated. Quite a few heads of other monasteries were executed and many sattras were relocated to patently unsuitable sites.

Soon enough the persecutions went out of control. The Bhandari Barua and his henchmen, after taking punitive measures against the higher ranks of monks, next went after the disciples. Bhakats were hunted down to be slaughtered; properties were confiscated and kinsmen killed; the soldiers derived amusement from making the monks eat beef, pork and mutton. Many of them were reduced almost to slaves for work at civic constructions; others were sent into exile. Some were offered as sacrifice to Hindu idols. The king was unaware of the extent of persecution his antipathy had brought about; when he learnt how severe the measures of his officers had been, he immediately ordered a stop to the persecution and recompense to the affected victims.

The month was February, the year 1696. It was the pleasantest season of the year; the harvest had been collected and the people, having feasted during the Bhogali Bihu festival, were taking a well-earned break from physical toil in the fields and elsewhere. Swargadeo Supatpha or Gadadhar Singha, renowned as a daredevil sportsman and skilled archer, was camping near a jungle by the river Dikhow for one of his favourite pastimes, a deer hunt. Numerous tents had been pitched adjacent to a stretch of floodplain grassland where deer herds came to graze; they had provided relatively easy pickings and in the few days they had camped at the spot, a sizeable number of stags and deer had been shot and skinned.

But that morning there was something wrong with the king. The royal bezbarua, who always accompanied the king wherever he went, had examined His Majesty but could not diagnose the nature of the ailment. It was something the physician had never encountered before; the king was almost delirious with fever and his body shook with uncontrollable spasms. A boil suffused with poisonous puss had appeared upon his throat; the more the physician and his assistants tried to decant the puss by piercing the boil, the larger it grew. Of course, the whisper going around the encampment amongst the retainers was that nemesis had descended upon the king because of his prosecution of bhakats and destruction of sattras. But the bezbarua, who was of a rational mind, understood that the king had picked up an unfamiliar disease from an unknown source. The physician had no antidote, though he lavished all his experience and knowledge in treating the king; within two days Gadadhar Singha was dead.

The entire kingdom mourned his demise. Although the king had taken many wives, his only children were the two sons he had fathered with Sati Jaimati. He had also made known his wish that his eldest son, Lai, be installed on the throne after his death. According to Shan custom, if a successor had been named, on the death of the incumbent monarch, the nobles must immediately bow before the new king and place him on the royal throne. Thus, even as Gadadhar Singha's corpse was being embalmed within the tent by a process and medicines known only to the Ahom priests so as to prevent it from decomposing, the nobles took Lai back to Garhgaon and formally announced that he would be the new king.

However, Lai deferred ascension of the Singorighar and forbade any sort of activity to celebrate his being made the king till his father could be given a funeral according to Ahom custom. The dead but embalmed body of the king, draped in royal robes, was carried on the back of an elephant to the capital, with thousands of citizens lining the route to bid final goodbye to the leader who had once again brought equanimity to a troubled realm. The body was kept in an incense-filled room made specifically for this purpose; both Brahmin and Ahom priests in turns recited holy verses without break through days and nights; as long as it lay in state, the royalty and nobles would refrain from festivities, rich food and drinks, while the subjects would also be in mourning.

Meanwhile, at Cheraidai, construction was started on a maidam or mausoleum where the mortal remains of the late king would be interred. In many instances, previous monarchs had built such maidams for themselves well in advance; but Gadadhar Singh had not envisaged such a premature death, so the maidam had to be built after his demise and his body lay in state for quite a long time. An official designated as the sheotiya phukan was in overall charge of building the mausoleum.

In the the earliest era of the Ahom kingdom, the structure of the maidams were built with bamboo and cane; later wood was used. Only during the past few decades were brick and mortar used for building the royal mausoleums, though the basic structures as well as rituals remained the same. Although indigenous masons had learned the art of making brick buildings from the Kacharis, they were not proficient enough to be fully entrusted with the job, and therefore master masons had to be brought from Bengal and Orissa to supervise construction.

But the Ahoms did have their own cementing mixture, which included ingredients such as molasses, lentil and lime, the secret of whose composition only they knew. Each item required for construction was supplied by members of individual khels or clans; similarly, workers engaged for construction too belonged to specific khels. The sheotiya phukan punctiliously kept a record of the quantities of materials that were used—in making the maidam for Swargadeo Gadadhar Singha, a two-storeyed structure, the list for the lower storey included 5,681 kolohs or pitchers of molasses, 696 large baskets of lentil, 14,700 baskets of limestone, 7,138 pitchers of lime, 24 large vats of oil, 240 seers of dhuna or incense, 1,25,000 pebbles and 1,99,600 pieces of brick; and 3,606 pitchers of molasses, 414 baskets of lentil, 9,220 baskets of limestone and 1,20,360 pieces of bricks, etc., for the upper storey.

It was the Deodhai head priest who chose the site for the maidam amongst the rows of previous mausoleums built for past kings and nobles in the sacred burial site of Cheraidai. A single row stretched for many miles and by now quite a few rows of maidams had been built; since Gadadhar Singh had been a king, a site in the very first row was selected. Workmen levelled the ground and the masons got to work, laying down the foundation and first constructing the lower edifice.

A blueprint of the structure had been already made by palace architects in consultation with the new king, patra-mantris, priests and the head mason. The lower floor, which would have many chambers including the burial vault in which the body of the monarch would be placed, had brick floors and walls, with each chamber connected by a passageway to the central vault. The various chambers were meant for the use of the retainers who would be buried alive along with the monarch in order to attend to the latter's needs while he ascended the golden stairs to the land of Lengdon, the almighty one. In the past, some of the queens, as well as the monarch's favourite animal such as a horse or even an elephant, had been buried in a maidam; but the new king decided against placing any members of royalty in his father's mausoleum. He also had the late king's retainers brought before him and individually asked each of them whether they would like to accompany their master in his ascent to Heaven. Surprisingly enough, quite a few of the devoted retainers did volunteer—these persons were accommodated in comfortable dwellings while they waited to be buried alive in the mausoleum to assist the monarch in his afterlife journey. This was a departure from past practice and testified to the humanism and kindness of the new king.

The mausoleum when completed was tall, enormous and impressive; it stood on a large plot of land and had a small temple at the very top; a ladder was provided for a retainer to climb from the ground floor to this temple to light the earthen lamp which would be placed there. He was also required to daily tend the tall lamp burning in the burial chamber where the king would be laid. As soon as the mausoleum was finished, it was fitted out with furniture and utensils. The central vault where the king would lie was furnished with a salpira or low bed lined with gold; a canopy of gold lace and cloth with seven folds was hung over it. The four bedposts to which curtains were fixed were plated with gold; pillows woven with threads of gold were placed upon the salpira. The weapon that an Ahom king always carried, the hengdang, was placed beside the bed in a gold sheath encrusted with diamonds. Also placed within the central chamber were five brass horais or trays; one large gold horai with a gold bowl containing gem-encrusted golden utensils needed to prepare betel nut for chewing, including a container for lime, one for tobacco, a golden knife and betel nuts made of silver. A casket containing expensive jewellery was also kept in the vault, perhaps in the expectation that the king, when he reached Heaven would have to offer gifts to Lengdon and the gods. Also, a great deal of the king's favourite food items, both cooked and uncooked, were stocked in one of the chambers so that he did not lack for nourishment during his journey.

In former times, a number of retainers used to be buried alive in a maidam, each required to cater to one specific need of the king. One of them was equipped with a long-handled, gold bichoni with which to fan the monarch; others were required to prepare betel nuts for his consumption and to hold a golden spittoon where the king could spit out the juice. Cooks, meal servers, retainers to assist the king in dressing or putting on his sandals—occasionally dozens of servants, both male and female, would be buried in a maidam.

Finally, when preparations for burial of the king were complete, his body was transferred into a wooden coffin. This was taken away from the capital to a temporary resting place close to Charaideo. From there, with paiks from a specific khel acting as pall-bearers, the flower-decked coffin was taken in a procession to the maidam along a route earmarked for this purpose and used for none other. A band of musicians playing upon the dhol, khol and other musical instruments led the procession; the pall-bearers were followed by chanting Ahom and Brahmin priests, the king's family, other members of the royalty, the nobles and their families, representatives of vassal kings and tribal chiefs, with the general laity bringing up the rear. The ululation of women periodically mingled with the music from the leading orchestra; at the rear the common folks let out cries of 'Long live the king!'

On reaching the burial site, the procession was received by the maidam phukan, the officer responsible for maintenance of the cemetery; as the musicians parted to make way for the coffin, with due solemnity, he led the procession to the small gateway through which the mausoleum could be entered. Here the main body of the procession stopped; only the new king, the patra-mantris, the Ahom and Brahmin head priests and the maidam phukan entered to inspect the site. The king indicating his satisfaction, the maidam phukan signalled to the pall-bearers, who now entered with the coffin. The body was transferred to the salpira and laid gently upon it, its head pointing to the east and feet to the west. The priests performed the final rites and the body was left alone in the chamber as everyone left. In the meantime, the retainers who were to be buried with the king were taking leave from their loved ones; when the functionaries had departed from the mausoleum, the dead king's final servitors, without hesitation, left the others and entered the mausoleum.

The sheotiya phukan closed the door and, while the crowd watched from a distance, hundreds of paik labourers now arrived with digging implements. They dug earth from a nearby spot already chosen for the purpose and carried it to be heaped upon the mausoleum, the small gateway being the first point to be covered. They also dug a moat around the maidam leaving only the narrowest of passage to it; the earth dug up from the moat was also used to cover the maidam. It took hundreds of workers and many hours, but finally the mausoleum disappeared under tons of earth and it began to take on the look of a small hillock. At a signal from the sheotiya phukan, the workers stopped piling the earth, while another group began to plant grass upon it to make the structure appear a vibrant green.

Long before sunset, the work was complete. The crowd broke up and people returned to their respective homes. Soon an eerie silence settled upon Cheraidai, the final resting place for kings and queens, broken occasionally by the chirping of cicadas.

THE NARRATOR

The frailness of the wizened old man was deceptive; it was late into the night but his voice remained as fiery as the flames of the bonfire lighting up the faces of his audience. Most of them had, of course, heard the entire tale before—of the myths that dimly illuminated the dawn of the Shan race and the establishment of a separate Ahom kingdom by Sukapha till its inevitable sunset—but the thirst within them to hear it again could never be quenched. If darkness could turn darker, it had done so; the flames of the bonfire were finding it increasingly difficult to battle the blackness of the night; yet the old man continued with his narration and his people continued to listen avidly.

'Gadadhar Singha redeemed the race from the depths it had fallen into after the glory that had been Saraighat. He acted without bias, punishing the high and mighty as well as the commoner if found guilty of misdemeanour. His first concern was for the welfare of his subjects; he gave strict instructions to his officials that the people of the realm should never be subjected to oppression; there was general contentment amongst the multitude, conducive to prosperity.

'Most important, the realm was no longer in danger of being invaded from the west; the Mughals had become a spent force. Most of the Ahom realm's resources since the time of Swargadeo Suhungmung had been squandered in defending the kingdom from the Mussulmans, but now, with the cessation of the threat, attention could be devoted to architecture and the arts, and it could be shown to the world that the Ahoms could engage in aesthetic and spiritual activities apart from fighting. The descendents of Gadadhar Singha of the Tungkhungiya phaid inherited a kingdom which was at peace with itself, economically self-sufficient. Rebellious tribes had been suppressed and order restored throughout the kingdom. The nobles had been put in their proper places and the sanctity and omnipotency of the Ahom throne irrevocably established.

'Thus, Gadadhar Singha's eldest son, Lai Gohain, had a stable kingdom which he could rule over; this enabled him to not only to embark on wide-ranging construction activities, but also to contemplate enlargement of his own kingdom, which now encompassed almost the entire Brahmaputra Valley. In deference to the memory of his father, though the nobles had declared him king, he had not ascended the singorighar; but once the interment of the late monarch was over, Lai completed such formalities in 1696, taking on the Ahom name of Sukhrungpha and the Hindu name of Rudra Singha. As I had told you earlier, it was this monarch who abolished the custom of beheading a man before ascending the singorighar and substituted a buffalo for the occasion. He declared the period of mourning to be over and ordered a month-long celebration to mark his ascension. He also made his beloved brother Lechai the raja of Namrup, as much as a token of his affection as to ensure that his brother was not tempted like some of his predecessors to conspire to grab the throne at Garhgaon!

'Because he had stayed away much of his life from Garhgaon and its politics, Swargadeo Sukhrungpha had an even better grasp of the general mood of the people than his father. True, there was a semblance of order in the kingdom, yet the new king had perceived certain undercurrents of disaffection which, if not dealt with quickly, might prove to be disastrous in the future. Though a Shakta himself, he, like his progenitor Chaolung Sukapha, understood the requirement for liberalness in matters of religion; it was the uncharacteristic illiberalness on the part of his father towards the adherents of the Vaishnav religion which lay at the root of the latent disaffection, for the larger segment of the subjects had turned to this faith. With great prescience, the new king, therefore, set about undoing the damage done by his father and quell the restiveness that might endanger the throne itself in the future.

'The Vaishnav gosains were reassured that they could return to their former calling and set up their sattras. They were granted land at Majuli and a cluster of sattras grew up at that place. The sattradhikar of Auniati was brought back from exile with great deference and the new king touched his feet to accept him as a spiritual mentor. The people were now allowed to worship in any way they pleased; aberration in such a wise policy, introduced by later rulers, as we shall see, led to the downfall of the Ahoms.

'Swargadeo Sukhrungpha was a devoted son who adored his parents and was determined to perpetuate their memory. He built a statue of Gadadhar Singha at Cheraidai, dressed it in royal robes, and appointed officers to make daily offerings of food and wine to it. His work to perpetuate the memory of his beloved mother, Jaimati, had greater permanence ...'

Rudra Singha the Great

～⌒～

HUNDREDS OF PAIKS WERE GATHERED AT JERENGA PATHAR, AT THE
very place where Sati Jaimati Kuonri, the mother of the present
monarch Swargadeo Sukhrungpha, was tortured and killed. The folks
around that area knew the exact spot where the stake to which the
lady had been tied was fixed. It was to be, if feasible, the central point
around which a huge tank would be dug to be called Jaipukhuri, as
a remembrance to her sacrifice—that had been the order from the
royal palace.

No less a person than the Dihingiya phukan was supervising the
digging operations, assisted by a group of technicians well versed in
the art of building large water reservoirs. These technicians, after using
two methods of determining groundwater sources, were astonished to
discover it to be close to the spot where the stake had been fixed, thereby
fulfilling the king's wish. The first method involved testing the soil for
moisture and placing lighted earthen lamps at likely spots. Stakes were
driven into the ground at those points where, despite there being no
wind and despite the lamp containing oil, the flame on the wick flickered
and went out. A bigger earthen lamp was next placed over each of the
stakes and the spot where it flickered out was estimated to be the source
of accessing ground water. The second method, to double-check the
original estimate since a great deal of labour was involved in digging

such a large pukhuri and a false reading would entail wastage of a great deal of labour, was to use a divining rod.

With both tests indicating the same source of access for groundwater that would keep the reservoir perpetually full even in the dry months, the central point was marked with a stake. It was to be an enormous pukhuri encompassing many acres of land, so digging commenced not from the centre but from the edges. A system of levees and ditches were dug so that the banks of the reservoir were higher than the ground around it; a similar system was dug on the inner sides—a technique that would ensure that however strong the wind, not even a ripple would disturb the surface of the tank's waters, giving it a placid look. The absence of waves would also ensure that there would be no erosion on the banks, thereby giving the tank a far longer lifespan.

Sure enough, there were a sizeable number of spectators every day, mostly women and children, who looked on with awe and wonder as the gigantic pukhuri began to assume shape under their very eyes. The expert technicians had the paiks dig evenly around the entire perimeter, just deep enough to ensure that no ground water seeped out. The dry floor of the tank was paved with a coat of concrete—the type invented by the Ahoms to cement their brick structures, made with ingredients such as molasses and lentil—and a circular area almost at the centre was left uncovered. Then, on a day presaged as auspicious by the Ahom priests, in the presence of the king and nobles, paiks began digging up the bare circle; this had been assumed to be the access source for the groundwater. Much to the delight of onlookers, soon water began to gush out of the hole that had been dug. A stake of sal wood, called naagmari, was immediately driven into the hole and a contraption attached to it so that, by raising or lowering it, the outflow of water could be controlled.

It took a couple of days for the mammoth tank to fill up completely. Outlets were built so as to let out water from the tank when it might overflow; these too had controlling devices to maintain the water at a desired level. Finally, the area around the large body of water was beautified; turf was laid on the high banks and the ground beyond; saplings were planted at various places of what once had been a bare field. The entire project from beginning till end had just taken forty-five days. Then, on another auspicious day as determined by the Deodhai priests, the king and his entourage came to Jaipukhuri for the consecration ceremony. Cries of 'long live Sati Jaimati' rent the air to drown out the sound of the Brahmin priests' chants.

The people knew that there were vast water bodies called sagars or seas far away from the Valley. They had heard of these from travellers; Mughal soldiers captured during the various battles had also spoken of such sagars. The enormous water tank consecrated to the memory of Sati Jaimati could not be deemed to be an ordinary pukhuri. In the perception of the ordinary subjects, it loomed as a sagar. Thus, in the course of time, in common parlance, the name of the tank as well as the area where it was located changed to Jaisagar, an abiding tribute to the martyr princess.

But Rudra Singha had other grand plans to commemorate the memory of his mother, structures that needed to be built with stones, bricks and mortar so that they would be able to withstand the ravages of time. Till now, most Ahom buildings and other structures had been built primarily with wood, bamboo and cane. According to prevalent laws, only the king could build with concrete; so there were very few buildings existent in the Ahom kingdom, and they were mostly temples. The new king was desirous that more brick structures should be constructed. The problem was that because of the paucity of masonry activity, there were hardly any masons in the region. The king therefore sent for a khanikar or mason named Ghanasyam all the way from Kochbehar to train a band of assistants.

At the moment Rudra Singha was in the audience hall of the palace along with the patra-mantris and other officials discussing other projects in mind.

'Summon Ghanasyam khanikar to our presence,' he ordered.

A tall, heavily built man, sporting a beard, entered and prostrated himself before the king.

'Are you ready to begin work?' was the only question put to him by His Majesty.

'Yes,' replied the mason with confidence. 'I've trained up two dozen men in the art of masonry, who can build with both stones and bricks. I've also stockpiled bricks made at the royal kiln and rocks from the royal quarry. The mortar your people make is indeed unique and excellent—I've procured all the ingredients needed to make enough for the task on hand.'

'Good,' said the king. 'Ask our priests to select an auspicious day to commence work.'

'Forgive me, Your Majesty,' said Ghanasyam, 'but I've already done so.'

The king was pleased at the initiative displayed by the khanikar. 'So, when can you start?' he asked.

'From today itself, Your Majesty,' replied the man from Kochbehar, a hint of a smile on his face.

The immediate objective was to build a temple dedicated to Lord Vishnu on one of the elevated banks of Jaisagar, to be followed by another beside it dedicated to five gods. The moment he left the presence of the king, the master mason gathered his troops and set off for the site. A miniature township had already been erected near the huge tank: temporary structures to house the paiks and the masons who would be engaged in the enterprise. As previously instructed by Ghanasyam, both Ahom and Brahmin priests were performing consecration rites to purify the land chosen for the two temples.

When the priests had completed their puja, the paiks and the masons set about to work under the supervision of Ghanasyam, who held a sheet of sanchi on which the design and dimensions of the proposed temples had been drawn. The foundations had to be dug first, and the stones built up from deep below. The floor or the plinth was laid out next. It was heavy going; the square slabs of rocks which had been piled up at one edge of the tank had to be manually carried to the site and laid in their proper slots with the help of a contraption of ropes and pulleys. The cutting and placement of the temple's walls was even tougher; a couple of paiks were crushed to death when a stone slab that was being lifted slipped from the hoist and fell upon them. The technical problem was that the walls curved upwards and tapered to a point as they reached the apex; moreover, there were no corners so that the walls had to be built in a perfect circle. But Ghanasyam proved that he was the right choice; with expert eyes and hands he drew chalk lines on stone slabs which paiks could chip away to proper shape and size.

As the days went by the temple began to take shape. Lower down, a quarter way up the wall, a ringed projection around the centre wall was built as a decorative feature. It had evenly spaced columns with short minarets atop each. Murals of gods and goddesses were exquisitely carved on the columns and walls to add to the temple's beauty. Also, without the king being aware of it, Ghanasyam had been making sketches of him. The king, indeed, was a handsome man, tall, well-built and imposing. Ghanasyam himself carved out a statue of King Rudra Singha, in full battledress, seated regally upon a horse, on a wall of the temple. After the plastering had been completed the rest of the wall of the temple was adorned with a pattern of repeated squares imparting it a unique look. Finally, a stone minaret was built at the top, upon which would be placed a koloshi of pure gold, was constructed.

Though it was a temple dedicated to Lord Vishnu, the king named it the Jaidol in memory of his mother. The temple to five gods was a less ostentatious affair and did not need very long to construct. On another auspicious day, in the presence of a huge number of royalty and commoners, the golden koloshi was lifted on top of the Jaidol. After it had been securely mounted, the bamboo scaffoldings, ladders, wooden hoists and ropes were taken away and the two temples revealed in their beauty.

With the waters of Jaisagar reflecting the rays of a setting sun and sunlight glinting off the gold koloshi atop the Jaidol, it was a spectacular sight. The Ahom realm had never had such wondrous structures before. The king was delighted.

Such an edifice needed consecration commensurate with its beauty. It would also be an occasion to flaunt the power and opulence of the Ahom realm before the rest of the world. On the instructions of Swargadeo Sukhrungpha, officers had fanned out to other parts of India such as Bengal, Bihar, Kashi and Kanauj to invite reputed Brahmins to attend the ceremony. The terms and conditions of the invitation were lucrative enough to induce many Brahmins of repute to undertake the arduous boat trip to the Ahom capital.

The day of the consecration arrived. Thousands of subjects had travelled from all over the realm to attend it and Jerenga Pathar was so packed with people that there was hardly any space to move. However, since the water tank's banks, upon which puja was being performed, were high and wide, the spectators had no problem in getting a view of the goings on. The king, his wives and children, as well as kinsmen, along with the nobles and their families, were seated in a special temporary enclosure beside of the temple. The palace Brahmin priests had lit a sacred fire and were busy with rituals involving pouring clarified butter into the flames and reciting mantras; at another spot, Deodhai, Bailung and Moran priests were preoccupied with their own consecrating worship of Shan gods.

However, the grandest of sight was the hundreds of brass kolohs or pitchers plated with gold or silver which were lined up from corner to corner on each of the four banks. Each of the pitchers was filled with holy water required for puja. A Brahmin sat behind each pitcher, muttering prayers and periodically dipping leaves of the mango tree in the water and spraying it into the Jaisagar. The pitchers flashed in the sunlight so brightly as to make spectators turn their eyes away from the brilliance.

The noise was deafening. Adding to the babble of voices and the chanting of hundreds of priests was the troupe of gayon-bayon performers from Auniati Sattra who played upon the dhol, khol, borkanh and other musical instruments. After the ceremonies had been performed and prayers offered for the well-being of Sati Jaimati's soul, the swargadeo personally handed over gifts in the form of gold, silver and land grants to each of the participating priests, as also the officers and paiks who had engaged in the construction of Jaisagar and Jaidol.

At a signal from the swargadeo, the sombre note which had prevailed despite the noise and the bustle changed to one of conviviality. Provision had been made to ensure that no one who had come for the consecration left unfed. At a spot next to Jerenga Pathar, a mammoth community kitchen had been opened; the people formed orderly queues with plates of cut plantain leaves in hand; servers heaped their plates with cooked rice, lentils, fried vegetables, pork and pickle. At another kiosk was being served laopani or rice beer which warmed up the convivial atmosphere further. Spontaneous shouts of 'long live Sati Jaimati' and 'long live Swargadeo Sukhrungpha' sporadically rent the air.

As the sun sank towards the western horizon and the revellers made their way homeward, everybody agreed that the consecration ceremony did justice to the valiant lady Jaimati. The Brahmins and other functionaries who had come for the ceremony would carry back tales of the grandeur of the Ahom monarchy and the opulence of the realm.

There was palpable excitement amongst the select few allowed to participate in the discussions of the king's latest project. It had been a dream with the swargadeo; had Ghanasyam khanikar proved less capable and industrious, it may have remained a mere pipe dream. But the master mason had shown his mettle in erecting the Jaidol and could be relied on to fulfill the swargadeo's dream.

Rather than simply describe what would be done, the master-mason had, in fact, created a miniature model of the project. It had been placed on the floor of the audience hall; the king, the patra-mantris and some technicians were gathered around it as Ghanasyam explained various aspects. The model was that of a new city that the king had dreamt of building to be named Rongpur or City of Joy. Local legend had it that in ancient days when this region was known as Pragjyotishpur, Emperor Bhagadatta had built a winter capital called Rongpur in addition to the summer capital. Swargadeo Sukhrungpha desired to follow the great Bhagadatta's example and build another capital in addition to Garhgaon. Though a majority of dwellings and workplaces in the new city would be made of wood, bamboo, ikora reeds, cane and thatch, a concrete palace of bricks would be constructed to house the king and his entourage whenever he chose to live in it.

'As you can see, Your Majesty, it would actually be two cities, one within the other,' Ghanasyam explained. 'Your kareng-ghar or palace of brick and mortar would be located in the city within the outer city. It will also have dwellings for your personal staff and security people. The entire palace compound will be surrounded by a wall of bricks with three gates manned by soldiers, situated south, east and west for entry into its exclusive precinct. This is to ensure your safety, Your Majesty.'

'Have you chosen the location for this new city, Your Majesty?' Laicheng Buragohain asked.

'Of course, I have.' The king replied testily. 'Can't you see those two lines snaking across the model? Well, one is the river Dikhow and the other the river Namdang. Rongpur will be built between the two rivers, at the place now known as Meteka. Namdang will lie to its west, Dikhow east. At the north, at the place called Bahgor, a protective rampart will be built. It is not too far from Garhgaon, just a few hours travel by elephant and even lesser by boat.'

'The rivers form natural protective barriers for the rest of the city,' Ghanasyam khanikar continued with his explanation. 'But, apart from the one at Bahbor, high earthen ramparts too can be constructed at other points towards Rongpur's south as additional safety measures if you so desire. The dwellings of the nobles will be situated just outside the wall of the royal city. The further a house is from the palace, the lower the rank of a noble or an official residing in it. A section of the city will have barracks where regular soldiers can be stationed. I've been told that you've had some difficulty in housing these at Garhgaon. Though I know that buying or selling things are not very prevalent here, yet I've made a provision for a marketplace, if required in the future. Also, at various spots, I will build bez-ghars or dispensaries to be manned by physicians to take care of the health of the residents.'

'Rongpur must be one of my most enduring legacies,' the king commented. 'It needs to have every convenience the citizens will require, including tanks for providing them with drinking water, and good, well-connected roads. You must build a number of dols at various points in the city so that citizens can offer prayers. Rongpur must be a city that glitters; the entrances to the city must have gates that proclaim its greatness.'

'I am contemplating something that might be one of the wonders of Indian stone work, Your Majesty, worthy of a city like your Rongpur.'

The king's ears pricked up. 'What is it, Ghanasyam?' he asked eagerly.

'An immense bridge made of a single stone, Your Majesty,' the khanikar replied. 'What in your language is called a silor sako. That's it, there, at that point on the model over the Namdang River. I've taken the measurements—it will span the entire Namdang River and be so wide and thick that three elephants would be able to cross it at the same time. It will have seven arches below it for the water to pass through. It will be carved from a single stone ... I've selected a stone from one of your quarries, though we'll need elephant-carts and paiks to have it transported to its designated spot.'

'You'll have these and anything else you need,' the king assured.

'I shall have stone masons trained by me to build the bridge and carve out figures on its sides. Since it will be made of stone, the silor sako at Namdang will endure for eternity, Your Majesty, and be an apt entry point for the City of Joy. I will also build another silor sako on the river Dimau.'

'Excellent.' The king signalled his approval by thumping the mason on his back. 'I have just two suggestions to make. First is provision for an area where wild animals can be kept—tigers, bears, untamed elephants as well as animals which we may, from time to time, bring from alien lands. Second, Rongpur would not be Rongpur unless it has a sports pavillion from which we and our nobles can watch sporting events. It need not be of brick and mortar—a wood-and-thatch structure would do. The field must have galleries around the central arena where the general public can sit to watch the entertainment.'

'A kind of rong-ghar, Your Majesty!' exclaimed Kamalakanta Bargohain admiringly.

'Precisely,' said the king. 'I shall pass the order and you can begin construction at once.'

The month was Bohag or April, the year 1707. The Assamese people, irrespective of ethnic background or religious affiliation, celebrated the festival of Bohag or Rongali Bihu, the biggest festival of the region, in this month. Preparations for this festival began well in advance and the actual festival spanned at least a week. Feasting and merriment, singing and dancing were the principal means of enjoyment during the festival.

Every year, the reigning monarch held a sporting tournament on the final day of Bihu. Since the construction of the capital city of Garhgaon, the tournament had been held there. But this year, the Swargadeo had made two important announcements. First was that henceforth Bihu would be the national festival in the Ahom realm. Secondly, the tournament would be held at the rong-ghar venue in the newly constructed capital of Rongpur.

On the day of the tournament, people made a beeline for the rong-ghar well in advance to acquire the best seats for themselves. Not all amongst the spectators were from the Garhgaon and Rongpur locality; in fact, people came from far-off places, travelling for many days, to watch this magnificent sporting event. This morning, amongst the crowd moving towards the venue, was the family of Baduli Bora, comprising himself, his wife Akoni and their thirteen-year-old son Tongsu. Baduli

was a farmer living in the Habung area on the north bank of the Luit;
Assisted by his son, Baduli had rowed across the mammoth river and
then up the Dikhow, mooring their boat at a ghat close to one of the
entry points of Rongpur. Then they had set off towards the tournament
arena, the stream of people moving in a single direction ensuring that
they did not have to seek directions.

Tongsu was in seventh heaven. He had never stepped out of his
village before; and now here he was, in the fabled city of Rongpur, going
to witness a tournament that he had heard so much about. Everything
about the city was strange and exciting. For one thing, Tongsu had never
imagined that there were so many people in the realm; for another, the
fine dresses worn by most folks at Rongpur marked him and his parents
as outsiders from some remote village, though he and his father were
dressed in fresh dhotis, with gamochas tied around their waists and
heads, and his mother in newly woven mekhela-chadar.

Tongsu's heart thudded with excitement as things he had not seen
before constantly caught his eye. The city itself was very well designed,
with broad, tree-lined avenues and fenced flower gardens with paved
walks in them. Since it was spring, the flower gardens were in full
bloom, enhancing the beauty of Rongpur. Their village had only a tiny
community pukhuri; here there were a number of them, ensuring that
the citizens did not lack fresh water. His own family was of the Vaishnav
faith propagated by Sankardev; yet he and his parents stopped as they
crossed the many temples and devalayas that had been built within the
city to prostrate themselves outside each gate.

Rongpur was in a festive mood. Sounds of laughter and music filled
the air. Young children, dressed in their best, hopped and skipped
down the streets. The Bora family gawked from afar, amazed at the royal
palace, the most prominent landmark in the entire city. They crossed
the marketplace; most of the stalls were closed on this day since it was
Bihu time.

'We need to reach the tournament ground quickly,' Tongsu's father
urged. 'By the looks of it, everybody seems to be headed for that place.'

But Tongsu demurred. 'My friend who had come to Rongpur before, says there is a poshu-ghar in this city. It is early morning yet ... and time enough for us to reach the tournament. Let's take a look at it first.'

His parents did not say no, for in truth they themselves were keen to see this unique poshu-ghar or zoo that Swargadeo Sukhrungpha had built in his city. But now they had to ask for directions and were pleased to discover that the city folks were extremely polite and obliging. A young lad, in fact, accompanied them to the entry gate to the zoo.

It indeed was a wondrous thing. The zoo spanned a huge area of around 350 bighas. The keepers manning the entry gate told them that there was no fee, which was a relief since the family had no money, with Akoni carrying some food in a bag for their sole meal of the day. The zoo contained enclosures shaped like octagons to keep the animals in. Each enclosure was surrounded by a deep and wide moat filled with water to prevent the animals from straying out, as well as a high embankment. Paths had been built on the embankments to enable visitors to watch the animals. The moats contained fish of various kinds, gharials or crocodiles, otters and turtles.

Tongsu gazed wide-eyed at animals with which he was familiar and ones he had never seen. Tigers, bears, leopards, panthers, wolves, deer and so on, of course, he knew about; but there were dozens of species he had not known of, imported by the swargadeo from other climes. There were animals with humps, some with manes, huge bulls but unlike the ones in Assam, covered with fur, and many species besides. At a few places, cane cages had been made to keep exotic species of birds. One enclosure had half-a-dozen rhinos. There were no elephants in this poshu-ghar; these, including the ones that would be used during elephant-fights in the tournament, were maintained in the official hatishal. The guards at the gate informed them that there were special officers to take care of the poshu-ghar.

Tongsu could have spent the entire day gazing awestruck at the animals in the zoo; but they were pressed for time and soon had to leave for the site of the tournament. The open ground in which the tournament was to be held was located beyond the main city. A fair had sprung up near the tournament ground. The traders were doing brisk business and there was much pushing and jostling. Tongsu craned his neck to see everything around him. The shrill cries of vendors shouting out their wares added to the din. Many of the stalls were selling eatables. Delicious aromas floated in the air but they possessed no money and had to be content with only feasting their eyes and noses!

But some things were free. A puppet show, for instance, was being performed in an open stall. Its theme was the battle of Saraighat and the two main puppets were those of Lachit Barphukan and Ram Singh, the latter naturally getting the worst of the bargain. Then Tongsu spotted a cock-fight and the family was forced to stop to watch it. A number of men sat in a circle, each with well-fed roosters in bamboo cages. A man squatted in the middle of the circle, holding the biggest fowl they had ever seen. A basket near him brimmed over with the bodies of dead roosters, victims of this powerful bird. The man constantly taunted the others, challenging them to put up a cock against his champion. Suddenly one man, unable to take the boasts, dipped into his cage and brought out a cock, a fine bird with many-coloured plumage and sharp beak and claws.

He placed his bird in front of the champion, whispered a few words of encouragement, and let go of the cock. Hackles raised, feathers glistening in the sun, the two cocks sprang into the fray. The spectators cheered the challenger on, urging him to teach the champion a lesson.

Alas, all in vain. The champion's claws suddenly flashed and sank deep into the challenger's throat. The bird fell onto the ground, thrashing its legs. The spectators let out a collective of sigh of disappointment. The champion's owner laughed, put the dead cock into his basket and began calling out again.

'We can't spend the whole day here. Come, let's head for the tournament ground,' urged Baduli.

'Whew!' exclaimed Tongsu as they neared the arena, his eyes round with wonder. 'I never imagined so many people lived on this earth. There must be thousands and thousands here!'

The arena was rectangular, enclosed on all sides by strong bamboo fencing. The only entry was from the eastern end, where there was a wide wooden gate over which officials and armed soldiers kept guard. Though the tournament's commencement was yet at least two hours away, the bamboo galleries half surrounding the central arena were packed with people and not a single empty seat seemed in sight.

'Oh,' Tongsu cried out in dismay. 'Where will we sit?'

But he need not have worried. It was clear to the people around them that this family was not from the city and must have come from far off to watch the games. 'Hey, you three, come over here!' cried a man who had apparently come with his own family too, comprising himself, his wife and half-a-dozen youngsters of both sexes. 'We'll make room for you.'

The three of them thanked their benefactor profusely. While Baduli struck up a conversation with the father, Akoni talked to the wife and Tongsu with the youngsters.

At the southern side of the arena, set slightly away from the barricade, was a tall, exquisitely designed building made of wood with a roof of thatch. A ladder was provided to go up, and another to go down on the other side.

'What's that?' Tongsu asked the children.

'Oh, that's the new rong-ghar built by our swargadeo,' one of them replied. 'He, his queens, princes and princesses, and the nobles with their families will watch the games from it.'

Tongsu's curiosity was limitless and he learnt a great deal about Garhgaon and Rongpur while conversing with the children. Time flew. Then, all of a sudden, two drummers entered the arena. Beating their drums, they announced the arrival of the ministers and other court functionaries. A sudden hush fell on the crowd, and all eyes turned towards the bamboo platform.

The nobles, escorted by soldiers and led by the king and the royal family, arrived in full regalia, atop caparisoned elephants. A band, playing drums, buffalo-horn flutes and other such instruments, welcomed them. The mahouts stopped the elephants beside the rong-ghar and the new arrivals stepped directly on to the upper floor and took their designated seats.

The swargadeo and the patra-mantris waved to the spectators. The people cheered and waved back. Then the king signalled for the games to begin. Tongsu looked around him. Every inch of sitting space was occupied. Women and children were present in great numbers. Many people, not finding room in the galleries, had climbed up trees growing in the adjoining area. Excitement filled the air.

The heralds beat a long flourish on their drums and announced that the first item was an aerial competition involving trained falcons. Half a dozen shenchowas or falcon trainers ran into the arena, with birds resting on their arms, held by thin leather jesses. The eyes of the fierce-looking falcons were covered with cloth hoods. The trainers bowed to the ministers and took up their positions. Assistants carried cages filled with game birds called kanua. The buragohain signalled and the assistants released the captive birds. Moments later the trainers took off the falcons' hoods, released them and set them after the fleeing game birds. The falcons soared up and were soon mere specks against the cloudless azure sky.

All eyes were turned towards the aerial competition high up. One of the specks grew bigger and bigger and soon a falcon glided down gracefully, a dead bird in its talons. After depositing the bundle of feathers on the cloth spread by its master, it soared up again in pursuit of another kill. A roar of appreciation erupted from the galleries. The cheering grew louder as other falcons appeared with their victims. The piles of dead birds on the sheets of cloth grew bigger and bigger. Half an hour later, the contest came to an end. Five of the falcons returned to their owners. The shenchowas cleaned the blood-stained beaks of the birds and hooded them. The unfortunate trainer whose bird had failed to return trembled at the thought of the punishment which would be meted out to him. After a count had been taken of the number of game-birds killed by each falcon, the trainer with the greatest number of kills was declared winner. The proud man ascended the steps of the platform and was rewarded with a gold necklace by the buragohain. The crowd clapped enthusiastically.

But the cheers turned to hoots and jeers as the luckless trainer whose bird had failed to return was tied to a whipping post and given ten lashes. The next item on the programme was announced—a fight between two elephants, a spectacular sport fraught with great risk. Soldiers armed with spears stationed themselves at various points along the outer side of the barricade. On several occasions in the past, a fighting elephant had broken the barrier and charged the spectators, killing and injuring many. The soldiers were there to drive the beasts away if they came too close to the fencing.

To the sound of drumbeats, two mammoth tusker elephants with their mahouts atop them came rushing in through a special gate. The animals were covered with ropes and a brass bell hung around the neck of each beast. They had been fed on hemp weed and as a result were extremely unruly. The mahouts upon their backs had a tough time controlling them. The entry gate was left open.

The two antagonists, long, pointed tusks gleaming in the sunshine, stood confronting each other at the two ends of the arena. Then, prodded on by their mahouts, they charged. The crowd held its breath. No one moved. No one uttered a word. Pin-drop silence reigned. The two animals clashed headlong. There were terrible, loud thuds as they battled each other, using their heads, trunks and tusks. The mahouts lay flat upon the elephants' broad backs, clinging on to the ropes for dear life. The beasts broke out of a clinch and retreated a few paces. The mahouts sat up and poked them with ankushas—elephant goads with iron hooks and spikes. Raising their trunks and uttering blood-curdling trumpets, the enraged beasts charged again. Moments before the collision, one of the elephants, guided by its mahout, slowed down and wheeled quickly to the left. The other beast, carried forward by its own momentum found itself at a disadvantage, having presented its rear to its opponent. Its opponent was quick to seize the opportunity. It moved swiftly, intent on burying its deadly tusks into the other's flank.

The spectators tensed, wondering whether this would be the end of the combat. But the second elephant made an almost impossible turn and swerved quickly away just as its adversary lunged at it. The sharp tips of the tusks, rather than sinking into its belly, simply grazed the skin. A fine trickle of blood appeared on its hide. The crowd erupted into cheers. They jumped up and down, shouting and gesticulating in excitement and appreciation. Tongsu cringed, but his newly made young friends applauded as lustily as the others. The beasts broke apart once again and circled each other from a distance.

'Fight, fight!' chanted the crowd. 'Kill, Kill!' they screamed. Again and again the elephants charged at each other, tusks and trunks repeatedly locking. All of a sudden there was a mighty, cracking sound and the audience gasped. The tusk of one elephant had broken into two. Trumpeting in pain and terror, the animal retreated. Finding itself having the upper hand, the other pressed home its advantage. The mahout on top of the injured beast tried to make it face the assault head on. But the beast obviously had had enough and was looking for a way to escape. Then to everyone's utter horror, the injured elephant, angered by the mahout's attempts to keep it in the fray, suddenly reared up and came heavily down. The man on its back, caught unawares, toppled onto the ground.

A horrible scream emerged from his throat as the animal placed a foreleg on his body, smashing him to pulp. Then the animal loped out of the arena, pursued by its victorious opponent. The spectators were stunned. They gazed in horror as assistants came rushing to the help of the fallen mahout. But he was dead. They picked up his battered body and carried it out. Tongsu was shaken to the core. He looked at the youngsters seated beside him. They too appeared to be deeply affected by the sudden tragedy. The blood had drained from their faces.

As if to ease the tension, a troupe of acrobats entered the arena. They were quaintly dressed, indicating that they were not natives and had been imported from other climes to entertain the Rongpur crowd. They performed seemingly impossible gymnastic feats and were warmly applauded. A buffalo fight was next. Two huge animals were dragged into the arena. The men, having released the beasts, scampered across the barricade to safety. The animals stood a few yards apart, pawing the ground and snorting in challenge. Then they rushed at each other, using their heads as battering rams. But all too soon one animal lost heart and ran away. The victor continued to trot around the arena to the cheers of the crowd.

A bihu huchari troupe, colourfully dressed in silk and equipped with numerous musical instruments, such as the mohor-singar pepa or buffalo-horn flute, dhols or drums, etc., now entertained the crowd. Half of the troupe consisted of women and the erotic songs exchanged between them made the elders in the crowd laugh uproariously. Many of the spectators stood up on their seats to sway with the music, others joined in the singing by the huchari group. Carried away by the hypnotic music, some of those sitting on the rong-ghar too stood up and danced.

The huchari troupe, a great hit with the audience, finally ended their performance by showering blessings on the king, his subjects and his kingdom. As it departed from the arena, the heralds beat their drums and announced the commencement of an archery contest with a grand prize awaiting the victor. Two dozen of the kingdom's finest archers entered the arena and the contest began. The competitors shot at stationary targets of strips of plantain stems. Tongsu was not very thrilled with this event for he himself was a crack shot with bows and arrows and could chop off mangoes by their stems; moreover, the proceedings of shooting by individual contestants and noting down of points was too slow. The boy, and perhaps a majority of the spectators, were relieved when the archery competition was over and the winner awarded by His Majesty.

The heralds announced the next item and Tongsu's heart lurched—a fight between two wild beasts, a tiger and a black bear, no doubt brought from the poshu-ghar. The spectators, who had grown somewhat restive during the archery contest, suddenly grew alert, and expectant silence reigned once again. Assistants lugged a huge cage made of solid bholuka-bamboo stems to the centre of the arena upon a large wooden platform on wheels. The bamboo bars of this cage had wide enough gaps between them so that the spectators could see the action within it, yet were close enough to ensure that the wild beasts could not wriggle out. The eyes of the onlookers popped out as two smaller cages were wheeled into the arena, one containing a huge black bear and the other a royal Bengal tiger. There were small trap doors in each of the cages through which the assistants could transfer the beasts into the bigger cage.

At first the two animals, perhaps more terrified by the crowd and the din rather than in a mood to fight, simply slunk at opposite corners. But they were constantly prodded from outside by men wielding long, pointed bamboo sticks; the tiger's temper was the first to flare; it had no other object on which to vent its fury than the bear slinking in an opposite corner. It emitted a blood-curdling growl and flung itself at the bear, going for its jugular. At the same time, the bear, anticipating the attack, stood up on its hind legs. Suddenly it appeared much larger than before; quite gigantic, in fact; with one paw, it swatted away the tiger as if it were a mere fly. It was its agility which saved the tiger from being fatally wounded as it swerved in mid-flight to avoid those razor-sharp claws, and moved as far as possible away from the bear's corner.

But there was no letting up on the part of the men with bamboo sticks who continued to harass the two beasts urging them on to fight. Finally, the infuriated animals set upon each other in a lethal combat; stark terror settled into the hearts of the spectators as the two brutes tore at each other, emitting growls and grunts. The bear, though monstrous and powerful, was in reality the more handicapped of the two; while the tiger was quick and agile, it was slow and ponderous. It fended off the tiger's attacks for almost half an hour but the final outcome was inevitable. With great cunning the tiger ensured that the bear had come up to the centre of the cage—then it deftly circled its adversary, leapt upon its back from the rear, and sank its teeth into the bear's throat, clinging on with all its might even as its adversary tried to shake it loose.

That assault had been deadly. The breath was squeezed out of the unfortunate bear and it suddenly toppled down, blood spouting from a wound in its throat. The tiger sensed its victory, but there was no indication of joy or triumph in the beast, unlike its human counterparts like the shenchowa or archery winners who had raised their arms in triumph. Discovering that the bear was dead, and having no need for food at the moment, the tiger slunk away into another corner and slumped down to recover from the exertion of the battle. The spectators let out a collective gasp of relief that the terrible conflict was ended. Tongsu felt dazed, and could see that his newly acquired friends, who must have seen the tournament before, were no less affected.

As though to allow the onlookers to recover from the grisly fight, a Deodhai dance was enacted, its slow, graceful movements and music designed to sooth the senses. Next, the drummers announced the final item of the day—the mal-juj or wrestling competition. It would not, however, be an open competition between participants with the losers being gradually eliminated till one winner remained. As explained by the drum-beating heralds, it would instead be a contest between the swargadeo's champion and anyone who dared to challenge him for a fabulous prize.

A giant of a man entered the arena: the swargadeo's champion! He was not from the region and must have been brought by the king from some distant land. The crowd gasped at the man's build. Almost six-and-a-half feet tall, his muscular body naked except for a short dhoti, this wrestler looked formidable.

'Come, ye brave wrestlers of Assam, and take up the challenge of fighting His Majesty's champion! Unimaginable riches await anyone who beats him. This is what Swargadeo Sukhrungpha has declared, O good people!'

The spectators were agog with excitement. A number of wrestlers who had come to the venue to participate in this annual wrestling competition entered the arena and squatted on the ground beside a large square, which assistants had marked on the earth. This was to be the wrestling ring within which the competitors must fight. Though their faces did not show it, the Assamese wrestlers were both surprised and dismayed at the change of format this year. They had come to battle each other—and here was the swargadeo putting up this giant of a man whom they needed to beat, though the reward would surely be worth the endeavour!

One by one, the competitors entered the ring to wrestle with the champion. One by one, they departed, accompanied by boos and catcalls from the crowd, having been knocked senseless and carried out of the arena. Then a tall and powerful man stood up and stepped into the ring. He was the local favourite, a wrestler of repute. If anyone had the slightest chance of beating the king's champion, it was he. The spectators greeted his arrival with loud applause. In their heart of hearts, they wanted their local favourite to win.

The two adversaries faced each other warily, looking for an opening. Suddenly the challenger sprang, caught the giant around his waist, and tried to trip him. But the man seemed to be made of rock. He put his palms flat on the other's shoulders and pressed hard. The challenger shuddered with pain, went down on his knees but, fortunately for him, was able to squirm out of that vice-like grip.

The giant laughed a full-throated laugh, beat his hands on his thighs, and pranced around the other wrestler. He looked more like a huge ape than a human being. His wily opponent sprang at him again, head bent low, trying to butt him in the belly. His head did hit the intended target, but had little impact. Before the man could retreat the giant's hands clamped around his waist, and squeezed. The challenger could not move. He was totally paralysed. Blood rushed to his head. He hit out desperately with his fists, but the pain caused by the squeezing hands soon became unbearable, and his legs gave way. When, finally, the giant loosened his grip, the challenger fell down unconscious.

He was dragged out of the arena by assistants. The remaining wrestlers lost heart at the drubbing of the favourite. They decamped from the arena as quickly as they had entered, much to the amusement of the crowd, which lustily cheered the swargadeo's champion. The king now stood up and, waving again to the crowd, signalled the end of the tournament. A procession of elephants arrived at the side of the rong-ghar and the royal entourage embarked upon them.

'Long live Swargadeo Sukhrungpha,' the people shouted, genuine spontaneity in their words. Tongsu and his parents shouted as loudly as the others.

By then the sun had crossed its zenith and was on its way down. So thrilled had they been with the spectacle that they had forgotten the hunger in their bellies. They lingered for a while on the gallery of rong-ghar to eat their meal and, having done so, made their way to the boat and back to the village.

Ghanasyam khanikar felt pleased with himself. He had spent many years in the kingdom of Swargadeo Sukhrungpha, away from his loved ones. Now the time had come for him to depart. He had been overwhelmed by the generosity and hospitality of the people of this land and much taken by the unassuming nature of the king. The swargadeo was endowed with a true aesthetic sense, and appreciated artists and wise men. That was why Ghanasyam had extended his stay beyond what he had initially planned and served the monarch far more than originally mandated.

He knew neither the king of Kochbehar nor the nawab of Bengal would be pleased with his protracted sojourn amongst the Assamese. When they had learned that no less an individual than the Ahom emperor had invited the khanikar to his capital, they had imposed upon him their own mandate. Ghanasyam khanikar had had no choice but to accede to their orders, or else he would never see his family alive again—that had been the threat the officer who approached him had made.

That assignment too had been completed; now he would be able to return home, free his family and continue on with his life. Due to the munificence of the Ahom monarch, Ghanasyam had become rich beyond his wildest dreams. But, true artist that he was, material things were less important to him than what he had achieved in the Ahom kingdom. These achievements would perpetuate his name for all time to come. Towns, temples, palaces, bridges—there were quite a few structures upon which he had put his stamp. The dols or temples of which he had supervised the construction had been many, as also the devalayas or places where Brahmin priests could stay and worship.

But none had been dearer to him, or for that matter to Swargadeo Sukhrungpha, than the Phakuadol at Rongpur. His Majesty's mother had been unceremoniously buried after she had been tortured to death, but her husband had made no move to give her a more fitting burial. It had been her son, the swargadeo, who had built her a maidam at Rongpur and had the Phakuadol constructed over it. In deference to the king's wishes, this temple was designed differently from conventional ones. Its plinth was octagonal, not rectangular in shape, and had eight series of steps leading to the top from the eight sides. Beside every stairway was a huge minaret, eight in all. In keeping with the ancient Shan belief that release from the mortal coil was not an occasion for mourning but celebration, the swargadeo would play phakua or holi once a year, with his family and select subjects, at the precincts of this temple; therefore, it was named the Phakuadol.

The king had a golden idol of his mother Sati Jaimati made and placed it in this temple. This required that another temple dedicated to Lord Shiva be built opposite to it. This was the Ranganath Shiva temple; built as an afterthought, it was completed within a night, and so it has plain walls without any carvings upon them. Ghanasyam had travelled to other parts of the Assamese country to construct edifices, the most significant being to the capital Garhgaon to build a brick palace there.

He had been highly impressed with the dynamism displayed by this Ahom king; it was quite a task keeping up with his imagination and enthusiasm for construction. The roads, water tanks and other civic utilities had been built by the kingdom's own engineers and officers, who were experts at the job; during the period he had been in this realm he had witnessed construction of the Kharikatiya, Dubarini, Darika and Barpatragohain alis or roads, as also pukhuris at Barkola, Sontola, Rongpur and so on. His task, on the other hand, had been to do the stone and brick works and train others in the same; an entire city had been created partly under his supervision; but if he were to name his outstanding achievement, it would be the two stone bridges made over the rivers Namdang and Dimau. As the chief mason of the realm, he had, of course, also been instrumental in constructing a number of temples and devalayas including the Baidyanath, Surya and Nandikeshwar temples and Phulbari and Jogeshwar devalayas.

Yes, his name would be inscribed for eternity in the history of this kingdom! An entire city had been built under his supervision; that had been an achievement which would abide in human memory. No wonder he was pleased. He sat in one of the outer rooms of the spacious chang-house he had been allotted at Rongpur, eating his morning meal, as the numerous retainers placed at his disposal began the task of packing his belongings. A huge maarnao, fitted out properly for the long voyage back to Kochbehar, lay in wait at the mooring ghat on the river Dikhow, generously gifted to him by the king along with its crew, to take him home. He would be leaving that very noon after a final audience with the swargadeo.

The head servant of the household entered the room and bowed to the khanikar. 'A phukan has come to our house, Your Excellency,' he informed. 'The officer seeks permission to speak with you.'

'Please show him in,' Ghanasyam, not suspecting a thing, ordered.

It was one of the security officers deputed at the palace. The khanikar knew the man well for he had met him numerous times before. He smiled and waved him towards a chair. But the officer preferred to remain standing.

'My apologies for intruding, Khanikar dangoriya,' the phukan said. 'But I have a task to perform. As you are no doubt aware, we keep a strict watch over people who come to or depart from our land, whether they be our own or strangers. Thus, we shall have to go through your personal effects before these can be packed and loaded on to the boat.'

Ghanasyam blanched. This had come as a bolt from the blue. He stopped eating and rose from his chair, trying to look as haughty as he could. 'This is an outrage! Am I, who have rendered such great service to your king, be treated like an ordinary trader? I shall lodge a complaint with the swargadeo. You will in no way touch my things.'

The phukan's response was a knowing smile. 'Oh, you can lodge any number of complaints with His Majesty, Khanikar dangoriya. But it will do you no good. You see, the directive to search your belongings has come from the swargadeo himself!'

Ghanasyam slumped down again into his chair. Even now there was hope that his perfidy would not be discovered, considering that he had taken precautions. He watched impassively as the phukan shouted out orders to the posse of guards whom he had brought along. They entered and made a show of shifting cursorily through the khanikar's personal effects. His impassiveness turned to inner terror as the officer himself went to the room containing the utensils Ghanasyam planned to take back to Kochbehar. The man scanned the items before unerringly picking up a brass bucket with a handle. The khanikar understood his end was nigh. He himself had witnessed how brutally the Ahoms treated traitors.

The officer shook the bucket and then nodded with satisfaction. He had one of his men split the bucket apart. It had a false bottom. Within it were sheafs of sanchi-leaf sheets, with drawings and text upon them. The phukan nodded to himself, seemingly satisfied. 'Tie him up,' he told his men. 'We'll drag him before the swargadeo.'

He had been such a fool—too late the khanikar understood. The deference shown to him by his hosts had made him forget how effective the Ahom secret service was and how it did not fail to keep watch over everyone, no matter of what rank or how powerful. The quickness and facility with which the officer had homed in on the brassbucket showed that he had prior information. Obviously, spies had been planted amongst the khanikar's retainers. Fool that he was, he had not seen this coming!

He was transported straight to the palace he himself had built and flung at the feet of the swargadeo seated imperiously upon the throne seven steps above the floor. It was a totally different individual who now looked down upon him, unsmiling and unforgiving. The sketches that Ghanasyam had himself drawn and planned to take back to Kochbehar had been scanned. They accurately depicted defensive positions, including moats, ramparts and guardposts, of various places in the kingdom, the focus being on the twin capitals of Garhgaon and Rongpur. The text contained equally accurate description of the defensive mechanism of the Assamese and figures detailing the army's resources of men and materials.

'They're holding my family hostage,' Ghanasyam pleaded, trying to convey his compulsions. 'I beg you, please let me go.'

'Behead him in public,' Swargadeo Sukhrungpha pronounced the sentence tersely. 'The people need to know the fate of one who betrays the realm.'

For the subjects of the Ahom kingdom, now referred to by everyone as the Assamese, it was the best of times. There was economic self-sufficiency, so necessary for the well-being of the people, as well as relative peace. The Ahom monarch Rudra Singha understood that the key to greater prosperity as well as cultural advancement was through increased intercourse with neighbouring realms and expansion of trade with them. Traditionally the Ahoms had discouraged outsiders from entering their kingdom from the west though migrants coming from the east had been generally welcomed. Thus, the outsiders allowed entry were mostly people whom the Ahoms wanted to import, in particular artisans skilled in crafts not known to the Ahoms themselves. Some of these skilled workers were even enticed with promises of land grants to come and settle here. Traders were strictly controlled; a few venturesome ones from Bengal had tried to smuggle out goods from the Ahom territory on previous occasions; their boats had been burnt and goods confiscated, while they themselves were put to the sword.

But Rudra Singha was an exception. He opened up the economy of Assam and encouraged native saudagars or merchants to carry on trade in indigenous commodities with outsiders, subject to revenue being paid to the state. Unlike his predecessors, who followed a policy of commercial insulation, Rudra Singha understood the potential of exporting exotic Assamese items of trade sought after elsewhere and importing diamonds, gems and other items to enrich the Ahom empire. Thus, the westernmost, well-located trading outpost called Hadirachowki or Assamchowki, as well as adjacent places such as Goalpara, became hives of business activity, thereby swelling the imperial coffers. Lac, made locally, was a famous item exported as far as China and Japan. There was bustling export of silk, agar wood, opium, ivory, cane and bamboo items and other indigenous products to mainland India, the sole significant item of import being salt. Occasionally elephants too were exported, subject to royal approval. Trade was established with Tibet, from where wool was bartered for gold collected from local riverbeds of the Brahmaputra Valley. Trading posts called Chaunahat and Jigonchurhat were set up on the route to Lhasa, which became the meeting point for Tibetan, Assamese and Chinese traders. Historically, the hill tribes of the region, as also the Bhutiyas of Bhutan, had engaged in barter trade with the people of the Brahmaputra Valley. Rudra Singha facilitated this by setting up haats or markets held at regular intervals at strategic places.

Sons of Brahmin priests of the palace were sent to educational centres in mainland India so that they could return and educate locals, especially Ahom princes. However, Rudra Singha was aware of the danger of allowing unfettered entry of outsiders into the realm, so he created three khels or professional clans to systemize his endeavour to increase cultural intercourse: the clans were named Bairagi, Kataki and Khaund after their occupations. The job of the bairagis was to travel in disguise and study people, customs and cultures of places outside the Ahom kingdom and inform the king about these. The king could then introduce the customs that he liked within his own realm. For instance, the festival of Phakuwa or Holi, which Rudra Singh celebrated at the temple at the maidam of his mother, had been imported from north India. The Katakis acted as ambassadors for the king—Rudra Singha sent his emissaries and gifts to different parts of India; potentates of central and north India were contacted; envoys were dispatched even to places as far as Rajasthan and Punjab. The khaunds, like the bairagis, were employed to keep in touch with other cultures as also purchase goods, such as precious stones, from the Indian mainland for the royal household. It was from the reign of this monarch that the khaunds had an additional duty to perform: they had to carry the ashes of members of the royalty and nobles for immersion in the river Ganges.

No doubt professions such as bairagi and kataki had existed before; but these were disorganized and the professionals were often conscripted for personal use by the upper classes rather than for work on behalf of the realm. Rudra Singha organized these into khels with a hierarchy of petty officials and gave each khel specific duties to perform. The bairagis, katakis and khaunds were also instrumental in bringing cultural items such as dance and music from other parts of India into the Ahom palace. However, he was not unaware of the cultural renaissance being brought about by the Vaishnav monks in the sattras, and encouraged these, appointing a functionary called the sattriya barua for the purpose. Empowered by royal patronage, the monks redoubled their efforts to bring about a socio-cultural renaissance, thereby making an enormous contribution to creating an Assamese community with a distinct identity.

He also created two additional khels for internal affairs, again from already existing professionals: Kakotis who kept the accounts of expenditure and Doleys who were required to make horoscopes and also predict the fortunes of the nation in addition to the ones made by the Ahom priests. The most significant aspect of Rudra Singha's reign was a revolutionary change in the system—till that time, important appointments were always made from individuals belonging to the Ahom community, in particular the nobility. Rudra Singha made no distinction between different communities with regard to appointment to important official positions. Except the topmost ones, he began appointing members of other communities, including those belonging to the Islamic faith, to posts such as phukans, hazarikas, rajkhowas, baruas, etc. This served greatly to enhance the feeling amongst the subjects of being one people and contributed towards the assimilation of people of different faiths and ethnic backgrounds.

The health of his subjects was of particular concern to the swargadeo. He created a cadre of health workers comprising a number of khels called Bihiya, Bihtola, Bez, Chang-Bez, Jora-Bez, etc., under the supervision of a bezbarua. It was ensured that a community health centre was set up in every village to treat the ill and the infirm. As for education, Brahmins living in villages were encouraged to teach children the rudiments of learning and tutors were appointed to teach Ahom princes. On learning that the great Ahom emperor was highly religious and patronized their caste, Brahmins from the Indian mainland, who otherwise would not have dared to venture into this seemingly dangerous region, now made a beeline for the Ahom kingdom. They were received cordially and many of them were employed to spread rudimentary education within the region.

Under the direct supervision of the king, artisans and professionals of quality, such as ironsmiths, brass workers, masons, goldsmiths, apothecaries, tailors, etc., were brought to the kingdom, given land and allowed to practise their profession here. For instance, to train local jewellers in the proper manner of encrusting gems on golden utensils and artifacts, jewellers and goldsmiths were brought in from the distant province of Marwar in northwest India. In fact, there was no aspect that did not concern the Ahom monarch—he even introduced new dresses styled in the manner of those worn by people of other parts of India and made it a rule that Assamese women should wear riha-mekhela.

It could be said that during the reign of this great king, Assamese society was emancipated and stepped into modernity from a medieval ethos. Though relatively illiterate himself, he had a scientific temper and encouraged individuals with enterprising dispositions. For instance, he brought a famous chemist from Biswanath to Rongpur and granted him hundred puras of land so that he could carry out his experiments. Like emperors in other parts of India, in particular the Mughals, Rudra Singha had scholars, musicians and seers grace his court, placing special seats for them whenever the monarch held a meeting of his council. The poet laureate in his court was Kaviraj Chakraborty, author of poetical works such as *Sankhachur Bodh* and translator into Assamese of classics such as *Geet Govinda*, Kalidasa's *Abhinayam Shakuntalam*, *Brahmabaibartya Puran*, etc. He also wrote a textbook on astrology titled *Bhaswati* to educate the sons of royalty and nobles. Rudra Singha himself had a poetic sensibility and wrote poems, lyrics and devotional hymns which he would recite during the periodic literary sessions held in a hall in the palace, specially built for literary and cultural activities.

The objective of this monarch was clearcut—to pick everything good about other societies and introduce them into Assamese society while encouraging local arts. In order to strengthen and enrich Assamese culture, he brought about an amalgam of local, classical and folk dances and music with their counterparts from other regions of India, using the remarkable cultural renaissance ushered in by the Vaishnav monks. Literary works were translated, art forms such as the creation of golden manuscripts reached their zenith and dance-dramas based on classical themes were composed. Also, the king drew not merely from other parts of India for cultural inspiration; he, more than anyone else, was aware of the rich cultural heritage of the various tribes of this region and tapped into their music and dances to widen the base of a broader Assamese culture.

A great patron of indigenous culture, he ordained that the traditional Assamese dances should not merely be performed in the sattras, but also in the temples and devalayas of the kingdom. Experimentation was carried out by artistes in fusing tunes and ragas from outside with traditional local tunes to create a unique musical combination. For the first time, Bengali songs, classical as well as folk, were sung during cultural performances in the royal court. To complement this, musical instruments imported from outside were added to the local ones that had till then been used primarily for folk music. He created khels of folk artistes and appointed an officer called Gayan Barua to look after their welfare.

Without doubt, during the reign of Swargadeo Sukhrungpha there was an economic, intellectual and cultural efflorescence unmatched by any in preceding periods. The monarch had successfully communicated his energy and enthusiasm to his people and taken them to the acme of prosperity. From then on, it could only be downhill for the Ahoms in particular and Assamese in general.

The Assamese society that had evolved during the four-and-a-half centuries of Ahom rule was a composite one, comprising numerous ethnic groups, some of which had migrated to the land long time ago and others that were relative newcomers. To have created a broadly homogeneous entity by uniting groups which had traditionally been inimical towards each other was no mean achievement. Though a sense of nationhood had been developed over the years, the apotheosis was reached during the reign of Rudra Singha. It had been noticed that the prevalent nationalism had its lacunae; if the central authority, meaning the Ahom monarch of a particular period, showed signs of weakness and vulnerability, some vassal or the other would endeavour to assert independence and had to be put down through force. Because Rudra Singha had the reputation of being a firm ruler, the first ten years of his reign were free from internal strife, thereby enabling him to take Assamese society to new heights of prosperity and cultural achievements.

However, towards the second half of 1706, this phase of unbroken peace came to an end when the Kachari King Tamradhwaj declared that he was throwing off the Ahom yoke and asserting his independence. It had been quite a while since the Kacharis were subjugated and their king made a tributary vassal of the Ahom monarch. However, during the intervening period, Garhgaon's focus had been Guwahati and its preoccupation the invading Mughals, so the kings then had not been able to attend to Kachari affairs. For some years, the Kachari king had stopped paying the annual tribute—on discovering that this had not elicited any hostile reaction from the occupant of the throne at Garhgaon, King Tamradhwaj misread the situation and declared himself an independent king.

Rudra Singha's response was immediate. He dispatched his army in a two-pronged attack against the Kacharis, the objective being capture of their capital Maibong. One wing under Boragi Barbarua, comprising around 37,000 soldiers, took the Dhansiri Valley route to enter Kachari country, while the other, of 30,000 men under the command of Koliya Solal Paniphukan, proceeded via Raha up the Kapili Valley. The campaign started in December 1706 and the Ahom forces attained a degree of success, though at the cost of many lives, less due to resistance by the Kacharis, more due to diseases and pestilence caused by a hostile environment of jungle and mountains. The barbarua's force finally reached and occupied Maibong, taking over a thousand prisoners and capturing a great deal of booty including a cannon and 700 guns. A while later, the paniphukan's force, which had confronted greater Kachari resistance, managed to join the barbarua and the Ahoms entrenched themselves near the Kachari capital.

The swargadeo sent word to his commanders that they press on towards Khaspur. But this they had difficulty in doing because many of the troops were down with fever due to the pestilential climate, with the barbarua himself having fallen ill. Moreover, provisions were running short, as was ammunition, so months were squandered without further progress. Rudra Singha, anxious that the campaign be concluded before the onset of the rainy season, sent repeated orders that it be recommenced, which induced the paniphukan to renew the offensive and progress up to a place called Sampani where once again he was forced to a halt. The gravely ill barbarua tried to return to Garhgaon but died on the way.

This made the king appreciate the crisis his troops were facing and he dispatched orders that Maibong be sacked and his men return, building fortifications on the way and leaving garrisons there to secure the country. Following his dictate, the Maibong brick fort was demolished, houses burnt down and the entire capital razed to the ground. A stone pillar was erected to mark the seizure of the township. With the soldiers left in fortifications erected in Kachari country dying from disease, finally the king had to abandon the entire idea and ask his entire army to return to the Ahom capital.

The Kachari King Tamradhwaj had fled in the face of the Ahom advance to the plains in the south, from where he requested the Jaiantia raja, another vassal of the Ahoms, for help to stave off imminent defeat. But even as Ram Singha, the Jaiantia raja, was mobilizing an army to help the Kacharis, Tamradhwaj came to know that the enemy had left Maibong and was retreating. He, therefore, intimated to Ram Singha that his aid was no longer required. It was at this time that the Jaiantia raja suddenly realized that if he kidnapped Tamradhwaj, he could take advantage of the disarray in the ranks of the Kachari army to annex their kingdom. He requested a friendly meeting with Tamradhwaj at Mulagul and by means of a clever stratagem made Tamradhwaj and his family members prisoners and carried them off to his own capital Jaiantiapur. He followed up this act of treachery with a campaign to annex Kachari territory.

Naturally, Ahom spies disguised as bairagis roamed all over the region; fortunately for Tamradhwaj one of them learnt of his plight and secretly contacted his wife Chandraprava. She sent a missive through the spy to Swargadeo Sukhrungpha begging forgiveness for her husband's past conduct and seeking Rudra Singha's assistance against his captors. Along with the letter, she also sent a strand of her long hair in a small container to testify to her identity. In response, the Ahom monarch directed one of his officers at an outpost to meet Ram Singha and convey a warning that unless his captive was released dire consequences awaited him.

However, Ram Singha sent a rejoinder that the Ahom king had no right to interfere in Jaiantia affairs; Rudra Singha's immediate response was to close down the haat or rural market at Gobha, upon which the Jaiantias were heavily dependent for supply of provisions. When this failed to move the obdurate Jaiantia raja, the Ahom king waited for the rainy season to end and sent a strong two-pronged assault force under the new barbarua and Pator Barphukan. The Jaiantias were no match for the well-trained and heavily armed Ahom army; some feeble resistance was offered but finally Ram Singha complied with the Ahom officers' demand that Tamradhwaj and his family be handed over.

Contrary to the Jaiantia raja's expectations, this did not stop the Ahom advance towards his capital and he was forced to mount cannons on the walls of the township to resist. However, on seeing the strength of the Ahom army, he sought to take recourse to flight, but was prevented from doing so by his nobles, who had advised him not to make enemies of the Ahoms. The barbarua laid siege to Jaiantiapur till he was joined there by the barphukan, and took Ram Singha captive. The royal treasury was emptied and taken back to the Ahom king, who ordered that it be divided amongst the troops who had taken part in the campaign. He also ordained that the Jaiantia raja's personal effects, including his elephants and horses, be brought to him as a symbol of submission. There were a number of households which had earlier lived in the Ahom kingdom but had fled to Jaiantia territory when Mir Jumlah invaded the land. They were ordered to return to their original places of habitation. It was decided that the Ahoms would maintain a permanent presence in Jaiantia and Kachari territory—katakis were sent to Mati Ullah, the faujdar of Sylhet, informing him that the Ahom swargadeo had annexed the principalities belonging to the Kacharis and the Jaiantias.

Even as Tamradhwaj and Ram Singha were being taken to be presented before Swargadeo Sukhrungpha, the Jaiantia nobles, aided by some members of the Khasi tribe, launched a counterattack to try and wrest their king back and restore the sovereignty of their principality. It was repulsed, though with some significant losses to the Ahoms; the Jaiantias gained some victories in subsequent skirmishes; but ultimately it was the might of the Ahoms which prevailed. Detachments from forts at various points, as also reinforcements sent by Rudra Singha under the leadership of Khampat Buragohain, combined to subjugate the uprising. The barphukan and barbarua stationed at Jaiantiapur too sent part of their forces to quell the rebellion; ruthless measures were adopted to cow down the hapless Jaiantia populace; villages were burnt down and at least a thousand Jaiantias were slaughtered. It was now surmised that since communications would be totally cut off once the rainy season commenced, the Ahoms needed to retreat from Jaiantiapur. Since the two rajas were being held as hostages, it was concluded that neither the Kacharis nor the Jaiantias would cause further trouble.

It had been an exhausting campaign, with the result not commensurate with the expense both in terms of men and material. Almost 2,500 Ahom soldiers had perished; though some amount of booty was captured, given the opulence of the royal coffers at the moment, they did not add significantly to it. At the same time, Rudra Singha understood that rather than treat the Kachari and Jaiantia principalities as territory under occupation, it would be wiser to give them back to their rajas after exhibiting to the latter the might of the Ahom kingdom and instilling in them such awe and reverence that they would stick to the terms of agreement. The Ahom king decided to return to Rongpur from Sala where he was temporarily stationed, and to hold a grand raj durbar, in the manner his bairagis and katakis had told him the Mughal emperors often did. There he would formally give the release orders for Tamradhwaj and Ram Singha, who were being held at a fortified camp near Bishwanath.

Preparations for the durbar went into full swing when the rainy season ended. Meanwhile invitations to the event had been carried to kings and potentates all over India, though without fail they sent back courteous notes stating their regrets at not being able to attend the durbar due to pressing engagements of their own. In truth, the fame of this Assamese race, which even the mighty Mughals could not conquer, and the charmed land which had killed a warrior like Mir Jumlah, had spread far and wide. No potentate in his right mind would even contemplate setting foot in that land of sorcerers! Only the Tripura maharaja, Ratnamanika, with whom the Ahom swargadeo had established cordial relationship by exchanging letters and gifts through embassies, though he could not personally attend, conveyed that he would send representatives to the occasion. The two katakis who had been sent to that principality had, on their return, not merely related the exciting nature of their journey to Tripura, but also written a manuscript titled *A Narrative about the Tripura Kingdom*.

However, the many vassal rajas and chiefs of the Naga and other tribes had sent in their acceptance of the invitation and arrangements were made in the city of Rongpur to accommodate them. The rajsora or audience hall within the newly built palace, despite its reasonably big dimensions, was considered to be inadequate for such a grand occasion, so an enormous temporary rajsora was built on open ground using pillars plated with gold and silver. Silver foil was used to cover up the thatched roof so that the rajsora shone like a jewel in the muted winter sunshine. The finest silks of a land famous for its high-quality paat and muga were used as screens to shade the sides of the structure; carpets covered the long and straight pathway from the entry where dignitaries would dismount from their elephants or horses. The path was lined with gold- and silver-plated flagpoles atop which fluttered countless flags and pennons. This was an official and not public event; even so, an open field, segregated from the rajsora area by bamboo barricades, was kept aside for the general public which was unlikely to miss such a grand occasion, even if the people had to watch the gathering from afar.

At the rear of the rajsora a huge stage of wood was built. At the centre of the stage was a seven-tiered wooden platform slightly higher than the floor of the stage. Upon it were two thrones made of gold, the legs of which were given the shape of lion heads, one throne bigger than the other. The thrones were cushioned and padded with bolsters of cotton covered with silk, and the bigger throne, meant for the swargadeo, had a gem-encrusted umbrella of gold over it, fixed to a golden staff—this umbrella was an emblem of Ahom sovereignty. There was space behind the raised platform for bodyguards as well as two bichoni- or fan-wielders to stand. Above the thrones were seven layers of cloth canopies, replicating the canopies over the thrones in the palace rajsora. The seven tiers of the platform were lacquered and decorated with indigenous herbal colours; the top of each step was plated in gold and encrusted with gems. Four large koloshis of gold were placed at the four corners of the raised platform to add to the ostentation.

Seats shaped like thrones, though less ostentatious than the ones meant for the swargadeo and the bor kuonri or chief queen, were placed on the stage on either side of the raised platform for the nobles and royal family to sit. Just below the stage were placed rows of similar throne-like seats facing the carpeted aisle leading to the stage stairs; these were meant for invited dignitaries. Beyond them were rows and rows of cushioned seats of bamboo and cane for other invitees; these faced the stage and were meant for officers and other important citizens of Rongpur. All in all, over 500 individuals could be accommodated in the makeshift rajsora.

Immediately outside it were placed telling symbols of Ahom might: seven rows of cannons captured in various wars. A phalanx of caparisoned elephants would also be in place on the actual day of the durbar to ceremonially greet invitees. Five hundred soldiers, armed with an array of weapons including the Ahom hengdang, would come to attention at the arrival of some of the important dignitaries, a list of whose names had already been prepared. An additional space had been created just behind the stage using silk partitions to form two compartments: one filled with gifts which would be given to some of the attendees from other areas and the other to store the gifts that would be brought by them.

A piece of bad news brought by messengers could not dampen the preparations for the raj durbar—the Jaiantia king, who had been kept in confinement at Bishwanath, had been afflicted with a severe case of dysentery and had passed away. Though his son had been incarcerated with him, he was considered too young for a durbar of this kind so it was decided that only Tamradhwaj should attend. A few days before the durbar, the Kachari king and the Jaiantia prince were ferried across to the south bank of the Brahmaputra on the royal barge; from there, they were taken to Rongpur on elephants and accommodated in a guest house within the palace complex.

Rongpur was agog with excitement on the day of the durbar. Nothing like this had ever happened in the Ahom realm; every citizen that day was proud to be an Assamese. The section earmarked for the public was so filled that there was real danger of some of them dying if a stampede took place, and officers and soldiers had a tough time controlling them. One by one, the guests began to arrive at the appointed hour; the tribal leaders came in their colourful traditional dresses. The nobles and their families were dressed in their best; the ornaments worn both by the ladies and the men sparkled, causing women in the crowd to gasp in delight. Only when all the invitees had arrived and were seated in their respective places was information sent to the king.

He and his family travelled to the venue on a procession of elephants, led by a troupe of singing and dancing gayon-bayon. Deafening cheers rose from the crowd as the procession was sighted; shouts of 'long live Swargadeu Sukhrungpha' emanated from it—the king was indeed popular with the public. A volley of small-arms was fired in the air by troops to signal his arrival at the durbar venue; the patra-mantris received him at the entrance and escorted the group across the carpeted aisle even as the audience rose to their feet in a show of respect. The king and his chief queen walked at the head with measured steps, waving their hands at the waiting audience. The other royal family members were guided to their seats while the monarch and his queen ascended the steps and sat down on the thrones. Once they were seated, members of the audience bowed to them and sat down.

The swargadeo, tall and handsome, looked imposing upon the throne. He had had seven royal costumes made for just such occasions, each cut in a style belonging to a particular region: Maandesh or Myanmar, Mungkong, China, Assam, Bengal, Delhi and Rajasthan. For this occasion, he had chosen traditional Ahom attire, requisitioned from the royal storehouse where these were kept: a churiya or dhoti made from the finest paat silk, a long, flowing shirt also of fine paat silk, a half-jacket on top with a vine-like pattern woven into it with golden thread, and a pair of shoes with curling toes imported from Bengal. On his head was a paag or turban made of white paat, wound around the head in a typical Shan style. The monarch had also requisitioned from the royal storehouse an entire set of ornaments for the occasion: all ten fingers of his hand had diamond rings, while gold bracelets encrusted with jewels were around his wrists, and gold and diamond necklaces hung from his neck. A huge diamond was affixed to the front of his paag, while rows of pendant jewels were attached to its sides so that they dangled lower than the king's earlobes. The swargadeo carried his ceremonial hengdang, which was sheathed in a magnificent scabbard of gold encrusted with precious stones; however, when seated upon the throne he had placed his sword on a spot by the side of the throne marked for the purpose.

The bor kuonri, the elder daughter of Sandikoi Barphukan, looked beautiful in her ceremonial dress consisting of a silk blouse and a skirt that reached down to her ankles, and a mekhela which covered the entire body up to the waist, with the end draped like a scarf over one shoulder. As for ornaments, they matched those worn by the king, but hers were far more feminine and delicate. Behind the seated royal couple were two damsels, dressed ceremonially, wielding bichanis with long handles with precious stones encrusted on them; the hand fans were merely props for effect since the season was winter and the weather cool.

A message had been sent to the palace that the king had reached the durbar pavilion; Tamradhwaj had been ready and waiting upon the golden howdah placed on the back of a caparisoned elephant. Escorted by royal guards on the backs of elephants without howdahs, the Kachari raja was taken to the durbar venue. The waiting crowd, learning who he was, flung a chorus of imprecations at him. Tamradhwaj, on beholding the durbar venue, was amazed at the splenduor confronting him; he had feared the worst, and so was pleasantly surprised when the soldiers at the venue saluted him smartly while the buragohain himself came to usher him to the king's presence.

The noble had apprised him of the protocol to be followed, and Tamradhwaj understood that he would have to follow it to the letter for his own good. The audience remained seated as the Kachari raja marched till he was close to the throne and then flung himself prostrate before the Ahom monarch. Swargadeo Sukhrungpha loudly told him to rise, whereupon his captive stood up, arms clasped in front of him, head bowed in submissiveness. The barbarua next made a speech, whereby he acquainted the audience of the preceding events and the crime of which the Kachari raja stood accused. As he heard the words, Tamradhwaj's heart sank—apparently, all the courtesy and hospitality showered upon him in the past weeks was a sham and severe punishment surely awaited him!

The king spoke next, and all of the Kachari raja's apprehensions disappeared in a trice. The king reminded him of the gravity of the offence, but pledged to set him free if he pledged undying allegiance to the Ahom throne and to assist it whenever called upon to do so. 'I have ambitious plans for our people,' he told the Kachari raja, though the words were equally meant for the ears of the audience. 'You will learn of them in the none-too-distant future. When the time comes, are you agreeable to assist me with men and materials?'

'Certainly, Your Majesty,' replied Tamradhwaj. His quick agreement was not merely due to the reality that he had no other recourse. He had been overwhelmed by the power and grandeur of the Ahom monarch and understood that it was to his own advantage to ally with him.

Much to everyone's surprise, the swargadeo stood up from his throne, descended the seven stairs and embraced the Kachari king. This was the type of gesture that elicited true loyalty. Escorting his new ally to a chair marked for him, the king ascended to his throne and, once more seated, raised his hand as a signal. One by one his vassals came up to the foot of the throne, knelt and offered gifts they had brought; the bargohain introduced each raja or chieftain individually, and the Swargadeo nodded his head to each in acknowledgement. When by these tokens, their allegiance had been re-affirmed, he asked if any of them had grievances and had brought petitions. A junior officer went around collecting the petitions to be later scrutinized by the patra-mantris.

Finally, Swargadeo Sukhrungpha addressed the entire gathering. A brilliant orator, he spoke about the glorious history of the Ahom race and the gallantry with which it had protected the kingdom the nucleus of which was begun by Chaolung Sukapha and which today had expanded to embrace the entire valley of the Luit. With due preparations, the time had now arrived to take the battle into the enemy camp; no longer would the Assamese people merely defend themselves from external aggressors; the time was now ripe to go on the offensive. The contours of these preparations would be revealed in the near future; the Ahom empire will undergo further expansion. He expected that those present in the gathering would vouchsafe every asset at their disposal to the motherland when asked to do so.

'But that is in the future,' the king concluded. 'Tonight is an occasion to eat, drink and be merry. I am inviting you all to a banquet to be held in this venue in honour of our latest ally, Tamradhwaj, the raja of the Kacharis. He will taste of our hospitality before being plied with gifts and escorted to his own realm tomorrow.'

The evening's banquet was a sumptuous affair, as much for the food and drinks served as for the cultural programme which accompanied the feasting. The throne and chairs had been removed from the stage and it now became a platform for a wondrous variety of cultural performances the likes of which many in the audience had rarely seen. Except for the swargadeo and his bor kuonri, who were served at a small table segregated from the others, the rest of the invitees partook of a buffet feast laid out on tables on the sides of the pavilion. The culture-minded amongst them came close to the stage with their food to hear and see more closely the items being presented, while those more comfortable with merely eating and drinking stood at a distance away. The royal family as well as the nobles mingled freely with the invitees; the officer for cultural affairs acted as the master of ceremonies, introducing the performers as also explaining some of the exotic items being performed.

The show began with a recital by the poet laureate Kaviraj Chakraborty, one of the jewels in Swargadeo Sukhrungpha's court, in honour of the present monarch. It was unabashedly sycophantic, but neither the king, nor the audience, appeared to mind. This was followed by a native song from Bengal, and then a folk dance by a troupe from the same region. Unusual performances, such as a recital of classical music by an ustaad brought by a khaund from faraway Delhi, whose ancestors had reputedly performed in the court of the Mughal emperor Akbar, were interspersed with local performances including those from hill tribes such as the Nagas. The evening ended with a Bihu-huchari dance, which had been deemed by royal authority as the national dance of the realm; the audience, including the patra-mantris, were induced to join in and shake a leg.

The very next morning, the Kachari Raja Tamradhwaj, after having been laden with assorted gifts, was escorted by Ahom troops up to the place called Demera, where his own soldiers awaited him. The Ahom monarch met the son of Ram Singha in a private audience; it was agreed that he would give his two sisters in marriage to the Ahom king in exchange for freedom and would also assist him in his expansionist designs.

As he grew older, Swargadeo Sukhrungpha, who had been a deeply devout individual from childhood, grew even more religious-minded. Questions of life and death troubled him. Not that he was dissatisfied with the life he had led or the work he had done. The kingdom was at peace; the Mughal wars as well as the dark days of conspiracy and killings within the royal palace were in the distant past; his subjects were content and prosperous. Yet, deep within him, was the fear he had not done enough to earn his path to paradise in afterlife. To some extent it had been the Brahmin priests who were responsible for the doubt and fear in his mind. For quite some years now, these priests, who had earlier enjoyed a status secondary to the Deodhai, Bailung and Moran traditional Ahom priests in the religious activities of the Swargadeo, had begun to dominate proceedings in the palace. Their version of afterlife differed from that of the Ahom priests; according to them, Indralok or the realm of the gods was not automatically attained by a swargadeo though he was of divine ancestry; it was through constant practise of rituals prescribed by the Brahmin priests and periodic donations to them that the king could ensure acceptance into paradise.* Although the Ahom kings, way back, had embraced Hinduism, they had not been actually ordained into the religion and had not taken 'sharan'—become a disciple of a Brahmin dharma-guru. This involved his prostrating himself before a Brahmin seer who would teach him the secret mantras or spells, and take him under his spiritual protection.

Also, there was another drawback—the Ganga was the holiest of holy rivers for a Hindu; the swargadeo had not taken a dip in it. He had not visited any of the holy tirthas, only one of which, the Kamakhya temple, lay within his realm. If he really wanted to attain salvation, he must make up for these drawbacks by immediately becoming an acolyte to a guru and going on a pilgrimage to holy places beside the Ganga and purifying himself in that holy river.

It had been such warnings from his Brahmin priests, which had disturbed the swargadeo and he grew determined to make good his shortcomings—in the way of emperors, naturally! Discussions with his patra-mantris made one conclusion obvious. Since all Brahmins within his kingdom were his subjects, he, as a king, could not prostrate himself before them—this was not quite what the Brahmin head priest of the palace had envisaged, but he could do nothing to resist it! The answer to the problem was to find a Brahmin seer from outside who could be summoned to Assam to give sharan to the swargadeo.

Khaunds were sent to the holy places of Bengal and Oudh to scour for a Brahmin seer worthy to be a mentor to the emperor of the mighty Ahom dynasty. However, there were few takers for the offer. Finally, however, the king's emissaries discovered a seer willing to come to the Ahom kingdom, but not to the capital. He would only come to Kamakhya and set up residence in that holy tirtha and the king, if he wanted 'sharan', could come to him there.

---

* Please refer to Rajkumar, *Itihashe Suonra Sashata Bachar* (2000); Barbarua, *Ahomor Din* (1981).

'His name is Krishnaram Bhattacharya Nyaybagis, Your Majesty,' the Khaund who brought the information told his king. 'He is a renowned Shakta priest who lives at Malipota, near Shantipur in Nadia district in Bengal. It is said that he is the performer of wondrous miracles. Once, when he was bathing in the Ganga, a singora fish is said to have pricked him with its spine. It is said that he cursed that all singora fish in the Ganga must die and from that day forth there were no such fish in that river! That is why this seer is also known as tengeramora or fish-killer!'

Krishnaram Bhattacharya was brought in state and installed as the Parbatiya gossain at the Neelachal Hill upon which stood the legendary temple of Kamakhya even as Swargadeo Sukhrungpha awaited an opportune moment to go and take sharan under him. Simultaneously, the Ahom king began preparations for his other plan—it was neither safe nor feasible for him to go on a pilgrimage and take a dip in the Ganga. Practical man that he was, he considered that the sole solution was to conquer Bengal and perhaps beyond so that a part of the river Ganga flowed through Ahom territory and other tirthas came under his sway.

This was not beyond the realm of feasibility. During his reign, the Ahoms had become a power to reckon with. Emperor Aurangzeb had died; the Mughal kingdom was in a state of disarray; his successors in Delhi were at each other's throats and Mughal outposts were extremely vulnerable. In fact, when he sent trusted emissaries to rajas of different parts of India, requesting that they not interfere in his design to usurp Mughal territory, some of them asked him as the potent swarga-maharaja of Assam to attempt a takeover of Delhi itself and teach those Mughal bullies a lesson. Rudra Singha also contacted vassals under him, including the Kacharis and Jaiantias, as well as vassal chieftains at the frontiers of Assam known as the Satrajas and Panchrajas, and received confirmation of their willingness to help in his endeavour.

The intelligent swargadeo quickly realized that in order to carry out his expansionist ambition, he needed to base himself in the strategically located city of Guwahati and organize his campaign from there rather than Garhgaon or Rongpur. Also, he could kill two birds with one stone by temporarily shifting to Guwahati—Krishnaram was already there and he could take sharan under him. So it was that, after gathering together all his military resources in Upper Assam, Swargadeo Sukhrungpha, at the end of the rainy season, set out for Guwahati, little knowing that he would never see his beloved Rongpur again.

It was a sight the inhabitants of the Ahom kingdom would never behold again. Hundreds of elephants and horses with the king at the front, thousands of infantrymen marching in step, and a huge armada of war boats sailing down the Luit! The army continued to swell as it proceeded towards Guwahati; once there, it reached 4,00,000 in number, with the allies and frontier chiefs throwing in their lot with him. The Kachari raja came with a force of 14,000 and the Jaiantia raja with 10,000; from Darrang district arrived tribal chiefs with soldiers including 600 warriors of the Dafla tribe. The ammunition manufacturing factories at Kharguli at Guwahati had to work overtime; cannons were collected from everywhere to empower the artillery wing. Such was the frenzy of war preparations that its tremors were felt as far as Delhi.

Even as he was framing his war strategy, on an auspicious day, Rudra Singha rode on horseback to Kamakhya temple for a preliminary audience with Krishnaram Bhattacharya Nyaybagis. He had gone with high expectations, hoping to encounter an impressive-looking saint who would explain to him the secrets of human existence. On the contrary, what he saw was an ordinary looking Brahmin who, though highly intelligent, appeared to be more a greedy upstart rather than a truly holy seer. The swargadeo consequently refused to prostrate before Krishnaram; whereupon the Brahmin was offended and returned home in anger.

A few days later, a severe earthquake rocked the area around Guwahati; though not many were killed in the disaster, some temples had been shattered; the Brahmin priests in the king's entourage told him that the gods were angry with him for having insulted the Shakta priest. By nature a superstitious individual, Rudra Singha grew convinced this was so, and implored Nyaybagis to return to Kamakhya offering a generous land grant. Krishnaram finally relented and came once more to settle in Neelachal and accept the land grant; but to show that he had been offended, rather than grant an audience to the monarch and teach him the bij mantra, the primary incantation which a neophyte must recite, he wrote it down on a leaf of the bel tree and had it delivered to him through an acolyte. It was now the king's turn to be offended; once again he refused to take sharan with Krishnaram, but advised his sons and nobles to do so. He also kept his pledge of bestowing a land grant upon Krishnaram on Nilachal Hill. Since he had settled upon a hill, Krishnaram became the progenitor of an order called Parbatiya Gossain or hill priests.

The news that the mighty emperor of Assam would pit himself against the redoubtable Mughals had spread like wildfire; it seemed that all of India awaited the outcome. Meanwhile war preparations were being redoubled, the intention being to begin the expansionist campaign in the month of November, 1714. But in September that year, tragedy suddenly struck. The Ahom king was afflicted with smallpox and bedridden. His eldest son, Shiva Singha, whom he had left in charge at Rongpur as prince-regent, rushed to Guwahati on learning of this. Sacrifices of 12 buffaloes, 100 goats and 150 pigeons were made at Kamakhya and gold donated to the deity there. Donations were made at other temples and devalayas praying for the king's recovery but his condition worsened day by day.

Various legends grew up around the death of the illustrious king. It is said that a Brahmin named Mukolimuriya Bhattacharya agreed to undertake deep meditation at the Bhubaneshwari temple and was rewarded for volunteering. While meditating various forces of darkness tried to distract him, but he resisted each in turn. Finally, the goddess herself appeared and said that the king would die in a year's time.

Unfortunately, this proved to be untrue and three days later, Swargadeo Sukhrungpha, also known as Rudra Singha, succumbed to his illness.

With his death died the Ahom ambition of conquering Bengal and bringing the Ganga within the realm. The huge army was disbanded and the rajas and chiefs returned to their own territories. The great king, deeply influenced by the Brahmin priests, had ordained during his final days that he should be cremated like Hindus on a pyre rather than be buried in a maidam in the manner of Ahoms. He was, therefore, cremated on the Manikeshwar Hill in north Guwahati, the last rites being performed with Hindu rituals by Brahmin priests, the first Ahom king to be so cremated. However, in deference to the objections of the Deodhai, Bailung and Mohan priests, his son Shiva Singha carried the ashes in an urn back to Rongpur. With due ceremony, along a route thronged with mourning subjects, the urn was then taken to Cheraidai and buried in a magnificent maidam befitting the status of Rudra Singha the Great.

Era of Queens

～

THE AHOM KING WAS IN A TERRIBLE DILEMMA. HE HAD BEEN unable to sleep the past few nights because of his preoccupation with a problem; so much so that he had had to ask the royal physician to provide him a nostrum to help him get some sleep. The more he pondered over the issue, the colder became the icy chill gripping his heart.

Was he fated to bring an end to the empire that Chowlung Sukapha had begun and individuals like his revered father Chao Sukhrungpha had taken to great heights? His dying father in Guwahati had given him two basic instructions—as the eldest son he must assume the emperor's mantle after his father's death and he must make Krishnaram Bhattacharya his religious guru. His father too had advised his four younger brothers to assume kingship in turn after one another's death rather than engage in conspiracies to grab the throne.

He had obeyed his father's deathbed wishes to the letter. He and his chief wife Phuleshwari had taken Krishnaram's sharan—he had no objection to this, for both of them were diehard Shakta Hindus. However, again in deference to his father's instructions, he had not bowed his head before the Shakta Brahmin, but took sharan in a somewhat peculiar manner. He climbed up a hillock in Guwahati almost to the very top. Krishnaram Bhattacharya Nyaybagis had climbed up

315

the same hill earlier and stood at its peak. Thus, he could tie a garland around the head of the king without the latter having to bow before him. Since that hill at Guwahati was the place where Shiva Singha had taken sharan, it came to be known as Sharaniya Pahar or hill where sharan was taken.

His father had already bestowed a land grant upon Krishnaram on Nilachal Hill. On Phuleshwari's advice, he built dwellings for the Brahmin and, taking away the power of managing the Kamakhya temples from the priests who had been traditionally doing so, vested it on Krishnaram. So powerful did this priest become during Shiva Singha's reign that his writ ran even in Garhgaon and Rongpur, the twin capitals of the Ahom kingdom.

Next, he had had to dismantle the huge army raised by his father—it had been a severe test of his tact and diplomacy to send the various rajas and chiefs back from the warfront without objections or complications. After cremating his father and leaving the barphukan in charge at Guwahati, he had rushed back to Rongpur carrying the urn containing the ashes. The king was familiar with the history of his race. If the throne was left unoccupied for long, jackals waiting in the wings would be tempted to take a bite at it!

There had been no problem however; his father had streamlined the administration and ensured that traditional Ahom protocol would be followed by the nobles in future; thus, in the winter of 1714, Shiva Singha had ascended the singorighar at Rongpur and taken on the Ahom name of Sutanpha. It was no surprise that he retained the Hindu name of Shiva Singha given to him by his father; after all, Shiva's consort Parvati, who had many forms including Durga and Kali, was the primary deity of the Shaktas. For eight long years, apart from some trouble with the Dafla hill tribe which had raided Ahom territory and was dealt with firmly—though he had to build the Dafla garh, a defensive rampart to keep that fierce tribe from raiding the plains-people in future—the kingdom was at peace with itself. He ruled in the manner his father had, firmly but fairly.

He was, however, no Rudra Singha. For one thing, he had an extremely suspicious mind, not trusting anyone apart from his wife. His very first action on becoming the king was to establish a fine network of spies throughout the kingdom. So effective was this network that no dubious act or word anywhere in the realm could remain secret from the king. At the same time, he was deeply superstitious and totally under the influence of his bor kuonri or chief queen Phuleshwari, who was a more ardent Hindu than even him. This was why, when the Brahmin priests of the palace came to him with their dire prediction, he had turned to her for a solution to the problem.

They had to remain formal in public, but within the privacy of their bedroom, well guarded outside, they could lay bare intimate secrets of their hearts.

'You seem deeply worried, my lord,' Phuleshwari cradled his head on her lap and gently stroked his hair.

'I am, my love. Our priests came to me with a terrible prophecy.'

'The Ahom priests, my lord? Surely you no longer believe in their mumbo-jumbo? Our Brahmin priests are the only ones who matter now.'

'You must not dismiss our Ahom priests so lightly, my love,' said the king. 'Their tradition of foretelling events has come down through centuries, and time and again they've been proven right. But, on this occasion, it is the Brahmin priests who have calculated my horoscope and come to very serious conclusions.'

Queen Phuleshwari too became grave. 'What do the astrologers foretell?'

'They surmise that the "Chhatrabhanga phase" has arrived.'

'Huh, what's that?' the queen, surprised, asked.

'The chatra or the gold umbrella which shades the royal throne and is an emblem of Ahom sovereignty will be broken if I continue to remain the king. That is what our Brahmin priests have warned me. It means that the Ahom supremacy might end unless I relinquish my kingship.'

A cunning glint appeared in the queen's eyes, and she took pains to avoid looking directly at her husband. 'Have you discussed this prediction with your nobles?'

'Yes. They too are concerned. Domai Buragohain dangoriya has advised me to give the throne to my brother Pramatta. Thanunath Bargohain agrees with him.'

'That, my dear husband, would be a foolish thing to do. Once a king lets go the reins of power, others wait in the wings to devour his carcass.'

'But there appears to be no alternative,' the king said ruefully.

'Of course, there is!' Phuleshwari asserted.

'So, what do you suggest?'

'First, my lord, you must send emissaries to Guwahati and get the prediction confirmed by our guru, His Holiness Krishnaram Bhattacharya. Only if he confirms that the calculations are correct should you think of taking the second step.'

'That would be advisable. I'll get our guru's opinion at the earliest. What about our Ahom priests? Should they not be consulted too?'

'There is hardly any need of that! If our guru confirms the prediction, that can be taken as the last word. You will need to reward the Brahmin priests for their diligence, and give them land and gold. Then you must take the most important step.'

'What is that, my love?'

'Place me on the throne as your surrogate and rule the kingdom through me. I have acquainted myself with the history of our people. When King Tyaokhamphti went to battle the Chutiyas, he appointed his bor kuonri to occupy the throne in his absence.'

The king remained silent for some time, mulling over the suggestion. The more he thought about it, the more attractive the idea appeared. He understood all too well the peril he would confront if he handed over the reins of the kingdom to his brother—there were too many examples of brothers killing or maiming brothers for the sake of power for him to assume otherwise.

'I'll have the Brahmin priests insist that this is sole solution,' the queen interposed, observing the hesitation in her husband. 'That will overcome any objections that might come from the patra-mantris.'

'They will need some convincing!' The king continued to remain dubious. 'My ancestor Tyaokhamphti had simply empowered his chief queen to govern in his absence ... she was not given the throne or allowed to sit on it. Also, Chowlung Sukapha had enjoined that only someone from his lineage can sit on the Ahom throne. You, my dear, hail from a commoner family.'

This was true enough. Before her marriage to the king, she had been a nat or professional dancer–musician and was known by the name of Phulmoti Nachoni. The king, while he was a prince, had become enamoured of her renowned beauty and married her, changing her name to Phuleshwari and making her the Parbatiya princess. Later, when he became king, she was made the bor kuonri.

'But I'll be the king in name only,' Phuleshwari assured him. 'You will conduct the affairs of the state and all I will do is put my seal of approval on your decisions. Surely the nobles will understand how sensible an arrangement this will be, particularly if we have the Brahmin priests backing us.'

The chief queen knew that the Brahmin priests would support her even without being told to, since she had them eating out of her hands. The king finally arrived at a decision. 'The emissary I send to our guru at Guwahati would also tell him about your suggestion. If His Holiness Krishnaram approves, it will be done."

The emissary to the Parbatiya gossain Krishnaram went to Guwahati and returned post-haste. The guru had made his calculations of the king's horoscope and come to the same conclusion as the Brahmin priests that the 'Chhatrabhanga phase' had indeed arrived. He too was of the opinion that it would be foolish of Shiva Singha to let go the reins of power. Instead, he should make Phuleshwari the nominal king and manage the affairs of the state using her as a front.

The conclusions of the Shakta Brahmin were communicated to the nobles. Quite a few of them had, under instructions from the dying Rudra Singha, taken sharan of Krishnaram. Thus, when the guru himself had asserted his opinion, it was not very difficult for Swargadeo Sutanpha to convince them that he must step down from the throne and install the bor kuonri in his place.

Little did the king know that Phuleshwari's personal and secret emissary had gone even more swiftly than the official katoki to Guwahati to apprise Krishnaram of the situation and instruct him as to what he should say.

The washing ghat was unusually devoid of women this morning. Only two of them, Akori and Saruai, were there, sitting side by side as they scrubbed their laundry upon flat stones set out on the riverbank for the purpose. Even as they worked, they discussed affairs of the state!

'What's the world coming to!' exclaimed Akori, imparting an extra-hard thrust upon the piece of cloth she was scrubbing to drive home her point. 'A woman placed on the throne at Rongpur! And the Swargadeo playing underling to her!'

'Oh yes, strange times are ahead, mark my words!' responded Saruai, nodding her head vigorously in agreement. 'They say the astrologers had predicted chhatrabhanga if the swargadeo did not step down. But he could well have given the throne away to his brother. Instead, he has placed on the sanctified throne that hussy he took as his wife and made the bor kuonri. Imagine, they have coined a new phrase for her since such a situation has never risen in the history of our people. She will be called Bar-Raja or Uthi-Raja. The swargadeo himself will be the Bohi-Raja and carry out her directives.'

'It's a shame that the patra-mantris agreed to the arrangement,' said Akori.

'Oh, they couldn't have done otherwise if they wanted to keep their heads on their shoulders,' said Saruai with a knowing wink at her companion.

'But at least they could have made less of a fuss of it. All that pomp and pageantry ... It's as if a real swargadeo and not a fake one were ascending the throne. Thank heavens they did not build a singorighar for her to climb!'

'If my sources at the palace tell me right, Swargadeo Sutanpha is the most henpecked of husbands. Everything that has happened is as she wished. So now our Phulmoti Nachoni who became Phuleshwari Bor Kuonri has now taken on the new name of Pramatheshwari after she was handed the throne. Do you know the significance of that name?'

'It's another name for Goddess Durga, isn't it?'

'Right you are. So, she imagines herself to be an incarnation of the goddess, does she? Mark my words, no good will come of it. The Brahmins have become all-powerful in the palace, and neither Vaishnavs like us nor the Ahom priests have any say any more.'

'Oh, she has already brought her folks to the palace and given them royal appointments. Just imagine, the new barpatragohain is Haranath, her younger brother, whom she brought from her native village of Kalugaon. It is rumoured that she has also struck coins in her name along with that of the swargadeo, using both Phuleshwari and Pramatheshwari while doing so. I've yet to see one, though.'

'As if the likes of us will ever get to touch gold and silver coins!' Saruai said wistfully. 'Some people, dear Akori, have all the luck in the world ...'

The nobles saw it, but the king did not. The chief queen was using her nominal position to get her own way, but the patra-mantris were powerless to stop it. She was highly intelligent, they acknowledged. Having been a dancer, she also had an artistic temperament and encouraged aesthetic activities. There were certain good undertakings she had embarked on. For instance, she was determined to spread education amongst her subjects and established a number of tols or educational centres for the purpose. But she wanted only children of Brahmin families to be educated and patronized the learned amongst them. A large institute providing rudimentary education was opened by her at Rongpur and was popularly known as Bar Rajar school. She issued a directive that any Brahmin who was illiterate should not be allowed into the pujas conducted in the palace.

She also displayed immense respect for learned individuals, her favourites being the poet laureate Kaviraj Chakraborty, and other intellectuals of her father-in-law's court, such as Ruchinath Dvij, the author of *Chandir Payar* and *Kalki Puran*, and Sivada Sarma, who wrote *Navaratna*. Under her advice, Kaviraj Chakraborty wrote the *Shakuntala Kavya* as also the drama *Sankhachur Bodh*, and translated the *Brihat Brahmabaibartapuran* and Jaydev's *Geet Govinda*. On her instructions Kabichandra Sarma wrote the play *Kamkumarharan*, and Ananta Acharya the *Anandalahiri*. She was also instrumental in getting a treatise written on horses titled *Ghora Nidan*. Her husband Shiva Singha had inherited a passion for composing poems and hymns from his father; not only did Phuleshwari encourage him in his literary pursuits, she also ensured that the royal palaces at Garhgaon and Rongpur became centres for literary and cultural activities, and books on various subjects were brought out. However, even the nobles realized that such activities were confined to Brahmin culture and were far removed from those with which the subjects were familiar. The Vaishnav sattras, for example, were hives of literary and cultural activities, and were producing new literature in Assamese and ushering in a cultural renaissance. But the palace was no longer patronizing the sattras; thus, an immense cultural gap was gradually developing between the royalty and common masses.

Endowed with the fanaticism newly ordained devotees often display, she inspired her husband to undertake extensive construction of Shakta temples and devalayas. On the lines of Jaisagar, she had the huge Gaurisagar tank dug in honour of the devi or goddess representing Shakti and on its bank were constructed three dols or temples which came to be known as Gaurisagar Bordol, Gossaindol and Devidol. She ordained that her brother Haranath, who had been made the barpatragohain, dig a similar water tank, to be called Lakshmisagar, at their ancestral village of Kalugaon and build two temples on its bank, a Shivadol and a Jagadhatridol. Instructions were sent to the barphukan to renovate the Ugratara devalaya at Guwahati and dig the twin pukhuris or water tanks called Jorpukhuri so that devotees could have a holy dip before worship. The same instructions contained a directive to build a temple at Ashwakranta, which Bijaya Duara, the barphukan, complied with. Numerous devalayas and thans, such as the Pingaleshwar

Devalaya, Gopeshwar Shiva Devalaya, Bhungeshwar Shiva Devalaya, Jagganath Devalaya, Siddeshwar Devalaya, Parihareshwar Devalaya and Agnibaneshwar Than, were constructed in different parts of the kingdom and there was a concerted attempt to take Brahmin Hindu religion to the subjects.

Apart from religious structures, a number of civic projects were also undertaken, such as the building of the Dhai Ali, a road constructed to commemorate the nanny who took care of Shiva Singha during his childhood. It was during this period that concrete bridges were built over some rivers, the Na-duarmukh Sako being an example. Extensive census and surveys of subjects were carried out in parts of the kingdom under the stewardship of two officers designated as darbadhara barua and jotokiya barua and the data recorded. These records, called pera kagaz, contained a list of all allotted land except homesteads, with size and other details. They were of great use in carrying out amelioration activities and were carefully preserved in archives for future reference.

The nobles had no objection to such activities; what they minded was the fact that the bor kuonri appeared to have forgotten that she was a proxy for the king and often behaved towards them as if she indeed was the empress of the realm. They were disconcerted to find that her uxorious husband ignored her transgressions and let her have her way. They were offended that she had become presumptuous enough to even place her name along with the swargadeo's on coins that were struck. Ever since 1543, following examples of kings of other Indian realms, when Swargadeo Suklenmung had struck coins in the fourth year of his reign, Ahom monarchs with few exceptions had followed the practice. The legend on Suklenmung's coin was in the Assamese language and characters, one side giving the name of the king, 'The great King Suklenmung, fifteenth year of cycle', and the other the name of his favourite deity: 'The king offers prayers to Tara'. Striking of coins was more a show of authority and power since coins were rarely used for purchase of commodities and the barter system prevailed, though later the use of cowries and conch shells was introduced for minor transactions. Thus, whenever a king with prospects of occupying the throne for a while ascended it, he would strike coins in his name to commemorate the occasion.

Only during the reign of Shiva Singha's father, the progressive Rudra Singha, did coins begin to be minted with greater frequency to be used for trading. An Ahom coin, following a practice adopted by regions in other parts of India, particularly Kochbehar, which had wielded some cultural and commercial influence upon the Ahom kingdom, weighed a tola or ninety-six rattis. Also, it was in the eighteenth century, during the reign of Rudra Singha, that smaller coins of forty-eight and twenty-four rattis were minted and circulated. Advised by Shiva Singha, his queen Phuleshwari began minting coins of even smaller dimensions of twelve and six ratis. However, as during the days of his predecessors, coins were of gold and silver and copper was never actually used. Three languages, Sanskrit, Assamese and Parsi, were used while inscribing coins on different occasions and of different denominations.

Unlike other parts of India, the coins minted by the Ahoms were not round but octagonal in shape. This was because the number eight held special significance for the community. The mythical progenitor of the Shan race, Lengdon, was the head of eight lakh gods and goddesses and had the power to unleash eight lakh thunderclaps; the great King Khenkham sat upon an eight-tiered throne; the serpent created by the Supreme Being Pha had eight hoods; Heaven was set upon eight pillars, etc. The Ahoms believed that a kingdom could expand on eight sides. The importance they gave to the number eight induced them to strike coins that were octagonal.

So far, only the name of the swargadeo had been mentioned upon a coin. But, as stated before, Phuleshwari, with the consent of the king, began to strike coins which bore her own name along with that of her husband, something which galled many of the nobles. A batch of coins which were struck under her orders in 1726 CE (1648 Saka era), for instance, had her name along with Shiva Singha's inscribed in letters on one side and those of Hara and Gauri (that is, Shiva and Parvati) on the other. Even more presumptuous seemed her experimentation with the minting of square coins in contradiction to prevalent Ahom practices—she had seen such coins being minted at Manipur and convinced her husband to do the same. Strangely enough, the lettering on these square coins was in the Parsi language with designations that were Islamic in nature; for instance, the batch struck in 1729 CE (1651 Saka era) read in Parsi: 'Shah Shiva Singha, sikka (rupee), struck by the order of Begum Pramatheshwari at Garhgaon in 1651'.

Her presumption in striking coins in her name alongside her husband's was merely a symptom of the authoritarianism that marked her behaviour; there were other issues, not the least being her constant overturning of counsel offered by the patra-mantris and getting her husband to act at her bidding. Her proactive championing of the Shakta religion and preference for Brahmins over all other religious priests, which she ensured that her husband shared, was disturbing the equilibrium in the palace. The Ahom priests were thoroughly upset; but even more sinister was the disaffection amongst her subjects, who were none too favourably inclined towards Brahmin-controlled Hinduism.

In the privacy of their bedroom, the king lay upon the bed, his head cradled on the lap of Bor Kuonri Phuleshwari. She stroked his hair and occasionally massaged his forehead.

'We're not doing enough, my lord,' she said suddenly.

'What are you talking about?' the king asked, surprised.

'Not doing enough about our religion. The bar raja and uthi raja are Shakta adherents ... the subjects must be the same. The religion of the rulers must be that of the subjects.'

'That's not the way we Ahoms think,' the king differed. 'The subjects in our realm are free to worship who they please. Such freedom enables you and me to be Shaktas, though our ancestors may have been adorers of the Somdeo.'

'Been a sore point with our palace's Ahom priests, that's for sure.' the queen's laughter was sweet as a temple bell. 'No, my lord, that should no longer be a tenet for the kingdom. Religious freedom offers a fertile ground for subversion. That is the reality of our Vaishnav sattras. The bhakats there follow the Ekasaran Namdharma preached by that heretic Sankardev—you may recall that he had escaped from the Ahom realm to take shelter in Kochbehar! A creed propounded by a heretic must not be the religion of the subjects. As I said, the religion of the subjects must be that of the rulers.'

'Let sleeping dogs lie, my love,' the king said, matching her laughter with his. 'Those monks have their faith, you and I ours. The salvation of the soul is a personal thing between each individual and the gods. No one else has a right to interfere.'

The bar raja decided she needed another argument to convince her husband. 'But what they preach is against the Ahom way of life,' she spoke with passion. 'They, for instance, wish their followers to abstain from meat and liquor. That is nothing but a recipe to make our Ahom warriors weaklings and cowards!'

'No, my love, that's a spurious argument,' the king replied nonchalantly. 'Sankardev's religion has been the main faith of the subjects for two centuries now. Yet our paik-soldiers, who follow that religion, have hardly been turned into weaklings and cowards. Else could my father have dreamt of conquering lands beyond Bengal?'

The queen conceded defeat. With her husband, at least. But, diehard Shakta that she was, she would carry on her endeavour to make the royal religion the subjects' religion all by herself. Let Durga Puja come. She will show these satradhikars and bhakats what it meant to follow a religion that was alien to the palace!

Akori and Saruai, neighbours as well as good friends, rushed frantically down a road in Garhgaon which led to the main gate of the city, their children and other family members in tow. The news had travelled fast. Four men from some alien world had come to visit the capital and were being granted an audience by Swargadeo Sutanpha. The grapevine asserted that the men had skins white as ivory and hair the colour of gold. The two women had, of course, seen men from other climes— soldiers who were captured during the war with the Mussalmans and brought into the realm to be settled here; traders who, having taken prior permission from the Ahom authorities, had come with their exotic wares from far-off places.

But those men, though taller than the average Assamese and possessing more facial hair, did not have ivory skin and golden hair. Surely the strangers, who waited at the gate this morning for the arrival of the king, were from some other heavenly body and not from the earth! Could they be emissaries from Lord Indra himself? Little wonder that the Deodhais had warned the king not to let them into the capital, and certainly not the palace, till he was sure of their antecedents! The king had granted them an audience, but would be meeting them outside the main gate.

Numerous citizens of Garhgaon, on hearing the news, were rushing towards the city's gate; the soldiers guarding the ramparts surrounding it had good-naturedly allowed the citizenry to climb onto them so as to get a better view of the proceedings. Akori and Saruai climbed agilely to the top and looked on at the scene unfolding before their amazed eyes.

Indeed, four of the men who waited with others at the outside of the gate had white skin and yellow-brown hair! They were also dressed in an outlandish fashion; they had come from the river ghat on hired dolas or palanquins, bearing along gifts for His Royal Highness. The men from Bengal who accompanied the strangers were dressed in traditional garb and appeared to be traders.

There was a sudden uproar amongst the crowd as the procession bearing the swargadeo was sighted; he arrived with fanfare, drummers and gong-beaters preceding the elephant that carried the Bor Kuonri Phuleshwari and the king on a gold howdah. It was a long procession— apparently all the folks in the palace wanted a glimpse of these strange beings from another planet! A wooden platform and two ornate thrones were being carried on other elephants; on reaching open ground outside the gate, servants unloaded these and set them up. The bar raja and uthi raja seated themselves on the thrones. The strangers were clearly surprised at the fact that the queen sat upon the larger throne, but knew better than to comment upon it.

The four strangers, as also the leader of the men escorting them, came up and prostrated themselves before the royal couple. The spectators, hundreds of them, raised a cheer at this. Surely these could not be divine messengers, since they had prostrated themselves before mortals. The queen signalled to the men to rise to their feet. 'Who are you?' she asked in Assamese. 'Where do you hail from?'

'We come from a far-away land, Your Majesty,' replied one of the strangers, a tall, strapping fellow with long, flowing locks like a woman's but yellow in colour. He spoke in the tongue of Bengal, which one of his native companions translated into Assamese. 'Like my companions here, we too are traders by profession. They spoke of a realm whose king was as powerful as the gods of heaven. It was our curiosity and sense of adventure which has brought us here.'

The stranger did not betray his astonishment that he had to address the queen, assuming that the monarchy of this realm, like his own, allowed for both men and women to be the monarch. 'And what is it that you call yourselves?' the queen, whose own curiosity was legendary, asked.

'We call ourselves British, Your Majesty. As for my personal name, I'm Godwin. With me are Bill, Lister and Mill.' The three other British gentlemen bowed. 'This is just a courtesy visit, Your Majesty,' Godwin continued. 'We have brought some gifts to show that we come with goodwill.'

'All right,' said the queen. 'We would have welcomed you into our palace and served you food and wine. But our priests have forbidden your entry into our city. So, we shall accept your gifts and you need to be on your way back to where you had intended to go.'

The rituals were quickly terminated. Servants came and took away the gifts which the strangers had brought along with them and presented to the royal couple. The men then bowed and withdrew and, embarking upon their dolas, headed for the river ghat where their trading vessels had been moored. The royal party too mounted their pachyderms and headed back for the palace.

'They were no katokis from Indra,' observed a disappointed Akori to Saruai. 'They were merely boga bangals, the white men from Bengal.'

The morning hours were the busiest for the bhakats or monks of the Moamaria sattra at Madarkhat. The morning prayer session had ended and the bhakats were occupied with allotted tasks; some were in the paddy fields and vegetable garden, some in the workshop making masks and utensils; a few of the more artistic ones were employed in inscribing holy texts on sanchi leaves using golden ink. The sattradhikar or the head of the monastery was within his private room absorbed in a one-act play he was composing when a teenage acolyte entered it.

'This is not the moment to disturb me,' the sattradhikar rebuked mildly.

'I realize that, Your Holiness,' the acolyte blurted out, worry and fright writ over his face. 'But there is bar raja's katoki at the gate along with a group of armed soldiers.'

Pausing his writing, the sattradhikar hurried to the spot. Indeed, a messenger from the royal palace was there along with soldiers. 'Are you the sattradhikar of the Madarkhat sattra?' the katoki asked.

That the bar raja had no love for followers of the gospel preached by Sankardev was an open secret. This was the cause of the trepidation the sattradhikar felt, though his face betrayed nothing.

'Yes. Is there anything wrong? Have we offended the bar raja in any way?'

'No, no,' the court official said with a smile. 'We have only come with an invitation. Exactly a week from now, you and half-a-dozen of your select bhakats are invited to the palace to join the Durga Puja celebrations.'

Try as he might, the sattradhikar could not conceal his relief. 'Please thank the bar raja for this kind invitation. We feel deeply honoured and privileged. Thank you too for taking the trouble to come to our sattra to invite us. May we request you to enter and partake of some food?'

'My apologies,' the katoki said. 'But we have other sattras to visit and cannot tarry.'

When he had stated that he felt honoured and privileged to be invited to the palace the sattradhikar was not merely being polite. It was, indeed, an unexpected gesture. It was well known that the bar raja was hostile towards the Vaishnav followers even though the masses were mostly adherents of Sankardev's faith. But apparently, she had had a change of heart. The royal invitation was an indication that she was willing to confer upon the Vaishnavs the same status as the Brahmin and Ahom priests.

Though pride had been considered a sin by Sankardev, yet the sattradhikar was but human. He could not help feeling proud that he was the keeper of a century-old legacy. Sankardev had many disciples such as Madhavdev and Damodardev to carry on the Ekasaran Namdharma movement; they in turn had their own disciples who spread out throughout the land to set up sattras and spread the gospel. Naturally, as the years rolled on, the main movement began to sprout different branches; the Mayamara sect, to which he belonged, was one such branch. It was founded by Aniruddhadev, a disciple of Gopaldev, an important figure in the Vaishnav movement.

Aniruddhadev was born in 1553 CE at Balikuchi village in North Lakhimpur. His mother, Ajoli Devi, was the daughter of Sankardev's youngest uncle. He grew up at a sattra in Kaljar, where he was educated and took sharan at the feet of his guru, Gopaldev. Soon he made his mark in spreading the Vaishnav movement and gathered disciples of his own. Legends of the wonderful powers he possessed began to grow up around him. It was said that he could, with the help of Dhatu Tamrakshwari Kalpataru Shastra gifted to him by Gopaldev, perform miracles. Along with his associate Jadumanidev, he came up the Brahmaputra and first set up a sattra at Nahorkotiya. Hearing about him, Khora Raja, who was the Ahom king in those days, had him brought to the rajsora to test the veracity of the legends. It was said that Aniruddhadev created an illusionary serpent before the king and then made it vanish. So impressed was the swargadeo with this maya or illusion that he bestowed the title of Mayamara upon Aniruddhadev. With the passage of time, his followers began to be called Mayamarias and later Moamarias.

There are other theories as to how the term Moamaria came about. It is said that because Aniruddhadev dwelt for a long time near the water body by the name of Moamari situated at Nowgong, his followers were called Moamarias.

Aniruddhadev and his followers set up Moamaria sattras at numerous places such as Puranimati, Na-pam, Dinjoy, Madarkhat and Garhpara. They were also called Motoks. A legend tells of how this came about. Prominent Moamaria disciples such as Laku Barpatragohain, Guimala Sholagohain, Neogphukan and others had informed Swargadeo Pratap Singha that they would not bow before anyone but their guru. The king tested them to see if this was true. He set up diagonally placed swords above a path and told the disciples to ride over it. Guimala and Neogphukan did as bid, but since they did not bow to avoid the swords, their heads were chopped off by them, which induced the king to end the test there and then. He called the sect Mot-ek, or single-minded, which in time became Motok. However, a more credible explanation was that followers of this sect were mostly concentrated in the area between the rivers Brahmaputra and the Buridihing called the Motok region, and thus were also called Motoks.

People from all tribes and creeds flocked to join the sect and the Moamaria sattras became powerful religious centres. Even some Brahmins and other upper-caste Hindus, as well as Ahoms, became members of the Moamaria community, though the bulk of it comprised people from the Moran tribe. The sattradhikar of Madarkhat was himself a sudra. However, though the Vaishnav faith was embraced by the subjects, the Shakta royalty at Garhgaon and Rongpur till now had chosen to treat it with contempt. That is why his gratification at being invited to the Durga Puja at the Rongpur palace was so great.

On the appointed day, the sattradhikar and six of his chosen disciples sailed down the Luit and up the Dikhau to be well in time to witness the puja rituals. The sattradhikar was open-minded enough to be curious about the practices followed by other faiths and was keen to see how the royal priests worshipped their deities. Rongpur was in a festive mood, though the common masses had no role in the actual puja. Their sole moment of participation would be when the idol would be brought ceremonially out from the palace compound for public immersion in the river Dikhau, and they would line up to witness the grand procession.

Though the puja was an exclusive affair within the palace compound, the open area before the palace temple was quite crowded—nobles and their families were there, as also the Brahmin priests, but the Ahom priests were absent. A huge idol of the ten-armed goddess Durga, seated upon a startlingly lifelike lion, one foot resting upon the figure of the demon Mahishasur who lay helpless on the ground, had been placed at the temple's altar. Artisans had been brought specially from Bengal to make this idol, which was robed in costly silk and draped with priceless ornaments. Priests were swaying in a hypnotic dance before the idol, loudly muttering esoteric mantras, the clay pots in their hands billowing incense smoke. A drummer squatted at one corner of the innermost sanctum of the temple repeating the same, monotonous beat upon a drum.

Close by the temple was the bolishal, or sacrificial altar, where buffaloes and goats brought for the sacrifice were tethered. Here too, Brahmin priests muttered mantras as periodically a beast was dragged to the altar and beheaded with a single stroke of a hengdang by a chaodang deployed for the purpose. Though most of the blood was collected in brass utensils, the ground at the bolishal was slushy red with gore.

Dressed in the plainest of robes, with not a single ornament gracing their bodies, the king and queen were seated on the floor of the temple, facing the idol. Their heads were bowed in supplication. Bereft of their royal attire and in that posture of humility, they hardly looked like a king and queen! The noise and the hustle and bustle were disorienting; the smell of blood and incense was sickening; it was an environment far different from the one in which the Vaishnavs prayed and contemplated. Somewhat confused and surprised at the fact that though they had been allowed to enter the palace compound at the gate after they had identified themselves, there was no one to welcome them and show them to their places, the Madarkhat sattradhikar looked around him. Then he saw them, at some distance away: monks and sattradhikars from other sattras, herded together like cattle in a separate enclosure, seated on the bare ground. Sudden suspicion that all was not what he had imagined snaked into the sattradhikar's mind; he fought it down and hastened with his disciples to join the Vaishnav monks in the enclosure.

His suspicions were not wrong. For an hour they were made to wait till, with the blaring of conch shells and ululation from the women present at the gathering, the priests concluded their worship. First to prostrate themselves before the deity were the king and queen. The Brahmin head priest showered blessings on the royal couple, sprinkled them with holy water, placed in their hands the nirmali or a red flower taken from those offered to the deity and with his thumb imprinted upon their foreheads a tilak or a mark with a red paste made of sindur and the blood of the sacrificed goats.

Things began to go horribly wrong after that. Having been blessed, the royal couple withdrew to their own special enclosure while everyone else prostrated themselves where they were. Confused mutterings broke out in the ranks of the Vaishnav monks and sattradhikars. Their religion forbade them from worshipping any idol. At the same time, Sankardev had insisted that all religions must be respected. They had come as guests and not as participants of the puja. Should they, therefore, in deference to the tenets of their faith, refrain from prostrating themselves before a clay idol? Or show the courtesy of guests by pandering to the hosts' faith?

Even as they were discussing this amongst themselves, the sudden appearance of a court official accompanied by a group of armed chaodang palace guards settled the matter for them. 'The bar raja commands that you prostrate yourself,' he barked at them. The monks and their mentors had no recourse but to obey. Much against their will, they hastily prostrated themselves as the Brahmin priests began showering their blessings upon the congregation.

Having received the blessings, members of the congregation led by the patra-mantris walked up one by one to the priests to be sprinkled with holy water, receive a flower and have the sindur-and-goat-blood tilak marked on the forehead. When even the most lowly of palace servants had been favoured with a tilak, the court official ordered the Vaishnav monks to proceed to the temple to accept nirmali and tilak.

'This goes against our religion,' the sattradhikar of Madarkhat objected loudly. 'On no account will we allow ourselves be marked with blood on our forehead.'

'Then prepare yourself to be chained and confined in the dungeon,' the official said nonchalantly. 'Then there will be a trial and perhaps death by beheading, just like those buffaloes and goats. The choice is yours!'

'We're guests here and must do what our hosts request of us,' interjected another Sattradhikar hastily. A murmur of assent from apprehensive throats broke out, seizing on the pretext.

One by one the monks, watched over by the palace guards, walked up to the Brahmin priests and had their head marked with a bloody tilak. Their sullen faces clearly showed inner revulsion, while there could be no mistaking the smile on the face of the bar raja: it was one of triumph.

The moment the ritual of receiving nirmali was over, the Vaishnavs did not tarry. The official and his guards did not try and stop them as they fled from the palace, angry and offended. The bar raja watched them scamper away, the same smile of triumph lighting up her face. Little did she know that she had, by her vindictive act, sounded the death knell for the Ahom kingdom.

THE NARRATOR

'Yes, that and other anti-Vaishnav actions of Phuleshwari planted the seed that later grew up into a giant weed strangling the banyan tree that had been the Ahom kingdom. When the ruler moves in a direction opposite of that of the ruled, anarchy is bound to be the result. True, the reigns of kings like Rudra Singha and Shiva Singha marked the social, cultural and economic heights reached by the Ahoms. Yet, in the period, primarily because of the deviation from the traditional Shan ethos and hankering after and aping ideas and customs imported from outside, the ground for decay and destruction too were laid. As I had said before, the wave which rises high must also fall low. But now there was to be no more rising again; the inexorable and irreversible end of the Ahom realm was nigh.

'To their credit, the Ahom Deodhai, Bailung and Mohan priests tried their best to resist the decline and guide their people towards traditional ways. Invoking the names of the great Sukapha, who at enormous risk had brought the holy Somdeo to the Valley of the Luit, they made the royalty and nobles worship it. No doubt the Ahom royalty abandoned burial for the Hindu custom of cremation on a pyre, yet the Ahom priests ensured at least the ashes were buried and a maidam built according to the Ahom custom. But the times were against them—Shakta Brahmins had a stranglehold over the royals; the subjects were mostly inclined towards the Vaishnav religion of Sankardev—the Ahom priests, and those nobles and Ahom subjects who tried to continue the traditional way of life and beliefs found themselves in a woeful minority and isolated from the political and spiritual mainstream.

'The hardcore Shakta, Phuleshwari, died in 1731. However, the superstitious Shiva Singha refrained from sitting on the throne and married her younger sister Draupadi, despite the fact that she was already married to someone else and had two sons. Official titles were conferred on her husband and sons, and she was brought to Rongpur to be deemed the bar raja and sit on the throne as a proxy to the king. She was renamed Ambika as well as Madanwika, and coins were struck in both the names. However, there were hardly any celebrations in the realm because everyone knew it was a marriage of convenience. The swargadeo could have married anyone else and made her bar raja. But he had been infatuated with Phuleshwari and married her sister because she would remind him of her!

'Yet Queen Ambika proved to be no mere figurehead; she displayed a fondness for learning and the arts as deep as her sister, though she was not as orthodox as far as religion was concerned. Two of her acts proved to be abiding. First was the construction of an enormous pukhuri which she named after her husband as Shivasagar or the Sea of Shiva. This water tank was far bigger than any constructed so far; the people therefore called it the Barpukhuri or big tank. Beside it, the queen had a mammoth dol or temple dedicated to Lord Shiva, which coincidentally, was the name of her husband too! Occupying an area of four-and-a-half acres, the Shiva dol had two sections, the garbhagriha and the mandap. Unlike other temples in the area, the main shikhar that rose over the garbhagriha had fluted, vertical lines, and was surrounded on all four sides by subsidiary shikhars called uramanajari.

'Soon the area around the tank and the temple came to be known as Shivasagar, the district where our village is located in the present. In course of time, the name Rongpur, which enjoyed the status of a capital during the Ahom era, became subservient to the name Shivasagar and today forms merely a part of the district. Ambika also constructed two smaller temples beside the Shiva dol. The first of these, occupying three acres and with a height of forty cubits, was dedicated to Lord Vishnu, while the second, of the same height and occupying two-and-a-half acres, to Goddess Devi.

'Also, Queen Ambika, in consultation with the king, was responsible for the penning of the classic called *Hasti Vidyarnava*. In the kind of terrain prevalent in the Luit Valley, especially in the rainy season, elephants were of essential use and thus highly cherished animals. Trained elephants were an important component of the swargadeo's army: they were used as transport and to haul heavy objects—occasionally younger ones were even used to plough fields! A man's wealth was measured in terms of the number of elephants he owned. Understanding the importance of this animal in Assamese society, Queen Ambika commissioned a scholar named Sukumar Barkath to collect all existing information on elephants and compile it in book form. This book is therefore a remarkable compilation on the various types of elephants, their habits and ways of behaviour, illnesses afflicting them and the cures, the training to be imparted to them and so on.

'Equally remarkable were the illustrations in *Hasti Vidyarnava*, done by two brilliant artists, a Muslim named Dilbar and a Hindu named Dosay. During the preceding centuries, great progress had been made in the art of manuscript painting, the sattras established by Sankardev and his followers being main centres where this was developed. Translations as well as original texts were supplemented by illustrations; when there was no space, illuminated margins were drawn to brighten up the tome. A great number of illuminated manuscripts, including the *Bhagavat Puran*, written and illustrated with colours that did not fade but whose formulas have been long forgotten, were produced during the Ahom era.

'*Hasti Vidyarnava* stands out both for its erudition as well as the illustrations. Through the latter, not only do we get a glimpse of the uses to which elephants were put, but also of the royal court and society of the times. Scenes such as an Ahom swargadeo holding court, royal procession on elephants, the playing of sports like falconry, various activities of the people, and costumes worn by nobility and the common masses, provide us with a vivid picture of contemporary life. The illustrations are in water colour and many of them are plated with gold—it is a wonder that, even after so many years, they have preserved their colour and the gold has not lost its lustre.

'There were many highly gifted artists like Dilbar and Dosay in the Ahom court—mention can be also made of Badh Ligira who illustrated the *Bhagavat Puran*, which was dedicated to Shiva Singha and Ambika Devi. As you all know, male servants in the palace were called ligiras and the female ligiris. So Badh Ligira was actually a retainer in the royal palace, testifying to the fact that many servants of the king were artistically gifted as well as literate.

'The women bar rajas, therefore, took the Ahom court to new aesthetic heights, but their religious fanaticism was the undoing of the empire. Ambika Devi died in 1738 and after her cremation, her ashes were buried in a maidam next to Phuleshwari's. As was the practice of Shiva Singha, he married another woman called Anadari and gave her the name of Sarbeshwari Bar-Raja. Not much is known about her; one achievement being the construction of the Keri Rajmao dol dedicated to the memory of her mother-in-law.

'In 1744, Shiva Singha, the man who chose not be king, died and was succeeded by his brother Pramatta Singha, who assumed the Ahom name of Swargadeo Sunenpha. Apart from a minor conspiracy against him which was detected and culprits punished, his brief reign of eight years was free from strife. Rudra Singha had indeed laid a firm social and economic foundation and the kings who immediately followed him could devote themselves to activities other than those of martial nature. Pramatta Singha was an enthusiastic builder and was responsible for a number of constructions, the most famous being the Rong-ghar we know in Rongpur. You may recall that a rong-ghar of wood and bamboo was already there in the city, from which monarchs could watch competitive sports and fights between animals. But the new king pulled that structure down and built in its place a rong-ghar of bricks and mortar which today stands as a testament to a glorious era of Ahom history.

'A temple and devalaya, called Rudreshwar dol and Rudreshwar devalaya, were raised at the spot in Guwahati where his father Rudra Singha had been cremated. Pramatta Singha was also instrumental in constructing the well known Sukreshwar devalaya and temple on the bank of the river Brahmaputra at Guwahati. In 1745, he undertook another census and survey of the subjects and ensured that these were properly recorded. The swargadeo had two sons named Malou Gohain and Madhav Gohain. Cognizant of the need to properly educate them, he brought a Brahmin from Bengal whom he later made a barua, who became the progenitor of the Bapu Barua clan.

'A story about Pramatta Singh illustrates the truth that though the swargadeos had become Shaktas, they retained their tolerant as well as superstitious nature. The king used to suffer from chronic migraine and the palace physicians were unable to cure it. One night he dreamt that if he offered a donation to a mosque, he would be rid of the affliction. The swargadeo gave ample gold to a maulana so that he could go to Mecca and offer prayers for the former's recovery. The maulana did as he was instructed and returned from his trip after two-and-a-half years. Unfortunately, before his return, in 1751, Swargadeo Sunenpha breathed his last.

'He was a good-natured man, very popular with his subjects. However, one of his actions, though unwittingly taken, had far-reaching consequences for the final destruction of the Ahom empire. During his reign, Rupchandra was the barbarua. Because he hailed from Bokota, his family came to be known as the Bokotial Barbaruas. The family was not of the nobility; Rupchandra's ancestors had been tailors who stitched 'jalam' or silken cords used to beautify palanquins. It was purely due to his courage and efficiency that he was appointed as a barbarua. After Rupchandra's death, Swargadeo Sunenpha appointed his son, Gendhela, as the new barbarua. Having been thus elevated, Gendhela changed his name to Kirtichandra. This, my people, was to be a fateful appointment, as you will learn later.

'After the demise of Swargadeo Sunenpha, in the normal course of things and as per the wishes of Rudra Singha, the third son Mohanmala Barjana Gohain should have been installed as the new king. But there was a problem in this, one which deeply divided the nobles. Mohanmala had been struck with smallpox when young and there were pockmarks on his face. As per Ahom tradition, a prince who had physical blemishes could not be made king. However, Mohanmala was popular with the subjects; also, it had been the wish of Rudra Singha that his four sons rule one after the other. Therefore, the buragohain and the bargohain were willing to overlook tradition and install him as the swargadeo, but Kirtichandra Barbarua, who had by now attained great power and influence, was dead set on retaining it and declared that Mohanmala could not rule.

'It was due to his insistence that the other patra-mantris had to concede that a prince who had blemishes needed to forgo kingship. Thus, the youngest son of Rudra Singha, Romanath Bonda Gohain, ascended the singorighar at Rongpur, taking on the Ahom name of Surempha and the Hindu name of Rajeshwar Singha. The wily Kirtichandra convinced the new monarch that if Mohanmala was to be allowed to stay in the capital, he would pose a constant threat to the swargadeo. So, the elder brother was exiled to Namrup. As we shall see, Mohanmala did indeed prove to be a threat, being at the centre of an armed uprising directed against Ahom hegemony.

'For many years, court intrigues and conspiracies had been the bane of the royal palace. But then the descendents of Chowlung Sukapha had managed to tide over all crises and take the Ahom realm on to heights of glory. The renewed authority of the swargadeo, attained during Gadadhar Singha's rein, the military, cultural and economic heights reached during the reins of Rudra Singha and his two sons—these represent the climactic era of Ahom rule. But the clouds of crisis were approaching once more and there would be no salvation this time. Yet, because of the heights already reached, it would be some years before the glory would grow dimmer as twilight approached ...'

Rajeshwar, the Godly King

⁓

THE RAJABHISHEK, OR CORONATION, CARRIED OUT ON A GRAND scale as befitted a son of Rudra Singha the Great, was finally over. Octagonal and square coins of gold and silver, in Assamese, with Sanskrit and Parsi scripts, had been struck to commemorate the event. His elder brother had been sent into exile to Namrup; his barbarua, Kirtichandra, had presented proof enough of Mohanmala's subversive activities, so the action was quite justified. The king was highly impressed with the intelligence, enterprise and zeal of the barbarua, though the man did have a violent temper.

Guided by the barbarua, new patra-mantris had been appointed: Numali had been made bargohain, Tamuli the barphukan and Langmaikolia Bholok the barpatragohain—they had been vouchsafed to be loyal to the king and not Mohanmala. But the king, who was a highly intelligent man himself and a good judge of character, could make out that none of them were of the same measure as the barbarua, and were therefore heavily dependent on him for counsel.

Thus, it had been Gendhela, now calling himself Kirtichandra Barbarua, who brought about changes in the paik system in an attempt to render it more efficient. Previously, four paiks constituted a got or unit; this was reduced to three paiks per got. The first paik was called mul, the second dewal and the third tewal. Unknown to the king, such a change, while not increasing efficiency in any way, served to induce an element of discontent amongst the subjects.

Each got had to render service to the state through the year, the paiks serving in rotation. When four paiks constituted a got, each paik had to serve for three months each, with the other three men taking care of his family and land while he was in service. But now each paik in the truncated got had to serve for four months, thereby causing an undercurrent of resentment amongst the subjects.

And, at the very commencement of his reign, the swargadeo was confronted with an enormous decision. He himself, like his father and elder brothers, was a stout Shakta and gave inordinate importance to the Brahmin priests of the palace. The Ahom priests had been chafing at this for quite some time; now, at the opportunity offered by the coronation of a new king, the Deodhais and Bailungs had brought their disaffections in the open and were at loggerheads with the Brahmins over an important issue.

The Brahmin priests were of the opinion that the swargadeo should retain Rongpur as the capital, since the inauspicious phase which marked the reign of his elder brother Shiva Singha had passed and there was no danger to the royal throne. But the Ahom priests vehemently differed; they had looked into the future using their traditional method of augury, and foresaw great danger for the kingdom if Rongpur was retained as the capital. It was not clear if the Ahom priests asserted their opinion simply to contradict what the Brahmins had said, or whether it was an actual augury. But the Deodhai and Bailung priests were unanimous that unless the swargadeo shifted his capital, preferably to Taimung in the Tipam area, or else to Garhgaon, the Ahom realm was destined for destruction.

When asked for his counsel, Kirtichandra Barbarua showed a way out.

'The question of building a new capital at Taimung doesn't arise, Your Majesty,' he advised the king. 'Rangpur has been developed through all these years and has become an ideal city, thus it must be retained as the capital. However, you must also declare Garhgaon to be endowed with capital status in order to placate your Ahom priests who have been of such service to the royal house in the past.'

'That's good advice,' Swargadeo Surempha said, impressed. 'The idea of having two capitals was pursued by no less a personage than my revered father. I have always had an ambition of building a new palace of bricks and mortar at Rongpur if I ever became the king. This I will now do. But, to show our Ahom priests that Garhgaon is equally important, I shall build another palace in that city too.'

Under the orders of Kirtichandra and the swargadeo himself, royal engineers drew up a blueprint for another palace at Rongpur the likes of which the Ahom realm had never seen before. Because it comprised many tiers, the structure began to be called the Talatal-ghar, which, loosely translated, meant a house that moved both up and down. It was a marvel of architecture, having as it did storeys which stood both above and below the ground. Within the palace the various rooms and corridors were so constructed as to confuse one who was unfamiliar with the interior about which corridor led to which room. The stairs that one might have thought led up actually led down, while passages which appeared to lead to the exit of the palace in reality led to the interior. As one went deeper inside, the doors became progressively shorter and narrower, so that the person had to bend low in order to progress. The objective of creating such a labyrinth was to confuse potential intruders and assassins and safeguard the king. Adjacent to the palace was the gossain-ghar, which the royals used as the prayer room as also to receive nirmali from priests from temples situated elsewhere.

The palace built at Garhgaon did not display the Talatal-ghar's architectural ingenuity, but was of conventional yet unparalleled beauty. Popularly known as the Kareng-ghar or royal palace, like the latter, it too had tiers both above and below the ground, as well as rounded ceilings that concealed the fact that there were more tiers above. Another safeguard provided to both the palaces was an underground passage which led to the river Dikhau, through which the king could escape from one to the other if he were subjected to attack by hostile elements.

Evidently, the reek of rebellion was already in the air and Swargadeo
Surempha was taking no chances with his safety.

The more Kirtichandra attained power, the more arrogant he became.
He had become notorious for throwing tantrums and, although the
other patra-mantris had complained to the swargadeo about his rudeness
and temper, the king asked them to tolerate it. The truth of the matter
was that Rajeshwar Singha, though able and efficient, was too fond
of the pleasures of life to spend time only in governance of the state.
This he left to his efficient barbarua while he himself indulged in his
passion for music and drama, as also construction of religious and other
monuments. To show that he commanded powers overriding those of
the other patra-mantris, Kirtichandra was given a special place to sit in
the rajsora, as also a gem-encrusted walking stick by the king.

Unfortunately, Kirtichandra's violent temper was responsible for
one of the most disgraceful episodes of Ahom history. Repelled by the
repeated insults heaped upon the patra-mantris by the barbarua, Numali
Bargohain brought out a buranji or chronicle titled *Chakari Pheti* in
which it was revealed that the Bokotial family to which Kirtichandra
belonged had been tailors who stitched 'jalam' or silken cords used to
beautify palanquins—thus, not only did he not belong to a noble family,
but he was not even an Ahom and was referred to as 'jalambata goriya' in
the buranji. The infuriated Kirtichandra first brought his kinsmen from
elsewhere to prove that his family was indeed of Ahom lineage; next he
told the king that if such lies could be written about him in a buranji,
there was no telling what could be written about the swargadeo himself
and his ancestors. In those days, apart from the official chronicle of the
court, prominent families and officials maintained their own buranjis.
Each and every one of these must be submitted to the court for inspection
to ensure that nothing scurrilous was recorded for the eyes of posterity.

The king, totally influenced by the barbarua, ordered that all buranjis
in the kingdom be submitted to the court to be examined. A majority

of the chronicles were submitted, but quite a few were secreted away. It took the barbarua two years to have a team of kakotis go through all the sanchi-paat manuscripts; those that contained the minutest reference that might be considered scurrilous were burnt and those responsible for their composition punished. A comprehensive historical legacy was thereby destroyed, though it did not in any way aid the barbarua from erasing the episode from the chronicles. Instead, it fanned the slow-burning embers of jealousy and anti-royalty feelings even further, with disastrous consequences which would unfurl in the next few decades.

The guards at the gate bowed respectfully as Kirtichandra Barbarua hurried through the outer gate of the royal palace. The show, to be held on the flat roof of the Talatal-ghar, must have already started and he was late. Ordinarily, this would not have worried the barbarua unduly; after all he was the most powerful man in the realm next to the swargadeo. But this show was different. It was the enactment of an ankiya naat or one-act play called *Kichak Badh* composed by Swargadeo Surempha himself. The king was an accomplished poet and had been given the title of Kavi Churamani or the Supreme Poet by his courtiers. Dozens of actors had been practising daily to enact the play in the bhaona or folk drama format. This evening had been set for enactment before a highly select audience. The swargadeo must be chafing that his right-hand man was not there to watch the fruit of his creation. There was no telling with these kings, thought Kirtichandra ruefully. At the moment he had the king eating out of his hands—but if he were to take umbrage at this seeming discourtesy, the barbarua might lose favour, something his all too many enemies in the court were striving at.

So preoccupied was Kirtichandra that he failed to notice that one of the soldiers guarding a closed door had a scarf covering his features. The barbarua was alone, but he was inside the palace and did not expect any trouble. Apart from guards placed at periodic intervals, the corridors were deserted. As he passed the guard whose face was concealed, the latter lunged at him with a short sword, attempting to stab him in the heart. The barbarua, with admirable instinct, swerved leftwards so that the blade missed his heart and pierced the area near his left armpit. With a scream that rang through the entire palace, he tried to grapple with his assailant, but the man, taking advantage of the complex design of the building, walked a few paces and turned right through another corridor, and was lost in the maze.

The scream ended the show. Chaodang palace guards came rushing to the barbarua's assistance; the king himself hurried up to the scene of the crime. A guest room was opened and the victim placed on a bed; the royal bezbarua, who had been watching the show along with others, examined the wound, cleaned it with herbal antiseptic lotion and stitched it up, the nobleman gritting his teeth and not letting out a whimper despite the agony.

'It's merely a flesh wound, thankfully,' was the royal physician's comment. 'The knife missed vital organs. You should be up and about in a day or two.'

The barbarua turned to the king. 'Your Majesty,' he said. 'The assailant knew his way about. So he must be someone from within the palace ... or at least has been here many times before. With your permission, I would like to make enquiries.'

'You're free to act in any way you please,' the king assured. 'Find the culprit and I'll order that he be executed.'

However, though Kirtichandra tried hard, the culprit could not be apprehended—that no one in the palace liked him enough to give evidence did not help! From that day onwards, the barbarua ensured that he was never alone when on the move, but accompanied by a couple of tangon-dhars or bodyguards armed with sticks.

'There was a Mughal emperor named Shahjahan,' Kirtichandra Barbarua said to the king. 'He was a mighty—'

Much to the secret delight of the other nobles who were present in the rajsora, Swargadeo Surempha peremptorily cut him off.

'You can be infuriatingly overbearing sometimes, Barbarua dangoriya,' the king admonished. 'Do you think I am an ignoramus? Can't you imagine that others apart from you have heard about Shahjahan?'

This was a gentle reminder to his close counsellor that the king was a learned man, indeed perhaps the most erudite amongst the Ahom kings. His court was filled with intellectual giants like Kavi Bidyachandra, the composer of the epic *Haribansa Pada*; he encouraged literary and cultural activities throughout the kingdom; in fact, Kirtichandra's own son, Chandrahas Dekabarua, directed regular performances of bhaona plays in the court, which often had casts of hundreds, plays like *Ravan Badh* being particular favourite of the swargadeo.

'I apologize, Your Majesty,' the barbarua, like all bullies, was exaggeratedly deferential to a superior. 'What I had wanted to point out was that Shahjahan was the greatest builder amongst all Mughal monarchs. We wish that posterity would call you the greatest builder amongst the Ahoms. You've already constructed the two marvels—the Talatal-ghar at Rongpur and the Kareng-ghar at Garhgaon. The royal coffers are full; trade with other realms is more lucrative than ever ... it is time that you build more monuments so that you'll be remembered as the Shahjahan amongst us.'

The king was pleased. The idea itself was sound, and he immediately began translating it into practice. Since he was a highly devout Shakta, he would, naturally, begin with building dols and devalayas. Also, he would ask his architects and builders to experiment, so that the structures did not appear imitations of those built earlier by other kings. He ordered the construction of a dol on the south bank of the Jaisagar Pukhuri to commemorate a nephew of the Parbatiya gossain whose sharan he had taken, so this temple came to be known as Naati Gossain dol, or the temple dedicated to the nephew of a gossain. Built of burnt earth and decorated with numerous hues and sculptures, this temple illustrated the aesthetic heights reached by temple-builders and sculptors during Rajeshwar Singha's reign. But people also know it by the name of

Ghanasyam dol, believing it was built by the famous master mason of that name during Rudra Singha's time.

Another temple was constructed at a spot between Rongpur and Jaisagar, west to the Rongnath dol constructed by Rudra Singha. It was built to hold an idol of Hara-Gauri or Shiva-Parvati, and was therefore known as Hara-Gauri dol or devalaya. A few years after ascending the throne, the king made a visit to Guwahati to meet his guru; he took this opportunity to select sites for new temples to be built and gave instructions to the barphukan to carry out the task. One of the sites chosen was Basisthashram situated beside the river Bharalu because it was said to have contained footprints of the great sage Basistha. A stone inscription stating that the temple was built on the orders of Rajeshwar Singha and completed in 1764 was erected to mark the occasion. While he was at Guwahati, a full lunar eclipse took place, which his astrologers declared to be a bad omen. To counter its ill effects, the Swargadeo donated to the temple at Asvakranta and donated land and money to Brahmins.

In ancient Pragjyotishpur, the name of which had over time changed to Guwahati, there had been a temple dedicated to nine heavenly bodies called the Nabhagraha temple on a peak of the Chitrasila Hills. Once a famous seat for astronomy and astrology research, the temple had fallen to ruins. Rajeshwar Singha had the temple rebuilt. Since a water tank could not be built on the mountain for devotees to wash themselves in before visiting the temple, a nine-cornered one called Shilphukhuri was dug at the foot of the hill and a stone inscription was erected to mark the occasion. Stone and brass inscriptions were also struck at the Kamakhya temple to commemorate the construction of a Durga dol, renovation work and donations made under the orders of Rajeshwar Singha.

One of the sites selected was at the Manikarneshwar Hill which stood at the point on the north bank of the Brahmaputra where the river Barnadi debouches into it. Construction of a temple was completed there in 1755, as also a water tank. Another temple dedicated to Goddess Dirgheswari was constructed around the same time on the north bank of the Brahmaputra. Phakuadols were erected at Bothakhana and Sukreshwar in Guwahati, and a mandir upon the Kedar Hill at Hajo, some distance from Guwahati. The Kedar mandir, made entirely from stone blocks, contained a Shivalinga believed to have been there since ancient times.

Quite a number of peeths and maths were constructed around Guwahati on instructions from the swargadeo. He also chose sites at Biswanath on the north bank near Tezpur where two dols dedicated to the gods Vasudeva and Govinda were built. He also donated land at Biswanath and elsewhere to private parties for worship of Shiva.

There was evidence that an ancient Shiva temple existed at a place called Negheriting at some distance from Rongpur. Legend had it that centuries ago a sage named Aubbarishi tried to establish a second Kashi, the holy site of Hindus, at Negheriting. He set up a number of Shivalingas at that spot and worshipped them, but was unsuccessful in his mission. Rajeshwar Singha constructed a Shiva temple there and installed a Shivalinga recovered from nearby. It is said that the stones of the earlier temple were used for constructing this one. It is the most magnificent of all the dols constructed in the immediate vicinity and has exquisitely curved statues upon its walls. Four smaller temples were built around the main one, each with its own covered approach or aagsora.

Rajeshwar Singha could not complete the entire temple complex at Negheriting in his lifetime and it was left to his successor Lakshmi Singha to do so. However, this temple was the most favoured one of the monarch and he would take nirmali sent from it before all others. So great was his reverence for this temple that he had a road called Borali built connecting Negheriting to Rongpur, and invested the responsibility of providing food and other essentials to its priest to villagers nearby. Since the area was dedicated to the god or deva Shiva, it began to be called the devargaon or village of the deva. In the course of time, this changed to Dergaon, the place where the temple is now situated.

Rajeshwar Singha was also instrumental in having large-scale civic works done by his officers, and many roads and water tanks were constructed during his reign. This swargadeo did turn out to be the Shahjahan amongst the Ahoms.

'Times have changed since we were youngsters,' said Rebakanta to his friend and colleague Hemadhar. 'The realm seems to have become a stranger to peace.'

The two men were paiks on military duty. They had received four months of intensive training in a military camp about this time a year ago. Now they had been called up since a campaign was in the offing and had been put up in one of the cane-bamboo-thatch temporary structures serving as barracks in the same camp.

'You're not far off the mark, Reba,' replied Hemadhar. 'My father tells me there had hardly been any strife for decades in the kingdom— since the time Swargadeo Gadadhar Singha sat on the throne. The realm was in peace during our teenage days, when Swargadeo Sunenpha was the monarch. More important, the palace too was at peace. But that seems a long way off now, since we've grown up into youths.'

'Tell you what, Hema, though we as paiks have been assigned to military duty, I was hoping we wouldn't actually have to fight. But trouble seems to have broken out everywhere, in the realm as well as in the palace!'

'You're not wrong, Reba,' conceded his friend. 'They say the upstart Kirtichandra has become all-powerful at the palace, what with the king being too busy enjoying life. They say he's addicted to opium—the Swargadeo, I mean.'

'Hush, not so loud,' cautioned Rebakanta. 'Someone might hear you and that might mean flogging at best and impalement on bamboo stakes at the worst.'

'Well, being sent to a war not of one's own making is as bad!' said Hemadhar, though he lowered his voice.

'I must say you have loads of information with you. Where do you get it from?'

'Oh, by keeping my ears open. Our officers talk a lot ... some brag how close they are to folks within the palace ... you can glean a lot from what they say.'

'And what do they say?'

'What you yourself had observed, my friend—trouble in the palace and the realm! When the steersman who guides the boat is weak or unconcerned, the craft is likely to be tossed about in the waters. The nobles, apparently, are disaffected by the undue importance bestowed upon the barbarua. In fact, when some of them were asked to lead this campaign, they refused. It has been a long time since such insubordination took place.'

'Could they get away with it? After all, our swargadeo is descended from heaven itself and defying him is akin to defying the gods.'

'Oh, he's a weakling in that way too. Despite the barbarua's urgings for stringent action, the king simply divested them of their office and property rather than taking off their heads. Finally, he managed to get an officer lower down in the order, Horonath Bhitorual Phukan, to lead this campaign after promising him land and gold.'

'So, that's the state of the palace! What about the realm?'

'The waters are getting choppy, my friend. First it was the Daffla tribe, which came down upon us plainsmen to pillage and loot, and then the Mikir tribe. Those two were taught a lesson and once again pledged allegiance to our swargadeo.'

'Which brings us to this campaign?'

'Yes. The Daffla and Mikir uprisings made the swargadeo realize that he needed to test others. So, he sent a katoki to the Kachari King Sandhikari asking him to present himself at the Rongpur court. Sandhikari not only refused to come; he, in fact, refused to meet the katoki at all. The swargadeo thereupon sent a mighty force to Raha, led by no less than our upstart Kirtichandra.'

'Ah, it must have been a battle royal! Did we win?'

'No, no one won or lost. You see, the very fact that our army was marching against him so terrified Sandhikari that he came of his own will and submitted to the swargadeo.'

'Oh, how I wish I'd been a soldier in such a war which never took place! But the one we're in promises to be far stiffer.'

'Unfortunately, it seems that way. You see, when the Kachari King Sandhikari came to make submission, he brought the raja of Manipur, Jai Singha, with him. Apparently, the kingdom of Manipur had been overrun by the Maans, forcing Jai Singha to flee and take shelter with the Kacharis.'

'The Maans? That's a new one to me!'

'That's because you don't keep your ears open, my friend. They are from our neighbouring realm in the west, the one they used to call Nara country and now Myanmar. Fierce as the tiger, these Maans! We've never had much trouble with them because our kings and their kings are, so to speak, kinsmen. But the Manipuri king wasn't as lucky. He's come asking our swargadeo for help.'

'So we've to fight his battle for him,' said Rebakanta ruefully. 'I only hope to God this one turns out to be a non-war just like the others!'

In a quirky manner, Rebakanta's hope was fulfilled. It indeed turned out to be a non-war. Yet the 20,000-strong Ahom force led by Horonath Bhitorual Phukan and accompanied by Jai Singha, the raja of Manipur, was vanquished, with over half the soldiers being killed. The main adversary was nature, as well as disease and pestilence. The mistake made by the Ahom commander was that, in order to save time, rather than make a circuitous trip to Manipur through Kachari country, he decided to take a direct route across the mountains lying south of Charaideo.

This was unfamiliar territory and soon the mammoth army encountered dense, almost impenetrable forests. The wisest thing would have been to retreat but the bhitorual phukan was hesitant to do so because it might evoke a negative impression of him with the swargadeo. So, rather than proceed with hengdangs in their hands, his soldiers had to use daos instead to hack through the thick vegetation. Progress was slow and strenuous; at night his army had to camp upon dank ground in unhealthy surroundings. Three months later, they were no closer to Manipur than they had been before; the guides had lost all sense of direction. One by one the soldiers began to die from lack of food, disease, and snake and insect bites. Hostile Naga tribes took the opportunity to launch guerilla attacks and kill as many Ahom soldiers as they could. Within six months, an incredible 10,000 men had died.

Messengers brought the news of the disaster to the king and he ordered an immediate retreat. The bhitorual phukan was dismissed in disgrace, though Jai Singha was promised another attempt to retrieve his throne. Because they had to fight Nature rather than an army, this battle came to be known as Lota Kota Ron or Creeper-Cutting War.

The two friends Rebakanta and Hemadhar died in this non-war, both from disease.

Once again Rongpur was in a festive mood. The swargadeo was getting married. The king already had a number of wives, but this marriage was to be special, because the bride was Kuranganoyoni, daughter of Jai Singha, the raja of Manipur. The swargadeo was determined to make it a special event since it brought together two powerful principalities in the region.

The disaster of the Lota Kota Ron did not deter Swargadeo Surempha from his resolve to help a fellow king. In November 1768, he sent another huge army under Kirtichandra Barbarua to assist Jai Singha in recovering his kingdom. While the main body of the troops encamped at Raha, Jai Singha took 10,000 men as far as the river Mirap. Such was the reputation of Ahom soldiers that as soon as the Maans learnt that an Ahom army was coming, they fled from Manipur, leaving Kelemba, the usurper whom they had put on the throne, in the lurch. With the help of Naga allies, Jai Singha easily dethroned Kelemba and wrested back his kingdom. As a gesture of gratitude for the help received from the Ahom king, Jai Singha had offered his daughter Kuranganoyoni in marriage to the former.

In the case of a marriage of a swargadeo, the groom did not go to the house of the bride; on the contrary, it was the bride who had to come to the palace for the wedding ceremony. However, Kirtichandra Barbarua suggested that the king make an exception in this case as a gesture of goodwill, and at least proceed to a camp by the river Sonari. The Manipur king too arrived there with his daughter and the marriage party, as also a huge dowry which included a troop of Manipuri men who would become bondsmen of the Ahom king. Another camp had been erected to host him and his daughter.

Although the Ahom royalty had taken on Hindu customs conducted by Brahmins in almost all spheres, in the matter of marriage, the Chaklang custom still prevailed if the bride was not a Hindu. Such a marriage was conducted by Ahom priests and Brahmins were not involved. Each day, for a week, womenfolk from the bride's side went in a group to the river ghat, singing songs and bearing gold pitchers. The bride was smeared with turmeric and other herbs and bathed in the water brought by the womenfolk. Meanwhile, the wedding stage, called a morol, in seven different hues, had been built at the groom's camp. The stage was marked with 101 segments and a lighted earthen lamp placed within each segment. On the day declared auspicious by the Deodhai and Bailung priests, the bride's party walked the short distance to the groom's camp, Princess Kuranganoyoni being carried on a palanquin. Women of the royal camp ululated as she alighted at the decked-up gate and the bridal party entered. The guests were escorted to their respective seats while the princess was led by the hand to the morol.

Swargadeo Surempha was already there, seated by the morol on a low wooden pirrah. Kuranganoyoni was made to circle him seven times and then sit by his side. Guided by the royal Deodhai head priest who recited incantations from the *Chaklang Puthi*, the groom and the bride took their marriage vows. At an instruction from the head priest, the duo stood up; a piece of cloth was loosely tied round the neck of the bride, with the other end being tied to the waist of the groom; they circled the morol seven times and then stood before it. The father of the bride came up and formally gave away his daughter in marriage to the groom. The bride was handed a garland of 101 flowers, which she put around the groom's neck. Swargadeo Surempha, like all grooms had to do during the chaklang ceremony, accepted the bride as his wife, placed his right hand on his hengdang, and promised to protect her in future.

The couple sat down. A phukan well versed in the buranjis recited the lineage of the king and the new queen, giving a heroic account of the exploits of the king. With the serious part of the ceremony over, the playful aspects began. These wedding games played by the newly wed couple included an exchange of knives, smelling the contents of a bowl containing milk, honey and rice, and dipping hands into a small basket of uncooked rice to find the rings hidden in it. The discovery of a ring first signified that finder's mastery over the other—the fact that, on this occasion, the queen found one first was greeted with loud cheers by the onlookers! These and other games over, it was customary for the groom and the bride to touch the feet of their elders; but since it was the royal couple, this custom was not observed.

Much feasting and merriment followed. A few days later, the parents of the bride returned to Manipur with sorrow in their hearts; while Swargadeo Surempha rode on an elephant back to Rongpur to be greeted by crowds on the roads cheering the new kuonri. The Manipuri bondsmen gifted to the king were settled near the mouth of the river Disoi at Magaluahat and provided with land and facilities for farming. Kuranganoyoni built a mammoth water tank at the spot where the Manipuris were settled, to be called Magalu's Jiyekar Pukhuri by the local people.

The festive mood and the celebrations in the palace were deceptive. Trouble was brewing within the kingdom and the grounds for challenging the rule of the Ahoms were being laid. Vassals such as the Jaiantia raja were displaying a defiant attitude and had to be subjected to constant warnings from Rongpur. The strife between the senior nobles, centred round the power Kirtichandra had been given, was assuming

serious proportions and once again the reek of plots and conspiracies
was thickening the palace air. But, more serious than these, was the
growing disaffection amongst a section of the subjects—the Vaishnavs
of the Moamaria sect. The contempt shown towards them by the Ahom
royalty had wrought an undercurrent of anger through the years; Bar-
Raja Phuleshwari's thoughtless act of humiliating them had fuelled that
anger; the highhandedness of Kirtichandra Barbarua and his constant
endeavour to belittle the sattras, sattradhikars and bhakats ensured that
a boiling point was about to be reached.

There were elements which were bent on manipulating this pent-up
fury to their own advantage. Mohanmala Barjana Gohain, who had not
been made the king because he was scarred by smallpox, and who lived
in exile at Namrup, was quick to seize the opportunity to avenge what
he thought was the injustice done to him. Also, the senior nobles were
ready to fish in troubled waters.

Thus, this morning, within the compound of Mohanmala's residence
at Namrup, a small band of people had got together. Significantly,
Bhagi Buragohain and Numali Bargohain too were there, as also the
sattradhikars of Moamaria sattras in the vicinity. The discussions were
to the point—the swargadeo at Rongpur was weak; the barbarua had
assumed overriding powers and had been using them to assail the
Vaishnavs. The solution, all agreed, was to kill Kirtichandra, dethrone
Swargadeo Surempha, and place Mohanmala on the throne with the
help of the Moamarias.

'You tell me that you have thousands of supporters,' Prince
Mohanmala spoke to the Moamaria sattradhikars. 'But how are we to
know that is true and you have their allegiance?'

It was the Madarkhat sattradhikar who put forward a suggestion.
'There is a wide, low-lying area nearby called Maloupathar,' he said. 'It
is neither settled upon nor cultivated because it is prone to flooding
during the rains. We'll announce to our followers that we intend to set
up another Moamaria sattra on Maloupathar. But, for that, the area
would need to be filled up with earth to obliterate its low-lying character.
We shall ordain that each and every able-bodied individual amongst our

followers must fling just a single clod of earth into the depression so that a raised plinth can be created for our sattra. That way you will be able to form an idea of how vast our following is.'

The suggestion was implemented. Prince Mohanmala was very impressed. Thousands of men and women had converged on Maloupathar to make a bor-bheti or high plinth upon which the Borbheti sattra would be set up. The nobles amongst the conspirators returned, assured, to the palace. There they were disconcerted to find that the barbarua's spies had got wind of the happenings and informed their master. Though for the moment Kirtichandra did not say anything to his fellow patra-mantris; he placed the small standing army on high alert and instructed officers close to him to be ready to mobilize forces at a command for him. The buragohain and bargohain sent word to Mohanmala that the time was not opportune to strike and he needed to wait for a while.

But the opportune moment arrived soon enough. In the month of May in the year 1769 itself, just a short while after marrying Kuranganoyoni, Swargadeo Surempha or Rajeshwar Singha, on a visit to the Shiva temple at Negheriting, fell ill and died. He was cremated on the banks of the river Luit and his ashes sent to be buried in a maidam at Charaideo.

THE NARRATOR

The flames of the bonfire were sinking. The fog, waiting like a pack of wild dogs circling its prey, was slowly closing in. The voice of the old Narrator too was tiring. Now it was tinged with a note of sadness.

'One relishes re-telling of glory. But when the sheen wears off, words turn bitter. Yet it must be told ... the dimming of noon's brightness and the falling of twilight. But you must forgive me if I do not dwell on it for very long. The time has come to end the tale of our race. I will keep it as brief as I can.

'Swargadeo Surempha or Rajeshwar Singha was the last of the great Ahom kings. The heights attained by Assamese society in terms of power, economy and culture during the time of Rudra Singha were to a great extent retained till the time of Rajeshwar Singha. But the seeds of downfall had already been sown. Conflict within the palace was at its fiercest; rather than listen to the subjects, the palace was compelling the subjects to listen to it; the faith of the royalty was in discordance with the faith of the masses. But the one factor which contributed most to the downslide was the presence of a tyrant who held the palace in his thrall.

'Yes, it was Kirtichandra Barbarua who, in 1769, backed the candidature of Kalshiliya Gohain, the youngest son of Rudra Singha, to be the next king. The other nobles supported the eldest son of Rajeshwar Singha. They questioned the legitimacy of the Gohain's birth, pointing out that he was very dark of complexion and could not have been Rudra Singha's son. But such was the barbarua's power that his candidate won the day. Kirtichandra insisted Rudra Singha had wished on his deathbed that his sons rule one after the other, and the dying king's wishes must be respected. The other nobles had no argument to counter this assertion, so Kalshiliya Gohain became the new king. He took on the Ahom name of Sunyeopha and the Hindu name of Lakshmi Singha. One of his first acts was to banish the two sons of Rajeshwar Singha to Namrup.

'The other patra-mantris were not the only ones to question the legitimacy of Lakshmi Singha's birth. Even the religious mentor, the Parbatiya gossain, did so and refused sharan to the new king. So Swargadeo Sunyeopha summoned from far-off Kanauj a Brahmin named Ramananda Pushpacharya, who had been his tutor as a child, and made him his religious guru. Ramananda was given the title of Pahumoriya Gossain but was popularly known as the Na-Gossain or the new seer.

'Though the king retained the patra-mantris, it was Kirtichandra Barbarua who held sway. A brilliant judge of character, the barbarua understood that Lakshmi Singha was a nervous, weak-willed, fifty-five-year-old man and could be kept on a tight leash. The swargadeo too was quite willing to enjoy the fruits of kingship and let the barbarua rule the realm as he pleased.

'The barbarua kept to the palace's tradition of contempt for the Vaishnavs and on many occasions heaped insults on them, particularly the Moamarias, who he knew were rebellious and needed to be kept in their proper place. As it happened, one day the king in the company of Kirtichandra was enjoying a pleasure cruise on the choranao or royal barge when he saw a Moamaria mahant or priest on the bank and asked the craft to be moored so that he could talk. The mahant was deferential towards the swargadeo, but intentionally ignored Kirtichandra. The incensed barbarua roundly ticked off the Moamaria mahant. The priest walked off in a huff, vowing revenge under his breath.

'The swargadeo's Moran subjects had the responsibility of supplying elephants and honey to him instead of paying revenue. A few days after the incident on the barge, the chief of the Moran tribe named Nahorkhora Saikia visited the palace at Rongpur to give three elephants to the swargadeo; Kirtichandra was incensed that the chief had gone straight to the king without letting him know. He had Nahor arrested and not only abused him with words, but also had his ears chopped off to teach him a lesson.

'The consequences of this senseless, brutal act were severe. As you know, my people, the Ahoms maintained a very small standing army for providing security to the royalty and the nobles. Whenever needed, a huge army could be raised because most Assamese males were trained soldiers apart from their customary professions. The aggrieved Moran chief went to his spiritual mentor, the Moamaria mahant, with his tale of woe; the latter asked his disciples to take revenge for the injustice meted out to the Moran chief. Thus, whereas previously in times of crises the subjects responded by reporting for military duty to the king, on this occasion, they did the same for their spiritual head. An army of Moamaria rebels was raised, with the mahant nominating his own son Bangan to lead it and appointing Nahorkhora Saikia and Raghav Neog as commanders. The exiled Prince Mohanmala and the sons of Rajeshwar Singha were roped in by the promise of restoring what was due to them.

'The first Moamaria rebellion, which began in November 1769, achieved overwhelming success. On the advice of Kirtichandra, the swargadeo removed Bhagi Buragohain, holding him to be sympathetic towards the rebels, and appointed Kuoigayan Ghanashyam in his place. For a while the force sent under the new buragohain succeeded in stemming the Moamaria advance at the river Dibaru; but Raghav Neog with a large band of men moved along the north bank of the Brahmaputra and made an assault on another front of the imperial army, putting it to disarray. Ghanashyam Buragohain advised the king to come to terms with the rebels, but Kirtichandra differed, and instead asked Lakshmi Singha to go to Guwahati and embark on an anti-rebel campaign from there.

'The king took this advice and departed from the capital post-haste. But he had left it too late. His decision to flee destroyed the morale of his soldiers and they gave in to the rebels, who strode triumphantly into Rongpur. Lakshmi Singha was pursued and easily captured. The helpless and cringing king was brought back to Rongpur and put in confinement at the Jaisagar temple. The arrogant, tyrannical Kirtichandra Barbarua too was captured and executed, along with his sons, and the women of his family members were allotted to the leaders. Some of the other nobles too were either put to death or imprisoned. On hearing the news of the Moamaria triumph, Mohanmala arrived at Rongpur to be crowned king, but had to confront the reality of betrayal. The Moamaria leaders, drunk with a sense of power, refused to make him king and he left the capital a disillusioned man.

'Raghav and Nahorkhora wanted to make Bangan the king, but his father the Moamaria mahant forbade him to accept; so, Ramakanta, a son of Nahorkhora, was placed on the throne at Rongpur. Oh, it was a merry time for the Moamarias, my people! The leaders occupied the spacious houses belonging to the nobles whom they had supplanted; most of the citizens of Rongpur had fled, and the common soldiers amongst the rebels occupied their dwellings. Raghav Neog made himself the barbarua and took the queens of the palace, including Kuranganoyoni, the Manipuri widow of Rajeshwar Singha.

'Ramakanta, who occupied the palace, even minted coins in his name, though, to be one up on the Ahoms, he made his nine-sided! The real power, of course, vested in Raghav who, in deference to his own Moamaria guru, called upon all Vaishnav sattradhikars to declare allegiance to him, an action which gave rise to much disaffection within the Vaishnav ranks. Also, the people considered the upstarts at the helm in Rongpur to be of the same social level as themselves, thus displayed little reverence towards them while maintaining their devotion to the Ahom swargadeo.

'Arrogance is the enemy of statesmen, my people. Their stay of around five months in Rongpur without the slightest signs of resistance made the Moamaria leaders arrogant, leading to carelessness. They failed to erect a network of spies, thus did not know that at Guwahati, still under Ahom occupation, the barphukan and other nobles were plotting to wrest Rongpur back and restore to the captive king his throne. They planned the timing with great care; it was to be mid-April, the time of the Assamese national festival of Rongali or Bohag Bihu, when many of the Moamaria soldiers at Rongpur would go home to be with their families for a few days. There could be no sending of a conspicuous force to Rongpur, for it would attract attention and alert the usurpers. The swargadeo's life was at stake, so subterfuge was of the essence. A bairagi was sent to confide in secret the plan and the time to Kuranganoyoni, for the nobles needed someone within the palace ...'

Twilight

⁓

THE SCENTS AND SOUNDS OF SPRING WERE IN THE AIR. IT WAS THE festive season when young men crooned love songs and danced the huchari with their beloveds. Huchari parties went from house to house, singing and dancing, with the elders amongst them blessing each household. As a mammoth huchari party made its way along the streets of Rongpur late in the evening, no one suspected these were no Moamarias although they were dressed as such or that, underneath their garb, they carried deadly weapons. Most of the houses wore a desolate look, with the dwellers having left for their villages to be with their folks during Bohag Bihu.

The guards at the gate of the palace complex, which also contained the houses of the nobles, were taken in. This Moamaria huchari party had come to bless the king, Raghav Barbarua and the others, they were told. The guards let the raucous party through. It first went to the house of Raghav Barbarua and, with resounding thrums of drums and clash of cymbals, announced its arrival. Although her new consort Raghav Barbarua lay fast asleep beside her on the bed, Queen Kuranganoyoni lay wide awake, waiting precisely for this signal. She got up and shook Raghav.

'Wake up,' she said in urgent tones. 'A huchari has come to our house to bless us. We mustn't keep it waiting.'

Raghav got up with alacrity. No matter that he had invested himself with the barbarua title; he was an ordinary farmer at heart. The throb of the huchari drums set his pulse throbbing. Putting on his official robe, he hurried outside. Kuranganoyoni followed close behind him, hiding an unsheathed hengdang at her back. As Raghav prostrated himself before the huchari party to accord traditional reverence to it, Kuranganoyoni raised the hengdang and severed his head from his body!

The rest of the operation went smoothly. Throwing off their camouflage, the nobles and soldiers disarmed the bewildered palace guards; the family of Raghav, including his mother and two sisters, Radha and Rukmini, were slaughtered on the spot; the usurper Ramakanta and those close to him were killed too and Rongpur was overnight cleared of all Moamaria presence. A signal was given to show that the capital had been retaken, and groups of loyal soldiers, who had been concealed near the capital, came rushing in to augment its defences.

A group led by Ghanashyam Buragohain and Bailung Bargohain left that night itself to Jaisagar dol to set Swargadeo Sunyeopha free. He was reinstated upon the Ahom throne with great fanfare in a bid to drive home to the populace his authority. The Moamarias were set upon with a vengeance; the mahant and hundreds of others, without considerations of guilt or innocence, were arrested, tortured and brutally killed. The equanimity which had prevailed for some time in the realm was irrevocably shattered.

Hammered into submission, the main body of Moamarias was quiescent for a while, biding its time. But, with the Ahom authority over the country being placed in doubt, other groups on the peripheries began raising their rebellious heads. Also, splinter groups of Moamarias revolted again and again, and much of Lakshmi Singha's reign was devoted to counter these with the help of Manipuri mercenaries. An official of the king was dismissed in 1774 for plotting against him; aware of the weakness of the ruling monarch this officer crossed to the north bank of the Brahmaputra and declared himself to be King Mirhang! A force had to be sent against him and he was finally captured and killed. The Chutiyas, led by a local landlord, rebelled and the sadiyakhowa gohain was killed; the royal army was finally able to put down the rebellion by means of severe repression, which further resulted in anger amongst the subjects.

The Moamaria uprising had severely disrupted social conditions. It was time for the Ahom priests to try and reassert their former pre-eminence. They told the king that if lawlessness prevailed in the country and the royal coffers were becoming empty due to prevailing circumstances, it was because the swargadeos had abandoned traditional beliefs and embraced the Hindu religion. They specially emphasized that some kings in the recent past had been cremated according to Hindu customs rather than buried as Ahoms should be. The Ahom priests said they wanted to perform rituals to undo the evil effects of such a practice. For a while, Lakshmi Singha was convinced of this and even allowed the priests to perform a weird ceremony. The Ahom priests made an effigy representing Rajeshwar Singha, performed the Rikkhvan ceremony to restore him to life, and then had the effigy buried in a maidam. However, this did not result in any marked difference in the situation and the wily Brahmin priests soon regained their hold upon the palace. They now insisted that Goddess Tara be worshipped in ostentatious ceremonies to bring prosperity back to the kingdom; a great amount of money was given away by the king to the Brahmin priests, while the Ahom priests refused to participate in the ceremonies.

Knowing that his health was failing, Lakshmi Singha made his son the prince-regent so that he could succeed him without problem. Thus, his son Loknath Gohain had the full support of the nobles when he ascended the throne after his father's death in December 1780, taking on the Ahom name of Suhitpungpha and the Hindu one of Gaurinath Singha. The manner in which he acted upon becoming the king revealed his true nature—he ordered the mutilation of all princes of noble blood so that they could not become rivals and also set one noble against another so that they could not conspire against him. Little did he realize that he himself would be the cause of his own downfall!

The Ahom empire was crumbling. With the controlling might of the central authority in doubt, the realm began to fall apart. As soon as he ascended the throne, the weak-willed but vindictive king began contributing to its destruction by beginning a campaign of atrocity against the Moamarias who had killed his father. Thousands, no matter how innocent, were impaled or beheaded; entire villages were razed on suspicion that they had sided with the rebels. A wise king would have attempted reconciliation with his subjects. But not Gaurinath Singha! He wanted revenge.

Nemesis was to overtake him soon enough. In April 1782, while the king was returning at night, a group of rebels, taking advantage of the darkness, carrying lighted flares like the king's men, covertly joined the party one by one. Thus successfully entering the well-guarded city of Garhgaon, they launched a surprise attack, cutting down whoever opposed them. Gaurinath Singha was fortunate that he was on the back of his elephant and could get away. While his loyal chaodang guards quickly whisked the swargadeo to the safety of the royal palace, Ghanashyam Buragohain summoned military resources and succeeded in driving the rebels out of the city. Thus ended the second Moamaria uprising.

But there was to be no respite. The very same year, Ghanashyam Buragohain passed away and his son Purnananda was made the buragohain. A brave, wise and resourceful man, Purnananda like his father advised the king to desist from persecuting the Moamarias and attempt reconciliation. But those whom the gods wish to destroy, they first make mad. There was no restraining the vengeful swargadeo. Atrocities continued to be perpetrated against the sect. Thousands more—men, women and children—were massacred, with suspected leaders being thrown into cauldrons of boiling oil.

The outcome was all too predictable. In 1786, the Moamarias raised another army and attacked Ahom entrenchments on the north bank of the Brahmaputra with the objective of crossing the river and taking Rongpur. A force was sent to repel them, but was defeated because most of the soldiers defected to the rebel camp. The Moamarias also attacked on the eastern front but were kept at bay by Purnananda Buragohain, who however was gradually forced to retreat from Sonarimukh, where he had met them, back to the safety of the capital Rongpur. The rebels followed him and laid waste the countryside, forcing the villagers to flee.

Leaving the buragohain to defend the city as best he could, the king, accompanied by most of his officers, fled towards Guwahati. In order to protect Rongpur, Purnananda hastily erected a fortification and succeeded in stalling the rebel advance for the time being. This fortification was called Bibudhigarh. Meanwhile, seeing the king flee, subjects loyal to him also followed, while some left their villages to hide in the hills. Finally, however, the resistance offered by Purnananda at Rongpur collapsed and he had to retreat towards Kaziranga. Meanwhile, Gaurinath Singha had proceeded up the river Kolong and set up an encampment at Rupahi. From there he sent emissaries to the Kachari, Jaiantia and Manipuri Rajas asking for their assistance; the former two refused assistance but the latter, reminded of the help the Ahoms had rendered once, came with a force of 500 cavalry and 4,000 foot soldiers to assist the king. The two met at Rupahi and the Ahom swargadeo requested him to proceed upstream to assist the buragohain. The Manipur raja, along with a detachment from Purnananda's force, made an assault to wrest back Rongpur, but lost heavily, depriving the raja of the will to make any more attempts. Leaving 1,000 of his men with the buragohain, he went back to Manipur.

Gaurinath Singha soon came to realize that the subjects around Nowgong too were displaying rebellious aggression, so he fled once more towards Guwahati. There he conferred with his barphukan and raised a 13,000-strong army which proceeded upstream to assist the buragohain. By then, both the principal cities, Garhgaon and Rongpur, were under Moamaria control and totally devastated by the rebels. Those amongst the subjects who had not fled from the cities and adjacent villages, discovering which way the wind was blowing, began out of compulsion to throw in their lot with the Moamarias. With Upper Assam under their control, the latter divided the land into two halves; a Moamaria leader accepted the throne at Rongpur, giving himself the name of Bharat

Singha, claiming that he was the descendent of Emperor Bhagadatta of Mahabharata fame, and minting nine-sided coins in that name. He appointed a man named Sukura as his barbarua. The other half was given to a Moamaria named Sarbananda Moran, who took on the title of bor senapati or commander-in-chief.

In fact, finding no effective central control, various chiefs all over Upper Assam, began to declare independence from the Ahom dominion and proclaim themselves kings in their own small domains. For instance, an ordinary weaver was made a king by the Moamarias at Japaribhita on the north bank of the Brahmaputra. Another person named Haulia declared himself the king of Majuli! Taking advantage of the prevailing anarchy, the Khampti tribe annexed the Sadiya region to be added to their kingdom, and even appointed a sadiyakhowa gohain of their own.

The suffering of the people can well be imagined. The Moamarias having razed villages and paddy fields, famine conditions prevailed. Many inhabitants died of starvation, while others managed to survive on wild roots and berries. Some fortunate families were able to flee to Lower Assam, some even crossing into Bengal. Had it not been for the inspiration provided by Purnananda, the remaining Ahom loyalists too would have crossed over to the Moamaria side, thereby providing a possible opportunity for the enemy to join hands with rebels in Central and Lower Assam. The reinforcements sent from Guwahati proved inadequate to oust the numerically superior and well-entrenched Moamarias from the Ahom capitals and the buragohain had to embark on a strategy of containment rather than assault.

The situation, for Gaurinath Singha, was not at all conducive in Guwahati. Some time previously, Gaurinath Singha had had Hansanarayan, the raja of Darrang, executed for treason, though the man was in fact innocent. A prince belonging to the Darrang royal clan named Vishnunarayan had been appointed as a vassal king in his place. Krishnanarayan, the son of the executed raja, sought revenge and imported a sizable troop of Hindustani and Bengali mercenaries called Barkandazes. With their help, Gaurinath's nominee in Darrang was ousted; now Krishnanarayan, learning of Gaurinath Singha's plight, raised the banner of revolt against him. His troops advanced as far as the north bank of the Brahmaputra opposite Guwahati.

Thus, the entire Brahmaputra Valley, from Sadiya to Darrang, had burst out in flames. Only Purnananda Buragohain clung on tenuously as a barrier between the rampaging Moamarias and Guwahati. But his position was becoming precarious. Absence of supplies meant that the men under him had to eat the flesh of their own mounts and scrounge from the jungles in order to survive. He had sent urgent messages to Guwahati for more reinforcements, but there were none to send. In desperation, Gaurinath Singha applied to the British in Bengal for help.

In 1498, the Portuguese adventurer Vasco Da Gama first laid out a sea route round the Cape of Good Hope from Europe to the west coast of India. Since then, there had been brisk trade between the two regions, with French, British and Dutch traders soon emulating their Portuguese counterparts in coming to the fabled land of Hindustan. In the year 1600, British merchants got together to form the East India Company and, setting up their base at Surat, obtained the permission of the Mughal Emperor Jahangir to embark on trade. In the course of the years, the company increased its reach to embrace a greater part of India and used its soldiers to exert political influence over regional powers. With the death of Aurangzeb in 1707, the disintegration of the Mughal empire began; the East India Company commenced taking advantage of the chaotic political situation to reveal its colonial designs and grab chunks of territory for itself. In the course of time, British hegemony spanned the entire subcontinent; the Battle of Plassey in 1759 brought Bengal under the Company's sphere of influence. However, the expansionist objectives of the British did not have Assam in its ambit primarily because the costs of retaining this remote outpost were not considered worth the revenue to be had.

But trade was carried out by British merchants with those in Ahom territory, the nodal point being Hadirachowki. The former's base was at Jogighopa; two European merchants, Bayley and Raush, had through prolonged competition attained monopoly of trade in Assam. The biggest item of import by Ahom merchants was salt, though some quantity of other commodities, such as cloth made in Europe and cotton linen manufactured in Bengal, carpets, brass, lead, pearls, iron implements, ornaments and jewellery, spices, etc. were imported. The exported items included the famed Assam muga silk, lac, ivory, agar wood, certain agricultural products like mustard and sugarcane, etc. Deals were made between traders through the barter system as well as with gold and silver. Both Bayley and Raush had huge warehouses at Dhubri and Jogighopa to store their stuff, indicating the extensive nature of trade with the Ahom kingdom.

On this autumn morning in the year 1792, a large boat moved swiftly down the Luit and moored at a wharf of Jogighopa. Three men, named Bika Majumdar, Dattaram Khaund and the erstwhile king of Darrang, Vishnunarayan, disembarked from the vessel and made their way to one of the warehouses. They were emissaries of the beleaguered Ahom Swargadeo Gaurinath Singha, sent to contact one of the European traders, Raush, who had been a resident of Jogighopa since 1768, so that he could put them in touch with the British authorities in Bengal.

Raush's warehouse was indeed huge and packed to capacity, though there seemed to be little activity going on within it. The reason became clear when they met the owner, a tall and burly fellow, unshaven and with the looks more of a pirate than a respectable merchant.

'Of course, I will help your king,' Raush stated after the pleasantries were over and the men got down to actual business. 'Apparently, your kingdom is in turmoil and all trading activity has come to a standstill, which does no good to my pockets, eh? Look around you. This godown is bursting at the seams!'

'Thank you,' said Bika Majumdar, who because he was of Bengali descent could speak the language and thus overcome communication problems with Raush, the latter being fluent in Bengali. He explained the broad situation in Assam.

'I shall immediately have some mercenaries dispatched to Guwahati,' Raush assured the emissaries. 'They can be sent further upstream to assist Purnananda Buragohain in his fight against the rebels. I will arrange to pay them in advance. Your king can recompense me later.'

'We need more than mere mercenaries,' Majumdar asserted. 'The backing of Her Imperial Majesty's government is vital if the grave situation is to be tackled.'

'Well, tell you what, I shall send the mercenaries anyway, so as to remain on the good side of your king. As for official assistance, I'll escort you to Mr Lumsden, the collector of this district. He can set up an appointment with representatives of the British government at Calcutta. Who knows, given the dire circumstances, you might even get to meet the governor-general, Lord Cornwallis. Also, I shall write a personal letter to another merchant friend of mine, who will arrange for your accommodation at Calcutta and assist you in getting around.'

The Jogighopa-based merchant clearly was an influential man and his recommendation carried weight, so much so that Lumsden lost no time in contacting the higher officials of the land and securing an audience for the emissaries with Lord Cornwallis himself. However, the governor-general was not convinced of the wisdom of meddling in the affairs of a remote kingdom.

'I'm afraid we cannot help your king,' he told the three ambassadors. 'We are pursuant of a policy of non-intervention in the affairs of other kingdoms unless our own interests are involved.'

Majumdar had been well tutored on how to reply by Dattaram Khaund, who had anticipated such a response. 'But your interests are indeed involved, Your Excellency,' Majumdar said. 'The mercenaries of the rebel, Krishnanarayan, who are causing depredation within the Ahom kingdom, are from your realm and are your subjects. It is thus your responsibility to ensure that their depredation is stopped and they be brought back to their native land.'

Lord Cornwallis smiled at such a specious argument. 'Yes,' he said, 'you're right. Those brigands are our subjects and need to be brought back. I congratulate you on convincing me and providing me with a pretext!'

The month was November, the year 1792. A flotilla of gunboats sailed up the Brahmaputra, carrying six companies of British sepoys comprising 360 soldiers, with Captain Thomas Welsh in command, accompanied by Lieutenant Macgregor as Adjutant, Ensign Wood as surveyor and Dr John Peter Wade as assistant surgeon. Welsh's mandate in September had been to sail from Calcutta to the easternmost British-held district of Goalpara, obtain from Raush a factual account of the Assam situation and report back to headquarters so that further instructions could be given. But, on reaching Goalpara on 8 November 1792, Welsh had been convinced by the account given by Raush that the situation was too grave for the delay entailed in sending a report to Calcutta and awaiting instructions. Prompt action was called for and thus he had at once set out for Guwahati to assist the Ahom King Gaurinath Singha, after having dispatched a missive to his superiors setting out the reason.

On 19 November, as they were approaching the Nagarbera Hill, the captain of his leading gunboat sighted another small flotilla moving swiftly downstream towards them. Soldiers were immediately put on alert as the flotilla was intercepted—but it turned out to contain Gaurinath Singha and his entourage who had fled from Guwahati after being attacked.

'It was a fierce assault by Krishnanarayan's men,' the Ahom king asserted before the British captain. 'They were so many in numbers that we could not withstand their attack.'

Welsh was both dismayed and surprised by the Ahom king's demeanour. The fame of the Ahom kingdom had spread far and wide and he had expected to confront a valiant warrior of noble bearing. On the contrary, he saw an extremely ordinary looking and terrified creature, noticeably addicted to opium, who addressed him with almost comical servility. Yet, as apparent in the behaviour of members of his retinue as well as the three emissaries, he was the undisputed monarch of this unfamiliar domain and the captain was determined to assist him.

Rather than rely on the king's version, he talked to those accompanying him and learned the truth. It had not been Krishnanarayan's army which had attacked Guwahati but a group of fishermen led by a bairagi who wanted to take advantage of the situation to acquire power. So demoralized had the Ahom king and his nobles been that they had panicked at this trifling assault and fled the city without offering resistance! The puny threat of the adversary was testified to by the fact that no sooner had Welsh and his troops reached close to Guwahati and moored their gunboats some eight miles away, the upstart usurpers fled, enabling the captain and his soldiers to march without interference into the city.

Captain Welsh advised the king to try and reconcile with Krishnanarayan by promising to return to him the principality of Darrang if he submitted to his authority. This strategy failing, Welsh began a campaign against Krishnanarayan on 6 December 1792. The Barkandazes who constituted the core of the rebel Raja's army were no match for the well-trained, well-armed and disciplined British sepoys and were soon routed with heavy losses. However, Welsh had simultaneously to deal with the vindictive nature of the Ahom king as well as the intrigues of his nobles, particularly the barbarua and the soladhara phukan. The captain threatened to stop assisting the king and to return to Calcutta if Gaurinath Singh did not stop the spree of cold-blooded murders he was carrying out on his presumed adversaries at the instigation of these two nobles. Such a threat had its desired effect; the swargadeo pledged to do the captain's bidding and the two conniving nobles were sent in exile to Bengal. By May 1793, Krishnanarayan stated his willingness to stop fighting if Darrang was restored to him; under the watchful eyes of Captain Welsh, who was concerned that Gaurinath Singha would renege on his promise, the rebel was formally restored as the raja of Darrang in lieu of an annual tribute of money and men.

With the acquisition of a further reinforcement of six more companies of sepoys sent from Bengal, with the permission of the governor-general, Captain Welsh in January 1794 commenced his campaign to restore order in Central and Upper Assam, having restored Ahom authority in Lower Assam and suppressed river pirates who had been disrupting communications.

Purnananda Buragohain sat in the prow of his war-boat and gazed sadly at the ravaged country around him as his vessel made its laborious way up the river Luit. The banks were totally devoid of human presence; not even stray cattle could be sighted. Only animals such as wild boar and buffaloes were to be occasionally seen at the sandy edge of the waters. Tears came to the eyes of the buragohain at the thought of the suffering his motherland had been subjected to. He firmly wiped away the tears and tried to erase the sinking sensation in his heart that the end of his race was nigh.

Some days back, saviours in the form of boga bangals at the head of native soldiers from Bengal had reached Jorhat, where the buragohain was making a valiant stand and keeping the Moamarias at bay. The noble was amazed at the skill and discipline shown by the British force as it quickly cleared the neighbouring region from the presence of rebels. He was mortified at discovering that Gaurinath had abjured all responsibility and thrust the burden of conducting the campaign upon Captain Welsh. But his was not to squander his energy on futile recrimination but to assist the white men in combating the enemy.

The sepoys brought by the white men were bolstered by what remained of his force, and the combined army was now moving up the Brahmaputra, the objective being capture of the capital Rongpur, which would be made the base from where to suppress the rebels. At Dikhaumukh, they disembarked from the unwieldy boats unsuited to proceed up the shallower tributary, and progressed on foot. The first resistance from the enemy came as they were twelve miles from Rongpur. A huge horde of Moamarias wielding bows and arrows, spears, daos, matchlocks, etc., suddenly appeared from nowhere and with bloodcurdling shrieks fell upon their relatively small group.

His own men might have fled before such a furious attack, but not the trained British sepoys. With almost supernatural calmness, the units closed ranks and knelt in formation, shooting with precision at specific targets, heaping scores of casualties upon the Moamarias. The adversaries, having never encountered such a disciplined force before and finding themselves being inflicted with heavy losses, fell back. But rather than chase after the retreating enemy with wild whoops of triumph as Ahom soldiers would have done, the sepoys, with the boga-bangals at their head, advanced at a steady pace, occasionally using the cover of defensive structures such as a brick bridge over the river Namdang. The Moamarias within Rongpur, growing panic-stricken at the relentless advance, evacuated the capital, enabling the advance party of the combined British and Ahom troops to enter it without resistance on 18 March 1794. Gaurinath Singha, who was encamped at Dikhaumukh, came to Rongpur three days later and was installed once again as swargadeo of the Ahom realm. Purnananda Buragohain felt ashamed at the servility displayed by his swargadeo towards his white saviours, in particular his supplication in public asking that they and their forces remain in Rongpur till all traces of rebellion were erased.

Had this request been granted, perhaps the Ahom dynasty might have lasted longer. Captain Welsh himself was aware that with his departure, anarchy would once again descend on the Ahom realm. He, therefore, had written to Calcutta giving an account of the prevailing situation and requesting permission for a longer stay. In the meanwhile, Lord Cornwallis had been replaced by Sir John Shore as the governor–general and the latter proved to be more stringent in following the policy of non-interference. Rather than accept the counsel of Welsh, he dispatched an order asking him to return to British territory by 1 July, which the captain expeditiously obeyed despite misgivings.

At the forcible eviction of the Moamaria encroachers from Rongpur, some of the original inhabitants had returned to the devastated and depopulated city; but their sojourn was not to be for very long. The buragohain had come to the conclusion that Jorhat, whose populace had displayed loyalty to the swargadeo, enabling Purnananda to hold his own against the enemy, was far suited to be the Ahom capital. His proposal that Gaurinath Singha move there was accepted with alacrity by the weakling king, who had been so demoralized by the departure of the British troops that he became incapable of taking decisions on his own. Almost as soon as he and his followers departed from Rongpur, leaving a garrison behind, the Moamarias, having learnt of the British withdrawal and evacuation of the royal party, descended in hordes upon the city. The Ahom garrison fled to Jorhat without offering resistance and Rongpur was once more under the occupation of the rebels.

Within the safety of Jorhat, Gaurinath Singha began to again reveal his brutal and sadistic nature, coming down with a vengeance on officers who had enjoyed Captain Welsh's confidence. The barbarua, appointed on the directive of Welsh, was dismissed while the barphukan and the solal gohain were murdered at the instruction of the king. Moamarias within the realm under Ahom control were hunted down and butchered; such was the brutality heaped upon the sect that entire families committed suicide rather than allow themselves to be arrested. Beyond the pale of Ahom control, a renewed state of anarchy prevailed and the fear expressed by Captain Welsh in his letter to his superiors, that if the British troops left 'confusion, devastation and massacre would ensue', started coming true. There was no effective Ahom control over a greater portion of the realm and a free-for-all situation arose.

Determined to put an end to anarchy and reassert Ahom control, Purnananda Buragohain undertook preparation towards that end. At Jorhat, a standing army, patterned on the model of the British sepoys and trained by two of Captain Welsh's native officers left behind for this purpose, was raised. Not only were the recruits given uniforms to induce the feeling of belonging to a unit, they were also armed with flintlock guns purchased from Calcutta. Slowly but surely, led by the buragohain, the imperial forces began to stamp their authority over the realm, subduing rebels both in Upper and Lower Assam. The intrepid officer showed that armed with the proper tools, it did not require British intervention to subdue unruly subjects and bring about peace, and an efficient native noble could do it as well.

With the gradual restoration of authority came a measure of prosperity and well-being. Subjects who had fled the Valley to the surrounding hills returned to their old habitats; new villages sprang up and farmlands which had been laid to waste grew green with paddy and vegetables again. Keeping the administration firmly in his hands, the buragohain took advantage of the deteriorating health of the swargadeo to attempt reconciliation with leaders of the Moamaria sect. Because the subjects of the realm were weary of the prolonged strife and anarchy, his overtures met with a degree of success and the flames of revolt began to die down. Though the Ahom forces could not reoccupy the area around Sadiya which had been taken over by the Khamti tribe, yet the period between 1794 and 1818 slowly began to mirror the Ahom realm of yore both in extent and imperial control.

The two haats or village markets, Macharhat and Chokihat, which gave Jorhat its name (the place was originally called Chong Sukat in the Tai language) were the focal trading points of villages in the region; Purnananda Buragohain erected his new capital close to them because of the strategic position afforded. The chief noble wanted that a river flow past the township; so, he gave bhog or offerings to the river Disai and dug a branch from it to flow beside Jorhat and debouch into the Brahmaputra. This came to be known as the Bhogdoi River. A number of pukhuris were dug to provide fresh water to the citizens; these included the Mithapukhuri whose waters were used to wash the deity in the royal temple, the Rajmaopukhuri dug by the mother of a king following Gaurinath, and the Bongalpukhuri dug by Rupsingh Subedar, a migrant from Bengal.

The royal treasury being almost empty, it was not possible to build up a capital matching the grandeur of Rongpur; in fact, the Rajbari or the king's abode at Jorhat was a relatively unpretentious though sprawling building of wood and thatch. On the evening of 19 December 1795, upon a bed in a chamber of the palace, the shrivelled figure of Swargadeo Gaurinath Singha lay gasping for breath. Around him stood the bezbarua and some servants, and the only noble present, Purnananda Singha, his face set in steadfast resolve.

The wretched king, who had contributed so much to the weakening of Ahom authority, was dying. Purnananda was cognizant of the power struggle which would ensue—the palace intrigues, conspiracies and killings! He was determined to nip in the bud any attempt at renewed disorder, even if it meant having to embark on actions distasteful to himself. The sole way of doing this was to take up the reins of absolute power so as to have total control over unfolding events. He wielded complete command over the other nobles—except one. Only Baskatia Barbarua stood in his way as one who could pose a challenge to him.

He stepped out of the bedchamber for a moment and signalled to one of his trusted officers waiting in the corridor. The man stepped up and was given whispered orders. He, in turn, hurried out of the palace to Baskatia Barbarua's quarters. 'The swargadeo summons you for urgent consultations,' he informed the dangoriya.

The barbarua suspected nothing. It was not unusual for the whimsical, opium-addicted king to summon his nobles and officers at the oddest hours. Putting on his official robes, he hastened alongside the officer. As they were about to reach the dimly lit gate of the royal residence, two chaodang assassins sprang out of the dark; while one put his palm over the noble's mouth to stifle any screams, the other slit his throat with a knife.

'Take him away and throw him into the Bhogdoi,' instructed the officer.

An hour later, Swargadeo Gaurinath Singha too was dead.

THE NARRATOR

'Only those who come afterwards have a true inkling of what happened before!' said the wise old narrator, in a voice that had grown tired. 'Yet

Purnananda Buragohain could sense the imminent setting of the sun on the Ahom empire. But a single individual cannot by himself alter the destiny of a race unless the conditions are conducive. In his case, they were not. The Ahom monarchy had become a hollow shell. The anarchy and violence of the preceding years had depopulated and devastated the land; the realm was healing, though the process was slow. There was every reason to fear that it would never again reach the heights of prosperity and glory attained in former times.

'But even the perceptive buragohain could not foresee that the Ahom empire, which had lasted for almost six centuries, would crumble within the span of another three decades!

'His was not to ask questions or make recriminations. His was only to perform his duty and try to revive his race as best as he could. The main problem was to find a successor to Gaurinath Singha, who could inspire the subjects as many of the earlier monarchs had done and imbue in them a spirit of nationalism. But the continuous maiming of princes of the different phaids, in order to make them ineligible for the Ahom throne, had resulted in numerous individuals of calibre being rendered unfit. Finally, almost against his wishes, he chose Prince Kinaram Gohain, a great-grandson of Swargadeo Gadhadhar Singha's younger son, the Namrup Raja Lechai, to be elevated to the Ahom throne. Because of the absolute power he wielded, none dared to challenge the buragohain's choice.

'The prolonged disturbances, looting by rebels, stoppage of trade, etc., had emptied the royal treasury, so much so that there was no money for Kinaram's coronation and he could not ascend the singorighar in true Ahom tradition. Thus, there was no public ceremony—Kinaram was simply placed on the throne with the nobles pledging allegiance to him. There was also no formal adoption of royal names; though he took on the Hindu name of Kamaleshwar Singha, his Ahom title of Suklingpha did not have much significance, being a literal translation of his Hindu name. On ascending the throne in 1795, Kamaleshwar Singha, with the consent of his buragohain, appointed his father Kadamdighala Gohain as the Saring raja, next in line to the Ahom throne in case he died, and Gangaram as bargohain. However, when his father died a couple of years later, Kamaleshwar's stepbrother Chandrakanta Gohain was made the Saring raja despite being of tender age.

'In truth, Kamaleshwar was merely the nominal ruler—the entire burden of governing the kingdom was invested with Purnananda. Though, during the short rule of Gaurinath, the buragohain had begun the process of restoring order in the realm and achieved a degree of success, much remained to be done. The most important task being to replenish the royal treasury, the Vaishnav sattradhikars were approached to help out, which they did, though unwillingly. There was also a need to bring back former subjects of the kingdom and increase its population— entire villages had been rendered barren during the upheaval caused by the Moamarias and other rebels—those who had fled to the hills and even to Bengal—were coaxed back with pledges of pardon and compensation. Merchants were encouraged to re-commence trade so that revenue could be collected for the royal treasury while a fillip was sought to be given to local cottage industry in order to increase the volume of export.

'Much of the wealth so acquired was spent by the buragohain in training up Ahom soldiers in the style of the British. Two divisions were created, one each at Guwahati and Jorhat, and placed under two 'captains'; firearms were purchased from Calcutta and thus equipped, the buragohain set about reinforcing the authority of the Ahom swargadeo in his domain. A good judge of character, he replaced the barphukan at Guwahati with an officer as efficient as himself; a man named Gendhela Koliabhomora. None too soon it proved, for a serious uprising broke out in Lower Assam. Two brothers, Hardatta and Birdatta of the Bujarbarua clan, helped by the rajas of Kochbehar and Bijni, raised the standard of revolt with an army comprising mostly mercenaries from Punjab, Hindustan and Kochbehar, and captured a large swathe of land in Kamrup. The British merchant Raush unfortunately was on his way up the Brahmaputra when the rebellion broke out. His boats were captured, looted and burnt by the rebels known as the Dumdumiyas, and Raush himself was killed.

'Displaying great enterprise, Koliabhomora Barphukan strengthened his own forces by importing Bengal mercenaries and, aided by the rajas of Beltola and Dimarua, succeeded in suppressing the rebellion, capturing and killing the two ringleaders and bringing order to Lower Assam. For his feat, the Ahom king honoured Koliabhomora Barphukan with the designation of Pratapballabh. It was a well-merited designation, for Kaliabhomora was indeed an able and progressive officer. Legend has it that he conceived of building a wooden bridge across the Brahmaputra from Tezpur to Kaliabar and even collected an enormous amount of sal wood for the purpose, but the project was shelved due to his demise. It had been the pragmatic Kaliabhomora who also recommended to the Ahom king that he accept the role of a monarch under the direct protection of the East India Company so as to receive immediate help in case of threat to the monarchy, as had come from the raja of Kochbehar. However, the recommendation, after consultation with the other patra-mantris, was shot down by the buragohain as demeaning to Ahom authority

'In the meantime, Purnananda Buragohain continued with his endeavour to restore order and stability to Upper Assam. Numerous smaller uprisings had to be quelled both on the north and south banks of the Brahmaputra including those by the Dafla tribe and Moamaria groups. He also had to proceed against the marauding Singpho tribe in 1798 and liberate Sadiya from the Khampti tribe in 1800. His endeavour did not cease with the death of Kamaleshwar Singha in 1811 through having contacted smallpox during an epidemic of the disease which had swept across the realm. The buragohain, using his indubitable powers, nominated Chandrakanta, the brother of the late king, to the Ahom throne.

'The objective of Purnananda Buragohain in nominating the new swargadeo, who was only thirteen years old at the time, was crystal clear— he wished to retain all power in his hands and use Chandrakanta as a puppet. This was a wise move, for the reign of Gaurinath Singha had been proof enough of the adverse outcome of allowing the king to act as he pleased. It is said in the buranjis that the young lad Chandrakanta, who till then had been living a carefree life with his playmates, did not wish to be elevated to the throne, and literally had to be dragged onto it crying and protesting. Finally, he agreed to sit upon it if his closest friend Satram, the son of a sarabjan or soothsayer named Kukurachoa Bora Bhut was allowed to sit by his side. Events later would prove that Purnananda Buragohain had made an error in acceding to this unusual request.

'With a boy king upon the Ahom throne, the buragohain took upon himself the task of administering the country. The paik-soldier system was abandoned and, for the first time in Ahom history, the job of fighting was vested on a trained and armed standing army. With its help, Purnananda and Kaliabhomora subdued the last vestiges of rebellion in Upper and Lower Assam and brought peace and stability back to the land. Purnananda's policy of reconciliation, pardon and leniency proved highly fruitful and thousands of subjects who had fled the realm returned to take up their former callings. Rongpur, the symbol of Ahom glory, was renovated though it was thought prudent to retain Jorhat as the capital. A number of roads were constructed to link this township with different parts of the kingdom.

'True to the spirit of the Shan tradition—a spirit forsaken by some of the other nobles in different, preceding periods—despite the unchallenged powers he enjoyed, Purnananda performed all his ameliorative endeavours in the name of the swargadeo. He would take the boy king along with him to different parts of the kingdom to show him to the subjects so that Chandrakanta's popularity would increase. He induced tutelary chieftains and rajas to come and pay homage to the new swargadeo, though financial constraints entailed that Chandrakanta, like his predecessor Kamaleshwar, could not ascend the singorighar.

'In every way this great Ahom patriot tried to stave off the inevitable and perpetuate the rule of his race. However, the degeneration had been too much for a revival. In a way, Purnananda himself was indirectly responsible on two counts for the terrible fate that awaited his beloved country just a few years later. First, in order to retain all-embracing powers and to prevent palace conspiracies against him and his king, he had removed most of the existing nobles and replaced them with his own kinsmen or men whose loyalty he did not doubt. When, just six months after the elevation of Chandrakanta to the throne, Kaliabhomora Barphukan passed away at Guwahati, he appointed a kinsman named Badanchandra, related to him by the fact that the latter's daughter was married to one of his sons, as the new barphukan.

'This was a mistake of irreversible magnitude which finally brought about the downfall of the Ahom rulers, and misery and calamity to the people of Assam. The usually perceptive Purnananda made this crucial error at a crossroads of his people's history, not realizing that Badanchandra had a vicious streak within him almost resembling that of Gaurinath Singha. As soon as power was invested with him, he began to display this latent oppressive streak; he and his sons began to extort the subjects of Kamrup and adjacent areas in order to enrich themselves. They were alleged to let loose upon the people an elephant named Balakdas after intoxicating it with bhang or hemp and derive amusement as the animal wreaked havoc by destroying houses and causing panic. He also imposed a rule that no 'dhekeri', a derogatory term for people of Lower Assam, could stay within Guwahati city after sundown, anyone caught doing so being subjected to severe punishment. Such was his reign of terror that Badanchandra Barphukan became a much-hated figure in Lower Assam—Purnananda realized his mistake too late and tried to rectify it by securing Badanchandra's removal.

'This became imperative due to events unfolding in Jorhat, and here again Purnananda was indirectly responsible. In adhering to the Shan code of loyalty to the king, he had overlooked some of the demands and whims of the young Chandrakanta, and tolerated the fact that Satram was almost the swargadeo's shadow. But, as Chandrakanta grew up in years, he began to chafe under the shackles imposed upon him by Purnananda. His disaffection was fuelled by Satram, who poisoned his mind by telling him that the buragohain had intentionally ensured that Chandrakanta did not ascend the singorighar and would not be worshipped as a genuine swargadeo by Ahom priests in the future in the ceremony of offering prayers and food to ancestors.[*] With the knowledge of the king, a conspiracy to kill Purnananda was hatched by Satram. This was discovered in the nick of time; the buragohain had all the conspirators arrested and summarily executed; but Satram, at the plea of Chandrakanta, was spared and banished to Namrup. However, soon afterwards, Satram was slain by some Nagas—on the orders of the buragohain, it was suspected.

'Enquiry into the conspiracy to assassinate Purnananda had revealed that Badanchandra Barphukan, now coveting power in the capital for himself, had instigated Chandrakanta and Satram to kill the buragohain. Also, the oppressions being committed by this barphukan and his henchmen were once again making Ahom rule unpopular with the subjects and unless he was reined in, there might be adverse consequences. To make matters worse, disturbing intelligence had reached Jorhat that the barphukan was hobnobbing with the British and a re-enactment of the Lalukshola Barphukan episode might be in the offing. Backed by incontrovertible evidence, Purnananda sent men to arrest Badanchandra and bring him to the capital for trial. But his daughter-in-law, Pijou Aideu, found out about the buragohain's intentions and sent her own emissary to warn her father about his imminent arrest.

'Badanchandra with his three sons Jonmi, Piyali and Numali, fled down the Brahmaputra on boats and escaped to Bengal. The new barphukan who replaced him, Ghanashyam, could not have them brought back despite his best efforts. Badanchandra, with the aid of people whom he had cultivated when he ruled Guwahati, made his way to Calcutta, and secured an audience with Lord Hastings, then the governor–general of the part of India ruled by the British. The fugitive tried to convince Hastings that the Ahom kingdom was in a state of turmoil and he needed to help by providing soldiers and arms to subdue

---

[*] Please refer to Ahom buranjis; Gait, *A History of Assam* (1905)

the uprisings. But Lord Hastings, citing the non-intervention policy, refused to assist.

'When destiny decides to work its magic ways, none can change the course of history. It seemed almost fated that Badanchandra would be the man who would be instrumental in destroying the Ahom kingdom. While in Calcutta, he met an agent of the king of Myanmar who had gone there with a similar purpose of having an audience with Lord Hastings. This man was taken in by Badanchandra's fabrications and assisted him to go to Myanmar and approach its king for help ...'

Sunset

AS HE WALKED THROUGH A PASSAGE TOWARDS THE HALL WHERE the Burmese King Bodau Phai and his courtiers awaited him, Badanchandra noticed that the palace of Amarapura was less ornate than that at Garhgaon, and made of only wood, bamboo and cane. It was also less lavishly furnished, while those occupying the hall were dressed relatively plainly when compared to the Ahom royalty and nobles. These pointed to the conclusion that the Burmese had had lesser exposure to more modern societies than the Ahoms and were thus more primitive in development. The faces of the men, including that of the king, were severe and their voices harsh, hinting that the race they represented was capable of cruelty and savagery beyond imagination. Badanchandra felt a shiver travel down his spine.

The moment he was escorted to the presence of the king, Badanchandra threw himself prostrate before him. Bodau Phai asked him to rise, speaking the local dialect, which one of his officers translated. The king next asked what his business was.

'Your Majesty,' Badanchandra spoke in humble tones. 'You are aware that your people are related to my people with ties of blood and history and that the Burmese and Ahom rulers are 'brother kings'. It is, therefore, your duty to ensure that a true Ahom prince sits on the Ahom throne.'

Bodau Phai was visibly surprised at this. 'Do not think for a moment that we do not know what is going on in our neighbourhood,' he spoke out a harsh warning. 'You have your spies, we ours. I've received no information that someone other than a member of the Shan brotherhood sits on the Ahom throne.'

'That's all a show, Your Majesty,' Badanchandra replied with all the conviction he could muster. 'Chandrakanta, the king, is merely a slip of a boy. The real ruler is Purnananda Buragohain—you can be sure that he is the one whose writ actually runs in the kingdom.'

'Is this true?' Bodau Phai asked his commander-in-chief, an individual with rugged features and a missing arm that he had lost in battle during an unsuccessful campaign against the neighbouring Shyamdesh or Thailand. There was a mocking hint in the king's tone.

'Quite true, Your Majesty,' the commander replied. 'Our spies confirm it.'

'So, what do you require of us?' the king asked in the same mocking tone, though he already knew. As soon as Badanchandra reached Amarapura, he had sought out an Ahom princess in Bodau Phai's harem. Her name was Rongili and she was related to him. He had explained the situation and requested her to intercede on his behalf with the Burmese king. Bodau Phai, therefore, was aware what Badanchandra's mission was.

The man standing before him was a betrayer of his country and could be made good use of. Bodau Phai had tried to expand his realm eastward by attacking neighbours but had been unsuccessful. So far, he had not contemplated an attack westward because he considered the Ahoms to be too powerful. But having a quisling who had once been no less than a barphukan gave him a distinct edge, and he was willing to empower the man in any way he wished.

'An army, Your Majesty,' said Badanchandra. 'I'll lead it myself. Together we shall attain victory against the Ahom forces. When I'm in power at Jorhat, I will ensure that the new Ahom king pays obeisance as well as tribute to you.'

'Your request is big, indeed. I don't think I have enough soldiers to spare to give you too large an army. But I shall request smaller kingdoms which fall on your way to help you out. They well know what will happen if they don't heed my dictate ...'

The traitor Badanchandra set out for the Ahom realm towards the end of 1816 with an army of 8,000 supplied to him by the Burmese King Bodau Phai. Messengers had been sent beforehand to the king's allies and additional soldiers from the chiefs of Mungkong, Hukong and Manipur joined the ranks and, by the time it reached Namrup in March 1817, its numbers had swollen to 16,000. A majority of the soldiers were from the Mong region, which lay south of the Patkai Hills; the Assamese used to call the inhabitants of Mong as Myan which was later corrupted to Maan. Thus, the approaching army was called by the locals 'the army of Maans'.

Such an attack from an unexpected direction caught Purnananda Buragohain unprepared. His spy network had failed to warn him early about the threat; the continued campaign to suppress internal discord and bring about stability to the Ahom realm had made his soldiers and officers weary and jaded; the Maans were fierce warriors. Despite these handicaps, the patriotic buragohain, though now old and without the vigour of earlier times, resolved to fight the invading army. He sent a force against the Maans and a battle was fought at Ghiladhari. Expectedly, the Ahoms were badly beaten and forced to retreat.

The old man was deeply worried. The Maans were not too far from Jorhat and approaching at a rapid pace. He knew what fate awaited him if he allowed himself to be captured by the enemy. They would not afford him the luxury of a quick death. After a lifetime devoted to the cause of his king, country and people, he would not allow it to end this way.

He summoned his eldest son, Ruchinath, as also the other chief nobles, to the inner chamber of his abode. 'I do not have the strength anymore to fight the new menace,' he told the gathering. 'Bear witness, all of you, that I appoint Ruchinath as the new buragohain. His first duty will be to raise another army to stave off the invaders.'

The other nobles nodded their assent. 'Your will would be done, Father,' Ruchinath said.

The old man gestured to everyone to leave the room. Alone, he pressed a tiny lever on the large, diamond ring he wore on his left middle finger. The diamond-encrusted lid flipped open, revealing a small depression between the ring's base and its lid, filled with a few drops of liquid. He had acquired this potion from a hill tribe: a potent poison, a small amount of which could even kill a tiger. He had worn the poison-filled diamond ring just for exigencies like this.

Without hesitation, he put his tongue to the liquid and licked it.

Moments later, Purnananda Buragohain, patriot and saviour thus far of the Ahom realm, was dead.

Ruchinath, accompanied by the other patra-mantris, walked rapidly towards the rajsora where Swargadeo Chandrakanta Singha awaited them. There was very little time to waste—they did not even have time enough to give a proper burial to his father. In the presence of the king, they prostrated themselves.

'All is lost, Your Majesty,' the new buragohain said. 'As directed by my father and ordained by you, I had sent a force to stem the advancing Maans. Unfortunately, this too has suffered defeat near Kathalbari east of the river Dihing. The enemy is now knocking at our door. You need to evacuate from Jorhat at once and escape to Guwahati.'

To not only his but everyone else's surprise, Chandrakanta took the news of the impending disaster calmly. Equanimity and courage were not virtues Ruchinath had associated with the swargadeo. On the contrary, this high-strung young man had a yellow streak in him which often seeped out in bursts of childish petulance. Yet here he was, not batting an eyelid at the fact that the capital of his kingdom was about to be overrun by a ruthless enemy.

'You need not fear on my account, Buragohain dangoriya,' the king said. 'Nor, in fact, for anyone else but yourself. After all, it had been your father who had engaged in a vendetta against Badanchandra. If he does wreak vengeance, it will be only against you and your family. So escape to Guwahati with your belongings and near and dear ones as quickly as you can. I'll face the future at Jorhat itself.'

The swargadeo smiled—a sly, crooked leer. All at once Ruchinath understood. It had been conspiracy and complicity all the way, the very bane of his race! It had been low curs like the one who now sat on the throne for whom upright individuals like his father had given their lives. However, he was careful not to let the inner contempt reveal itself on his features. He bowed and withdrew from the rajsora.

So, Chandrakanta Singha had proven himself to be the biggest traitor of them all!

Ruchinath did not tarry. Scores of menials ferried his essential belongings as well as immediate family members to the boats which lay moored on the bank of the river Bhogdoi. By the same afternoon, he was on his way to Guwahati.

On their way, the Burmese soldiers had struck terror amongst the Assamese subjects, wantonly burning villages, slaughtering menfolk and raping women. The news of their brutalities had travelled quickly; thus, the people of Jorhat cowered as, in the month of March in 1817, Badanchandra entered the capital on an elephant, accompanied by the Maan commander-in-chief on another elephant, and a body of soldiers on foot, hard-featured brutes who could strike terror in the stoutest of hearts. They made straight for the rajabari and, dismounting, Badanchandra and the Burmese commander strutted towards the rajsora where Chandrakanta, seated on his throne, awaited them.

Neither Badanchandra nor the Burmese commander bothered to even bow to the monarch; but Chandrakanta, quaking inside at the fact that events were no longer in his control, did not remonstrate. 'Welcome back, my dear Barphukan,' he said, with his habitual false, leering smile. 'I see you've performed as I'd desired. I shall reward you for this.'

'Not quite, Chandrakanta,' Badanchandra Barphukan replied haughtily. 'It is you who'll perform as I desire! You can remain the swargadeo as long as you wag your tail at my bidding.'

The king seethed inside at the humiliation being heaped upon him in front of his nobles, but knew any objection on his part would bring about instant retribution from the egomaniac confronting him. 'Yes,' he said humbly. 'I shall act at your bidding. What is it you wish?'

'First, I am no longer the barphukan. You will appoint me the buragohain ... I'll be the rajmantri—chief amongst the nobles whose advice you will unerringly follow. Second, we need to send the Maan army back to Myanmar. Its commander must be adequately rewarded.'

'Well, there is not much in the royal treasury,' Chandrakanta replied. 'But he can have whatever there is left.'

'I see. In that case, there is hardly anything of monetary value that we can send as tribute to the Maan King Bodau Phai. So, this is what you must do. Send one of your daughters as a gift to him, as also at least fifty elephants."

'But I've no daughter who can be sent,' objected Chandrakanta.

'Then we'll have to invent one,' Badanchandra laughed and said openly, aware that the Maan commander could not understand what was being said.

Subsequent events unfolded as Badanchandra, now the supreme power in the realm, wished. Hema Aideu, renowned for her beauty, the daughter of Boga Kuonr, a royal of the Tungkhungiya phaid, was palmed off as the king's daughter and dispatched as a gift to the Burmese king. After her marriage to Bodau Phai, her name was changed to Atan Miri Borkuonri. A number of servants as well as a group of Assamese soldiers were also sent as part of her retinue.

Unbridled power corrupts the most decent of individuals. What it could do to a vicious traitor like Badanchandra can well be imagined! Having sent the Burmese commander and his soldiers back to their native land, he quickly took firm grip on the affairs of the realm. Treating the swargadeo as a doormat, he ruled like a tyrant. His early targets were the family members of Purnananda and Ruchinath Buragohain. Hundreds of these were arrested and either beheaded or impaled on bamboo spikes. Their households were sacked and looted, and the valuables added to the new rajmantri's own wealth. Next, he dismissed numerous officials and appointed in their place individuals owing allegiance to him, bestowing on the latter confiscated land and property. In order to replenish the royal treasury, he confiscated the valuable possessions of merchants, sattradhikars and even common subjects. Badanchandra had been a hated figure when he had been the barphukan in Lower Assam; within a matter of months, he became a hated figure in Upper Assam too. Not only the common subjects, but almost everyone, began to deridingly refer to him as the 'Maan ona barphukan', or 'the Barphukan who had brought the Maans', behind his back.

Two men stealthily entered the section of the palace kept aside for the rajmao, mother of Swargadeo Chandrakanta. A servant led them into an inner sanctum, where the queen mother reclined on a couch, a worried frown on her features.

One of the men was Dhani Barbarua. Though newly appointed by Rajmantri Badanchandra in place of the dismissed Srinath Barbarua, he did not consider that he was in any way indebted to the former for his elevation. On the contrary, Dhani Barbarua was repulsed by the crude and barbaric streak displayed by the rajmantri and understood that as long as he was alive, no one in the palace was safe.

His repulsion was shared by the rajmao, which was the reason why she had summoned the barbarua for a secret tryst with her. The queen mother knew how noble a man Purnananda Buragohain had been.

She was grateful that he had made two of her sons swargadeos and sacrificed everything for king and country. In comparison, the traitor who ruled the roost at the moment, and held Chandrakanta under subjugation, was an insufferable impostor. She knew that her contempt for Badanchandra was universal—even Chandrakanta hated him. He must be got rid of. She was well aware that not a tear would be shed if the tyrant was assassinated.

But the planning had to be meticulous. Failure might bring about ruin for her and her son, not to mention her co-conspirators. The problem was that Badanchandra had a group of soldiers whose loyalty he had purchased through handsome compensation; he knew of the threat to his life, carried weapons on his person and was always surrounded by bodyguards wherever he went. Any murderous assault to be successful had therefore to be attempted when he was alone and without his weapons.

The rajmao had her own intelligence service. It was made up of the domestic staff—ligiras and ligiris—in Badanchandra's household who fed her each and every detail of his daily routine. There appeared to be one window of opportunity for the briefest time. Also, the attempt would have to be carried out by a single individual and not a group—someone totally unconnected with the palace as well as the nobility, so as to distance them if it proved a failure.

The barbarua had brought just such a person with him. His name was Rup Singh. There was a troop of Hindustani sepoys in Chandrakanta's army. Rup Singh was a subedar in that troop. He had been given a hefty sum to carry out the assignment and promised more if he was successful.

'You will have just a few minutes to kill the target,' the rajmao told the hired assassin. 'The man wears amulets on his person which give him extraordinary protection. When he is wearing these, he cannot be killed. Also, he is a powerful man and can defend himself well with the arms he always carries. So, we must select a moment when he is neither wearing the amulets nor has arms with him.'

'That's a difficult ask,' said the barbarua in a voice steeped in pessimism.

'Oh, but my informants tell me that such a moment does exist,' the rajmao said with a smile. 'Badanchandra gets up at the crack of dawn and he goes to the toilet in his backyard to relieve himself. There is an enclosed bath shed a little distance away from the toilet. Badanchandra first goes to this bath shed and leaves his amulets and weapons there before entering the toilet. Having relieved himself, he returns to the bath shed for the mandatory bath and then wears his amulets and picks up his weapons. It is within this brief period that we must strike.'

Rup Singh nodded. 'It shall be as you desire,' he said tersely. Dhani Barbarua also nodded, amazed at the resourcefulness of the rajmao.

The advantage of a residence possessing a large compound, from the point of view of an assassin, was that there were many places to hide. Also, the oil flares lighting up the complex, though numerous, since it belonged to the rajmantri who was the de facto ruler of the realm, could not quite illuminate every nook and corner. Thus, despite the fact that the place was very well guarded, Rup Singh had little difficulty in silently climbing over a bamboo jeura, or fencing, in the backyard and slipping into the compound. The black blanket in which he had draped himself helped in merging into the overwhelming darkness. The assassin wafted like a ghost towards the bath and toilet sheds and hid himself behind some bushes. With the patience of a leopard stalking its prey, he waited. Dawn was just a couple of hours away. It would bring its own dangers but the fearless subedar would take things as they came.

As usual, Badanchandra awoke at the crack of dawn and began his morning ablutions. There was a servant to assist him in every activity, even one such as putting on his slippers as he got out of bed. Also guards accompanied him almost everywhere. As the rajmao had so cunningly grasped, it was during his visit to the toilet that Badanchandra would be truly alone and unarmed. He emerged into the backyard in the predicted time and first went to the bath shed to take off his amulets and lay down the short dagger he carried with him and then entered the toilet. The moment the toilet door opened once again and Badanchandra stepped out, Rup Singh was upon him, his sword striking the surprised and helpless man again and again.

The victim's cries rent the air, making his sons, servants and guards come rushing to his aid. The assassin Rup Singh would have been killed there and then—but the swargadeo's soldiers, who had been concealed behind the backyard fence, now jumped into the scene and called out to the others to lay down their arms in the name of the king. This they promptly did. The rajmantri's sons and loyal guards were chained and taken away while the king's men, as instructed, looted the residence of all its valuables.

Thus perished Badanchandra, the one who inexorably dug the grave of the Ahom empire.

Events moved at a quick pace after the assassination of Badanchandra early in the year 1818. Chandrakanta, realizing that his mother was behind the killing, made no move to bring those involved to justice. In fact, the king himself had grown terrified of the man and was secretly glad he was dead. On the advice of his mother, he sent news to Guwahati of the death of the traitor and requested Ruchinath Buragohain to return to Jorhat.

The latter heeded the request, but not with the intentions Chandrakanta or the queen mother had desired. The buragohain did not trust the king an inch, retaining his suspicions that he was responsible for bringing the Maans to the Ahom kingdom and ordering the death of his father. So, he was determined to remove Chandrakanta, by force if necessary. He had sought out an Ahom prince named Brajanath Gohain, a great-grandson of Swargadeo Rajeshwar Singha, who was living in exile at Silamara in Bengal, and could be elevated to the Ahom throne. Unfortunately, Brajanath had been earlier mutilated and therefore, as dictated by Shan tradition, could not be placed on the throne. It was then decided that his son Purandar Gohain would be made the swargadeo in place of Chandrakanta.

Ruchinath Buragohain had already raised an army comprising Hindustani mercenaries and some loyalists so that he could make an attempt to retrieve power from Badanchandra. Thus, on receipt of the news of the latter's death, he could proceed immediately to Jorhat along with his army, and Brajanath and Purandar in tow. Too late Chandrakanta understood what the objective of such a hostile approach was; he also knew that he was in no position to offer resistance, so fled with his retinue from Jorhat to Rongpur leaving a low-ranked officer in charge. The officer, Luku Dekaphukan, bravely offered whatever resistance he could, but soon his small force was overwhelmed by Ruchinath's army and he himself was killed. In February 1818, the buragohain occupied the Ahom capital of Jorhat and Brajanath's young son was placed on the throne with little ceremony, taking on the name of Purandar Singha.

In deference to the queen mother, Ruchinath would have allowed Chandrakanta to remain undisturbed at Rongpur. In fact, the buragohain did everything he could to make the deposed king's stay in Rongpur comfortable. But Ruchinath's younger brother and Purnananda's third son Oreshnath still burned with the thought of revenge for the death of his father. He sent soldiers to Rongpur to forcibly mutilate the erstwhile king, which they did by cutting off his earlobes, thereby ostensibly making him unfit to be a king. But for this, Chandrakanta may not have become vindictive and remained content to stay undisturbed at Rongpur. But he felt extremely humiliated by the mutilation and resolved to respond in kind.

He now took full advantage of Ruchinath's generosity in not destroying him and his followers once and for all. With all due secrecy, emissaries were sent to the king of Myanmar giving details of the happenings in the Ahom realm and asking for help. King Bodau Phai was not only grieved at the death of Badanchandra, but also enraged that Chandrakanta had been dethroned. In February 1819, he sent another force, even bigger than the previous one, to set things right in the Ahom kingdom. This force was commanded by a general named Alamingi.

Purandar Singha's army put up a spirited resistance, but was defeated at Phulpanisiga on the bank of the river Jhanji. The king was forced to flee along with his family and nobles to Guwahati. Chandrakanta, who had joined Alamingi on the way, was ceremonially reinstated as the king for a second time. The fate of this king had been always to play second fiddle to others. It had been Purnananda Buragohain who had made him the swargadeo; Badanchandra had been the de facto ruler when alive, and now actual power vested on Alamingi. The Ahom king chafed under this dominance of others upon his authority, and secretly resolved to break free given the least opportunity.

However, it took a while for such an opportunity to arrive. Meanwhile, the Burmese commander was preoccupied with setting things in order. Not only did he have all the relatives of Ruchinath Buragohain, Dhani Barbarua and Nirbhainarain Bargohain, murdered, his troops hunted down the three and killed them. A force was sent to Guwahati to capture or kill Purandar Singha; the latter tried to resist but his followers were routed by the Burmese, putting the exiled king once more in flight, obliging him to flee to Silamara in British-ruled Bengal after appointing Ghinai Bhoga as the barphukan to defend the city. In Bengal, Purandar Singha made repeated supplications to the British authorities for help in expelling the Burmese from Ahom territory and restoring the throne to him. The British replied as before: their policy of non-intervention forbade them from giving a positive response to his pleas. When Chandrakanta and Alamingi petitioned the British governor-general for extradition of the fugitives sheltering in British territory, the answer was the same.

At Jorhat, Alamingi was changing the entire Ahom administration after his troops had slaughtered the buragohain, the bargohain and the barbarua, and their kinsmen. A man called Kalibor was made the buragohain; another, Govinda, the borgohain and a Kachari named Patal, the barbarua. Having achieved the main objectives of his campaign, Alamingi left for Myanmar. The Maan commander did not make the earlier mistake of departing en masse. He left one of his commanders named Mingimaha Tiloa Boju at Jorhat as well as a sizeable number of Burmese soldiers to keep a check on the Ahom king. However, in 1819, the Burmese king Bodau Phai died and his grandson, Bagyodoa ascended the throne. The political changes taking place in his country induced Mingimah Tiloa Boju to depart for Myanmar in early 1820, after leaving 1,000 Maan soldiers behind at Jorhat.

This was the opportunity Chandrakanta had been waiting for. In a way, it was the last throw of the dice for the Ahoms. The king's plan was to secretly build a huge fort at Dighalighat on the bank of the river Buridihing and station a large troop of soldiers there so that any more invasions from Myanmar could be resisted. He assigned to Patal Barbarua the task of building the fort, to be named as the Jaypur fort, which was to be around 350 metres in width. Like most Ahom forts, it was to be square in shape and possess deep moats and ramparts surrounding it from all sides.

Naturally, the new Burmese king, Bagyodoa, had eyes and ears in the Ahom capital. Even before the Jaypur project had begun, he was already informed of it. A huge force was sent for the third time under the command of Mingimah Tiloa Boju. The Burmese ruler no longer had intentions of merely aiding his 'brother king'. The ease with which the Burmese had reached the Ahom capital Jorhat on two occasions earlier had revealed that Ahom authority in the realm was like a gourd with only the shell. The worms of greed for power and internal rivalry had eaten up and hollowed the inside. The new Burmese ruler, like his father, had ambitions of expanding his empire and bringing Assam into his dominion. The mandate of Mingimah was made absolutely clear. Wreak havoc upon the Ahom realm and teach its delinquent ruler a lesson.

The unprepared Ahom forces could not resist the fierce invasion. The Maans levelled the Jaypur fort to the ground and killed Patal Barbarua. As they advanced towards Jorhat, Chandrakanta Singha, not knowing how they would treat him, given that he had tried to erect defences against their attack, escaped in the nick of time and reached Guwahati. On learning that the Maan general had sent soldiers after him, he soon left Guwahati and took shelter at Hadirachowk on the extreme western bound of the kingdom so that he would be able to escape to Bengal if the need arose.

Having occupied Jorhat, Mingimah Tiloa Boju sent emissaries to Chandrakanta asking him to return to the Ahom capital to be reinstalled as the swargadeo. The Ahom king knew better than to come back! Seeing his unwillingness, Mingimah elevated the son of Boga Kuonr and the brother of Hema Aideo, Jogeshwar, to the throne. Jogeshwar Singha was merely a puppet in the hands of the Maans and, in effect, the Ahom era, when it was the patra-mantris who selected the swargadeo, had ended. Mingimah Tiloa Boju stayed on in Jorhat and directed affairs from there. But the thousands of Maan soldiers he had brought with him could not be accommodated in one place. They were ordered to spread out in groups all over the kingdom and fend for themselves till they were summoned for active duty.

The nightmare for the subjects of the realm had begun.

That ill-fated morning, the villagers of Samoshal on the north bank, situated between Lakhimpur and Biswanath, did not know what hit them. A village of long standing, it had withstood the vagaries of time, reaching prosperous heights as well as depths of poverty, particularly in recent times. It had been most adversely affected during the insurgency by the Moamarias, being caught in the crossfire in the war of attrition between the royal forces and the rebels. But of late, its inhabitants had been able to rise up again, thanks to the liberal policy pursued by Purnananda Buragohain. Cultivation had recommenced; the paddy fields were green with young plants and household gardens with vegetables; the various professionals in the village had resumed their activities; and the self-sufficiency and sense of contentment which had pervaded the village in earlier times had returned to a great extent.

Because it was located on the north bank of the Brahmaputra, and the Burmese army had marched across the south bank, Samoshal village had not felt the impact of the Maan invasion so far. But this morning things were to suffer a drastic change. Some youngsters who had gone fishing and swimming in a nearby stream saw them—a sizeable group of armed strangers coming towards the village.

'We've never seen anyone dressed like that,' they ran to the village and informed the headman. 'They're still at some distance but are clearly headed for our village.'

'There's nothing to worry about,' the headman replied nonchalantly. 'Must be just a band of the swargadeo's soldiers on some assignment or the other. Perhaps they are weary and hungry and desire to stop for some rest and food at Samoshal. I shall talk to the leader and offer our hospitality.'

The fact that, reaching closer, the band of armed men suddenly broke ranks and spread out so as to encircle the compact, residential section of the village perplexed but not unduly alarmed the headman. The strangers suddenly came to a halt as three from their group walked up the mud path that snaked through Samoshal, dividing the village into two halves. The headman strode out with some of the elder members of the village council to meet the trio.

'Welcome, strangers,' he told the newcomers. 'Our village Samoshal is renowned for its hospitality. We would be obliged if you partake of our food and rest here for a while.'

Without warning one of the intruders took out his sword and decapitated the headman. His companions unsheathed their weapons and cut down the group of elders.

Curious village men, women and children had gathered in groups to see their headman's meeting with the strangers. At the totally unexpected and ghastly turn of happenings, the women let out squeals of terror and children began wailing, while the men raced to lay their hands upon their weapons. But they had no chance. The strangers were fierce and well-trained Maan warriors. While some of them held the women and children captive at swordpoint, the men were massacred, with little injury to the assailants. After the last man standing had been put to the sword, the younger and comelier of the women were taken inside huts and brutally gang-raped, even as the horror-stricken elderly women and youngsters watched.

Having satiated their lust, the Maan soldiers separated a few young women from the rest and held them prisoners within one of the hutments. The rest of the women and children were herded into the village naamghar, or house of prayer. The soldiers detached bamboo walls from some of the cottages and placed them around the open sides of the naamghar so that the structure was completely enclosed from all sides, with no outlets through which those inside could escape. Then they set the wood, bamboo, cane and thatch building on fire.

The screams of agony were so piercing that they made roosting birds rise up into the air. The stench of burning flesh choked their nostrils, but the strangers were not bothered. They engaged in a macabre, satanic dance, their howls of laughter as loud as the agonized wails. Finally, the cries subsided; the fire burned out; the Maan devils ceased their satanic dance. Only the stench of burning human flesh continued to pollute the air.

The Maans chose the cottages where they would stay. The women who had been separated and kept alive would slave for them, cooking, washing and satisfying their lust. The Maan men would remain in the village till summoned once again by their leaders.

The gruesome scene witnessed in Samoshal village, had been enacted and reenacted throughout the realm. Not that Assamese people did not hit back. In many villages, the inhabitants grouped together to fight the Maans. But, in the absence of backing by the Ahom military, such uncoordinated defensive action soon petered out and the Burmese overcame all similar resistance. The men at Samoshal had been fortunate in being delivered a quick death. In other villages, they had not been so lucky; the savage Maans derived pleasure from torturing men and castrating them, roaring with mirth as they bled to death. Pregnant women were disembowelled and the foetuses eaten by the killers. Some of the soldiers would use young toddlers as missiles; toss them up at clumps of coconut growing on palms and hold competitions amongst themselves as to who could dislodge how many coconuts. Boiling people in oil was a favourite pastime with the Burmese soldiers; one of their sources of amusement was to give a person a chance to flee and then hunt him down as though a wild animal.* Young men and damsels had their palms pierced and rope strung through the holes and knotted; they were then herded like cattle back to Myanmar to work as slaves. These diabolic acts emboldened native marauders to pose as Maans and also inflict unimaginable barbarity upon the people. Such was the extent of slaughter that the Ahom realm was deprived of almost one-third of its population, with a lucky few being able to escape to the hills or Bengal.

The entire land wept. The land was sunk in pain and darkness. Without doubt the 'Maanor Din', or the 'Days of the Maan', was the bleakest period in the entire history of Assam. The Ahom royalty too was not spared the misfortune that had befallen their country, and were tortured and slaughtered wherever they were found. While Purandar Singha, with the help of Robert Bruce, a British trader–adventurer based at Jogighopa, was raising a force of mercenaries to give battle to the Burmese, Chandrakanta was doing the same with a similar objective. Meanwhile, meeting no resistance, the Burmese had spread their reach to Guwahati in Lower Assam, but Chandrakanta, with a force of 2,000 mercenaries, mostly Sikhs and Hindustanis, was finally able to counterattack and wrest Lower Assam back from the Burmese in January 1822.

Meanwhile, Purandar Singha was confronting the Burmese with his troops coming through Bhutan, though with limited success. Yet the combined assaults had placed the Maans on the back foot, enabling the stronger army of Chandrakanta to progress further upstream towards Central Assam. It may have well reached the capital Jorhat, had not, towards May 1822, another Burmese commander named Mingimaha

---

* Please refer to the chronicles written in Assamese; in particular, Dewan, *Contemporary Assamese Society* (1990).

Bandula arrived from Arakan with a sizeable force. A decisive battle, the very last fought by an Ahom swargadeo, was waged in June 1822 at Mohgarh which Chandrakanta lost, with at least 1,500 of his soldiers killed. The victorious Maans, in order to capture him alive, gave hot pursuit but Chandrakanta was able to escape from Burmese-held territory into Bengal. The failure of Chandrakanta also made Purandar realize that it was futile to try and retake the Ahom realm with such limited resources and he too withdrew from the fray.

Mingimaha Bandula returned to Myanmar and informed King Bagyodoa of the disgraceful conduct of the Burmese soliders under Mingimaha Tiloa Boju and the ruinous state to which they had reduced the Ahom realm. The Burmese ruler recalled Boju and sent a more benign commander to replace him. Meanwhile, Chandrakanta, through intermediaries, had been pleading with the British authorities to assist him in getting the Burmese out of Assam, without receiving a positive response. Simultaneously, the new Burmese commander had been continuously wooing Chandrakanta Singha, sending to him emissaries with reassurance that he even now considered him as the true king and that Jogeshwar had been enthroned only because he had not returned to occupy the throne. Finally, a frustrated Chandrakanta, disillusioned with the British, took the bait offered by the Burmese and returned to Jorhat. The treacherous Burmese promptly arrested him and imprisoned him at Rongpur.

Chandrakanta stood alone upon the high ramparts of the royal palace at Rongpur, watching the sun sink with astonishing rapidity in the western sky. A light breeze wafted across, touching his cheeks. The city of Rongpur, which his ancestor Rudra Singha had built with such care and affection, spread out like an unfurled carpet before his gaze, wasted and almost depopulated. The rong-ghar stood desolate; the crowds that had once burst out in raucous cries at the sight of a descending falcon had vanished into thin air. Only jackals and hyenas roamed where once there had been vibrant life.

As the sun hovered at the very edge of the horizon, the light lessened perceptibly. With his mind's eye, Chandrakanta could see the ghosts arise—those of Sukapha, the founder of the Ahom dynasty; Suhungmung, the tiger of a famous country; Pratap Singha, Rudra Singha and all the rest; brave women like Mula Gabharoo and Jaimati; warriors and statesmen such as Lachit, Atan and Purnananda. Six hundred years of almost uninterrupted rule. Those spectres of the past seemed to point their fingers at him, as though blaming him that things had fallen apart and a glorious era was about to come to an end.

Endowed with a sense of history, Chandrakanta had no more illusion that even the least possibility of revival remained. He understood that no longer would men and women of flesh and blood keep a heritage alive. It would be mirrored only in the sanchi-paat pages of buranjis, the highs and the lows, the victories and the defeats. But he was not the only one to be blamed. He had been merely a pawn in the hands of destiny, the final victim of causes and consequences, actions and reactions.

The sun, almost magically, dipped suddenly from sight. Darkness settled over Cheraidai, over Garhgaon, over Rongpur, over the land that had once been the kingdom of the Ahoms but was no longer.

THE NARRATOR

'There is only one, insignificant chapter left in the history of the Ahom race,' said the Narrator wearily. 'It can be soon told.'

In truth, weariness had gripped everyone not yet asleep—it is only the tales of conquest and glory that can keep minds avid for more, not of defeat and dissolution. The youths tending the fire had grown tired of their task; the flames of the bonfire had died down and it was a pile of glowing embers; the night was bleaker and darker than ever.

'The Burmese now held sway over what had once been the kingdom of the Ahoms,' continued the Narrator. 'Their writ ran right up to Hadirachowk at the western edge. Over a quarter of the population of the Brahmaputra Valley had been slaughtered, thousands of Assamese men and women led away to Myanmar as slaves. The land was so ravaged that cultivation had almost ceased. But the power they commanded over the Valley made the Maans so arrogant that they imagined they could take on the might of the British who by then ruled over much of Hindustan. Their delusion was compounded by a misconception that was funny, if you think about it. As I had told you, my people, in the final stage, the Ahoms had a standing army patterned on the sepoys of the British. They were dressed in the same way and carried similar arms. This force, as we know, proved ineffective against the marauding Burmese soldiers. This induced in the Maans the misconception that the British army was similarly inefficient and they could take it on.

'How wrong they were was soon proven! Many subjects of the erstwhile Ahom kingdom had fled to British territory when it was assailed by the Maans. The Burmese king sent instructions to his commander-in-chief that they were to be captured and brought back to Assam. Soon Burmese forces were intruding into British-held areas and carrying out raids, forcing the East India Company to abandon its non-interference policy and declare war against the Burmese on 5 March 1824.

'The Maans quickly realized that they had bitten off more than they could chew ... it was now their turn to flee as two British forces, one by land and the other by river, under the command of David Scott and George Macmorine, began a campaign against them. The British soldiers were better armed, trained and disciplined; their gunboats were faster; despite being outnumbered, it took them but a few days to capture Guwahati. Hostilities ceased during the period of heavy rain, in which Macmorine died of dysentery and Arthur Richards was appointed in his place. The campaign resumed as the dry spell set in and on 17 January 1825, Jorhat fell to the British and Jogeshwar Singha was apprehended. By end-January, Rongpur had been taken and Chandrakanta Singha set free. Both were transported to Guwahati. Jogeshwar Singha moved further on to Goalpara where he died soon afterwards.

'Knowing that their cause was a lost one, the Burmese now entered into a pact with the British and agreed to leave the Brahmaputra Valley.

However, that did not end the war and the British continued the campaign against the forces of the Burmese king, which finally ended with the signing of the Yandaboo Treaty on 24 February 1826. By the terms of the treaty, the king of Myanmar ceded the territory of Arakan and Tenaserim to the British, as well as agreed to abstain from any attack on the newly occupied British territory of Assam.

'Can't you appreciate the tragedy of this, my people? Two foreign forces, the Burmese and the British, determining the fate of the Brahmaputra Valley and the adjoining hills, with the once mighty Ahoms having no role to play? Only one more time did an Ahom swargadeo get to play a minor role in this sad drama. Having established some sort of order in the realm through martial rule, the British, in 1833, for a while reinstated Purandar Singha as the titular king of Upper Assam on condition that he paid an annual tribute of Rs 50,000 to the British. However, in 1838, under the pretext of failing to pay his tribute, the British caused him to abdicate and took up direct control of the region. The once-omnipotent Ahoms finally lost a realm that they would never again regain ...'

The old Deodhai priest's voice trailed into silence. He had nothing more to say. He turned his back upon his audience and walked away into the dark night. The villagers too stirred and left the spot, all too aware of the heritage that had been lost. Soon the bonfire's embers stopped glowing and only the light of the fireflies flickered amidst the gloom.

Select Bibliography

IN ENGLISH

Acharyya, N. N. *The History of Medieval Assam*. New Delhi: Omsons Publication. 1992.

Barpujari, H. K. *The Comprehensive History of Assam*, Volume 1 to 5. Assam: Publication Board Assam. 1992.

Barua, B. K. *A Cultural History of Assam*. New Delhi: Archaeological Survey of India. 1969.

Barua, S. L. *A Comprehensive History of Assam*. New Delhi: Munshiram Manoharlal Publishers. 1985.

Barua, U. N. *A Glimpse of Assam*. Jorhat: Published by Indibar Barua.1928.

Basu, N. K. *Assam in the Ahom Age*, 1228–1826. Calcutta: Sanskrit Pustak Bhandar. 1970.

Bhuyan, Suryya Kumar. *Atan Buragohain and His Times*. Guwahati: Publication Board Assam. 2010.

Butler, J. *Travels and Adventures in the Province of Assam*. Reprint. New Delhi: Nabu Press. 1854.

Chatterji, Suniti Kumar. The Place of Assam in the History and Civilization of India. Guwahati: Department of Publication, University of Gauhati. 1970.

Dutta, Ajit Kumar. *Maniram Dewan and Contemporary Assamese Society*. Jorhat: Published by Anupoma Dutta. 1990.

Gait, Edward. *A History of Assam*. Reprint. Guwahati: Bina Library. 1905.

Gogoi, P. *The Tai and the Tai Kingdom*. Guwahati: Department of Publication, University of Gauhati. 1968.

Gohain, Nilutpal. *The Legend of Lachit Barphukan*. New Delhi: Locksley Hall Publishing. 2021.

Gohain U. N. Assam under the Ahoms. Reprint. New Delhi: Spectrum Publications. 1999.

Hamilton, F. B. *An Account of Assam*. Reprint. Guwahati: Powershift in association with Faculty Books. 1814.

Hunter, W. W. *A Statistical Account of Assam*. Assam: Trübner & Company. 1879. E-book.

–*Lachit Barphukan and His Times*. Guwahati: Publication Board Assam. 1947.

Montgomery, M. *The History, Antiquities, Topography and Statistics of Eastern India*. 1838. E-book available on Digital Library of India, Item 2015.283662.

Nath, R. M. *The Background of Assamese Culture*. Shillong: Published by author. 1948.

Robinson, W. *A Descriptive Account of Assam*. UK: Ostell and Lepage, 1841; Reprint, Guwahati: Sanskaran Prakashak.

Shakespear, L.W. *History of Upper Assam, Upper Burma*. London: MacMillan and Co Ltd, 1914. Digital version available on Central Archaeological Library, Acc. no. 1537.

Wade, J.P. *An Account of Assam.* Edited by Benudhar Sharma. Published by R. Sharma, 1880.

IN ASSAMESE

Barbarua, Hiteshwar. *Ahomar Din.* Guwahati: Publication Board Assam, 1981.

Barua, G.C. Ahom Buranji. Edited and translated. 1930. Digital version available at SOAS, University of London.

Barua, L. *Kamarupar Itikatha.* Guwahati: Publication Board Assam, 1985.

Bhuyan, S. K. Assam Buranji (1228–1826). Edited by Harakanta Barua Sadaramin. Directorate of Historical and Antequarian Studies, Government of Assam, 1962.

Choudhury, P.C. Assam Buranji. Directorate of Historical and Antequarian Studies, Government of Assam. 1844. Edited by Kashinath Tamuli Phukan. 1964.

–Deodhai Assam Buranji. Directorate of Historical and Antequarian Studies, Government of Assam. 1932.

Neog, H., and L. Gogoi. Asamiya Sanskriti. Guwahati: Assam Sahitya Sabha & Banalata. 1966.

Rajkumar, Sarbananda. Itihase Suonra Soshota Bachar. Dibrugarh: Banalata. 1980.

–Satsari Assam Buranji. Edited. Directorate of Historical and Antequarian Studies, Government of Assam. 1974.

–Tungkhungiya Assam Buranji. Edited. Directorate of Historical and Antequarian Studies, Government of Assam. 1933.

About the Author

~⌒

Arup Kumar Dutta is an author, freelance journalist and social commentator based in Assam. He writes fiction, non-fiction, newspaper editorials, articles and columns, satirical pieces and so on for adults, and adventure novels for young people. In his five-decade-long career, he has authored thirty-five books including *The Anagarika's Swansong* (2009), *The Bag* (2018), *The Brahmaputra* (2001), *Unicornis* (1991), *Cha Garam: The Tea Story* (2001), *The Roving Minstrel* (2002), *The Kaziranga Trail* (1978), *The Blind Witness* (1983), among others. He has been conferred numerous awards, including the Padma Shri by the Government of India (2018), and DLitt (honoris causa) by the Dibrugarh University (2018) and the Gauhati University (2020). His website is www.arupkumardutta.com.

Printed by Libri Plureos GmbH in Hamburg, Germany